Issachar Bates

Issachar Bates

A SHAKER'S JOURNEY

CAROL MEDLICOTT

UNIVERSITY PRESS OF NEW ENGLAND

Hanover and London

University Press of New England
www.upne.com
© 2013 University Press of New England
All rights reserved
Manufactured in the United States of America
Designed by Richard Hendel
Typeset in Arno by Passumpsic Publishing

For permission to reproduce any of the material in this book,
contact Permissions, University Press of New England,
One Court Street, Suite 250, Lebanon NH 03766;
or visit www.upne.com

Library of Congress Cataloging-in-Publication Data
Medlicott, Carol.
Issachar Bates: a Shaker's journey / Carol Medlicott.
     pages cm
Includes bibliographical references and index.
ISBN 978-1-61168-419-3 (cloth: alk. paper) —
ISBN 978-1-61168-434-6 (pbk.: alk. paper) —
ISBN 978-1-61168-408-7 (ebook)
1. Bates, Issachar, 1758–1837. 2. Composers — United
States — Biography. 3. Shakers — Biography. I. Title.
ML410.B2662M43   2013
780.92 — dc23
[B]   2012051384

5 4 3 2 1

CONTENTS

Appendixes

PREFACE

The preparation of this work has taken me on a long and circuitous journey, similar in some ways to Issachar Bates's own. I entered the world of Shaker scholarship at middle age, after an abrupt career change took me into academia. During graduate school in the Department of Geography, University of California at Los Angeles, I focused on issues of historical geography in the Early American Republic, but with no expectation of ever pursuing Shaker research. As a midwestern native, I had been vaguely aware of the Shaker presence in Kentucky, and I had developed a casual interest in Shaker music. It was that musical interest that brought about my first encounter with Issachar Bates. During a post-doctoral fellowship at Dartmouth College, I joined the Enfield Shaker Singers in nearby Enfield, New Hampshire, where one of New Hampshire's two Shaker villages had been located. I first saw Issachar Bates's name on the sheet music of several of his songs that the group's director, Mary Ann Haagen, had researched for the group to perform. One of these songs, "Ode to Contentment," spoke to me in a special way:

Come contentment lovely guest
Reign unrival'd in my breast
Thou alone wilt do.
Thou alone canst fill my soul
Ev'ry passion canst control
When the stormy billows roll,
Thou canst bear me thru.'

At that time, I was in a professional and personal limbo, searching for an academic job, adjusting to a major residential move, unsure of whether my career change had been wise. It was autumn of 2004, and the country was experiencing a turbulent election season. Discontent seemed to be all around me, and I immediately wanted to know more about the man who had written those words. Later I would learn that that "Ode to Contentment" reflected a time of painful transition in Issachar Bates's life and his effort to become reconciled to new challenges and new demands. I felt a bond. And I began to realize that Issachar's story deserved to be shared. The long journey leading to the completion of this work then began.

Upon learning that I would be moving to the region that constituted the

"Shaker West" in the nineteenth century, I decided to try to develop some research interests in the somewhat less studied communities of Ohio, Indiana, and Kentucky. Because of my training as a historical geographer, I was interested in how the Shakers initiated territorial expansion beyond the eastern seaboard states, how they maintained some degree of cultural unity across great distances, and how they adjusted to environmental differences in the various regions where they settled. Initially, biography was very far from my thoughts. But I soon realized that Issachar Bates's great mobility made his life an ideal window into a very geographical story, namely, the story of the Shakers' great territorial expansion of the early nineteenth century. I also found precedent for my work in several recent biographical projects undertaken by other historical geographers. Indeed, geographers are recognizing the value of "bio-geography," an approach that uses personal narratives about inhabiting and negotiating particular places as tools to reconstruct and better understand the landscapes of the past.

This work has benefitted from the insightful comments provided by Steve Miller, Glendyne Wergland, and Steve Paterwic, with whom I shared drafts of particular chapters. I am also grateful to the acquisitions editor at UPNE, Richard Pult, for his patient support and encouragement. I received valuable critiques, commentary, and suggestions from two anonymous reviewers, which brought immeasurable improvement to the work. I alone am responsible for any errors, inaccuracies, and analytical lapses.

From the beginning of my modest research efforts in the Shaker field, I have encountered a convivial atmosphere and a delightful and diverse collection of people bound together by their common enthusiasm for "things Shaker," past and present. I now feel blessed to be able to count many of these witty and creative people among my closest friends, and I have been the fortunate beneficiary of their generous assistance, encouragement, and guidance. My most earnest gratitude goes to my good friend Christian Goodwillie. I have come to depend on his endless assistance, insights, and support, as well as his bountiful humor. Also indispensable has been the unwavering support and assistance of Glendyne Wergland, Steve Paterwic, and Steve Miller, all fine scholars who have gone to no end of trouble to guide me to sources, impart their insights, listen to my problems, suggest solutions, and correct my misunderstandings. My friend Mary Ann Haagen has been a patient and tireless mentor, particularly in the area of Shaker music. Because music was such a critical part of Issachar Bates's life, my research has taken me into hundreds of music manuscripts, requiring me to become fluent in Shaker music notation.

It was Mary Ann who introduced me to joys and challenges of transcribing Shaker music from the original letteral notation.

I have repeatedly drawn on the support of the professional staff at various Shaker sites, as well as institutions that house Shaker primary sources. I am particularly grateful to Jerry Grant of the Shaker Museum and Library at Old Chatham, Larrie Curry at the Shaker Village of Pleasant Hill, Tommy Hines and John Campbell at the Shaker Museum at South Union, Jeanne Solensky and Richard McKinstry of the Winterthur Library, Randy Ericson of Hamilton College, Lesley Herzberg of Hancock Shaker Village, Roben Campbell of the Fruitlands Museum, and Lenny Brooks of the Shaker Library at Sabbathday Lake. The many close friends that I have made in the "Shaker world" have also generously shared their experiences and insights, especially Dorothy Jones, Martha Boice, Mary Allen, Liz Baker, Bill Mooney, Stephen Stein, Rob Emlen, and the members of the annual "seminar" sponsored by Hancock Shaker Village.

My research has brought me into contact with other delightful people who have assisted me in myriad ways. The Bates Association, an organization that promotes genealogical research on the Bates family name in American history, has been very generous in helping to locate information on Issachar Bates's descendants. I am particularly grateful to Sandy Bates, one of the group's officers. I also benefitted from the kind and generous assistance of Thomas Posey, Jr., a descendant of eighteenth-century General Thomas Posey and of his wife Mary Posey. Mr. Posey shared with me the insights he has gathered from his research on Mary Posey, who became acquainted with Issachar Bates in 1808. Finally I want to express gratitude to Rev. John Pastor and Officer Robert Hall, owners of a historic home in Petersham, Massachusetts, who allowed me to see the spot where a pivotal event in Issachar Bates's life occurred. This was a precious opportunity that I will never forget.

Though I have not actively involved my mentors and advisors from the UCLA Department of Geography in the preparation of this work, their wisdom and guidance were a valuable resource, especially that of Michael Curry and John Agnew. I am grateful to my colleagues at Northern Kentucky University for encouraging and showing interest in my work, as well as for assisting me with occasional research puzzles.

Three friends deserve special mention. Over several years, my friend Mary Lou has helped me develop greater insights into Issachar Bates. Lois Madden and Dennis Delaney and their passionate interest in the world of the early Shaker West have sustained me, and the many lively discussions we share about the lives and events addressed in my work have led me to better clarity in my analysis.

I am grateful to the Shaker family of Sabbathday Lake, Maine. It is both a privilege and a humbling experience to study the people and events that they look to as their spiritual heritage. And this work could never have proceeded had I not been able to rely on the love and support of my husband, Bob, who has girded me up, sympathized with my frustrations, listened to my ideas, read my drafts, and patiently assisted in countless ways.

Finally, I must thank Issachar Bates for launching me on this journey. His energy, resilience, humor, eloquence, conviction, courage, and determination — to say nothing of his music and poetry — have inspired, entertained, and moved me. Issachar Bates made a difference, both in his lifetime and afterward. Would that we could all achieve as much.

ACKNOWLEDGMENTS

I am grateful to several institutions for their support of my research and writing, in the form of research fellowships and other financial assistance: Special Collections Library at Western Kentucky University, Bowling Green, Kentucky (2007); Winterthur Museum and Library, Edward Deming Andrews Fellowship (2010); Hamilton College Communal Studies Collection Research Fellowship (2012); Northern Kentucky University, faculty summer research (2011) and sabbatical leave (2011–2012). I also wish to acknowledge the support of the editorial staff of *Timeline*, Ohio Historical Society, who encouraged my early research efforts by assisting me in preparing my article "Issachar Bates: Shaker Missionary" (*Timeline* 26:3, September 2009), which represented my first stab at biographical writing.

The research for this work has taken me to the manuscript collections of many institutions, large and small. The following have graciously granted me permission to quote from the Shaker manuscripts in their holdings: Winterthur Museum and Library, New York Public Library, Ohio Historical Society, Western Reserve Historical Society, and Hancock Shaker Villages. I am grateful to other institutions for giving me access to their collections, either through onsite use or microfilm: Library of Congress, Shaker Museum and Library at Old Chatham, Kentucky Special Collections Library at Western Kentucky University, New York State Library, Filson Historical Society, Communal Studies Collection at Hamilton College, Dayton Metro Library, Petersham Historical Society, Athol Public Library, Washington County Historical Society, Special Collections at Dartmouth College Library. Several institutions and individuals have generously permitted the use of illustrations: Western Reserve Historical Society, Ohio Historical Society, Hamilton College Special Collections, Shaker Museum and Library at Old Chatham, Winterthur Museum and Library, Joslyn Museum of Art, Dayton History, Smithsonian Museum of American Art, Filson Historical Society, and the American Antiquarian Society.

■ In my use of quoted material, I have generally retained writers' misspellings and grammatical inconsistencies. However, I have made some silent corrections for the benefit of the reader. I have made every effort to ensure that these corrections do not affect the writer's meaning.

"Now here's my faith I'll speak it plain"

The life of Issachar Bates is an extraordinary American story. It opens a window onto the dynamic richness of a young and growing America, from its late colonial "signs and wonders" and the upheaval of Revolution to the religious turmoil of the Second Great Awakening and the expansion of the western frontier.[1] Issachar Bates both witnessed and participated in this rich drama. One critical factor brings his life journey into focus: Issachar Bates was a Shaker. But he was not just one face among the thousands to pass through the movement. Rather, he was an early Shaker convert who happened to be utterly pivotal to the movement's successful expansion beyond the Appalachian Mountains in the early 1800s. And Issachar Bates was a conundrum. He was both a patriot and a pacifist; he fathered nine children and embraced celibacy; he pioneered and preached, built new communities even as he sought the solitude of the woods, helped establish a separate Shaker "Zion" yet kept to the road whenever he could. In short, Issachar's life was as filled with tumult and contradictions as America itself. Tracing his life's journey illuminates the Early Republic from which the Shaker movement was launched, follows the Shaker story to the "western" United States, exhibits the growth of the Shaker "West," and reveals the ways in which the Shaker movement remained coherent across vast distances. It also exposes an irony that Shaker scholars have begun to observe: within this religious order where individual identity was subsumed within collective "union," individual gifts, character, talents, and achievement still mattered enormously. As a believer who played a key role through a long and formative period of Shaker history, Issachar Bates left his mark on the movement — as a preacher, evangelist, poet, songwriter, dancer, and community leader. Given the influence of Shakerism on American culture, it is not too much of a stretch to say that Issachar also left his mark on America.

This is his story.

■ The Shaker movement was already decades old in America when Issachar Bates converted in the summer of 1801. For Issachar, formal Shaker conversion involved making a personal confession of sin to a Shaker elder. To do this, Issachar rode away from his home in Hartford, New York, on the southern edge of the Adirondack Mountains and headed south to New Lebanon, the center of the growing Shaker movement in the Berkshire Hills on the New York–Massachusetts border. It was not an action he undertook lightly. At the age of forty-three, Issachar was the sole provider for a large family. He had been married to Lovina Maynard for twenty-three years, more than half of his life, and most of their nine living children remained in the household. Never noted for work in any particular trade, Issachar made a somewhat meager living as a woodsman and farmer. But he was a popular figure in the community and an active member of the local Baptist church, where he had been the choirmaster for about a dozen years. Through a dramatic religious experience around 1795, Issachar had discovered that he had a gift for preaching, and by the late 1790s he often accepted preaching appointments in the surrounding area. One of eleven siblings, Issachar maintained loving relationships with several brothers and sisters, and he remained concerned for the welfare of his aging and widowed father, who lived in western Massachusetts.

Issachar Bates lived an exceptional life by any standard. With late colonial Massachusetts as the backdrop of his childhood, he was profoundly affected by the climate of his times and eager to join in the fight for American independence. Enlisting as a teenage fifer, one of his earliest experiences was the Battle of Bunker Hill, and before the war ended, he participated in many other engagements, from Vermont to New Jersey. After the war, he was drawn to the frontier, first to the wilds of Maine and later to wooded mountains near Saratoga, New York. Becoming a Shaker continued his frontier life, when in 1805 he was chosen to be one of the movement's first missionaries to carry the Shaker message beyond the Appalachian Mountains. The next thirty years found him moving throughout the Ohio Valley, intersecting with some of that region's most spectacular people and events, from Tecumseh and William Henry Harrison to the cataclysmic New Madrid earthquake. His journeys trace the evolution of American transportation of the period, from the Wilderness Road through the Cumberland Gap to river steamboats and barges on the Erie Canal. He returned to New Lebanon, New York, in 1835 to live out his final years. At the time of his death in 1837, the Shaker movement had grown exponentially through his effort, and three of his children were assuming important roles within the rising generation of Shaker leaders in the East.

In many ways, Issachar's life itself embodied the major expansion phase of Shaker history. By happenstance, he was witness to Ann Lee's earliest proselytizing efforts in central Massachusetts in the early 1780s; later, he himself carried on those efforts in the Shaker West. Issachar was present when Shakerism reached its geographic apex in western Indiana and began to contract. He helped establish each of the seven major settlements in the West, seeing the Shaker world reach its probable numerical high point in the mid-1820s. Even at the end of his thirty years in the West, he remained in the thick of thorny changes, as the pioneering generation of leaders aged and began to be displaced by a younger generation. With his return to New York in 1835 and his death in the spring of 1837, Issachar's life closed at the same time as a critical early phase in Shaker history. But his personal influence persisted.

Almost immediately after his death, Issachar Bates began to represent to believers across the Shaker world the "pioneering" generation that had overseen Shaker expansion. In fact, within just a few months of his death, conditions in the Shaker world took a momentous turn when a group of girls began having inexplicable visions. These events would take the Shaker world across a threshold into what would eventually be called the "Era of Manifestations," a dozen years or more during which Shaker villages were pre-occupied with spectral visits from Ann Lee, other early Shaker leaders, angels, and a range of historical figures. While Issachar's life offers a valuable window into the Shaker world prior to the diversions of the Era of Manifestations, that era also serves as a signpost to Issachar's legacy. For decades after his death, Shakers attested that Issachar's spirit visited their worship meetings, bringing messages, counsel, and songs. Issachar became one of the symbols of an earlier, more heroic phase of Shaker history. Death did not soon diminish Issachar's influence, and he remained a popular character in many Shaker visions for years to come.

The common understanding of America's Shaker heritage implicitly assumes that a large degree of uniformity existed within the Shaker movement: uniformity of belief, of behavior, of worship, of lifestyle, of creative practice, of material culture. The Shaker world stretched across a thousand miles of the American landscape — from Maine to the western Indiana frontier, hardly a homogeneous region. And Shakers have been part of America for each and every day of America's 234-plus year history as a nation: from the movement's beginnings in 1774 with nine newly immigrated English radicals, swelling to thousands in the early nineteenth century, and dwindling down to a tiny handful in the early twenty-first century. Along the way, a separate Shaker culture emerged, a culture that shared certain characteristics even while it exhibited sharp regional differences. Today, "Shaker" is understood mostly as a design aesthetic, a pared-down fusion of form and function expressed through simple natural materials in objects ranging from furniture and baskets to cabinetry and architecture. To the degree that Shaker uniformity existed, it was hard won. Particularly in the movement's earlier decades, it was a work in progress. Paradoxically, Shaker uniformity drew its raw ingredients from the many creative individuals who gave their lives to the movement during its growth period, who participated in the hard work of expanding the movement, and who rose to the challenge of teaching others what it meant to be "Shaker."

For these reasons, it is remarkable that biography has played such an insignificant role in Shaker scholarship to date. The sum total of Shaker scholarship has addressed the collective society in its many spiritual and material dimensions, implying that the contributions of individual Shakers — for good or ill — need not be examined at length. After all, Shakers themselves were enjoined to lay aside their egos and submerge their personal qualities within the collective. But as Shaker scholar Glendyne Wergland succinctly states, "There is no such thing as a generic Shaker any more than there is a generic American."[2] With a solid foundation of basic descriptive history already established, one turn in Shaker scholarship is toward increasingly sophisticated analytical and critical explanatory studies. Biography is a key part of this explanatory turn. Biography literally enlivens our study of the Shakers, allowing us to flesh out the uniform ranks of believers with real faces, personalities, idiosyncrasies, and singular experiences. And biography also helps fill in a stubborn contextual gap that always arises in any study of the Shakers, namely, the question of why. Many simply cannot conceive why individuals would renounce spouses, children, sexual love, personal wealth, and property to join a radical, celibate, and persecuted religious order. Our failure to understand that basic question still consigns the study of the Shakers to America's cultural margins, even as we ironically enshrine Shaker material output within America's cultural center. Scrutinizing individual Shakers, their kinship and friendship networks, and the faith and livelihood struggles that both brought them into the Shaker movement and informed their existence within that movement brings us right to the heart of the matter: namely, understanding how Shaker culture was created and has been sustained against such odds.

The Shakers of the past clearly believed that biography was important, and they seemed to place special value on Issachar Bates's life story. Many individual Shakers wrote autobiographies at the urging of the Ministry and elders. Issachar wrote his autobiography in the early spring of 1832, evidently at the urging of Richard McNemar, a prominent Ohio Shaker and Issachar's longtime friend. It is a remarkable work — lively, witty, emotional, direct, sometimes blunt, laden with rich detail. With attention to many phases of his long, interesting, and well-traveled life, both before and after becoming a

Shaker, Issachar's account was probably considered gripping reading by other Shakers. It was copied and recopied many times, mostly in bound manuscript volumes together with other duplicated material authored by or associated with Issachar: poetry, hymns, letters, and commentaries. Of the many surviving versions, no two are quite alike, and each one reflects a distinct amalgamation of material illuminating this singular man. In some cases, copyists omit some of Issachar's stories, possibly because they were considered graphic and therefore unsuitable. Some of his more colorful turns of phrase are altered in some versions, probably because they were considered too vulgar for the general community to read. But Issachar's use of direct and vivid language made his narrative all the more appealing. Evidence from extant manuscripts suggests that no other Shaker's autobiography was copied as enthusiastically. Several Shaker communities held copies that were worn and well-thumbed, and nearly fifty years after his death, portions of his autobiography were edited and serialized in the *Shaker Manifesto*, a magazine circulated throughout the Shaker world. And the memory of Issachar Bates was kept alive in other ways, too. He left scores of songs and poems, many that contain lively accounts of journeys, of adapting to frontier life, of struggles to establish new settlements amid hostile social and natural environments. Many of his letters survive, spanning much of his long Shaker life. Texts written by other Shakers also contain abundant anecdotes about Issachar Bates, pointing to a colorful and energetic personality that balanced charisma with coarse humor, features that seldom co-existed in Shaker preachers but traits that were ideally suited to engaging the rough conditions of the frontier. Perhaps because of his indelible association with Shakerism's "pioneering" phase, or perhaps because he was simply a larger-than-life figure that left a strong impression on whomever he touched, Issachar Bates and his memory captured the attention of later Shakers in a unique way.

During his time as a Shaker, Issachar often stood both literally and figuratively at the center of Shaker worship because of his talents as a singer, dancer, and songwriter. Music sustained him throughout his long life. From the time that he taught himself to play the fife as a teenager, providing an entry to the Revolutionary Army, music was one of Issachar's tickets into the broader world. As a Shaker, he drew on his many years as a popular Baptist choirmaster to bring musical animation to Shaker worship. For the Shakers, music was even more integral to worship than it was in other Christian congregations, because the trademark Shaker dance was accompanied by various sorts of "laboring" songs. Issachar wrote, "As I was a singer it always fell to my lot to sing the first laboring song in breaking the way to worship God in the dance."[3]

By the end of his life, Issachar had become a major contributor to Shaker hymnody, which first flourished during the western expansion period. With his deep love of music and his proven ability to retain countless songs learned throughout his lifetime, he helped to ensure that music would continue to stand at the center of Shaker spiritual life.

Issachar also was adept at expressing himself, both orally and in writing. His education was unremarkable, but he was an avid reader of the Bible and religious tracts. Once he began to preach, his persuasiveness and appeal to listeners can be ascertained more through the many surviving anecdotes than through any written record of his sermons. Issachar's words touched people, and the thousand-odd conversions that he personally oversaw in the West are eloquent testimony to his talent as an orator. He was also a reasonably good poet. Like many educated people of his period, he often used poetry to express his most private thoughts, mark the major transitions in his life, and record his most profound observations about life and his fellow human beings. Unlike many Shaker contemporaries, he did not keep a journal, but he left a rich "paper trail" nonetheless, in countless hymnals, letters, and other manuscripts.

Issachar was a gregarious man, given to warmth and affection. But he also was well accustomed to being alone, and many key events of his life occurred when he was alone in the woods or accompanied by only two or three other people. One of eleven siblings and father of nine children, Issachar was deeply familiar with life in a large and eclectic household. No doubt this equipped him for Shaker existence. Yet as an adolescent he was often forced to "hire out" to other families, a circumstance that may have found him in lonely and dismal conditions among strangers whom he needed to please. Such experiences, together with his soldiering life, may have helped him develop the resourcefulness and leadership abilities that would guide his Shaker life.

Yet despite youthful separation from family and a penchant for solitary revelation, Issachar was emotional, capable of deep love and friendship for both men and women. He enjoyed drinking, particularly in the company of his friends, and he may have been an alcoholic. Perhaps because he spent most of his Shaker life apart from his biological family, his friendships were acutely important to him. Some of his closest friends were men with whom he seemed to share little in common. Benjamin Seth Youngs, probably his dearest friend, was much younger, unmarried, small and delicate, and had joined the Shakers at twenty — quite the contrast to the physically robust middle-aged Issachar at the time of his conversion. Other friends were older married men and fathers, latecomers like himself to the Shaker order. One important friend was Ohio convert Richard McNemar, who would become a key figure in the Shaker West. Similar to Issachar, Richard converted as he approached middle age and was the head of a large family, a popular preacher, a poet and singer. But the jovial Issachar and the intellectual Richard were miles apart temperamentally, even as they forged a crucial relationship during their thirty years together in the West. Other vitally important friendships were with women. Issachar openly forged affectionate bonds with several young women in the West, each of whom seemed to consider him a father figure. Perhaps these friendships formed partly as a vicarious expression of the paternal affection that he could no longer give directly to his daughters who remained in the East.

No images or drawings of Issachar Bates are known to exist. Some Shakers recalled him as a handsome man with arresting features, who paid careful attention to maintaining "tasty" — or tasteful — grooming and appearance. This may have contributed to his charismatic preaching persona. His son, also named Issachar and a Shaker elder at Watervliet, New York, by the 1870s, was photographed several times; but no one is known to have remarked upon whether the son resembled his father. However, one Shaker sister from Ohio wrote of Issachar senior that:

> His forehead was a little retreating but large and full, his brows jutted over his eyes, had a large Roman nose which looked grand to me, had an exquisite mouth with a look that could only say delicious things, a broad full chin with a dent in the middle on the lower side dividing it in two lobes ... the ends of the curls which hung over his clean shirt collar had a silky reddish hue (it is said he was very tasty in arranging his toilet) ... Issachar's height was five feet nine inches, and his general weight about 150 pounds, he was very thick through the breast, (and) stood erect.[4]

Writing at another time, Moses Eastwood, a Shaker brother at Watervliet, Ohio, where Issachar was an elder for several years, also recorded this description of his physical appearance in the early 1830s: "In person he was about five feet eight inches in height, of a dark complexion, and dark colored hair and but little inclined to be gray or bald for a man of his age ... He was a man about middle size, a firm close made body and a strong hardy constitution well calculated to bear fatigue and hardship of which he had been much inured all his life before he came among believers."[5]

Issachar did indeed possess a hardy constitution, which he put to use in the Shakers' service. He walked thousands of miles, contracted malaria, suffered frostbite. He needed spectacles, and he developed a tremor in his head and neck. But his hands remained strong and steady enough for both writing and skilled work. Later in life, he became a keen gardener and basket-maker. He learned to weave large willow hampers, which he produced in the dozens. And at seventy-nine Issachar continued to sing and dance, conforming to the best expectations of the Shakers' lively worship, as one of his final songs attests with its memorable line, "I'll take nimble steps, I'll be a David."

Issachar Bates's music has informed this project in many ways, not least of which is the title for this introduction, taken from an untitled hymn written by Issachar sometime during his years at the Shaker settlement in western Indiana (see appendix 2 for full text and tune):[6]

> Now by my motion I will prove how much the work of God I love
> For ev'ry tree what fruit it shows is 'round the limbs on which it grows
> So let my limbs with fruit be strong while lab'ring such a lively song
> Come all my active powers wise and make a living sacrifice.
>
> Stand up my soul and clear my way, And give me room to dance and play
> O cut me loose from every drag, As Samuel hew'd the base Agag.
> For why should sluggish flesh control And bind my ever living soul
> Such lawless bondage shall not be, As God is true I will be free.
>
> Now here's my faith I'll speak it plain And let my feet the sense explain
> With zeal to labor and unite With every gift that comes to light.
> If in back order there I'll spring If in step manner or to sing
> If shuffling I will do my best To keep my union with the rest.
>
> The reason why I sing so long And step the notes so quick and strong
> Is just because that God has done What he has promised by his Son.
> He's sent the everlasting Key That opens heaven where I be
> This animates me while I move For this strong Key is truth and love.

These verses exude energy, exuberant effort, and — above all — *movement*. Issachar Bates was a man in motion. The motion of his life took him through the birth of America, into the expanding frontier, and into the heart of a religious order that has become a quintessential part of the American experience. As a Shaker, his "motion" can be read on several levels, from his preaching on the revival circuit, to his work on the construction and growth of communities, to his active leadership of song and dance. Indeed, the dynamic motion of people like Issachar — whether at work or at worship — reminds us of just why Shakerism has been called a "*movement*." In one verse, Issachar identifies what it is that sustains and animates his long life of "motion," namely, God's promise of a key into heaven.

This book generally follows Issachar Bates's life and times chronologically. First it explores Issachar's youth alongside the coming of the Shakers to New England. One chapter examines Issachar's dramatic years of service in the American Revolution, and another follows his young-adult years and the growth of his family. Most of the rest of the book traces Issachar's life as a Shaker. After a chapter on his conversion and early missionary travels, it turns to Issachar's life in the Shaker West: his early travels and preaching in the region; his leadership stints at the West Union (Busro), Indiana, and Watervliet, Ohio, communities; his contributions to life in the West as seen through his many friendships and travels; and the onset of a troublesome transformation in the Western communities in the early 1830s. One chapter examines members of Issachar's family and descendants, including the lives and contributions of some among Issachar's many kin who were Shakers: his son Issachar Jr.; his daughters Polly, Betsy, and Sarah; his wife, Lovina; and several siblings, nieces, and nephews. Later, the book follows Issachar back to the Shaker East, exploring his return to New Lebanon and his struggles to cope with separation from his beloved West. The book concludes by looking at the significant shadow that Issachar casts across the Shaker movement, examining his legacy to Shaker culture and the ways in which he has been remembered.

Many of the manuscripts used in this study, including those written by Issachar, use erratic spelling and punctuation. In quotations, I have made silent editorial changes sufficient only to ease the comprehension of a contemporary reader. I use the forms of address for Shakers that they used for each other, which in most cases meant first name only, sometimes preceded by a gender-specific title such as elder/eldress or brother/sister. I have chosen, in most cases, to refer to Issachar Bates using his first name only—a name that was unusual even in his lifetime. Of the few other Shakers named Issachar, one was his son and namesake, and the others were obscure young men in Ohio who may have been named in his honor. Most Shakers signed their letters and other writings with simply their first names, Issachar included, and in countless manuscripts, Ministry, elders, and rank-and-file believers refer to him by first name only, and with no title. Other manuscripts do attach the title of elder or brother, but Issachar's title changed during his years as a Shaker. He was an elder for periods of time at two different western villages, and for the last several years of his life he was again a brother. During most of his Shaker life, he was simply one of the "brethren." Still, many referred to Issachar as "elder" after he no longer held that title; a few even referred to him as "Father Issachar," a title to which he never held legitimate claim. But his strong and unusual name paired well with his strong and unusual personality.

There has been some debate over the derivation of "Issachar" and its correct pronunciation. As a man's name, "Issachar" is found in the book of Genesis, and it was the name given to the ninth son of the Hebrew patriarch Jacob. Consequently, it is the name of one of the twelve tribes of Israel, but its exact Hebrew derivation is murky.[7] Within the Shaker studies community, some believe today that Issachar Bates's name should be pronounced with a long "I" vowel sound and the emphasis on the second syllable. But evidence suggests that during Issachar's lifetime, at least in the Shaker West, his name was pronounced with a short "I" vowel sound and the emphasis on the first syllable. Several poems written by western brothers and sisters include Issachar's name in meters that would make any other pronunciation exceptionally awkward. A journal kept by Brother Nathaniel Taylor of Watervliet, Ohio, names Issachar consistently as some variation of "Elder Isker," "Elder Isiker," or even the mellifluous "elderisker."[8] Together, this evidence points to a first-syllable accented pronunciation, quite different from how some pronounce it today.

Debate over the pronunciation of Issachar Bates's distinctive name should not interfere with our appreciation of his delightfully complex life story. One of Issachar's close friends, South Union, Kentucky, Shaker songwriter Sally Eades, poignantly expresses the love that Shakers in the West felt for both Issachar and for his unusual name: "Your bright example we adore / We love to even speak your name / May heaven bless you evermore / We thank the Lord that here you came."[9] Issachar's name and his story deserve to be remembered. His life journey can teach us much about the Shakers, the unique experience of the Shaker West, and the rich tapestry of life in the Early Republic.

Issachar Bates

CHAPTER 1

"Signs and Wonders"

EARLY LIFE, SPIRITUAL PREPARATION,

AND THE COMING OF THE SHAKERS

*I was afraid that God would come up on me some day in Judgment
because I was not good. This caused me to watch the heavens above
and the earth beneath for signs and wonders. — Issachar Bates*

As Issachar Bates looked back on a childhood filled with memorable events and experiences, he interpreted many of his youthful circumstances as preparation for his later life as a Shaker. His family life was unsettled, forcing him to develop personal qualities of adaptability. He lived entirely in unsettled regions, barely removed from wilderness conditions. He witnessed great social transformation. Unbeknownst to Issachar as he was growing up in rural Massachusetts, the people who would soon turn his life and the lives of multitudes in New England upside-down were developing their radical ideas in an industrial town in far-off England. About the time that Issachar was leaving behind his own childhood, these "Shakers" left the place of their nativity to migrate to America, where their remarkable behavior would soon be interpreted by many as some of the "signs and wonders" that had gripped New England for years. The young Issachar Bates was deeply affected by many of these "signs and wonders," various natural phenomena widely interpreted as divine portents of grave future occurrences. These experiences made him vigilant during his childhood and beyond, and prepared him for the singular life that would follow.

*I was born in the town of Hingham County of Suffolk State of
Massachusetts 14 miles south east of the city of Boston on the Atlantic
shore the twenty ninth of January in the year of our Lord 1758.*[1]

The town of Hingham marked the southeastern reach of the Massachusetts Bay Colony when the ancestors of Issachar Bates arrived there in 1635. Clement Bates hailed from Norfolk, England, near the English town of Hingham, and he emigrated with a large group that included the first American ancestors of at least two other important nineteenth-century figures, Abraham Lincoln and poet Katherine Lee Bates. Clement Bates was granted an acre of land and named to a town office; he also became a fish merchant. In the late 1670s, his grandsons migrated some four miles to the east and helped establish Cohasset, a second enclave or "precinct" within Hingham.[2]

David Bates, the great-grandson of Clement Bates, was Issachar Bates's grandfather and a substantial and ambitious citizen of Cohasset in the first half of the eighteenth century. Known locally as "King David," David Bates had his hand in a range of enterprises. He farmed and raised sheep on a thirty-acre parcel that lay on King Street, Cohasset's first thoroughfare, plotted by surveyors in 1670. He also owned a small fishing vessel, probably used to fish for mackerel in the local waters outside Cohasset Bay.[3] He was a mason and among the chief builders of Cohasset's first meeting house in 1747. He also served as the town constable. David Bates married Patience Farrow, and the couple had twelve children. When Patience died, David remarried a widow with many children of her own.

In 1752, David Bates and other Cohasset householders voted for formal separation from the town of Hingham. The few miles between Cohasset and Hingham could be traversed only by rough paths, arduous for going to market and grueling for school children. The journey by sea from Cohasset Bay around Nantasket Peninsula and into Hingham Harbor was longer and more difficult than sailing to Boston. Moreover, Cohasset families were large and interrelated, and they formed an autonomous community distinct from Hingham.[4] However, by the time of Issachar Bates's grandfather David, the expansive Bates kin network had spread through the twin communities, and Bates had become a common family name in both townships.

The father of the Shaker Issachar Bates was William Bates, born in 1725 as the third son of David Bates and his first wife, Patience Farrow. Another son was born to David and Patience in 1734, and they named him Issachar, but this child died within a few months. At the end of 1735 a further son was born to the couple, and again named Issachar. This was William Bates's closest sibling, a younger brother Issachar Bates, whose name William would later give to his own son. William's interests were less eclectic than his father's, and his trade is simply identified as "bricklayer." In 1748 he married Mercy Joy, daughter of Prince Joy, another important Cohasset citizen and farmer, who often held school in his home for local children and was instrumental in attempting to establish Cohasset's first school. In 1749 William's assets consisted of a house, with no acreage recorded. But the family soon began to grow, and between 1750 and 1760, six children were born in Cohasset to William and Mercy.[5]

Cohasset was Hingham's robust "second precinct" of 160 households, but was not yet officially a separate community when Issachar Bates was born there on January 29, 1758. Issachar was the fifth child of William and Mercy, and their third son. Their first, Noah, had lived only a few months.[6] Adhering to a pattern followed by William's parents in the previous generation, the next male child born became the deceased child's namesake. Issachar was their next son, some four years younger than Noah. No baptism is recorded for Issachar, although two of his siblings were baptized in the local Congregationalist church. Even in colonial New England, Issachar's name likely would have been noticed as unusual.[7] At that time, no one in Hingham or Cohasset outside the Bates family bore that name.[8] "Issachar," which comes from the book of Genesis, is the name of one of the twelve sons of the patriarch Jacob, from whom the twelve tribes of Israel are derived. But because the name was so obscure, it is more likely that Issachar was in fact named for his uncle, his father William's younger brother, than for Jacob's son — especially because at the time of Issachar's birth, his uncle Issachar happened to be courting Hannah Joy, the younger sister of Mercy Joy, Issachar's mother. That couple married in 1760. It was not unusual in the period for families to become intertwined through the marriages of siblings to siblings. Just as Issachar's father and uncle had married sisters, Issachar and one of his own brothers would later also marry sisters.

When I was about three years old, my father (William Bates) with my Mother (who was Mercy Joy) moved their family into the county of Middlesex, township of Sherburne, about 24 miles west of Boston, where we lived about nine years.[9]

William Bates's family was growing, and he was finding good work as a bricklayer in Cohasset. He built the chimneys on Cohasset's first school, near the home of his father-in-law.[10] His family and his wife's family were close and growing increasingly interconnected through marriage. And Bates kin were spread throughout the community. But nonetheless, sometime around 1762, according to Issachar Bates's own account, William chose to uproot his family and move to the tiny village of Sherborn, a journey of about forty miles to the west. The reasons for William's decision are not explicit. But William's father, David, had died the previous year, and David's second wife had remarried.[11] Moreover, William's younger brother, Issachar, also moved from Cohasset at about the same time, but farther afield to eastern Connecticut. It is possible that upon David Bates's death whatever residue remained of his estate passed to his heirs, providing his sons and their families the assets necessary for resettling elsewhere.

Sherborn, then called "Sherburn," was a farming community of about 110 families in the woods along the main route leading from Boston to the communities of the Connecticut River Valley region to the west.[12] Sherborn adjoined Natick, a town of "Praying Indians," only three miles away. Small cottage industries produced baskets, tools, and small articles for markets in Boston, but the area was not particularly prosperous.[13] A first cousin of Mercy Joy Bates, Benjamin Joy, had also left Cohasset in the early 1760s and come to Sherborn to work as a storekeeper and farm a small piece of land.[14] It is possible that William Bates partnered with him, or that William tried to find work as a bricklayer, building chimneys as brick was not used locally to build houses.[15] The Bates family continued to grow, and at least three more children were born in the Sherborn area.[16] But supporting a large family of at least nine children was difficult with little extended family to rely upon for help. Tax records show that in 1767 William Bates paid a real estate tax of under five shillings and a personal property tax of under three shillings, very low sums relative to the other households in Sherborn.[17] The family probably struggled. In 1768 Benjamin Joy declared bankruptcy, and around the same time, William Bates moved the family about twelve miles west to Southborough, a slightly larger town just inside neighboring Worcester County,[18] where they lived for about two years. Writing of the move away from Sherborn and Southborough three years later, Issachar would remark that the family came to realize what it was to "fare hard." By that he may have meant that while the family fared hard in Sherborn and Southborough, after their move conditions grew even worse.

> *I shall now make some remarks how my little mind was exercised in those days. Altho I was a mischievous boy yet I thought much about God … (M)y parents were Presbyterians, and taught me all the good things they know of such as the little praise cradle hymns catechisms and creeds, which I attended to regular.[19]*

Although there is no record of Issachar Bates's formal education, we can be certain that he learned to read and write during his time in Sherborn and Southborough. His mother probably valued education, since her father, Prince Joy, had been instrumental in establishing local schools, and she likely worked to educate her children. From Issachar's own brief allusions to what he learned under his parents' tutelage, we can infer that the family probably owned a copy of the *New England Primer*, which had been the universally favored children's school book across Massachusetts since before 1690.[20] By the 1760s, editions of the *New England Primer* also integrated the Westminster

Catechism, the popular doctrinal text for Calvinistic Protestants, including Presbyterians.[21] Issachar's remark that his parents were Presbyterians, is a bit puzzling because Presbyterians were not numerous in Massachusetts in the 1760s. (Many colonial New Englanders that ascribed to Presbyterianism — which was distinguished by its ideas about church governance and its conviction that church and state should be united — were formal members of Congregationalist churches and enforced strict Sabbath observances in their own households.[22] This was possibly the case in the Bates home.) It is clear that religious doctrine loomed large in Issachar's early education.

Issachar probably also attended school for at least part of his childhood. Massachusetts law had long required that towns over a certain size provide free schools. Sherborn records reflect the presence of both men and woman teachers in the 1760s, not unusual for Massachusetts in the mid-eighteenth century.[23] Additionally, rural towns like Sherborn with diffuse populations and no concentrated town center often held "moving schools," in which an itinerant schoolmaster would travel through the region offering temporary schools in short increments of a few weeks or months.[24] Issachar described himself as "mischievous," but he also indicates he was an obedient child and a dedicated pupil. Clearly, some of his accomplishments as a youth — such as mastering the fife and composing poetry — suggest he was a boy of keen intellect and creativity. His later writing also reflects a fondness of numbers and a general fluency with mathematics, so his early education must have included basic arithmetic. Massachusetts law dictated that towns establish "grammar schools" to prepare young boys for college by offering Latin and other advanced subjects, but Sherborn was fined by the Massachusetts General Court in 1767 because its schools did *not* comply with that directive. In fact, no grammar school was established in Sherborn until 1773, several years after the Bates family left the town.[25] It is therefore unlikely that Issachar's formal studies ever went beyond basic reading, writing, and ciphering. Besides the *New England Primer* with its catechism, Issachar's literacy and worldview developed through use of the Bible and popular hymn books of the day, such as the hymns of Isaac Watts.

> About the year 1771 my Father moved his family into the new country about 40 miles to Worcester county in the state aforesaid where we soon found what it was to fare hard. Now nothing worth naming took place for about two years, only that we had to work hard to get a living in that new country. For there was a large family of us — my Father and Mother and eleven children (viz) Mercy, Noah, Hannah, Issachar, Sarah, Theodore, Olive, Molly, Dolly, Caleb, and William.[26]

It is not clear why William Bates moved his family again after some three years in Southborough, this time to the far northern part of Worcester County and the newly incorporated towns of Templeton and Athol.[27] Possibly William Bates was attracted to the area because land was still available and populations were relatively low, affording opportunity for families willing to endure life in a primarily unsettled area. The mountainous region was still thickly forested; most homes and town buildings were log cabins. Athol, where the last two Bates children were born, did not complete its first meeting house until 1773; in the adjacent town of Templeton, where several of the Bates children would later marry, neither meeting house nor school was built until the 1780s.[28] The rugged geography kept the area isolated, the few roads were poor, and the climate was harsh. Altogether, these were by far the roughest conditions the Bates family had faced.

For Issachar Bates, life in the wooded mountains of Templeton and Athol meant the abrupt end of his childhood. He writes that during the family's first few years in the area, "Some of the time I lived with my Father and some times hired out." From the age of thirteen, he was sent to work as hired help for other families and his wages used to support the still growing Bates family. Indeed, "hiring out" was such a common experience for boys and young men of the period that working as a servant was ubiquitous in colonial New England.[29] In communities just beginning to carve themselves from the wilderness, households with fewer able-bodied males readily hired paid labor from households where males were more numerous. In such conditions, hired hands faced such physically demanding work as felling and clearing trees, preparing logs for building, constructing cabins and fences, and digging out stumps and stones to make way for fields and orchards. This was exhausting work even for most full-grown men, but the practice of "putting out" adolescent boys was regarded as an important feature of their preparation for adult life in colonial New England.[30] There was no stigma attached to working as a hired hand and no mantle of shame for the families who allowed their sons to do so. But Issachar's life as a hired hand may have meant the end of his formal schooling. Templeton and Athol did expend modest sums for education in the 1770s, and they organized school districts; but as a hired hand, Issachar might have had little opportunity to attend classes.

While many young hired hands were subjected to cruel treatment by their employers, Issachar Bates left no evidence that his experience of being a hired worker was a particularly unpleasant one. He may have been absent from his own family's household for long periods of time. Indeed, Issachar's son and namesake, Issachar Bates, Junior, later recorded that his father had left William Bates's household entirely as a young teenager: "When young he left his Father and went to Garry, Massachusetts, now called Phillipstown."[31] While this statement contradicts what Issachar writes about his own childhood, it suggests that his children grew up hearing him recount his adolescence spent substantially independent of his parents. He may have slept in the homes of strangers, or his sleeping quarters may have been in barns and outbuildings. In any case, he probably faced conditions that would have encouraged him to develop resourcefulness, self-reliance, and a congenial demeanor. Issachar would certainly exhibit all these qualities later in life, and they became some of his greatest assets as a Shaker. What little he recorded about his early moral training at home suggests he developed the diligence and obedience that would have satisfied his employers. And he may have been a physically robust youth. Some sixty years later in the 1830s, a Shaker in Ohio described Issachar's physical condition this way: "He was a man about middle size, a firm close made body and a strong hardy constitution well calculated to bear fatigue and hardship of which he had been much inured all his life."[32] Issachar was physically suited for hard labor, and he grew accustomed to a life of daily exertions. As a boy called to do a man's work in the woods, he also began learning some of the tasks that he would later tackle when he helped carve Shaker settlements out of the Ohio, Indiana, and Kentucky frontiers.

Although the Bates family migrated to communities that were successively more isolated during Issachar's childhood, the overall climate of ongoing and impending change was inescapable. Whether it was continuous humnan transformation of the once wilderness landscape, the subsequent social transformations as people throughout the region migrated to "new settlement" areas, the accompanying ideological transformations as the realities of frontier life in the "new settlements" diverged from the establishment churches, or the coming political transformation as the clash with the British loomed, change was the order of the day.[33]

> I could read some and heard my parents read that God would show wonders in the heaven above and signs in the earth beneath. And when I was about eleven years of age these frightful signs began to appear. A few years before the revolution war and the opening of the gospel in New England, many of those wonders were seen ... For in all ages God in his condescending goodness whenever he was about to build up and bless a people, he gave them previous signs of his intentions that the wise might be encouraged thereby. And whenever he was about to bring living destruction upon any people, he

gave them warnings before hand by signs and wonders that the wise might be prepared to meet the event.[34]

From childhood Issachar Bates had developed a Calvinist view of the natural world that recognized nature as God's handiwork. For the Calvinist, because God created all things, God could intervene in the natural world at any time, and the processes of nature could reflect divine will.[35] As political tensions mounted in colonial New England, pointing to a clash between colonists and Crown, and as peculiar religious sects proliferated in number, many New Englanders retained the conviction that God worked through nature to prepare humankind for great changes that were soon to come. Consequently, the newspapers, broadsides, and pamphlets of the time were filled with reports of "signs and wonders," as people sought to make sense of unusual natural phenomena.

The many signs and wonders that Issachar witnessed during his childhood and youth — beginning about 1769 when he and his family lived near Southborough and continuing through the Revolutionary era and later — left their mark. Although he did not write about them for over sixty years, his early witness of these signs clearly cemented a lifelong conviction that unusual events in the natural world were God's way of communicating directly with humankind. And because his life would be forever changed by the Revolutionary War and the arrival of Ann Lee and the Shaker gospel, he interpreted certain natural "wonders" in his childhood as signposts pointing to both. Many of the phenomena that Issachar describes in his autobiography can be corroborated by contemporary newspaper and pamphlet accounts of observations made in the Boston area. Most are easy to identify; some are more perplexing. A typical account, this one occurring about the time that Issachar's family moved to Southberry, runs as follows:

> The first [sign] had the appearance of what is called northern lights — night after night, for weeks flashing from east to west, till at length one night it spread over the whole horizon and the whole heavens appeared to me like a flaming brush heaps. No sleep that night for it lasted all night. The next was [a] blazing Comet which could be seen every clear night for weeks. The tail of it appeared to be about a rod long. It was bell muzzled in perfect shape of a trumpet. Some nights it would look as red as blood at other times more pale.[36]

Boston newspapers of the period regularly reported sightings of the Aurora Borealis across the region.[37] John Winthrop, a Harvard professor and astronomer (and descendant of the founder of Massachusetts Bay Colony), kept a "Journal of Meteorology" from 1742 to 1779, in which he recorded Aurora Borealis episodes and their intensity. The period from 1768 through 1771 identifies over fifty Auroras, many characterized as "bright," "very bright," "great," or "considerable."[38] A comet during the period is also well documented, appearing in September 1769 and eliciting excitement through-out the Northeast.[39] Although mainstream New England church leaders had been trying to distance themselves from the more Calvinist-inspired interpre-tations of such natural spectacles, the reaction of common people was still to regard such extraordinary sights as "prodigies" portending dramatic changes in social order.[40] The young Issachar Bates seems to have been surrounded by people who strongly believed that God communicated through such "prodi-gies." In the press of the day, factual accounts of unusual astronomical events, such as the 1769 comet, were often combined with narrative accounts of fan-tastic dreams and visions, accompanied by apocalyptic and scripture-laden interpretation, and published as pamphlets. William and Mercy Bates owned one such pamphlet, published in 1769 (figure 1.1), and it impressed Issachar deeply enough that he was able to describe it and quote from it over sixty years later.[41] Of this vision that corresponded with the 1769 comet:

> It was printed in a pamphlet and we had it. I remember so much of the contents as this. [T]wo Angels descend from heaven and came down and stood each on a separate fort and one cried to the other with loud voice saying, "Watchman what of the night what of the night," who answered "Midnight midnight." And cryed aloud to the other "What of the times. What of the times. Who answered, Doleful times! Doleful times, for the judgments of God shall begin in old England and shall spread into New England and there shall be wars and great calamities and darkness shall cover the whole face of that land."[42]

Of the signs and wonders that played such a vital role in Issachar Bates's childhood, perhaps the most unusual occurred in Southborough, Massachu-setts, probably during 1769 or 1770. Issachar's recollection of the incident is both gripping and mystifying:

> We lived in a large house with a beautiful green dooryard. One Sabbath evening a little before sunset my Father and Mother took their chairs and sat in the green yard, it being a beautiful clear pleasant evening. We chil-dren went also and regaled ourselves on the green. I happened to look up and called on them to look up and see what was in the air. There was

1.1 *The cover of* The American Wonder, *by Samuel Clarke (1776), reprinted several times in 1760s and 1770s New England and recalled in detail by Issachar Bates. (Courtesy American Antiquarian Society.)*

a black vane about the thickness of a common stove pipe and appeared to be about five rods long and crooked like black snake and in the same shape tapering at both ends. It began to draw up like a horse leech till it gathered into a round ball about the size of an eighteen inch bombshell and then exploded and the fire flew in every direction, and the report was as loud as any cannon I ever heard only not so sharp. And in one moment the sky was as red as blood. O how doleful was the color of that green grass and how awful we felt. We all thought it was the day of judgment.[43]

It is impossible to know what Issachar and his family observed in the sky that early evening, when their interlude of pleasant relaxation abruptly turned to terror. Unlike Issachar's other accounts of "signs and wonders," this description bears little resemblance to a known natural process. He interprets whatever he saw using metaphors drawn from his own life experience: common objects and creatures, military ordnance. But the event itself defies categorization. Yet as bizarre as it was, even that terrifying scene was consistent with events of the day. A Boston newspaper records an incident that bears a strong resemblance, in which a peculiar dark cloud remained "suspended in the air and quite motionless" for an entire day before beginning to move over the town, whereupon it "swelled, looked excessively black and fierce, and . . . began to roar, and blow, and bellow, and thunder, and to vomit smoke and fire, and raged like Aetna in ten thousand flames."[44]

Although we can never know exactly what Issachar Bates saw in 1769 or at any other time, his writings clearly assert that whatever the natural wonder, it could best be explained as a portent, given as a divine gift to help the observer make better sense of the relationship between God and humankind. Issachar never deviated in this conviction. His experience of the natural world told him that it offered a set of tools through which one could both experience the wonder of direct communion with the divine and also discern divine will. In his writings about his childhood, he communicates this theme plainly to his readers.

Issachar regards himself as a witness to events that may soon be lost to history: "I am now in my seventy-fifth year of my age and I was but a boy in those days, so I may justly suppose that the greater part of those who were eyewitnesses of those things which took place in New England are gone the way of all the earth and perhaps have left no account of those wonders behind them."[45] But Issachar is also concerned that people are growing less likely to accept divine explanations for natural phenomenon. He is obviously well aware of the rise of science and the appeal of scientific explanations. And using the sarcastic and slightly off-color tone for which he became so well known in the Shaker world, he mocks those who would omit God from their interpretation of the natural world:

> But in these latter times if God is pleased to show any wonders in heavens above or signs in the earth beneath, the next news you will hear of the matter some perfect ass star-gazer has hoisted his Telescope and reached as far into the heavens as he was able and come down with the pleasing news that he can account for it all by natural causes, and the multitude mock you if you presume to contradict his divination.[46]

Although by the time Issachar Bates recorded his account of these childhood events he had traveled far in time, space, and experience from his rural New England roots, in at least one respect he never changed: he was just as likely in old age as in childhood to use his observations of nature to achieve an understanding of divine will. For the aging Issachar, it is clear that the "signs and wonders" of his childhood stayed with him. They shaped his worldview. As his life experiences accumulated through the tumultuous times of war, encounters with the Shakers, and beyond, Issachar's impressions of the natural world were tinged with the conviction that its workings were signals of God's work in the world.

> And as it is the woman's day Through my first Daughter I began
> To make that great and last display That ever God will shew to man . . .
> The order of the second birth Is thro' the daughter now made known
> The only way of God on earth Which all created souls shall own.
> And thus the eternal Mother saith Ye that despise my Anna Lee
> Are such as shun my pleasant path Yea such as always hated me.[47]

While Issachar Bates was growing up in Massachusetts, events far away across the Atlantic were moving on a trajectory that would later converge with the arc of his life. Ann Lee, considered the spiritual founder of the United Society of Believers in Christ's Second Appearing — or "Shakers" — was born in 1736 to a working-class household in Manchester, England. As a young woman, she worked in textile mills and was drawn into a small radical religious sect that bore enough superficial similarities to the Quaker faith to garner the nickname "shaking Quakers." In addition to rejecting all the liturgical and priestly trappings of the Church of England, the group practiced a bodily active form of worship, including physical convulsions, dancing, singing, and speaking in tongues that, among iconoclastic sects like Ann Lee's, were considered the evidence of genuine spiritual outpouring. Because these Shakers also participated in illegal acts of dissent against the Church of England, persecution forced their migration to America. On August 6, 1774, Ann Lee's trans-Atlantic voyage ended in New York City. With her were her brother William Lee and seven other companions. Soon they acquired a piece of land near Albany, New York, in a place called Niskayuna. The land was swampy and unimproved, and the Shakers toiled to eke out a living.[48]

On the frontier of the colonial interior, the Shakers were hardly the only unusual religious sect. Indeed, the atmosphere in less settled interior communities seemed conducive to nonconforming religious practices. And roughly coinciding with the onset of the Revolutionary War, religious revival broke out in the region and spread in a wide swath of the colonial interior from Nova Scotia to Pennsylvania. The spiritual emphasis of this "New Light" stir was salvation achieved not through adherence to established church doctrine but through individuals' inward conviction and renunciation of sin.[49] Ann Lee and her followers were initially on the sidelines of this movement, although they did draw the attention of colonial authorities in Albany, being recent British arrivals who condemned the fighting that was then under way. But they did no active proselytizing. Still, stories of Ann Lee's prophetic gifts and her powerful preaching began to spread. A Baptist revival in 1779 drew some New Light Baptists to nearby Niskayuna, Christians curious to see this "prophetess" for themselves. That encounter led the Shakers to Joseph Meacham, a New Light Baptist preacher from New Lebanon, New York, who was to become their first American convert. Meacham's conversion took place close to New England's "Dark Day" of May 19, 1780, a day that remained inexplicably dark although there was no eclipse. Now explained as a natural phenomenon and likely a consequence of distant forest fires, the "dark day" was believed by many at the time to be a portent of profound social and spiritual upheaval, perhaps even the end of the world. Seizing this opportunity, Ann Lee and the Shakers set out to evangelize in earnest. Ann Lee's preaching in Niskayuna, New Lebanon, and through the Berkshires of western Massachusetts, was electrifying. More people embraced the faith and joined the Shaker ranks, many moving with their families to resettle near other converts. Members of a millennial sect in Harvard, Massachusetts, significantly to the east in Worcester County, heard of Ann Lee and came to see her for themselves. Many of these new adherents were the disillusioned followers of Shadrach Ireland, a recently deceased visionary who had prophesied that the millennium had arrived and that he would never die. They urged Lee to carry her message to people living farther afield.[50] So in 1781 Lee and several followers set out on what would become a missionary trip of more than two years.

They followed a meandering route through southwestern Massachusetts, into northern Connecticut, back into central Massachusetts, and up to Harvard in northern Worcester County.[51] Along the way they were hosted in the households of kin and friends of new followers, and Ann Lee preached to new audiences. She also began to draw opposition. At Harvard they found refuge with the remaining members of Shadrach Ireland's sect, who lived together in a large house called the "Square House." That house, which would later loom large in Shaker culture as a hallowed and favorite residence of Lee, became Lee's base of operations for more preaching trips in the region. She visited the nearby communities of Petersham, Athol, and Templeton, and it was there that the life journeys of Ann Lee and Issachar Bates would intersect, when Issachar was a young man in his early twenties.

During Ann Lee's lifetime, becoming one of her followers was a radical and even mysterious act. To the Shakers, Lee was the "woman clothed with the sun" foretold in the book of Revelation, whom God had drawn into the wilderness for protection, signaling the arrival of the millennium. She seemed to corroborate scripture, with her abilities of prophecy and miraculous discernment. But the conception of God and Christ that Lee promoted deviated sharply from that of other Christian sects, even in the more nonconformist backwoods regions where the Shakers found their audiences. Rejecting the Trinity as a human-invented doctrine, Lee instead emphasized dualities — male and female, body and spirit. For the Shakers, the "Christ spirit" was God's anointing presence in people and in the collective body of believers. While they did not reject such standard features of Christian theology as the miraculous birth of Jesus, the Shakers emphasized the sinless life of Jesus and his physical suffering — "the cross" would become one of their most powerful metaphors.

From the beginning of the Shakers' expansion in New England, the sect's many radical elements left audiences thunderstruck and drew strong persecution. For the Shakers, Ann Lee's own physical and mental suffering drew ready comparison to that of Jesus, especially a widely recounted episode in which her prayerful anguish was so great that she sweated blood, similar to Gospel accounts of the despair of Jesus in Gethsemane.[52] And paralleling the standard image of Jesus as a "second Adam," undoing the sin that Adam brought to humankind and offering a rebirth, Ann Lee represented for the Shakers a "second Eve," sharing in this task and completing it. During worship, the Shakers invited the workings of the Christ Spirit into their midst and into their own bodies, and they believed that dancing, whirling, and glossolalia (speaking, or babbling, in unknown tongues) were the confirmation of the

Spirit's "labors" among them. During Ann Lee's lifetime and in the opening years of Shakerism in America, becoming a Shaker entailed simply making a verbal confession of one's sins — across one's whole lifetime — to one of the Shaker leaders, embracing the collective "labors" of worship in the dance, and pledging to live without sexual immorality. Ann Lee preached that sexuality was the source of original sin and that complete freedom from sin could only be found in celibacy, a sacrifice that was referred to as "bearing the cross." Most early believers continued to live in their own households with their spouses, but forsook further sexual intercourse. They pooled some of their resources, worshipped together, and shared the conviction that they were freed from further sin and were enjoying the promised Millennium in the presence of the Christ Spirit.

When Issachar Bates first learned of the Shakers, they were not yet organized in fixed communities with their own collective economy.[53] But the number and influence of Shakers were growing across the rural Northeast nonetheless. Further, the Shaker teachings and practices were sufficiently radical within the religious climate of the region that they reinforced the conviction held by many that sweeping changes of divine origin were the order of the day.

> *Now these things created doleful feelings in these parts for a while ... I still kept a sharp look out ... I thank my God who has spared me to this present time and has ... suffered me (when a wicked man) to stand on earth and be a witness of his marvelous work. O thou Infidel — O thou Deist. O thou skeptic. O thou nothing. What will become of you who believe in nothing but the work of your own hands?[54]*

The mid-1770s found a teenage Issachar Bates living in Athol, Massachusetts, in northern Worcester County. Having been profoundly affected by a succession of astounding "signs and wonders," young Issachar fully expected momentous events to engulf his life in the very near future. In part, his expectations would be fulfilled through the tumultuous circumstances of impending war. Though the region was isolated and poorly connected by road to other parts of the colony, the male population mustered and prepared to do its part in the hostilities. As the Bates family worked to help build the local community, they were unaware that in adjacent New York the newly arrived Shakers were struggling to make a home in the swamp lands outside Albany, where they would live as a spiritual family. Soon the paths of these two families would cross, with far-reaching implications for both.

Issachar emerged from childhood with a firm conviction that God was a real force in the world around him and was preparing to do great things. The children in the Bates family now numbered eleven. Issachar's youngest siblings were born in the mid-1770s when their mother was in her early forties, establishing an age span of almost twenty-five years among the siblings. The older Bates children began to marry and establish their own households. William Bates and his eldest son, Noah, both turned out for wartime service, along with second eldest son, Issachar, and, later, a younger son, Theodore. From 1775 to 1781, Issachar's life would change dramatically. The war formed a bridge from boyhood to manhood for Issachar, forcing him into leadership roles among his peers. Though he had probably never before left Massachusetts, the war took him through New York, New Jersey, and Vermont and exposed him to famous people and pivotal events. In between stints in the army, he married young and began his own family. And Issachar Bates would soon have his first personal encounter with Ann Lee, the woman who was to forever change his world.

CHAPTER 2

"Take the bloody track of war"

A FIFER IN THE AMERICAN REVOLUTION

Rights of freedom we'll maintain,
And our independence gain
— Issachar Bates, "Rights of Conscience"

Issachar Bates was a young teenager in Templeton, Massachusetts, some sixty miles west of Boston, when preparations began for war with England. After the Boston Tea Party and the arrival of British troops in Boston, communities throughout Massachusetts began organizing militia units. Men and boys of all ages turned out to train on village greens, using the standard military manuals of the day to conduct the drills necessary for going into battle; and fife and drum were an integral part of the preparation, as they were necessary to regulate movement. Like other young men in his family and community, Issachar Bates was caught up in the fervor of the times and wished to serve the cause of American freedom. Perhaps because he was only fifteen when war preparations began in earnest or perhaps because he was drawn to music, he showed the initiative of buying himself a fife and learning to play it. For more than a year before the "alarm" went out in April 1775, he spent as many as six hours a day fifing for the "minute men" of his community, as they paraded on the town commons.

The fife was one of the most popular musical instruments in colonial times. Because of the piercing and even ear-splitting tone that it produced, the fife played an indispensible role in military life, delivering tactical communications on the field.[1] Fifes were made of wood—usually boxwood, ebony, rosewood, or mahogany. By the 1770s, they were marketed throughout the colonies. Many were English made, but American cabinetmakers also produced fifes as a cottage industry. Issachar Bates would have had little trouble finding a fife to purchase, possibly using wages earned as a hired hand. Fife manuals were also widely marketed, and in some towns instructors advertised to give lessons. Issachar would have owned a fife that was about seventeen inches long, with six finger holes and meant to be held transversely. The tone in the upper register would have been exceptionally loud and shrill, made more so depending upon the lung capacity of the player.

In addition to mastering the fife, Issachar Bates was trained in what he calls the "old Norfolk manual exercise," a reference to one of the European military manuals that contained standard instructions for military training, deportment, and battlefield maneuvers. Several were in use in 1770s America. Issachar probably used *A Plan of Exercises for the Militia of Massachusetts; Extracted from the Plan of Discipline of the Norfolk Militia,* by Windham and Townshend and published in 1768 and again 1771 by Richard Draper in Boston. This was adapted from an earlier English publication from 1759, which praises the importance of the fife in military training, saying that foot soldiers perform "with the greatest order and regularity, to the sound of the fife; keeping the most exact time and cadence . . . The effect of the musick in regulating the step, and making the men keep their order, is really very extraordinary . . . it is the best and indeed the only method of teaching troops to march well."[2]

Issachar Bates served as a fifer throughout his several tours of duty. Musicians in the American Revolution experienced the war somewhat differently from the ordinary soldier, and their roles varied constantly. The Continental Army and colonial militias alike adapted many customs regarding the function of military musicians from British and other European military tradition, but at different times and to varying degrees. Each colony had slightly different practices relative to musicians' status, duties, and expectations. Also, the regulations affecting musicians changed during the course of the war, as officers sought to enhance military efficiency by improving and standardizing music. Still, many general impressions can be drawn to illuminate Issachar Bates's experience as a fifer.

In peacetime, fifing was considered suitable for young boys, as it involved primarily the drilling of troops or ceremonial appearances. But with the outbreak of war, the demands of a fifer changed considerably. Paired fifes and drums are commonly perceived as a staple of the Revolutionary Period. But at the outset of the Revolution, fifes and drums together accompanied only the elite British "grenadier" units, with drums alone accompanying units of foot soldiers. "Grenadiers" led charges and were responsible for delivering heavier ordnance ("grenades"). Such units needed fifes, whose piercing tone could be better heard over the greater din of heavy weapons; consequently, fifers marched into the thick of battle with the grenadiers. Military orders at the outset of the war reflect remarkably few fifer positions: only two per unit of grenadiers. But soon other units wanted fifers, and their use became more widespread.

On the American side, there is no indication that fifers were limited to grenadier units. Instead, fifers and drummers generally worked in partnership in all units, but with twice the number of drummers. The musicians were organized and led by a drum major and fife major, respectively. The position of fife major, which Issachar Bates held during part of his service, was not necessary unless a unit had at least three fifers. The fife major was responsible for instructing the fifers in the many tunes they needed to master, and he conducted their daily practices and disciplined the slackers. As musicians were under orders to practice daily at specific times in military encampments, fifers and drummers would have done a great deal of their practice together.

The "Norfolk manual exercise" identified by Issachar Bates included a specific set of nine drum "beatings," corresponding to standard tactical maneuvers (i.e., "The Reveille," "The Parley," "To Arms," and "The March). Drummers had to master these beatings, and fifers had to adapt specific tunes to accompany each one. The manual did not stipulate specific tunes, nor did any of the fife "tutors" or instructional manuals available in the colonies. But most of the fife tutors recommended appropriate tunes to be used for each specific beating. In addition to the nine beatings, drummers were charged with mastering a much wider array of signals (i.e., "cease firing," "fix bayonets," "form battalion," or "to secure your arms"), for which fifers likewise had to fashion appropriate tunes. Individual fifers had significant latitude to choose and adapt tunes, and circumstances often required hasty improvisations, as the surviving diary of one New Hampshire fifer shows.[3] They also tended to take into account the preferences of the men in the unit, as well as the suggestions of the drummer. Many tunes became closely associated with specific drumbeats or signals not by the application of regulations but because fifers adopted preferences expressed by soldiers, or they borrowed tunes from popular culture. For example, a popular tune called "The Rogue's March" was commonly played for the signal "drumming out of camp," which accompanied punishments. And the drum signal "to go for provisions" was paired with an adaptation of a popular song called "A Song in Praise of Old English Roast Beef," and came to be known simply as "Roast Beef."

Yet company musicians also had to be prepared to function as soldiers, and after 1777 they were equipped with weapons. Musicians in the Continental Army might have been more likely to play for ceremonial occasions. But in the militia units, such as those Issachar Bates served, the musicians necessarily played an integral battlefield role because their function was to communicate orders in the thick of battle. Consequently, musicians' pay was slightly higher than that of the common private and similar to that of a corporal. The pay of fife majors and drum majors was higher still. After 1778 the fife major of an infantry unit was paid nine dollars per month. For an artillery unit, the fife major drew more than ten dollars per month. Fifers lived with the units they served rather than being quartered with other musicians. Because music could enliven "down time" or cheer the wounded, company musicians were also pressed to join in social situations or play in the hospital area, sharing wine and spirits with their fellow soldiers. In the work of Raoul Camus on military music in the American Revolution, the discussion of company musicians' potential to be popular and convivial figures — fifers' uniforms varied, but generally included hats adorned with cockades and feathers — is completely consistent with Issachar Bates's description of his own experience: "I was merry and lively . . . I had a kind wit that would catch the ears and draw the attention of every class of people . . . I could sing nearly every song that was going . . . and I could make as much music on the fife as any of them."

In addition to fifer and fife major, Issachar Bates also notes that he served "occasionally [as] drill sergeant, or fluglemaster" during the war. Because drills were accompanied by fife or drum anyway, it was probably logical for Issachar as a fifer to be pressed into service to oversee drills in the absence of a drill sergeant. By "fluglemaster," Issachar is probably referring to the military musicians' function as bugler or trumpeter. Field commands for mounted units were issued by trumpeters, who were themselves also mounted. The music played by trumpeters was less demanding than that mastered by fifers, consisting mainly of "fanfares and flourishes." As many trumpeters were required to learn the fife so that they could play tunes suitable for marching and drilling, it stands to reason that the reverse might also have been true, explaining Isacchar's possible role as a trumpeter.

Issachar Bates was part of several critical actions in the Revolutionary War. During his first tour of duty in the spring and summer of 1775, his militia unit participated in the Battle of Bunker Hill, where he played the fife. During the rest of that tour, Issachar was stationed at Cambridge, where the camps took frequent fire from the British that were occupying Boston. Early in 1776, Issachar's second enlistment took him back to Boston, where he assisted in the emplacement of artillery on Dorchester Heights, a tactical move that is credited with precipitating the British withdrawal from Boston on March 17. Thereafter, Issachar marched with his unit south to New Haven, Connecticut, and traveled by ship to Long Island. There and in nearby New York City and Harlem Heights, he and his unit were caught up in the complex series of efforts directed by General Washington to hold onto New York City, then gradually retreating north, and culminating in the Battle of White Plains in October. During this period, Issachar was part of the famed "flying camps," a strategy by Washington to protect units and supplies through nimble and frequent nighttime movements.

Issachar's third enlistment began at the end of 1776 and included marching to New Jersey, where his unit narrowly missed the battles at Trenton and Princeton. In early 1777, Issachar's unit built and manned a fort near Bound Brook, New Jersey, and skirmished with British and Hessians. Later that year he was attached to a unit that marched to Bennington, Vermont. From there his unit unexpectedly changed plans and marched west to occupy a strategic location near Albany, New York, called "Half-Moon" (presently Waterford), where the Mohawk River joined the North River. Just as abruptly, they were ordered back to Bennington, but arrived in mid-August to find the historic Battle of Bennington just concluded. Issachar was part of a group set to guard a multitude of several hundred Hessian and British prisoners in the Bennington meeting house. Soon after, Issachar's unit participated in the campaign against the forces of British General Burgoyne. As Burgoyne retreated north, Issachar was with a regiment sent to Fort Edward in the southern Adirondacks to cut him off. His unit also marched to Saratoga, where it was present at Burgoyne's surrender. After a short enlistment in 1778 during which he guarded prisoners in Rutland, Vermont, Issachar's final involvement in the war came in 1780, when he joined a unit for three months' service at West Point. He was there when Benedict Arnold assumed command and prepared to hand over the fort to the British, the act of treason for which Arnold is infamous. In between these enlistments, Issachar had married and his family was beginning to multiply.

Issachar's service brought him together with other men of his community, including his future father-in-law, Bezaleel Maynard, and other members of his future wife's extended family.[4] In fact, his service was probably a key factor in his marriage, as Lovina Maynard's family was far better off socioeconomically than his. Issachar's service also overlapped with that of other members of his family, such as his older brother Noah, who appeared to serve in the same unit at the beginning of the war in 1775, and his brother-in-law, David Train, who served alongside him in 1777 in Bennington, Vermont.[5] Bezaleel Maynard, a comrade-in-arms of both Issachar and Noah Bates, would become the father-in-law of both: Noah married Lovina's older sister shortly after Issachar and Lovina married. Issachar's brother Theodore also served in the war, despite his diminutive height of five feet. Because Theodore was younger, his service came somewhat later in the war, beginning in 1779 when he was only seventeen years old.[6] Consequently, Issachar and Theodore did not serve together.

The war expanded Issachar Bates's sphere of experience in many respects. His various enlistments gave him the opportunity to travel. He was attached to units that marched as far as coastal Connecticut and southern New Jersey to the south and central Vermont and the upper Hudson Valley to the north. He saw New York and Boston, two of the most sophisticated American cities in that period. He saw many famous generals, and he probably saw George Washington, at least from a distance. He witnessed violence, bloodshed, and death; and he experienced fear, hunger, and privation. Already inclined to recognize spiritual significance in natural events around him, Issachar continued to interpret some of the most striking and unusual sights he saw in wartime as signs and wonders with divine purpose. And during his first enlistment, he was exposed to a coping mechanism all too popular among soldiers, namely, alcohol. By his own admission, he "began to partake of the substance," and his account implies that he drank to excess. He also picked up incredibly colorful swear words, whose use became a habit that he found almost impossible to break. But despite the stress and anxieties of military life, Issachar seemed to revel in certain aspects of it: the camaraderie, the music-making, the exposure to new people and new experiences.

Like thousands of men of his generation, Issachar Bates was irrevocably changed by his service in the American Revolution. He would carry aspects of his experience with him to the end of his life. Although he renounced violence as a Shaker and strongly repudiated later acts of warfare when he witnessed them, he retained a strong inclination to use military metaphors and expressions, both in his poetry and his everyday speech. It is possible that the strong tendency in early Shaker discourse to describe spiritual struggles using military metaphors could be due to the influence of the many veterans, like Issachar, who joined the early Shaker communities. This connection is especially plausible when one considers the influence of early hymn poetry on Shaker discourse, by providing a foundational arsenal of metaphors. Issachar Bates, for example, was among the most prolific early Shaker poets, and he had ample opportunity to imbue Shaker discourse with military metaphors through his verse, as well as his use of military expressions in his public preaching. And Issachar brought other aspects of his military experience to the Shakers, besides turns of phrase. The same skills he used as a fifer to launch field drills and guide the soldiers in specific exercises and battlefield maneuvers were easily applied to Shaker worship. As a principal singer, Issachar was responsible not only for beginning the singing but also for setting the style and tempo of the singing to suit the various modes of Shaker dancing: march, shuffle, round dance, back order shuffle, and so on. He made no secret of his military inclinations; they were plain for anyone who read his poetry, heard him use military jargon, or heard him use the vulgar language he had first learned as a soldier. The fact that Issachar was still associated with soldiering, and specifically with playing the fife, long after his death affirms that he may have taken ample opportunity to tell tales of his military past. When he left the Shaker West in 1835, his parting song was one he called "Issachar's Retreat," and it clearly harks back in both title and tune to fife signals that he had employed in the war sixty years before.

In early 1832 while living at Watervliet, Ohio, Issachar Bates sat down to write his autobiography. He completed the task in short order, producing a document that recounted his life to the present (he would augment it periodically over the next four years). Of the eighty-five pages completed by the end of March 1832, just under twenty, or about 20 percent of the total pages written, deal with his experience in the war. It is the only section of his autobiography to which he gives a separate title, "The Revolutionary War." This animated and richly detailed account, written much more than half a century after the fact, testifies powerfully to the indelible mark the war left on his life. Soon after completing his autobiography, Issachar unexpectedly encountered another opportunity to recount his war experience. In the summer of 1832 the Ohio Shakers learned, probably through newspapers, of the passage in the U.S. Congress of the Revolutionary War Service-Pension Act (4 Stat. 529). That law was the latest and most liberal in a series of congressional efforts to provide monetary recompense for the dwindling number of Revolutionary Era veterans. Issachar took action swiftly. He wrote a second testimony of his service, which he submitted as part of an application to receive his military pension. These two separate accounts of his Revolutionary War experience together amount to about 4,600 words. Both narratives are presented below in full.[7]

Some explanation of the differences between the parallel wartime narratives is warranted. Each one contains unique insights and slightly different perspectives. Of the two, the narrative Issachar prepared for his pension application is the more succinct. I have chosen to consolidate the two versions, by breaking the pension application narrative into short passages, distinguished by italics, and interspersing these at appropriate junctures throughout the longer narrative. In this way, Issachar's words from the more succinct version provide springboards into the successive sections of the more elaborate narrative. I present his accounts mostly verbatim and uninterrupted, save for occasional notes identifying officers or locations.[8] In some places I have made silent changes in punctuation to ease the flow of the narrative.

The Revolutionary War
When about 13 years of age, my father moved his family into Worcester county,
62 miles from Boston, where we lived at the commencement of and during the
Revolutionary War. I was rising of 15 years of age when General Gage landed
his troops at Boston. I then, with other boys of my age, entered the military
school, learned the manual exercise, and also learned to play well on the fife . . .

About the first of May 1773 General Gage landed his army at Boston.[9]
Now <u>War</u> was all the topic of conversation. Every man that was able to
lift an old rusty Gun, and every boy that was big enough to carry a little
wooden gun, were all learning War. Perhaps one fourth part of the time
was spent on the parade ground learning the old Norfolk manual exercise.
For <u>my</u> part, I got me a fife and learned to play well. Minute men turned
out to be in readiness; and I turned out to fife for them. Every preparation
was made for war.

I shall here mention two more signs that appeared. A few days before
the alarm, a few of us were on a hill called Mt. Ararat. We saw two very
black clouds rise — one from the north, and the other from the south.
They met in the west, within a short distance of each other, and there
stood like two armies, and fired at each other as regular as in any pitched
battle; at the same time it thundered and lightened most dreadfully for
about twenty minutes; the clouds then vanished out of my sight. Nextly
I will mention about a strange flock of birds.

On the day of the battle at Lexington, a wonderful flock of birds flew
over us. They were not to be numbered. No one, to my knowledge, has
ever pretended that they ever saw that kind of bird before or since. They
were seen by thousands, and flew in open sight about sixty miles in a
straight course to Lexington, where they disappeared. They flew in as
good order as any band of soldiers ever marched and in profound silence.
They resembled a kind of hawk the most of any bird. They all stopped at
Templeton pond, a small lake about sixty miles west by north from Boston, and went on.

The next day the alarm came of the battle at Lexington, and the men
appeared about as numerous in the roads, as the birds were in the air.

Now I shall digress a little, and leave the track I have been pursuing,
and show the reason why I have been so particular in describing these
signs & wonders which I have seen, before I enter on my journey into the
revolutionary war.

Firstly, I am now in my seventy-fifth year of my age and I was but a boy in those days, so I may justly suppose that the greater part of those who were eyewitnesses of these things which took place in New England, are gone the way of all the earth and perhaps have left no account of those wonders behind them.

Secondly, I am so well acquainted with the spirit of man that I am forced to be jealous over him; that even those who still survive have so little feeling to acquaint themselves with God and his wonderful works, that they either thought light of them at the time or thro' negligence let the whole matter fly off with time from their minds, into forgetfulness or oblivion, so as to be forever hid from the knowledge of future eyes.

Thirdly, because my soul has been grieved to see the goodness of God (which leadeth to repentance) not only treated with neglect, but with ridicule! For in all ages, God in his condescending goodness, whenever he was about to build up and bless a people, gave them previous signs of his intention, that the wise might be encouraged thereby. And whenever he was about to bring destruction upon any people, he gave them warning beforehand, by signs & wonders, that the wise might be prepared to meet the event.

But in these latter times, if God is pleased to show any signs on earth, or any wonders in heavens, the next news you will hear of the matter is, some puffed up star-gazer[10] has hoisted his telescope and reached as far into the heavens as he was able, and down he comes with the pleasing news that he can account for it from natural causes, and the multitude mock you, if you presume to contradict his divination.

At about the age of 17 with the consent of my father, I enlisted for 8 months under Captain Dexter[11] of Worcester aforesaid, and about the first of May 1775 marched with his company of independent Rangers to old Cambridge where the main army was collected. I was too young to pass muster but served as a musician. The company to which I belonged was attached to Colonel Patterson's regiment and General Sullivan's brigade.[12] During that summer I was stationed at the edge of the marsh between Cambridge and Boston in open view of the city; where we were often saluted from the old Somerset a 70 gun ship that lay anchored in the bay. On the 17th of June, I was in the battle at Bunker's hill, and in several skirmishes during that campaign.

Now I shall return home from my digression & pursue the bloody track of war,[13] not with pleasure to my spirit, but at the request of my friends. When the minute men (before mentioned) started for Boston,

I started with them, but my Father took me back, and this was a great grief to me. However, in about two weeks he consented to let me enlist (which I did, under Captain Dexter) being then about seventeen years and three months of age, not old enough to pass muster into the ranks, but could pass as a fifer, and continued a fifer and fife major thro' out the war.

It was about the first of May 1775, when we took old Cambridge where the main army was collected. We, being an independent company of rangers, were stationed at the edge of the march,[14] in open view of Boston, and the old Summerset, a 70 gun ship lying in the bay between us & Boston, who often saluted us with her metal.

Here I found that I had got into a fix, where I had no need to look for signs, for I began to partake of the substance. Nothing remained for me but to shut my eyes and harden my heart and enter freely into that school of vice, in which, alas! I was not slow to learn. And until we had got well hardened, this old Summerset troubled us very much with repeated firing at us, during the summer, for we kept this post all summer. Our annoyance from the Summerset, after a while, became a matter of mere sport, for we would dig the balls out of the ground & take them on a wheelbarrow up to the college, and old General Putnam would pay us for them in rum by the gallon.[15]

We kept this post all summer and until we got well hardened to this. I always did my duty, and I was merry and lively and never had an angry word. I made as much music on the fife as anyone. Drums and fifes! Blood and whiskey! What drinking and shouting! And what of it all? We were free volunteers. I can now say with Solomon, "This also is vanity."

Thus times went on very well till the 17th of June, when the battle was fought at Bunker Hill. On that day we were ordered to take post at the foot of the hill by Mystic river, between Charleston & Boston bay, and there stand, openly exposed to the Summerset, the Glasgow frigate (a most furious instrument of war), and three floating batteries, & we had to take our full share of all their pot-metal, cannon balls, grape and canister shot. We stood where we could see all the movement of the army, and the battle on the hill; and here I saw the fulfillment of the battle between the two clouds, for it literally appeared like the same thing.

But all the horrors of this day (June 17, 1775) did not look so doleful as those of the night. For after the Hill was given up, & our army had retreated, just as dark commenced, the British began to burn Charleston. And Oh! the horrible sight to stand & behold their hot balls, carcasses, & stink pots flaming thro the air,[16] for the distance of more than a mile, & in less than half an hour, that beautiful town all in flames. The smoke of the blaze lightened the whole heavens as far as we could see. And here I saw the literal fulfillment of the flaming heavens, of which I saw the sign before mentioned.

At the close of this battle our army retired from Bunker Hill to Prospect Hill, about three quarters of a mile distant, and began to fortify, & the British immediately began to bombard & cannonade with all their powers to prevent the progress of this new fortification, and kept it up for about three weeks, even until the fort was finished and completed, and then they quit.

I was a part of the time at these scenes & would see their great nasty porridge pots flying through the air, and crammed full of devils as they could hold, come whispering along, with their blue tails in the day time & their fiery tails by night; and if they burst in the air, they would throw their hellish stuff all about our ears, and if they fell on the ground, they would hop around just as tho' the very devil was in them till they had burst and then look out for shins and all above: and at the same time cannon balls flying, about once a minute.

Now to view these wicked inventions of men to shed the blood & bring destruction upon their fellow creatures, it is no wonder that I was favored with the sight of these signs and wonders which I saw in the heavens, while my mind was young and tender, that after I had hardened my heart and gone thro' the literal fulfillment of these things, I should know how to hate them.

Now after the fort at Prospect Hill, fort Patterson, and one at Rocksbury (a small breastwork where our company were stationed, and a few other small works), there was no more forting nor battle that season, except some little skirmishes.

In the spring of '76 I enlisted again for three months under Capt. Boucher of Worcester, and on a certain night in the month of March we were marched over Dorchester neck on to Dorchester hill, where we planted three posts, and in a few days routed Lord Howe from Boston, and, on Sabbath morning, had the pleasure of seeing his mighty fleet of 150 sail of vessels weigh anchor, hoist sail, and clear out. Next morning we marched into the city and took possession of what the enemy had left.

But in the spring of 1776, a large body of troops marched at Dorchester. I was then in Capt. Bunker's company.[17] Every plan was then contrived to drive Lord Howe out of Boston,[18] and to get both sides of him was the object, and preparations were made accordingly. Thus in the month of March, one Wednesday night, about ten o'clock, we took our march over Dorchester neck, on to Dorchester hill, with one hundred and fifty carts loaded with frames of forts, and fosheens (bundles of brush) & we planted three forts on the Hill that night (they were not all as yet filled with dirt) and as the day began to break we left the hill for the British to fire at. The next night we went on again, and did likewise the next morning, only left a guard. The next night we went on and kept the hill, and the next day which was Saturday they did their best with cannon from every battery, firing all night and killing but four men; and we were none afraid of their landing, for we had seventy barrels filled with sand on the hill, to roll down upon them, which would have broken their ranks to slivers, and they knew it.[19]

On Sabbath morning, about ten o'clock, they hoisted their canvas sails of 150 vessels in our sight and cleared out.

On Monday, we marched into Boston & took possession of what they had left, which was of no great value. A number of starved horses, mortars also, and cannon all spiked up. The meeting houses were gutted, the insides all tore out to the ground, in order to train their light horse in them. We went to work regulating the fortification, and turning them all to our own advantage.

Soon after this tour, I enlisted again under Capt. Benjamin Gates of Worcester for five months, and marched to New Haven in Connecticut. There we went on board of a sloop commanded by Capt. Fips,[20] crossed the sounds and landed at Burlingslip New York city, where his Excellency Lord Howe with his great fleet again appeared in sight. We remained a few weeks in the city, and were then moved up the North river about three miles and stationed in barracks.

We then marched to New York, where we had another view of his Excellency General Howe, with his great fleet in sight again, and his red coats on Staten Island. Here I was in Captain Gates' company, in what was called the flying camps.

Now to make a long story short. The first attack the British made was on Long Island, which they took by the sacrifice of much blood. This laid the City of New York very much exposed, yet every exertion was made to defend & keep it. But when this was found impossible, the next plan was to clear the city of its treasures, particularly the continental stores, which was completely done out of sight of the British by means of a large number of battens which General Washington ordered to have made & put into the North River, which were kept silently running every night for two weeks, from the City to Kingston.[21]

Nothing now remained in the City of the continental stores, except about 50 cord of wood which was in the upper part of the city, on what was called the holy ground (a large common, encircled with poor washer women, and some base women). General Washington then ordered a herald to mount the fence, and proclaim to the poor that they might have that wood. And here was a sight worth looking at, for in about fifteen minutes that wood was in as many divisions as there were poor persons, which you must know was not a few. Now General Fellows brigade to which I belonged, was at this time stationed in barracks three miles above the city.

I then belonged to Colonel Hollman's regiment and General Fellows' brigade called the new bevy of Continentals. Sometime in the month of August, after the British had taken Long-Island, General Washington evacuated the city, and retreated back to Harlaam heights. I witnessed that whole scene, was left among the city guards to cover the retreat of the army; and after being surrounded by the British on all sides, narrowly escaped with my life and my fife and the clothes on my back . . .

In the latter part of August (if I mistake not), one Friday morning, the guards were drawn out as usual and sent on to the city. It was my turn to fife them on, and stay with them. All of us were expecting to be relieved in 24 hours. No victuals came that day. Saturday the same, no relief, no victuals. And on Sabbath morning eight British ships hoisted sail and came on; five up the east, & three up the North River. The three that came up the North River, each gave us a broad side, as they passed by the brewery guards where we were. We gave them back the best we had, two eighteen pounders, which were played well.

In about two hours the earth shook terribly, & whether it was thunder or an earthquake I could not for awhile decide. But now the mystery began to open why we had not been relieved. Our army had been these two days preparing for a retreat, and had this morning started, and the British were pouring in the metal upon them on both sides of the Island to cut off their retreat,[22] but they missed their aim altogether. Yet the guards were entirely cut off, for the British had landed an army on the Island, who were marching down to take possession of the city, & us in it. But by some means General Putnam rushed thro' and came & dismissed all the guards (about 400 men) and told us to clear ourselves any way that we could. A number of them pushed off to an old sloop that was condemned, and started across the river, and were helped from the Jersey shore after she sank.

For my part, I took my little drummer, a pretty boy named James Ellet, then about 14 years old, and started up the North River to get our clothes, but behold but behold, when we came on the ground there were neither barracks nor clothes, they were all thrown into the river and rafted up to Kingsbridge. And instead thereof, a body of distressed men waiting to surrender to their enemies. Here was trouble enough, and our number still increasing, small parties running back to us that had met the enemy. "What the news?" Ans. "We are all cut off; and we have had no commander." At length there came a colonel of some regiment who advised us to parade rank and file & when the enemy came in sight, if we were willing, he would give orders to ground our arms, and lay our hats a top of them, to which we all agreed, about 200 of us, and here we stood for some time.

Now I shall just mention the simple means by which we escaped. By this time a number left the ranks, and took their choice to swim the river, but how they came out I know not, the river was three miles wide. But while we stood here waiting for the ceremony of surrender, an Irishman stepped out of the ranks, and addressed the Colonel in these words. "Dear Colonel, I am thinking it will be of no use for us to stay here and wait to be taken, for I am thinking we'll be taken fast enough if we go along." Very well, replied the colonel, I will make a proposal. We will all march into yon grove (a horrid thicket), and all lay flat on our bellies. There will be nothing come thro' there except perhaps a small flanking party, and we will rise and fire and force our way thro.' This was done, but no flanking party came thro' and we lay and heard them all go by, and then up and ran. So we attributed our deliverance to the speech of that half-drunk Irishman.

We ran about a mile and a half, & it being extremely hot, we made a halt on the top of a hickory nole, and the first we knew we received a shower of potmetal, from the three ships in the North River. We then scampered down the cliffs and halted no more, till we finished our nine mile race, and came into the main road & found some of our own army.

Then I took my little drummer and went on to Kingsbridge. Here we begged a slice of cold beef, the first food we had taken for three days; then went into a barn that night.

[T]he next day we overtook the army at Harlaam, and were ready for the grand battle which was fought about two hours after our arrival. I then continued with the flying camps moving back and skirmishing from place to place to protect the military stores till we passed Crump Pond, Quaker Ridge etc and reached the White plains. There we had another severe battle, and kept the ground for three days till the stores were moved ahead out of danger. Thence we started by night and continued our march till we reached Croton's bridge, and there on the hill made a final stand. Here my five months ended and I was discharged by Capt. Gates and returned home.

The next day which was Monday, we found a company on Harlem Heights; nothing there to eat. And in about two hours after we arrived the British came upon us, and we had a heavy battle; but we drove them & kept the ground, losing a number of our best men.

We staid but a few weeks in this place, before we moved back into the country, and it is out of my power to tell of the curious moves we made, before we made a stand. For it was General Washington's policy to keep the stores and baggage always ahead, on which account we were rightly named the Flying Camps; for we hardly ever staid more than three days in a place without having the stores removed. We would march in the night and come up with them, then stay and guard them till they were again moved on ahead.

But at White Plains the British came upon us stores and all, and there we had to fight, and a sore battle it was; but we kept the ground and defended it for three days, long enough to get our stores out of their reach, alltho' we lost a number of men.

Thus we kept on with these night marches till we got to Croton Bridge up the Hudson, near the Sappan Bay about forty miles from New York, & there on the hill made a permanent stand.

Now according to the arts in war, this prudent retreat was worth notice. Here were all our stores and baggage, covering more than an acre of ground. Hundreds of barrels and hogsheads of liquors of all kind: rum, brandy, wine, sugar, molasses, pork, flour, &c, all brought out of the City of New York, and the whole underwent no less than twenty removals, with the British at our heels all the time for a number of weeks. And yet I do not suppose that in all that time they ever got from those stores one dollar's worth.

Here I staid till late in the fall, and my time being out I was discharged & sent home with a number of others.

*In February 1777 I enlisted again under Capt. Warner of Worcester for three
months and marched to the Jersey's, about the times of the grand battles at
Trenton & Princeton, but those battles were fought just before our arrival.
Our march was thru' Rama — and Pluckhomin [town names are very
indistinct], and Morristown to Roundbrook where we were stationed & built
a fort, the British then lying in Brunswick. Here we had various skirmishes but
no pitched battle; and here I finished my three months tour, was discharged &
returned home.*

I stayed at home but a short time, before I enlisted under Captain Warner, and went to the Jerseys in the time of the battle of Princeton and
Trenton 1777. But the battles were fought just before we arrived. And
General Washington had taken Governor Hessians at Trenton and defeated the British at Princeton, and they had retired to Brunswick.[23]

We were then stationed at Bound Brook, where we build a fort called
Fort Staats. Here we had a number of skirmishes with the British and Hessians but no pitched battle. They came out one day and paraded in battle
array, horse in front, face to face. And there they stood nearly an hour, looking each other in the face. At length our right wing let off two field pieces,
and a heavy flank shot with rifles. And they soon sounded the French horn
for retreat, and went back to Brunswick, and we were glad to get rid of
them so, for they had a superior number to us, but they did not know it.

*Soon after, in the same year, I enlisted under Capt. Hockwell and went to
Bennington, Vermont. Thence with General Lincoln to Half-moon point on
the North river. Thence we were recalled in haste to Bennington, to aid in the
battle at Maloomscork, which battle was fought the day before our arrival;
and General Stark had taken 500 Hessians, 82 British regulars and 87 Tories.
Here we staid and guarded those prisoners till they were marched under guard
to Old Rutland and Northampton.*

Now my three months were out and I went home. And in a few days
I enlisted under Captain Stockwell, and went to Bennington, Vermont.
From there I went with General Linkhorn to Half-moon (now Water-
ford) at the junction of the Mohawk with the North River. But in a short
time we were sent for, to return with all speed, to assist in the Battle at
Maloonscoak.[24] But we were one day too late; for the battle was fought,
and General Starks had taken 500 Hessians, 62 British regulars, and 37
Tories. These were all put into Bennington Meeting House. The Tories

were soon taken out, yoked together with ropes around their necks, and drove off to North Hampton Jail, but the rest we guarded till they were removed sometime afterwards.

Thence we were marched under Major Wilder to Saratoga, at the time that Burgoyne was defeated at Stillwater and was on his retreat to Canada. Thence three regiments of us were ordered to leave the barrack (for Burgoyne to enter who was just at hand), and wade the North river and march with all speed to take possession of Fort Edwards in order to cut off Burgoyne's retreat. After crossing the river we had some skirmishing with an advance party of British and succeeded in getting possession of the fort, and three days after we received orders from General Gates to return speedily to Saratoga to deal in taking possession of the ground, and the arms & artillery and the 5700 prisoners which Burgoyne had surrendered on a final defeat. After this pleasant piece of business was settled, a number of us were discharged and returned home, out on this tour 3 or 4 months.

Our next call was to Saratoga to help take care of the rest of Burgoyne's army: for having been defeated at Still Water, was making his way to Canada. Three regiments of us were ordered to march with all speed up the North River about 18 miles and take possession of Fort Edward to cut off his retreat. This we accomplished, and kept the fort & kept out scouting parties in the pine woods to prevent anyone from escaping.

In three days we received orders from Gen. Gates to return as soon as possible, for Burgoyne had capitulated, and we soon took a lively step you may be sure; and my fife seemed to have an uncommon joyful sound.

On our arrival, here were 5000 of our enemies soon marched off the ground under guard, to old Rutland, instead of going back to Canada from whence they came. We took their grounds and their arms into our possession. Our regiments were soon discharged from the ground, and soon went home: I with the rest, for there were no more enemies to conquer in these parts.

After this I served a short tour at old Rutland in guarding those last mentioned prisoners, and I fifed them on as far as Springfield, on their way to be exchanged —

After I got home I began to grow sick of a soldier's life, and got into a notion of marrying. Tho' I first went a short tour to old Rutland to help guard the Burgoyne prisoners.

Finally in 1780 I turned out with a volunteer company of young men under Capt. Attern for a three month tour to West-point, and was there when the traitor Arnold sold us all to John Bull.[25]

Then in 1780 there was a call for men to go to West Point for three months, and the young men would turn out if I would go. The committee also offered me a great price, and I turned out with about 25 young men for West Point, and there served out our time, and altho' Benedict Arnold sold us all to the British, the bargain was disannulled, and we were all returned safe home, & here the war ended with me!

And the result of this important campaign terminated my services in the revolutionary war, which according to martial law were faithfully rendered, first as a fifer, and for the last three terms fife major, and occasionally drill sergeant, or fluglemaster, and often as a substitute to ease my fellow soldiers in their several camp duties or scouting enterprises.

And now whoever may read this little history of my experience in the war, may have some ruminations in their minds, about what kind of a soldier I was, & what character I supported.

Well I will candidly tell you, and you will only have my word for it. It cannot consist in greatness nor goodness, but this I can say in good conscience, that I always did my duty thro' the war like a man, altho' I was but a beardless boy. I was merry & lively, but never had a wry word from an officer, & but very few from a soldier thro' the war. I had a kind of wit that would draw the attention of every class of people, from the clergyman down to the ruffian. I could sing nearly every song that was going, whether civil, military, sacred, or profane; and I could mimic almost anything that moved; and I could make as much music on the fife as any of them. And this was not all. I was as generous as the day with my messmates. For I would stand their watch tours to ease them, and often take their place in going out on scouts, and on fatigue, while my only calling was to blow the fife. And what of it all? I can say with Solomon, "This also is vanity."

Thus I served seven tours in the revolutionary war, and during the whole term of service never asked for a furlo — never was under guard — nor never received a wry word from an officer, to my remembrance.
I hereby relinquish any claim whatever to a pension or annuity, except the

presents, & declare that my name is not on the pension Roll of the agency of any State, that he has no documentary evidence & knows of no person whose testimony he can procure who can testify to his service.

Sworn and subscribed the day and year aforesaid in open Court.

Issachar Bates, September 11, 1832

CHAPTER 3

"I'm journeying with those who I love in the flesh"

ISSACHAR BATES AS HUSBAND AND PROVIDER

And after I got home I began to grow sick of soldiering life,
and got into a notion of marrying . . . — Issachar Bates

Issachar Bates was certainly not the only young man in New England for whom the Revolutionary War marked a turning point. Events in Issachar's family life during the war years and its aftermath set him on an eventful path that would lead to new frontiers in a literal sense, as he sought to relocate himself and his growing family to the fringes of New England. For him, this period opened with the abrupt and definitive end of his early life at home with his parents and siblings. At the same time, he faced a host of personal challenges. He struggled to find and establish a living through which to support his own growing family, he was drawn to new creative avocations, and he enjoyed popularity among his friends and neighbors. Privately, however, Issachar suffered from depression and deep insecurities, which came to a head in a series of momentous spiritual crises as he reached midlife. After a chance encounter with Ann Lee, James Whittaker, and a group of Shaker converts soon after the war's end, he continued to harbor thoughts of the Shakers throughout the long interlude of his postwar life, from the early 1780s until the end of the century. During this time, as he transformed from a youth to a middle-aged man, he struggled to establish a home in the wilderness for his growing family, yearned for greater spiritual meaning, and sought comfort in a deeper religious experience.

■ William and Mercy Bates were approaching middle age when they settled in Athol, Massachusetts, in 1771 with their nine children, including thirteen-year-old Issachar. In the war's early years, three more children were born into the family. Twin boys, Caleb and William, arrived in September 1775.[1] The following February, baby William died, even as the grieving mother, Mercy Bates, now forty-three years old, was pregnant with yet another child. That child, another son and the family's last child, was born in June 1776 and was also named William.[2] Not long afterward, Mercy Bates died,[3] possibly from the complications of childbirth in middle age, leaving her husband William with seven children under the age of sixteen, among whom two were babies. Widowers with small children invariably remarried quickly in the eighteenth century, as a wife was utterly essential to the smooth running of a household.[4] Issachar's father, William, was no exception. For reasons unknown, his new marriage prospect came from the distant community of Chesterfield, Massachusetts, some fifty miles to the west. In April 1777, his marriage to Sarah Stockwell of Chesterfield took place in Athol, but the couple moved almost immediately to Chesterfield, taking several of the younger Bates children with them—eight-year-old Dolly and the babies, Caleb and William. Before his twentieth birthday, then, Issachar Bates saw the death of one infant brother, the death of his mother, the remarriage of his father, and the breakup of his father's household.

How the older Bates children—including Issachar—got along in Athol in the face of their father's departure is not entirely clear. Issachar's older sister Hannah had married a young Athol man named David Train in 1774; his family, like the Bateses, had also migrated to the area from Middlesex County to the south. It is quite possible that Hannah opened her household to her several siblings, including Issachar, who were still minors. But in any case, the teenage Issachar was in and out of the army almost continuously during 1776 and 1777, with only a few interludes at home. Perhaps having spent much of his earlier teen years hiring out to other households before mustering into the army at seventeen gave Issachar a self-sufficiency that helped him to cope with the loss of his mother, the departure of his father, and the absence of a stable family home.

Now about my marriage and the change in the course of my life. In the month of May 1778 I was married to Lovina Maynard, daughter of Bezaleel Maynard of Garry, the town in which we both lived. By her I had eleven children. The first was stillborn, one lived but a few minutes.[5]

As a sign of this self-sufficiency, Issachar took the initiative to establish his own household early in 1778 by declaring his intention to marry Lovina Maynard, daughter of Bezaleel Maynard and Elizabeth Keyes, who had migrated to neighboring Gerry (adjoining Athol), with a large family from Shrewsbury, Massachusetts. In Shrewsbury, the Maynards and Keyes families were early English settlers and both families of "some rank."[6] At least two of Bezaleel Maynard's siblings were officers in the Revolutionary War, serving in Worcester County units, though Bezaleel himself served as a private.[7] Lovina was Bezaleel's fourth daughter, and by early 1778 only the eldest daughter,

Elizabeth, was married. But contrary to the normal eighteenth-century practice of daughters marrying according to birth order, Lovina had two older unmarried sisters when she and Issachar Bates were wed. She had just turned eighteen and he had just turned twenty, both young in light of the region's standards at that time.[8] Perhaps they were genuinely in love, but scholars of marriage patterns in colonial New England have noted that daughters marrying out of birth order indicated strong parental involvement in a match.[9] In Issachar's case, such involvement is likely. Having served in the same regiment with Bezaleel Maynard in 1777, Issachar would have had ample opportunity to get acquainted with his future father-in-law and make a good impression. Moreover, the Bates and Maynard families became legally interconnected later that year when Noah Bates, Issachar's twenty-seven-year-old brother, married Lovina's older sister, Ruth.[10] In Issachar's new household, children were soon born — the first stillborn, and the second, a daughter, on Issachar's birthday (January 29) in 1780.[11] The couple named the baby Lovina. More births followed, roughly every two years, for a total of nine surviving children.[12]

The Bates and Maynard families may also have been drawn together on religious grounds, too. Issachar Bates writes that they all lived in Gerry ("Garry"), but that town did not yet exist when either of the families moved to the area. Rather, the towns of Athol and Templeton shared a long border. Not long after the Bates family arrived, the Baptist religion began to make inroads into the area, the consequence of several Baptist families moving to Athol and Templeton from northeastern Connecticut. In 1773 residents of the eastern portion of Athol and western portion of Templeton petitioned to leave the local Congregationalist church and establish a separate Baptist church congregation.[13] That congregation was the basis for the town of Gerry, which was later renamed Phillipston in the early nineteenth century. Since both the Bates and Maynard families are reported to have lived in Gerry, it is very likely that they all held Baptist inclinations. Given that Issachar Bates later united with a Baptist church when he moved his family to Hartford, New York, it is possible that his Baptist leanings began when his family included itself in the group of residents that left Athol to form Gerry (figure 3.1).[14]

⤳ *[M]y mind was again plagued with another phenomenon — the literal fulfillment of Green's vision, the Dark Day all over New England. This baffled all human skill, for it was given up by great and small that there were neither cloud nor smoke in the atmosphere, yet the sun did not appear all that day and that day was as dark as night. No work could be done in any house without a candle, and the night was equally as dark accordingly, altho' there was a*

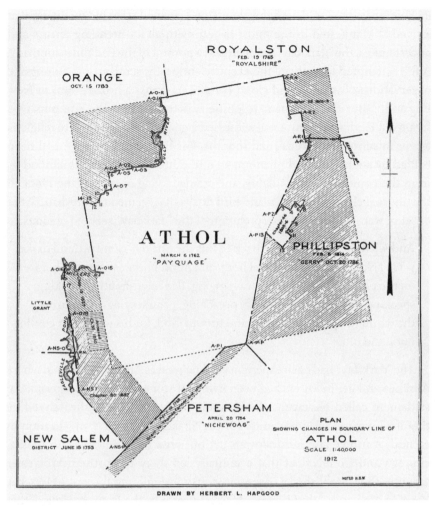

3.1 *Herbert Hapgood, "Plan Showing Changes in Boundary Line of Athol," 1912. (Courtesy of the Athol Public Library, Athol, Massachusetts.)*

well grown moon. I was going to one of the neighbour's houses in company with a young man, and as we passed by several houses the people were out wringing their hands and howling, "the day of judgment is come." This made the young man look pale. I made as light of it as I could, but it felt awful. Here was Green's vision literally fulfilled, for darkness covered the whole face of the land of New England.[15]

May 19, 1780, was a day that struck terror and awe throughout New England. In northern Worcester County, as in other parts of the region, the inclination was to "mark well the gloom" and conclude that judgment day had arrived.[16] Manifested in the midst of war, with all its attending terrors and uncertainties, the "dark day" resonated as a portent of the end times for many. A few attempted to evaluate the event scientifically, scrutinizing it alongside observations of weather and cloud conditions across a broad swath of New England.[17] But the dominant response was to interpret the darkness as a sign from God, and many areas witnessed a general revitalization of religious fervor in subsequent weeks and months. For Issachar Bates, who had been baffled by strange natural phenomena intermittently since his childhood—from the comets, northern lights, and strange flying objects of the 1760s to the unusual cloud formations and bird flocks that seemed to foreshadow the onset of war—a spiritual interpretation of the "dark day" seemed obvious.

> And what next, right on the back of this the Shakers came on, and darker yet . . . Now such confusion of body and mind I never witnessed before on the part of the Shakers. It was singing, dancing, shouting, shaking, speaking with tongues, turning, preaching, prophesying, and warning the world to confess their sins and turn to God, for his wrath was coming upon them.[18]

The "dark day" had been experienced as far west as Albany, New York, where Ann Lee and her followers had been living for some five years in a peripheral settlement called Niskayuna. Interpreting the religious revival catalyzed by the "dark day" as an opportunity for the Shakers to begin evangelization in earnest, Ann Lee and her followers set out on a peregrination into Massachusetts and Connecticut that eventually led them to northern Worcester County. They established a base some thirty-five miles to the east of Issachar Bates's home area—in Harvard, Massachusetts, at the "Square House" that had recently been inhabited by the peculiar followers of Shadrach Ireland. From there, Ann Lee, James Whittaker, and a growing band of enthusiasts made several extended forays into the adjoining communities of Petersham, Athol, Gerry, and Templeton. So frequently did the Shakers preach in those communities that a local resident reported that in the early 1780s Shakers outnumbered other travelers on the local roads.[19] It was the geography of these roads that conspired to bring Issachar Bates and the Shakers together. In December 1781, he found himself, along with his friend and fellow army comrade Moses Mixer, among a crowd of two hundred gathered to hear Ann Lee preach. The venue was the home of wealthy Petersham resident David Hammond, whose house lay along the main road connecting Petersham with Gerry.[20] The Hammonds had grown sympathetic to the Shakers, and the Hammond house was a favored location for Shaker worship, including professed miracles, speaking in tongues, and ecstatic dancing.[21] Issachar's account of what happened on that occasion, shared orally, was integrated by others into various written remembrances and passed down among several generations of Shakers. It appears in several versions, among them the following account, which was probably written down by Ohio Shaker Susan Liddell a century later. "Mother" is the title Ann Lee was given by her followers:

> Issachar was present at David Hammond's in Petersham, with Moses Mixer, at a time when the Believers were assembled for meeting. Mother being there, and Elder Issachar having a great desire to see her, made it known, and was admitted into her presence, and heard her sing. But soon the house was beset by a disorderly mob, and by some means Issachar was placed in the door to keep them out, and for a time effected it. But shortly after they succeeded in clearing him from the door, and rushed in, intending to seize Mother and drag her out; but the sisters clung round her so thick, and seeing the brethren and some others so ready to protect her, they relinquished their object and instantly left the house. Father James Whittaker had been preaching to those present, but seeing this conduct he dismissed the meeting, and the world people went off, and the believers retired to their homes.
>
> But Mother by the spirit said the mob would return again. And it did return, and dragged Mother off in that shameful manner we have on record.
>
> Aftewards Moses met Issachar and asked him what he thought of those people? I think, said he, that they are the people of God. I never saw a woman that looked so beautiful to me as that woman that they call Mother, nor heard any singing that sounded so heavenly as her singing; it fairly charmed me.
>
> He expressed much displeasure that he could not have had the privilege of seeing and hearing her longer, but was disturbed by the mob. He and Moses deeply regretted their having left the house, after learning of the mob's return, and both said they should have defended her, and believed that they could have protected her from the abuse she received from the hands of her terrible persecutors on that occasion.
>
> Issachar ever afterwards testified that he received faith in Mother Ann's gospel at that time, which always continued with him.[22]

Issachar had been captivated by Ann Lee's preaching and singing. Caught up in the frenzy, he had tried to shield the Shakers from a mob that swarmed into Hammond's house and broke through the doorway into the room where Ann Lee was gathered with other women. Her followers prevailed, but only temporarily. The mob later returned to Hammond's house,[23] and Ann Lee suffered injury and humiliation when she was dragged down the stairs and into the yard, where she was hung from a tree and stripped, allegedly so that the mob could see proof of her gender. Whether Issachar and his friend Moses—who would also later become a Shaker—truly nursed regret over the incident is uncertain. And that Issachar actually converted to the Shaker faith on that occasion is unlikely. His own writing indicates that the encounter planted a seed that would lie dormant for nearly twenty years. What he did carry with him was the satisfaction of knowing that he was never among Ann Lee's persecutors. Although profoundly affected by what he witnessed in Petersham in 1781, Issachar concluded that his own life path was already chosen. He had a wife, his family was beginning to grow, and the frenetic life of those early Shakers, however appealing, was not for him.

> Now when I saw all this I was convinced it was the work of God among the Shakers, but I was not ready yet. For I had married a wife and therefore I could not come. But I thank my God who has spared me to this present time and has kept my hand from ever persecuting this blessed people, and that he suffered me when a wicked man to stand on earth and be a witness of his marvelous work.[24]

Having married and begun a family, Issachar Bates needed to establish a means for making a living. The loss of his parents—his mother's death and his father's remarriage and move to distant Chesterfield—may have been a disadvantage as most young men relied upon their parents to help set them up in a farm, trade, or business. But as Issachar had begun working as a hired hand at the age of thirteen, it is also possible that the loss of his parents' household meant less to him that to other young men. Marrying into a relatively affluent family almost certainly benefitted Issachar and may have given him some of the assistance necessary to launch his own household. Several of his married siblings remained in the area, too, which was probably both help and comfort to him. There is evidence that he shared warm relationships with his siblings Hannah, Noah, and Theodore, all of whom may have pooled their household resources.

Issachar's choice of livelihood was not clear to him. He later wrote that he dreamed of becoming wealthy. Farming a small piece of land was hard solitary work for a gregarious young man whose lively personality had blossomed in the army. Issachar possessed abundant talents: a self-taught musician, gifted singer, and comical storyteller adept at mimicry. Yet none of these translated readily into a lucrative profession. He was also generous, outgoing, and filled with initiative. Admittedly, he had picked up vulgar habits of speech and drinking in the army, but his life experiences—as a member of a large family moving from place to place, as a frequent hired hand, as a soldier—had equipped him to undertake a wide range of tasks, adapt to difficult situations, and deal with a range of contentious and adversarial people. Discouraged by farming, he tried to set himself up in a business as a merchant trader, without much success.

> After I was married I bought a small plantation and went to work. But I
> could not get rich fast enough at that and went to speculating in goods,
> horses, cattle, sheep, hogs, and everything a fool would take a notion to
> ... I spared no pains by hard work and speculating in every thing that was
> lawful (and some more) to make gain and get rich. But I will thank God
> that he blasted the whole of it. Being unacquainted with the tricks of trad-
> ing men I verily thought that what a man promised to do, that at any rate
> he intended to do it. For I knew that I did. But I found to my sorrow that it
> was not so, and by fraudulent tricks of trading men I lost as fast as I gained.
> So I found that this trading industry would not answer my purpose.[25]

Perhaps influenced by his father, whose solution to economic difficulties had been to move on to a new and less settled area, Issachar determined to re-settle his family in the hinterlands of Maine, still a territory of Massachusetts in the 1780s, where land was cheaper and more plentiful. Strong in body and resourceful, Issachar was both physically and temperamentally equipped to live in a wilderness area. He found opportunity deep in the interior of Maine, in the fledgling community of Norridgewock on the Kennebec River. Once an Indian settlement, Norridgewock had been decimated by the French in the 1720s and resettled by the British in 1773. Issachar had originally acquired a supply of store goods and hatched a plan to travel to Norridgewock, where store goods were scarce, and sell them to the new settlers for a profit. While there, he saw opportunity in this new region, so he negotiated to purchase two hundred acres. He began clearing the land and put in a crop, with the intention of moving his family here.

> Then I took a quantity of store goods which I had taken in payment for
> shipping horses and started for Kennebec River in the State of Maine.
> And one hundred miles up the river at an old French and Indian settle-
> ment Norridgewock I purchased 200 acres of land and paid for it all

down and got a good deed and put in a crop and returned home 300 miles expecting to move my little family in the fall, but my wife was so much opposed to the move that I swapped it with a man in good standing for fifty acres of good land nigh by. I made him a deed of the land at Norridgewock and he sold it soon. He had to finish the last payment on the fifty acres before I could get a deed and I had great confidence in the man. But the next I know of the matter he had slipped off between two days and I never got one cent for my land from that day to this. This with other misfortunes left me about 150 dollars — worse than nothing.[26]

The ease with which Issachar was tricked out of his acreage in Maine, along with his chance for a smaller piece of land back in Worcester County, suggests that his good nature made him astonishingly naïve. This trait seems a bit out of character with his military experience, which should have helped him develop rather more insight into reading people. But one thing is clear from the way that Issachar recounts the loss of his land and assets so many years later: he felt the injustice of the situation bitterly "from that day to this," indicating that the experience was an intensely formative one. This was just one more episode that contributed to Issachar's keen sense of justice, of balance, of effort expended for just reward. Whether in respect to his military service, his life as a trader and landowner, or his later life as a Shaker, Issachar Bates saw the world as a balance sheet — an orientation that would later manifest in his creative expressions as a Shaker — his preaching, poetry, hymns, and other writings.

> And when I was about twenty-eight years of age I moved my family into the state of New York into the woods and went to work with all my strength and made a living for my family. And my creditors were patient with me, and I paid them all honestly and made a comfortable living.[27]

The year 1786 found Issachar Bates trying to recover from impoverishing his growing family. Once again, he sought a move to a newly settled region, this time the woods of Washington County, New York, in the southern Adirondacks (figure 3.2). Issachar was no stranger to the area. In 1777, he had been attached to a unit dispatched to Saratoga to intercept British troops under General Burgoyne. That unit had been redirected to occupy nearby Fort Edward, a frontier outpost in Washington County near the falls of the Hudson River,[28] which afforded Issachar and other men an opportunity to see this unsettled area firsthand. It was rich in timber resources, close to mountains and lakes that supported game and fish populations, had fast-moving

3.2 *"A chorographical map of the Province of New-York in North America, divided into counties, manors, patents and townships. . . . Engraved and published by William Faden,"* 1779. Issachar Bates migrated to Hartford, New York, when much of the region remained an unmapped frontier. (Library of Congress, Geography and Map Division.)

streams suitable for operating mills, and was relatively accessible to population centers further south along the Hudson Valley. Among the area's earliest
residents were young men who had seen the area as soldiers and recognized
its potential for settlement.[29]

Issachar's reasons for moving to the area were twofold. Not only had he
been there himself, two young unmarried men from Worcester County to
whom Lovina was related by marriage went there in 1782, broke ground, and
built a small cabin, establishing themselves among the first settlers of the
town of Hartford. These men were Aaron and Eber Ingalsbe, brothers of John
Ingalsbe (who married Lovina Maynard's sister Louisa). In 1786, Issachar
Bates and his family followed these Ingalsbe brothers to Hartford, along with
several of Issachar's in-laws — John and Louisa Ingalsbe, as well as Francis
Maynard, youngest brother of Lovina.[30] A few years later, Lovina's uncle
Gardner Maynard migrated to Hartford with his family, augmenting the kinship cluster still further.[31] The tendency for family groups to join forces in set-
tling a frontier area is well known. For Issachar's wife, the prospect of moving
to the wilds of upstate New York with her sister Louisa, her brother Francis,
her uncle, and other in-laws was obviously much more appealing than the
prospect of moving to the interior of Maine territory had been. In addition,
since Issachar was in debt — having lost both his Maine property and his land
in Massachusetts — moving to a new area along with family members was
probably the best option.

Although Issachar and his family lived in Hartford, New York, for about
fifteen years, there is no record of him owning property there. Hartford was
laid out as a roughly rectangular site midway between Fort Edward and the
Vermont border, and many Hartford residents leased property from landowners. Families who migrated together tended to reside near one another,
and — as Garner Maynard and Aaron Ingalsbe, both related to Issachar by
marriage, each owned property in the southern part of Hartford, south of the
town center[32] — it is possible that Issachar's family lived adjacent to some of
his kin.

At nearly thirty years old when he arrived in Hartford, Issachar still lacked
a steady profession. He writes of working at "moving logs," so it is likely that
much of his employment consisted of cutting trees and handling logs, work
he had likely first done years before when he was a hired hand. But he had also
worked at farming, trading, and hauling goods and animals, and he probably
had learned some masonry from his father. Still, with all this varied experience, Issachar had no set livelihood. For a New England man reared during
the late colonial period, finding one's life vocation was crucial to a sense of

identity and even a sense of manhood. One scholar of men's domestic lives in late colonial New England notes that men were pitied if they reached Issachar's age without a settled career: "The worst thing to befall a man seeking his way in the world was to remain unsettled . . . A settlement assured a productive and secure manhood."[33] Moreover, men who openly nurtured a desire to become wealthy, as Issachar had done, could be morally suspect. The fact that Issachar had plunged his family into debt through his poor choices and that at nearly thirty years of age he was apparently relying upon his wife's siblings and in-laws to help him stabilize the situation of his own growing family strongly suggests a man who was wrestling with inner demons. By his own admission, Issachar had begun drinking while a teenager in the army, and his writing indicates that he was dependent upon alcohol at some points in his adult life. Whether his drinking seriously interfered with his ability to earn a living is uncertain. But a man's pride hinged upon his ability to be a good provider, and alcohol was "often the handmaiden of the poor provider."[34] What is certain is that Issachar seemed to struggle with depression during this period of his life: "I had many serious thoughts, more than anyone would judge I had by my common deportment, for I was what is called in the world a clever, jolly, honest fellow. But it did not always feel so to me . . . for I was very full of serious thoughts. But I always hated conviction. It plagued me at night, hindered me from sleep."[35]

Outwardly Issachar Bates was cheerful and popular among his neighbors, but inwardly he struggled with dark thoughts, insecurities about his children's well-being, and doubts about his own salvation. By "conviction" Issachar meant the overwhelming realization of God's presence and capacity to judge. A consequence of his parents' Calvinistic teachings, his schooling from the *New England Primer*, and his early experience of apparent "signs and wonders," Issachar had harbored since childhood a certainty that the world and everything in it had fallen from God's grace and was subject to judgment. It followed that if he was likable in the world's eyes, then he must be a miserable sinner in God's eyes. Yet Issachar's popularity in Hartford partly accrued from his service to the community. He attended the local Baptist church, founded in 1788 and established in a log meeting house in 1789 that he may have helped to build.[36] He wrote of his personal acquaintance with the church's founding pastor, Amasa Brown. In about 1790 Issachar began to teach singing at the church, probably serving as its first choirmaster, a role he held for many years.[37]

Considering his father's pattern of frequent moves, it is possible that Issachar had developed a restless nature and that his inner emotional struggle intensified as he and his family grew more and more settled in Hartford. He writes of deep spiritual struggles beginning when he was about thirty-seven. At that time, his family had lived in Hartford about nine years, quite possibly longer than Issachar had resided in any one spot in his life. Having married young, seeing his family growing larger and larger around him, unable to find satisfaction in his employment, and plagued with spiritual doubts, Issachar may have had what is currently called a midlife crisis:

> [W]hen I was about thirty-seven years of age, one morning as I opened the door to go out to my work, I cast my eyes back on my children (which were seven in number). An awful feeling struck my mind — what will become of them children? Ah, and what will become of me — for I had often made use of the same vile language before them which I learned in the army. I then determined to begin to mend my life. So I went to my work, moving some large logs. One of them acted very ugly (as I thought), and I broke out in my usual manner — "damn the thing." Here I was all alone, nobody to hear me but God. Oh, the horror! It is all vain for me to think of being any better! I went behind the fence and fell on my knees. I prayed, I cried, I begged for Almighty power to help me to govern my tongue, if no more. For I had tried till I was beat. But I found that it must go deeper than the tongue. The disease was in my heart, and that had to be broken up from the foundation.[38]

Thus began Issachar Bates's earnest toil toward spiritual transformation. A few points from his account are striking. First, he was burdened with worry for his seven children — particularly for their emotional welfare and spiritual sustenance. He carried guilt for exhibiting to his children the rough habits and vulgar language of his army days, indicating he was a genuinely loving and concerned father. Second, he believed that his vulgar habits and his inability to control them were a symptom of a deeper problem. Curbing his tongue was not a solution. Rather, he needed a complete alteration of character. This impulse is thoroughly consistent with the Christian conversion process experienced by people for centuries. And third, Issachar experienced this transformative moment alone and in the woods. Thus began a pattern apparent during the remainder of his life, whereby events and interludes of strong spiritual import happened to Issachar when he was out-of-doors and in near solitude.

Interestingly, Issachar seemed to maintain a sense of shame, even in the isolation of the forest, which drove him behind the protective barrier of a fence where he fell to his knees and poured out his anguish. From this wrenching day alone in the forest, Issachar was set on a long and rocky spiritual conversion process that would persist for several years, although the next few months would prove the most tumultuous. Issachar would later write revealingly about this interlude, and his narration deserves to be recounted at length.

I did not think of mercy. I did not ask for mercy. I pled for judgment and torment to be poured out on me till I was broken to pieces . . . I had lived all the days of my life transgressing God's Holy Law . . . But it was not comfort and joy that I was seeking after. Nay, it was to come to an honest settlement with God if possible. I was perfectly willing that God should take my life, and all that I had, if that would make an atonement. But I abhorred myself to that degree that it appeared to me that God wanted nothing to do with me. And whenever the tears ceased to flow freely, I was in keen despair. Oh my wicked heart — the words of the poet suited me well: "my thoughts on awful subjects roll, damnation on the dead, what horrors seize a guilty soul, upon a dying bed."[39] But I had it upon a burning bed. Oh Hell, I have been in your bowels . . . I kept my mind to myself and did not open it to any mortal, and I am glad I did so. For if the preachers had found out my state they would have ruined me . . . But I had been then five or six weeks in such trouble that I had created a sore lump in my breast. It felt to me like a three pound cannon ball, and I did not care if it killed me.[40]

Issachar had reached a bitter low point, gripped with despair. Any sense of self-worth had disappeared, replaced by an overwhelming conviction of worthlessness, sin, and rejection by God. His thoughts were so self-destructive that he dared not voice them to anyone. His allusion to a "burning bed" suggests that some of his anxiety stemmed from undisclosed sexual issues. Taken together with other remarks about this period of religious conviction in his life, it is possible that strong sexual impulses were among the habits that Issachar felt powerless to control. His description of self-hatred, a chronic sensation of bodily heaviness and pain, and a desire for death all conform to symptoms of serious clinical depression. Given his time and place, virtually the only source of relief available was couched in the trappings of religious conversion. Consequently, Issachar continued to look for a solution through the church.

I then concluded that I would go the next Saturday to a Baptist meeting. Accordingly, I went and sat in a pew and heard them all open their minds . . . After they all had got through, the way was opened for anyone to be free that had anything on their minds. A young woman in the pew urged me to rise and speak, which I did . . . And then they began to urge me to go forwards into the water. I told them I had no such intention. Then they began to warn me. One Job Picket among the rest warned me not to delay, for he did so and he had to go seven years into captivity among the Shakers for his disobedience . . . But I told them I felt very far from being a Christian and I should wait till I was better satisfied. So I returned homeward and felt worse than ever. The sore in my breast, or rather in my heart, was in tormenting pain, and I concluded that I must cry for mercy or give up the ghost.[41]

Even as Issachar's neighbors and fellow Baptists found spiritual satisfaction through meetings, testimonies, and baptism, comfort still eluded him. Job Picket's advice against an entanglement with the Shakers served only to remind Issachar of his encounter with Ann Lee nearly fifteen years before. Unable to share the spiritual contentment enjoyed by his fellow Baptists, Issachar was dejected and discouraged, so depressed as to be in physical pain. As he headed home alone from an evening church meeting along a deserted road, he experienced an epiphany that changed him.

And . . . right there in the middle of the road in one moment, in the twinkling of an eye, a hot flash like lightning struck me between the shoulders into my heart and drove out the sore lump and every weight that was about me and left me feeling as light as nothing with my hands stretched opened on my tiptoes and expecting every step to leave the earth and step into the air. Here I had the perfect knowledge of joy unspeakable, and full of glory, for no being in heaven or on earth could be any happier. And it was truly unspeakable, for I could not utter the half of it then, neither can I describe the half of it now. But I went home to my own house and told them what great things the Lord had done for me and went skipping across the floor singing psalms and hymns, which astonished my family very much. Thus I kept up my exercise until one o'clock at night and then laid me down in perfect peace and death and hell were removed far from me.[42]

Issachar Bates's experience alone on that road through the woods is not unlike many other religious conversions, from that of the Apostle Paul, to the eminent seventeenth-century English preacher George Fox, to the nineteenth-century American evangelist Charles Finney. All refer to a defining moment of insight while journeying in solitude. The book of Acts tells of Paul's conversion while traveling on the road. Fox writes of achieving spiritual clarity through hours spent alone in the woods and walking on the road.[43] Charles Finney's conversion occurred while walking from his home to his office, and was the culmination of a period of deep depression and doubt.[44] Other prominent religious figures of Issachar Bates's lifetime, such as the hymn writer John Newton and American itinerant preacher Lorenzo Dow, write of abrupt transformations from the depths of despair to states of indescribable bliss.[45] English evangelist George Whitefield, whose celebrated preaching tours of the American colonies affected tens of thousands of people in the 1760s and would have been known to Issachar and his family, relentlessly emphasized the need for a specific moment of spiritual transformation in order for a person to be certain of salvation.[46] Whitefield's basis was the New Testament scripture John 3:3, where Jesus remarks, "Except a man be born again, he cannot see the kingdom of God." Certainly the idea of one's salvation being tied to a moment of profound personal transformation was a familiar one to people of Issachar's time and place. Still, the sudden reality of it was astonishing both to Issachar and to his family. People in his church and community, too, were amazed at the unexpected change in his entire demeanor.

> In the morning I arose praising God . . . and when the people came along to meeting I went with them preaching and praising God to their astonishment. And when I got on to the common before the meeting house there were a large body of people collected, and there I poured out a testimony. I know not what it was, for it was none of mine, but I knew it was the power of God and it throwed them all into tears, Deists and all. Then I passed by the north end of the meeting house to the burying yard (the sight of which had always filled me with dread) and stretched out my hand over the fence and bid defiance to the grave, to death, and to hell, and I have never been afraid of that monster (so-called) from that time henceforth, even forever. And as I returned and passed by Elder Brown I told him I was now ready to go into the water or anything else, for I was prepared to serve God forever. So all gathered into the meeting house. And I took my seat which was the fore seat in the front gallery (for I had been their chorister for some time), and as I rose up to pitch the tune I broke forth in the power of God to the singers. I told them I had been four winters learning them to sing with the understanding, and now I could learn them to sing in the spirit, and so went on till the whole house was in tears. Now one may judge how wonderful this new thing appeared . . . for one so unexpected as I was to come forth with the flaming power of God.[47]

3.3
*The Hartford, New York,
Baptist meeting house, where
Issachar Bates was active
throughout the 1790s, stood a
few yards south of these graves
that date from the period.
The site is now occupied by
the Hartford Post Office.
(Photo by author.)*

Whatever propensities Issachar Bates was known for within his community, public expression of religious fervor was not among them. People knew Issachar as a jovial and boisterous man, slightly crude though well-meaning, with enough natural singing talent and enthusiasm for music to make him an acceptable choirmaster for the Baptist church. But he was certainly no orator. The specter of him abruptly pouring out a testimony on a Sunday morning, spontaneously addressing the church so dynamically as to move people to tears, was almost unimaginable. Likewise the sight of him in public making exuberant gestures over the gravestones next to the meeting house (figure 3.3) was more than peculiar. Issachar Bates seemed to be a new person. Writing later, although he did not recount this interlude by specifically saying he had been "born again," it is clear that he saw his new spiritual reality as tantamount to a second childhood, wherein he was returned to a childlike state of complete trust, openness, and simple faith. Issachar explained his reversion to a spiritual childhood using the analogy of the "prodigal son. He insisted, too, that his recognition of God's grace came not from education or from immersion in religious doctrine, but rather as a direct spiritual insight:

For I had returned to the days of my youth [and] had the same little child-like faith that I had when I was a little boy — that God is good, yea, and I have proved his goodness to me . . . Now let the vain disputer of this world come forwards and labor to make me think that I received all this by my education or by tradition and his labor will be in vain. For I never received one trait of it from that quarter, for I was always a free agent, and I received this my portion from God when a child. But I played prodigal with it and wasted it like another fool and had to go through dreadful suffering to get back to my Father's house. But when I began to return don't you see how the Father ran and met me and kissed me. Well, I can see it and feel it now.[48]

Because he had undergone a profound spiritual transformation, Issachar may have been unable to come to grips with some of his natural inclinations that remained. It seems, for example, that he had difficulty reconciling his sexuality with his understanding of Christian faith. In writing about his uncertainties, he indicates that he was surprised and horrified when, after his dramatic conversion interlude, he again experienced sexual desire. He refers to this in the parlance of the day as "motion of the flesh."

Now I must go a little back after my three happy weeks had passed away, behold the motion of the flesh began to return, which felt more deathly to me than the bite of a rattlesnake. And this was not all, but all my past sins were set in order before me and had all got to come out of my mouth, altho' I thought they were canceled. So I left my work and went to Elder Brown and took him out to the sugar camp and told him my distress and that I wanted to confess my sins.[49] He replied, "You do not mean your 'secret sins.'" "Yea, that is my distress," said I. "Well," said he, "I shall not hear you, it might ruin your family." I said my soul was more to me than my family. I begged of him to hear me. He said he would not. Then I began to tell him how I felt in relation to the works of the flesh. He said such trials as them were just an imposition of the Devil, for it was the great command of God. So I had to take my load back again with this hope, that my wife would hear me. But she flew and left the room after the first motion. Here I was, poor distressed creature, no man to guide me and no woman to help me. I often opened my faith to individuals how I felt and what I believed concerning the works of the flesh, bearing arms, swearing of oaths, dressing in the fashions of the world, but it was generally treated with contempt . . . I kept up pretty good spirits for about four years and after passing through several revivals, but all ended in the flesh.[50]

As a father of many children and a former army soldier with an admittedly vulgar tongue, Issachar Bates was obviously no stranger to sexuality. But his evolving religious convictions were propelling him to a new understanding of sexuality namely, as incompatible with an ideal Christian life. Having already witnessed Shaker preaching, he would have been exposed to Shaker tenets of celibacy years before. In addition, Issachar began to be persuaded to the notion that only through confession of sin to a clergyman could he find true absolution. Baptists did not practice individual verbal confession of sin at that time. Yet Issachar begged his minister in Hartford, Amasa Brown, to hear his confession, including his "secret sins" — sins so abhorrent that revealing them would have had the capacity to ruin the standing of Issachar and his family in the community. Exactly what these "secret sins" were is unknown, but they must have included sexual behavior that, by the standards of the time, was beyond the pale: adultery, fathering a child out of wedlock, acting on homosexual impulses, or even masturbation. Whatever he had concealed and longed to confess, even his wife did not want to hear; she ran from the room when he attempted to confide in her. In the end, Issachar became so frustrated that he began to speak to anyone who would listen to him about his convictions on what he considered sinful behaviors. Yet even as he battled to balance his sexuality with his new understanding of Christian rectitude, two additional children were born to Lovina, bringing their living offspring to nine. And Issachar was able to subsume his doubts and carry on as a lively presence in the religious affairs of the community.

> There were a great stir among the people in these times, so that we had society meetings three nights in a week. I always attended and was very lively preaching and exhorting in turn, till they began to charge me with preaching, which was far from my thoughts. But they insisted on it, that I could never be justified one side of taking up my cross and preaching. Accordingly, four Baptist preachers were appointed to hear me, and they licensed me to preach anywhere, and I did preach the best I knew sincerely.[51]

As one powerful consequence of Issachar Bates's conversion experience, he found literally a new voice — a verbal eloquence that he had never before displayed. In part, that eloquence manifested itself in a clear talent for preaching. People in the community were captivated by his preaching, beginning the day after his conversion on the road, and he soon was urged to begin preaching as a regular avocation. Issachar almost certainly traveled far afield from Hartford to preach in other communities of the southern Adirondack region.

His daughter Sarah, writing in 1875 when she was nearly eighty-four years old, notes — somewhat emphatically — that her father was a "Baptist Licensed Elder: had a Church, and was greatly beloved by the members."[52] While there is no direct evidence to suggest that he was placed in sole charge of a Baptist congregation, it is possible that he may have briefly been assigned by the area Baptist clergy to preach at the new Baptist church in Schroon, New York, about fifty miles from Hartford. According to a short family history recorded by Issachar Bates Jr. about twenty years after his father's death, Issachar briefly moved his family to Schroon, which was at that time a tiny unincorporated community on the banks of Schroon Lake. (It was there that Betsy Bates, the youngest child of Issachar and Lovina, was born in 1798.) After living in Schroon for less than two years, the family returned to Hartford, New York, in 1799.[53]

Another dimension of Issachar Bates's new verbal eloquence is found in his written expression. There is no evidence to suggest that his formal education was anything but meager. Yet he certainly possessed enough innate intelligence to comprehend and retain what he read: Bible passages, the *New England Primer*, catechism, a few printed pamphlets owned by his parents. Because of his musical talent, which had blossomed when he was a fifer in the army, he was motivated to learn and retain lyrics for all manner of popular songs. As a choirmaster, he would have been well acquainted with the printed hymnals of the period, which contained the rich religious poetry of such hymn writers as Isaac Watts, Charles Wesley, and John Newton.

At some point after his initial conversion, Issachar decided to try his hand at writing poetry, and he intended that many of his poems be sung as hymns. He was encouraged in this pursuit by the fact that a number of New Englanders who were his contemporaries were then enjoying success as hymn composers. Following in the pattern of Massachusetts musician William Billings, a composer and singing-school master with little formal musical training whose choral music enjoyed raging popularity, amateur musicians and singing-school masters from Connecticut and Rhode Island in the south, to Maine in the northeast, to upstate New York and Vermont in the northwest, were busily producing some of America's earliest hymn collections in the 1780s and 1790s.[54] As an enthusiastic musician and choirmaster, Issachar may have dreamed of joining the ranks of such regionally popular New England composers as Daniel Read, Jeremiah Ingalls, Supply Belcher, Nehemiah Shumway, and Jacob French,[55] when in 1800 he published a short collection of hymn texts titled *New Songs, on Different Subjects*.

The eight poems that comprise *New Songs, on Different Subjects* reflect a blend of local history, regional observation, and spiritual reflection. All seem intended for singing.[56] One includes the annotation "To the tune of Major Andre," and others include choruses and refrains, indicative of hymns. All but one of the poems appear to post-date Issachar's spiritual conversion around 1795. One of the poems, titled "Composed on the death of Mr. Isaac Orcutt, who was kill'd by the fall of a tree, in Hartford, state of New York," recounts an incident that likely took place around 1790. Fashioned as a seventeen-stanza ballad, the poem tells the story of a tragic accident in wintertime, when a young man went out alone into the woods to cut some timber only to have a part of a tree fall on him. According to the text, Isaac Orcutt sustained a mortal head injury, lay crushed and bleeding in the snow, undiscovered for the better part of a day before he was found by neighbors, and soon died. The fact that Issachar Bates so carefully reconstructed Isaac Orcutt's sad end in what could have been one his earliest poems suggests that he not only knew the young man,[57] and perhaps was among those who tried to save him, but also that he empathized deeply with the experience. Issachar, too, spent long hours alone in the woods working with logs, a risky undertaking. He may have nursed a fear that he, too, might suffer a similar fate. Another poem, titled "Composed on the late sickness in Hartford, state of New York," tells of an epidemic in Hartford in which a distressing number of households suffer the loss of parents, spouses, and children. No date is identified in the poem, but it may refer to an epidemic that had occurred not long before the poem's publication in 1800. Issachar's sister-in-law, Louisa Maynard Ingalsbe, who had been part of the family group that migrated to Hartford in 1786, died in 1799 at the age of forty-one, possibly a victim of "the late sickness." With his own family affected, Issachar would reasonably be motivated to write about the incident. Other poems point to Issachar's customary experience of solitude and his familiarity with the forested wilderness of the region. "The Hunter's Midnight Prayer" includes the notation that Issachar "compos'd this song near Schroon Lake where he encamped for a night," more than fifty miles from Hartford. Hunting was probably a necessary activity for the men of Hartford,[58] and wild game likely constituted an important part of a family's diet. Another poem, "A Prospect of Lake Schroon, Compos'd on its banks," consists of a detailed description of the lake's remote setting, the surrounding topography, the natural resources of the area, its wildlife, and a projected vision of how settlement might proceed someday, with roads, mills, and fields.

Did Issachar's hymns receive much attention once his little collection was published in 1800 by Dodd in nearby Salem, New York? Clearly, there was some regional circulation. One of his hymn texts, "The Harvest," was included in a hymnbook published in Boston in 1804, though without attribution to Bates.[59] The same text was included in *The Christian Harmony*, published in 1805 by Vermont choirmaster and composer Jeremiah Ingalls.[60] Of all the texts, the one that has received the most attention was the ballad recounting the death of Isaac Orcutt. As a folk ballad, it was circulated through New England during the nineteenth and early twentieth centuries, though the authorship by Bates was apparently unknown, and some names and places were altered.[61] Even if the hymn texts in Issachar Bates's little booklet of 1800 are only eight in number and only a few were circulated to any degree, they nonetheless marked a very important milestone. From that modest beginning, Issachar would become a remarkably able and zealous poet and hymn writer, one of the most prolific poets among the Shakers, and would be remembered by Shakers even decades after his death for reveling in "poetry run mad."[62]

> I began to testify that salvation was not among us nor never would be in that way of going. Then I began to look all round the world to see if there were any that did good and I found that they all lived after the flesh except the Shakers. And there I hated to go. Here I was for three years my faith with the Shakers and my union with the world, and I a tormented Baptist preacher . . . And if I said or hinted such a word as going to see the Shakers, I had the awfulest warnings to keep away from these deluded creatures. And there were none of them nearer than 70 miles. And how to break these bands and get to them I could not contrive for some time.[63]

Although years passed after Issachar Bates's initial religious conversion during which he harbored doubts, sought a public confession, struggled with what he regarded as sexual sin, found a calling as a preacher, and discovered a gift for composing eloquent poetry, genuine assurance of salvation still eluded him. Inevitably drawn to the Shakers and never having forgotten his initial exposure so many years before, Issachar was gradually convinced that only the Shakers offered a path to salvation that would satisfy him. This situation alarmed Issachar's friends and associates, who reminded him of the abundant anti-Shaker testimonies then in circulation in the region. By the late 1790s, the Shakers had many detractors, including one-time members whose published diatribes excoriating Shaker beliefs and practices were circulated throughout New England and beyond.[64] Issachar and others in his family and community no doubt would at least have heard of such accounts. Still, Issachar was determined to learn more about the Shakers firsthand. In 1800 he visited the Shaker community of Watervliet, New York, established at the site of Ann Lee's original settlement location outside Albany. The circumstances that took him there are not clear, but the reaction of the Shakers to his presence is recorded in an 1878 Shaker publication:

> In the year 1800, Issachar Bates came to Watervliet as an inquirer; and the whole settlement was roused to a high pitch of excitement over the fact that the gospel had sufficiently opened to attract a single individual who wanted more salvation than he could get elsewhere! The news soon reached Mt. Lebanon, and Asenath Clark, then a youth, (but afterwards presiding Eldress of the Societies,) ran from room to room, and from individual to individual, with the joyful tidings: "The gospel has opened, for a man has come!"[65]

Issachar does not write explicitly about this 1800 visit to Watervliet. But his published booklet of poetry does contain subtle indications that he had recently visited the Shakers. One poem bears the lines, "It is for Sion I do sigh / Though absent from connections dear," a possible reference to a visit to one of the Shaker communities, which the Shakers referred to collectively as "Zion." Elsewhere in the booklet, a stanza reads, "And Father if it be thy will / That I once more on earth shall meet / Thy children, I will praise thee still / And my devotion shall be sweet." For the most part, however, Issachar struggled to conceal his growing attraction to the Shakers and privately connived to find a way to steal off to New Lebanon to talk with an elder directly. His account of what transpired deserves to be read in full.

> At length I fixed on a plan and made it work. I told my wife that I believed it was my duty to go and see my poor old Father. She was very willing . . . I went and visited my Father. And then went to New Lebanon. I found my sister Dolly on the way, who had lately confessed her sins, and a sister's daughter of mine, also Hannah Train, with whom I had some conversation. They told me when I got to Lebanon to inquire for Elder Cooly at the North House. So I went on a while with two minds, one for Lebanon, the other for home, awfully afraid of being deluded. At length I broke the snare. I appealed to God that he knew my heart, he knew it was salvation that I was after, and he would not suffer me to be deluded. So I went on, lodged at a turn off Tavern that night on the mountain between Hancock and Lebanon. Heard dreadful stories about the Shakers. Next morning I arrived at the north house, knocked at the door, and Stephen Woodward opened unto me. I told him I wished to see Elder Cooly. He soon came forward. He asked me what I wanted. A: I want to talk with you. Qus: What about? A: Religion. Qus: Do you profess religion?

A: Yea. Qus: What order? A: Baptist. Qus: Are you satisfied with what you have got? A: Nay, I am not. "Very well," said he, "go and take some breakfast and then we will talk." Stephen told me after I confessed my sins that he went and told the cook to get some breakfast for a man that was going to confess his sins and preach the gospel. After breakfast Stephen conducted me to Elder Ebenezer's room . . . Then he went through all the work of God from the beginning of the world down to this very time in which he and I now stood. And it was the first straight testimony that I ever heard out of the mouth of a man. It seemed as though my soul was perfectly acquainted with it. Then I told him what a fix I was in — that I had stole away from home . . . and I wanted his council whether to confess my sins now or go home and settle matters and come again. He replied, "Count the cost well, Issachar." So he went to the gate with me and after I was on my horse, these were his last words: "Farewell Issachar, and remember that there is but one Christ." This sounded strange to me, for I thought I always knew that. But these words stuck to me till it was opened to me that I never had understood this scripture — one faith, one Lord. And there must be a Christ to every faith. And I knew that there were many faiths. Then I had an open vision of this great Babylon all in confusion and I bid adieu to it forever. Now my whole stay at Lebanon was not much over an hour, for we did business quick — I ate quick and talked quick and heard quick and started home quick for I was quickened. I went home and kept myself as close as possible. But they soon smelt me out, and before night the news was all through the country that I had joined the Shakers.[66]

Issachar Bates was forty-three years old. He had been married to Lovina for twenty-three years — more than half of his life — and he had fathered nine children. Against a backdrop of great change in the first generation of post-Revolutionary America, Issachar had waged his own struggle to make a stable home for himself and his family, to earn a living, and to find some inner satisfaction. Along the way he had unexpectedly encountered Ann Lee, the woman whose teachings would change the lives of Issachar and his family forever. Before yielding to the summons of the Shakers, however, he had endured years of severe depression and spiritual crisis. But in overcoming that, he discovered within himself vital gifts that would sustain him through the rest of his life: the verbal eloquence to undergird both charismatic preaching and expressive poetry. Drawn to the controversial Shaker order, a group both celibate in its lifestyle and radical in its theology, Issachar faced an impossible dilemma. He was a married man with nine children and an obvious yearning for the freedom and autonomy of the frontier, yet he had yielded to the spiritual call of the Shakers and he now sought to commit himself to the narrow restrictions of Shaker life. The prospect of Issachar Bates embracing the Shakers seemed incomprehensible to most who knew him. But in reality it was simply the inexorable end of one tumultuous phase in his life journey.

CHAPTER 4

"A testimony as hot as flames"

SHAKER CONVERSION AND EARLY TRAVELS

In this flood, I must either sink or swim . . . Salvation
was mine and I would have it. — Issachar Bates

Issachar Bates's solution to the restlessness, personal uncertainty, and spiritual despondency that had plagued him his entire adult life was to do the unthinkable — to turn to a marginal sect that was so deeply repudiated by mainstream Christians throughout the region that its very name conjured horrifying images of practices that no reasonable person would sanction. Accounts then in circulation portrayed Shaker worship as a hellish frenzy, with drunken men and women dancing naked together.[1] Shakers were alleged to kidnap and enslave people, and their reverence for Ann Lee — who had died in 1784 — was portrayed as the most shocking blasphemy. Yet Issachar set himself on this path. In 1801, "becoming" a Shaker was an ambiguous process. It was necessary to make a complete verbal confession of one's lifetime of sin, to reject further sin by certain practices of self-denial — forswearing oaths, arms, fashionable clothing, sophisticated speech — and most of all, to renounce all sexuality and lust. Shakers preached that people should live as Christ had lived. This would come to mean communal living concentrated in one of some twenty economically independent villages, spread across a thousand miles, under legally binding covenants and presided over by hierarchical Shaker authorities.

But this "gospel order" was not yet established when Issachar Bates turned to the Shakers. The movement was still small and fluid, confined to a portion of the Northeast. After riding some seventy miles to New Lebanon and confessing his sins, Issachar simply returned home and began to work out what this decision would mean for himself and his family. He could not know that his short journey to New Lebanon was actually the start of a very long journey that would take him from both his home region and his wife and children. Issachar was about to be enlisted in yet another campaign, a campaign to preach the Shaker gospel to an unbelieving world. It was a campaign that would bring him into union with new friends and comrades and take him to new places, first deeper into the margins of New England and later into the far western frontier along the already celebrated Wilderness Road.

*My greatest trouble was at home, with those of mine own household.
But soon a committee was sent from the Baptist Church to labour with me.
O the flood that they poured out of their mouths against the Shakers. And I
told them that I knew the greatest part of them reports to be lies eighteen years
ago ... So they went away and gained nothing of me ... Then I got on my horse
and went to New Lebanon and confessed my sins. August 1801. And then I was
ready to meet any of them and have been ready ever since to meet any flesh
bug on this earth. But when I returned home none but a well tried believer can
sense what I had to endure. Not one in my family nor in the neighborhood nor
within 70 miles but what was opposed to me, and the children in the streets
that used to reverence me when I was a preacher now mocked me.*[2]

Joining the Shakers was a decision that cost Issachar Bates dearly. His family and church community were appalled, and he was hurt by their scorn and
rejection. Undeterred, he stood by his choice. Indeed, he drew energy from
the resistance he experienced in his neighborhood. Having already preached
as a Baptist for some years, he developed a remarkable zeal that was virtually unmatched even among the Shaker preachers and that intimidated his
detractors: "[I]n a few months they were willing to keep out of my way, for I
had a testimony as hot as flames and I stood in the power of God. And they
did not much like that. I was soon after sent by the Church to preach to the
world in company with Benjamin S. Youngs, who was a loving companion
and a blessed little strong man of God. He went with me first to my family in
Hartford and gained their feelings and respect which they have retained unto
this day. Then we went to Pittsford, Vermont."[3]

So began Issachar's long career of preaching "to the world" on behalf of the
Shakers. It was the latter part of 1801, probably within just a few months of his
own confession of faith. Yet he was entrusted with the vital task of representing the Shaker faith to a suspicious and hostile public. He would not venture
out alone; rather, he was introduced to a companion, Benjamin Seth Youngs.
Theirs was a momentous meeting. From that initial trip to Vermont in 1801,
Issachar's passion for preaching the Shaker gospel to the world never flagged,
and Benjamin would remain his closest friend, fellow preacher, and traveling companion. Later, Issachar would refer to him as his dearest "friend and
fellow traveler," would reflect upon their shared experiences from the beginning of his Shaker life, and would compare their friendship to the legendary
devotion of Old Testament characters David and Jonathan. He even indicates
that he looked up to the physically diminutive Benjamin in spiritual matters,
despite the difference in their ages.

But as I was with little Benjamin (now Elder Benjamin) from the beginning I always felt safe with him: for you know he is the son of the right hand. But whom I esteemed the father of my right hand in all matters. We traveled many thousands of miles together thro' tribulation and sufferings; and many were the snowbanks & deep waters thro' which we waded together, & love & union were always our staff. Besides I am persuaded that there never were many Davids' & Jonathans' hearts more closely knit together: and I learned many good things of him.[4]

Born in 1774, Benjamin Seth Youngs was part of a large family from eastern New York State that came to the Shakers in the early 1790s.[5] Benjamin had grown up with Presbyterian influence, then joined the Methodists when he was seventeen.[6] Benjamin's father, Seth Youngs Jr., was initially a devoted Shaker, but committed suicide in 1815. The unmarried Benjamin confessed his sins in 1794, when he reached adult age. By 1801 when he met Issachar Bates, Benjamin was still a young man, fifteen years Issachar's junior. As an adult he was remarkedly small, less than a hundred pounds, and so boyish in appearance that he was often mistaken for a child.[7] Possibly Benjamin reminded Issachar of his younger brother, Theodore Bates, also a small man, whose physical description contained in his Revolutionary War record is reminiscent of Shaker descriptions of Benjamin.[8] This chance similarity may have helped the two men forge a strong bond. Like Issachar, Benjamin was fervent believer and an eloquent and persuasive preacher. Though he had only a "common school education," he probably shared an intellectual bent with other members of his extended family. Some years later, he would be instrumental in producing the first elaborate book-length account of Shaker theology.[9]

The multiple points of contrast between the two men could also help account for why the Shaker Ministry paired them together.[10] Issachar was fiery and zealous, while Benjamin was mild and soft-spoken. Issachar's demeanor was blunt and even crude, while Benjamin appeared "harmless, innocent . . . and his deportment exemplary."[11] Unlike Issachar, Benjamin harbored no particular interest in music so although he was an excellent preacher, he was unable to lead potential converts in song. Issachar was an excellent singer who had led a choir for many years. Well accustomed to the frontier — able to hunt, handle horses and guns, make camp in the forest — Issachar was likely seen by the Shaker leaders as someone who was physically well equipped for journeying in remote areas. And another part of the Shaker Ministry's initial motivation in pairing the two together may have been to afford Benjamin some protection as the two men traveled through a region with which Issachar had some familiarity, having lived fifteen years not far from the Vermont border. But the biggest initial benefit from the newfound friendship between the two was that Benjamin came to Issachar's home in Hartford to counsel his family. Somehow Benjamin was able to win over Lovina Bates, the Bates children, and other extended family members and convince them to accept Issachar's choice. Indeed, he was so persuasive that the entire family — even those members who would remain outside the Shakers — developed permanent respect and admiration for Benjamin. After assuaging the fears and concerns of the Bates family, Benjamin and Issachar together proceeded another fifty-odd miles to Pittsford, Vermont, on their first missionary journey together.

> There we found wonderful things, they had a wonderful revival caused by a marvelous light on top of one James Wickers house. The whole neighborhood were awakened . . . they called on us to speak, and I arose first and felt zeal & freedom, for I felt confident that this effectual door was opened by divine Providence . . . And when I was through Elder Benjamin [spoke] with the same impulse and clinched the nail completely. And when we were through a man rose up and looking me right in the face, putting his hands on my shoulders, said, I want you should go with me and hear me confess my sins. Another went to Elder Benjamin in the same manner and so they kept it up one after another, 'til I think there were 12 male and female that confessed their sins that evening. At the close of these openings there came one into the room and told us there was a wonderful sight she seen in the sky. We all went out, there was a light across the centre of the Horizon from East to West about two rods wide, as it appeared of a palish red, and a bright border on each side. O how soon we interpreted this sign, that the same light and power was soon going to reach those waiting souls in the West. But not one thought that we had got to travel this bright road. Now the people kept on confessing, 'till I think there were 26 that set out. But oh! the battles we had with the Methodist preachers, they were all but raving.[12]

The Shaker leaders probably sent Benjamin and Issachar to Pittsford, Vermont, in 1801 because they were aware of existing believers' kin living in that area, who were possibly open to hearing Shaker testimony. Census records for 1800 show that the town's residents included Cooleys, Hammonds, and Harwoods, all related to previous or recent Shaker converts, including Shaker elder Ebenezer Cooley at New Lebanon, with whom Issachar had spoken when he went to make his inquiry earlier in 1801.[13] The Hammonds and Harwoods in Pittsford were related to families in northern Worcester County, in or near Petersham, where Ann Lee had preached in the early 1780s; several members from these families had already joined the Shakers.[14] Pittsford residents had formed a Methodist congregation by about 1799 and were served by circuit-riding preachers when Issachar and Benjamin visited.[15] The two were invited to preach, and they were both gratified and stimulated when a dozen men and women requested to make their confessions on the spot. On the same occasion, Issachar and Benjamin, along with the new Pittsford converts, witnessed a strange cloud formation in the evening sky, which appeared to be a shining road leading from east to west. Issachar reflected later that he interpreted this as a sign that the Shaker gospel would eventually be carried to the unsettled western lands.

Another account of the first missionary journey of Issachar Bates and Benjamin Seth Youngs comes from the testimony of Cassandana Brewster, a Hancock, Massachusetts, Shaker who spent her childhood in Pittsford, Vermont, and whose family hosted the Shaker missionaries in 1801 when Cassandana was nine years old. She writes of being inexplicably captivated by the two men, of giving them her rapt attention, and of learning the Shaker manner of "laboring" (dancing) by positioning herself between the two of them.

[W]hen I was about 9 years old, as I was returning from School one afternoon in company with my cousins ... I saw in the road, west of our house, two men on horseback, that looked to me just like Jesus Christ, & they were going towards our house ... I dropped my dinner pail, left my cousins, & ran home as fast as I could & told my Mother that Jesus Christ was coming. Then I hastened out of the house & ran to meet them. When I got there, they stopped their horses, & Elder Benjamin asked me if I knew where Justus Brewster lived? Said I, "He lives right there in that house!" "Are you his little girl?" said one, — I replied that I was ... I went along by their side. I loved them so I did not know what to do ... I took hold of one with one hand, & hold of the other with my other, & so walked between them to the house, feeling greatly delighted. As we were going up the steps, one of them said to the other, "This is a good omen" ... It was Benjamin Youngs & Issachar Bates ... My attention was so fixed on them that I took no notice of anything else that was said or done. And I then received as real Faith according to my understanding as I ever had, & have kept it ever since ... I knew nothing about the order of laboring, but found I could always dance the easiest next to the Elders. So when we had meeting & labored, I always took my place to labor next to them, & danced right between them.[16]

Together, Issachar and Benjamin were able to establish rapport with children and adults alike and gain a considerable number of converts, many of whom later moved to Watervliet, New York, and elsewhere. The little girl "Dana," as she was later called, would write that "several families thot they could be Shakers & remain there (in Pittsford), but they lost their Gift & fell back."[17] This would be a response that Issachar would typically encounter in his missionary work—that converts who resisted moving to a settlement of other Shakers found it virtually impossible to uphold the Shaker principles apart from the mutual support of other committed believers.

Because he was a both father and a sibling of youngsters and clearly had ample experience with children, Issachar Bates may have related easily to young Dana Brewster. His own daughter Sarah Bates was also then nine years old. It was common practice among Shaker converts for minor children to accompany their parents into the order, irrespective of whether they were themselves old enough to understand the Shaker faith. Of Issachar's nine children, only the oldest daughter, Lovina, was over twenty-one years (and possibly married) when the family contemplated Shaker life. His eldest son, Artemas, was about twenty, and his two sons Oliver and Nahum were in their teens. The remaining children—Polly, Issachar, Sarah, William and Betsy—ranged in ages from thirteen to three.

> Now about fourteen months after I set out, my wife confessed her sins; this was a great relief to me. After this I had the privilege to sell my plantation and move my family . . . so that in March 1803 we moved to Watervliet, all but my two oldest sons with whom I settled. After we arrived my family were soon satisfied and the children all confessed their sins and were all very comfortable. This began to feel like my Father's house, which I had been looking for for 7 years. I thought I had got home, but I did not know what was yet before me. Here I went to work as comfortable as any being could wish for—part of the time out preaching to the world and visiting those we had gathered and the rest of the time at work till the year 1805.[18]

The arrival at the Shaker village of Watervliet, New York, of Issachar Bates, his wife, Lovina, and seven of their nine children[19] took place in the midst of a flurry of in-gathering, a period when large families from all over the region were converging to transform the small holding originally settled by Ann Lee and her followers into a substantial Shaker community.[20] The new converts came from disparate locations—some from Long Island, others from central New York, others from central New Hampshire and western Massachusetts.

Many, like the new believers from Pittsford, Vermont, had been converted through Issachar's earliest missionary efforts. According to a letter written to Sarah Bates in 1871, discussing the arrival of early families at Watervliet, New York, Issachar and his family moved into a portion of a house that was already occupied by the family of David Train.[21] The Trains were kin to the Bates, David Train having married Issachar's older sister Hannah in Athol, Massachusetts, in 1774. The same letter identifies the arrival of the family of Jason Harwood, the husband of Issachar's younger sister Dolly.[22] So in becoming a Shaker and moving to Watervliet, Issachar was enjoying a reunion with members of his family whom he had likely not seen for many years. It is no wonder that in writing of his contentment with his new situation he characterizes it as being "like my Father's house."

Like other adult men among Shaker converts, Issachar Bates was put to work to help support the community. At this time, much of the work would have consisted of expanding the physical infrastructure of the Shaker property to permit the support of so many people: clearing and draining land, constructing farm buildings, expanding housing and kitchen facilities, and building fences. Issachar would certainly have participated in this sort of labor. But he also possessed a set of abilities probably even more valuable to the Shakers, namely, his gifts for charismatic preaching, poetry, and song. As more and more believers were gathered at Watervliet and New Lebanon, worship meetings grew larger and the dancing — or "laboring" — more elaborate. Singing grew more and more important to sustaining the dance, and designated singers sometimes stood off to one side.[23] Those Shakers with greatest musical gifts, such as Issachar, were instrumental in worship and encouraged the laboring process. Although a "young believer," the term used by the Shaker hierarchy to denote those who were more recently converted to the faith, Issachar was such a zealous and effective preacher that he was increasingly relied upon to act as a preacher at "public meetings" at the Shaker communities,[24] in addition to undertaking journeys to seek more converts or revisit the regions where converts had already been gained.

Issachar Bates's preaching garnered mention in a published account from Shaker apostate Thomas Brown, who in 1812 published an account of his impressions gleaned from visiting and living among the Shakers over several years. Brown quotes Issachar's evangelization philosophy as, "Catch them any how, so as we can but catch them," suggesting his methods were initially excessive.[25] In fact, Issachar's preaching and his demeanor both came under scrutiny, and sometime in 1803 or 1804 Brown was so appalled at Issachar's preaching to the public at Watervliet that he solicited Shaker elders' reactions:

But what I most disliked, was a speech of Issachar Bates about this time, to a Methodist minister, who sat on the fore seat. This man appeared to be very attentive to Issachar's discourse, and most of the time, he looked him in the face. At this, Bates appeared to take offence. Accordingly, he left the subject on which he was discoursing, and stretched out his hand toward the clergyman, and cried out — "Brute, brute, brute, you are beneath the beasts of the field." After meeting, the Methodist preacher went and stood before the fire to warm himself. Bates went and stood by the side of him; and by his looks, I thought he was like a dog that was ready to snap. Oh! thought I, what a spirit you show . . . After meeting, I went home with the family of which Seth Wells had the lead. To him, I expressed my decided disapprobation of Bates's conduct; and told him that Bates had greatly insulted the man . . . I observed that the Methodist preacher bore it with calmness, and showed the spirit of a Christian — whereas, Bates had exemplified the spirit of the Devil. All Seth said in reply, was — "I don't know that we have any right to condemn Issachar's gift." Astonishing! thought I, do you call scurrility and abuse, a gift. But I must not omit mentioning here, that, sometime afterwards, Elder Ebenezer received information of Issachar's conduct . . . Stamping his foot, he several times said to him in an accent of disapprobation — "What! do you abuse people? What! have you no more sense of the order of the gospel than to abuse people?" I was pleased to hear of this. It raised Elder Ebenezer in my estimation.[26]

Here the contrasting reactions of Seth Wells and Elder Ebenezer to Issachar's preaching are evident. Seth Wells had come to the Shakers about the same time as Brown, in the mid-1790s. An Albany, New York, school teacher, Seth Wells' conversion had been a coup for the Shakers because he brought with him into the movement his parents, nine of his siblings, and several members of his mother's family, the Youngs, including Issachar's close comrade Benjamin Seth Youngs.[27] Seth Wells also shared a warm friendship with Issachar. Although this warmth would become more strongly apparent in the many letters that the two men wrote in later years, this passage from Brown's account is nonetheless telling. It points both to Seth's fondness for Issachar and to his appreciation for Issachar's "gift," which the Shakers could not discount, however problematic his behavior might be on specific occasions. The Elder Ebenezer mentioned in Brown's account is probably Ebenezer Cooley, who counseled Issachar on his first visit to New Lebanon and helped convince him to convert. Because Ebenezer Cooley's specific charge was ministering to young believers, perhaps he felt he had greater license to censure Issachar's abrasive preaching.

> *Now from 1801 to 1805 we had wonderful accounts in the newspapers of an extraordinary revival in Kentucky and other western States, and about which my beloved companion and fellow laborer used to talk and converse a great deal while in our journeys and traveling.*

In the generation following the American Revolution, expansion of settlement beyond the Appalachian Mountains coincided with tremendous religious revivals throughout that region. Sometimes called "America's Pentecost," this was a prolonged period of spiritual uproar remarkable for its geographic scope and cultural impact.[28] In regions where towns were yet few and most settlements numbered only in the dozens, "camp meeting" events drew astonishing crowds in the thousands. Where revivals were most active, such as Cane Ridge and Gasper River in the northeastern and southwestern parts of Kentucky, respectively, observers estimated ten thousand people at time would gather in the woods around makeshift preaching "stands" and log meeting houses where thunderous sermons would last hours and onlookers would erupt into frenzies of shouting, barking, jerking, and whirling.[29] The religious tumult was unlike anything ever witnessed in the eastern states, even in the Baptist "New Light" revivals around New York and New England in the 1780s. In Albany, New York, *The Albany Gazette* reported of the ongoing revival in Kentucky and Tennessee that "abundant evidence has been given, that its author is God . . . The aspect of an extensive country has been changed from levity to seriousness, scoffers silenced, and thousands convinced."[30]

For the Shakers, this news was momentous, indeed. The preaching meetings conducted by Ann Lee and her first followers in the early 1780s had included very similar spiritual exercises: people speaking in tongues, bodies seized by inexplicable jerks and spasms, trances followed by sensational outcries. Issachar Bates had witnessed some of this personally. Together with Benjamin Seth Youngs, the two were increasingly the initiators of spiritual conversions that were dramatic in their own right. Having witnessed "signs" that the divine work they were participating in would soon reach westward, it was not surprising that the Shakers were captivated by news of the Kentucky revivals. They reasoned that God was at work in the West in exactly the same marvelous manner as had been felt by Ann Lee and her followers. Besides, Ann Lee herself had prophesied that the work of the Shakers would reach America's "southwest."[31] But unless Shakers went west to interpret the revival events, how would people there know the events' true significance? As Issachar would remember:

> I wondered why the Church did not send messengers with the gospel to them poor souls, for I pitied them in my heart. But I concluded that the Church knew better about them than I did. But in the latter part of December 1804 I was sent for to go to Lebanon. Soon after I arrived Elder Ebenezer invited me into his room. We sat and talked a while about common matters. At length he asked me how I felt towards them precious souls that God was at work with in the west. I told him I had wondered why they had not been visited before this time . . . Said he, "I want to know your faith supposing the lot should fall on you to go. For one, are you man enough to leave your family once for all, and all your friends in these parts, and hazard your life in that part of the world for Christ's sake and for the sake of them poor souls that God is preparing for salvation?" I answered thus: "My faith is in the gift of God that is in the Church and that faith I will obey come life or come death." "Well," said he, "that will do, for the Church have appointed Elder John Meacham, Benjamin S. Youngs, and Issachar Bates to start for that country the first day of January 1805."[32]

The decision of the Shaker Ministry at New Lebanon, New York, to dispatch three men to journey across the Appalachians in the winter of 1805 was both bold and risky. The region was then America's western frontier. Traveling conditions were rough and dangerous.[33] News of the religious revivals was already a few years old, and the Shakers had little idea of where the men should go and what people they should seek. The success of the undertaking depended partly on serendipity and partly on the initiative and resourcefulness of the three men themselves. The Ministry trusted that they would be able to withstand the physical conditions of the journey and cultivate acquaintances along the way that would help them locate receptive audiences. They were well aware that Shakers had already acquired a dubious reputation — even as far away as the young cities of America's interior, where some of the scathing accounts by Shaker apostates had been circulated — and that this alone could result in the men being harassed, assaulted, or worse. But at a time when the Shaker leaders were utterly convinced that theirs was a truth that could alter the spiritual face of America, the rewards well justified the risk.

At the time that Ministry contemplated a missionary effort, the eleven Shaker communities in the East numbered close to 1500 members.[34] Of these, around 300 lived at the largest community of New Lebanon and another 300 were divided among the nearby communities of Watervliet, New York, and Hancock Massachusetts. From the late 1790s, the Shaker communties had experienced sharp growth, owing in part to the evangelistic efforts of brethren like Issachar Bates and Benjamin Youngs. As to which three brethren to send, among the many able-bodied Shaker men at the time, the Ministry faced an interesting choice. However, any debate that might have taken place has been lost to history. The leader of the trio was John Meacham. He was the eldest son of Joseph Meacham, Ann Lee's first American convert, whom she termed her "first born son."[35] Though a child when his father converted in 1780, John Meacham regarded his faith as having come directly from Mother Ann.[36] At thirty-four years old, he was already an elder among the Shakers, a leadership appointment that reflected the esteem in which he and his family members were held among the Shakers for their spiritual substance and reliability. It was clearly important to the Ministry that one of the men dispatched for this vital mission be someone who had known Ann Lee herself and, as such, could effectively represent the Shaker church as it was fast becoming institutionalized in the East. As for the other two, it is quite possible that Benjamin Seth Youngs and Issachar Bates were chosen on the basis of their track record of recent missionary successes. Granted, they had never traveled as far afield as the trans-Appalachian wilderness, but they had managed to fulfill several preaching assignments in the rough margin of New England and upstate New York. They worked well together and trusted one another. Benjamin was part of the large Wells–Youngs kinship network that included several individuals, such as Seth Youngs Wells, who already occupied influential positions among the Shakers in the two New York communities of Watervliet and New Lebanon. Both Meacham and Youngs were unmarried men in their early thirties who had been Shakers for all of their adult lives. Issachar, in contrast, was nearly forty-seven, a married man with nine children. With less than four years as a Shaker, and much of that time spent on preaching trips among strangers, Issachar held scarcely any notion of what it was like to live a settled Shaker life. Yet, of the three men, Issachar was physically the best suited to withstand the journey because of his hardy nature and his long years inhabiting frontier areas. Moreover, as a veteran soldier with skills as a hunter and woodsman, Issachar could well protect the group if necessary. Perhaps the Shaker leaders also hoped that, as a plain-spoken and earthy man of the world, Issachar could appeal to frontier westerners in a way that Meacham and Youngs could not, especially considering that both younger men were soft-spoken and even delicate. And, because Issachar was a zealous preacher and singer who held "somewhat of a poetical genius" in contrast to his meager education, it is

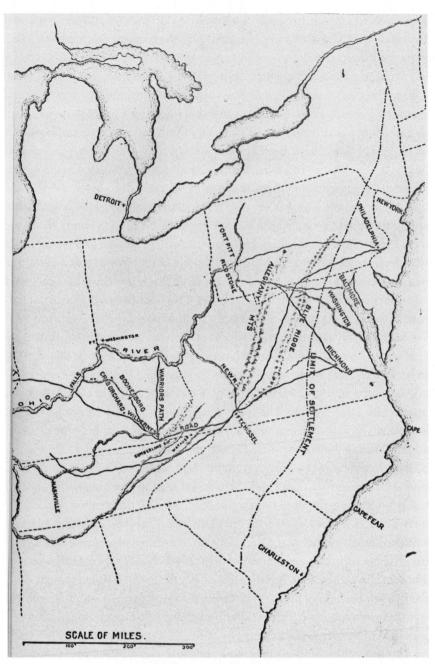

SCALE OF MILES.
100'   200'   300'

4.1 *Issachar Bates and the other Shaker missionaries followed the Wilderness Road
route from New York State through the Cumberland Gap and into Kentucky. (From*
The Wilderness Road, *Thomas Speed, 1882. Courtesy of the Filson Historical Society.)*

possible that the Shaker leadership believed he would be a particularly effective worship leader in the West, should the men's missionary efforts begin to bear fruit.[37]

    On the first day of January 1805 at three o'clock in the morning we started . . . we loaded our horse and went on our journey of which I shall not state any particular journal, only that it was a tedious cold hard winter . . . the back roads were not passable by reason of ice, snow, and water, for we had rain, hail, or snow the most of the time. We made no stay of any account exception of on the Sabbath.[38]

Leaving the Shaker village at New Lebanon on that dark and bitterly cold morning was emotionally wrenching for the missionary trio. Benjamin would later write, "I well remember, too, that early Tues. morning, when going down the hill at the North House, I will say that I went down weeping — but I had a great mind to throw away my staff."[39] For Issachar, a loving and affectionate father, the departure was even more traumatic. According to an oft-told anecdote recorded decades later by an Ohio Shaker, Issachar's youngest daughter Betsy had stolen away into the woods to see her father off: "Issachar's youngest daughter was sitting on top of the gate post looking for her father to come. And when he arrived, she reached out her arms to him and said, 'You will come back again won't you.' Issachar detained by the child's embrace, his companions went on. When having catched up with his company again, he said 'The parting with that child was one of the hardest trials of my life.'"[40]

Why Tuesday, January 1, was chosen as the missionaries' departure date is unknown. But it was a choice that would echo decades into the future, giving Shakers in the western states an additional reason to mark New Year's Day for celebration.[41] The Shaker leaders likely had access to descriptive materials about the "wilderness road," the route that led from the major cities of the mid-Atlantic west to the Blue Ridge Mountains of Virginia, then southwest to the Cumberland Gap and northwards into Kentucky (figure 4.1). Since the route had been pioneered decades earlier, several promoters had generated guidelines for potential travelers, and these included estimates of travel times.[42] A midwinter departure helped ensure freezing temperatures for most of the journey, keeping road surfaces hard, and hopefully an arrival before spring rains swelled creeks, making crossings more dangerous and transforming roads and trails into a mire of mud. Another factor might have been to ensure the trio's arrival well before the heavy spring work of plowing and planting would begin for the western settlers. Farm work in the spring was so demanding that people had little free time to contemplate matters of religion, and the Shaker leaders likely saw late winter and early spring as more opportune seasons for missionaries to find audiences.

The "principal clerk" for the group was Benjamin Seth Youngs.[43] It fell to him to carry letters from the Shaker leaders introducing the three emissaries and describing their intentions as representatives of the Shaker church, as well as to chronicle the journey in a diary. Benjamin was meticulous in recording the daily distance traveled, weather conditions, and amounts paid for lodging and food for themselves and their one horse. He also commented regularly on the road and trail conditions, recording such difficulties as high water, ice, and mud. Despite their progress south, the weather remained uncommonly cold and snowy; people along the way remarked that the winter was unusually severe. Still, the men sometimes covered over thirty miles in a day, even as their progress was often slowed by various unforeseen difficulties. At one point, they needed to find a cobbler to repair their boots; later, their horse became ill and they feared it would die.

For the three earnest Shakers, overnight accommodations could be vexing, and a room to themselves was a luxury. Along the road, a wide variety of households lodged travelers, but the host families were often not considered fit company by the devout trio. Ostentation repelled the men. At overnight stops in Pennsylvania and Delaware, they were put off by the "grand appearance & unnecessary attendance of the house" and a supper that consisted of "baked fowl & much needless attendance." Later, at a stop near Baltimore, Benjamin noted of their lodging: "The popular & lofty spirit that reigns here is distressing to our feelings beyond expression." Some of the accommodations in Virginia were scarcely better. Annoyed by a "table prepared in fashion," Benjamin remarked that for the group to "eat a crust of bread in a cottage with plain & decent people would have been abundantly more agreeable to our faith & feelings."[44] On the other hand, the men felt conflicted when they were invited to lodge without charge with a courteous and hospitable Quaker family, with whom they felt reasonably at ease until they realized that the family owned many slaves: "we could not feel freedom though it was without cost."[45]

A typical day's travel involved departing early in the morning before any meal, stopping several hours later to obtain breakfast, resuming travel until early evening, pausing only to consume a little food they carried with them, and finding the next night's lodging and an evening meal by six or seven o'clock. On most Sundays they stayed in their lodgings, rested, read scripture, and wrote. The three men conferred on writing the travel journal, and about a month into the journey they prepared a long letter to send back to New

Lebanon reporting their progress.[46] Issachar included a short personal note: "I desire that my family may be informed that I am well, & send my love to Levina, and the children."[47] Food was a daily concern. The men carried butter with them and bought bread when they could. As they got farther south, food grew more meager. Wheat flour and bread became scarce or contaminated by weevils and was "generally not fit for dogs to eat."[48] Venison and pork were the customary meats, when they could be had. In Tennessee they treated themselves to peppermint candy and bought sugar to sweeten their drinking water. But the men all suffered sickness from exertion and bad rations.

As January turned to February and the trio reached deeper into the mountains of southwestern Virginia and eastern Tennessee, still they withheld from preaching, even the few times they were invited to do so. They grew increasingly alert to news of unusual spiritual exercises matching those of the revivals reported in Kentucky and elsewhere. By late February, they began to encounter people who had experienced dramatic episodes of "the jerks." But the trio was cautious, because the people seemed unchanged by the manifestations and consequently would probably not be receptive to the Shakers' message. Benjamin wrote, "Notwithstanding these powerful operations — the people are yet lost in sin & joined with the world in most of their pursuits & many even who are powerfully wrought upon by outward operations, when ever these are off remain the same carnal creatures in all their conversation & conduct!"[49] Finally, on February 20, the men ventured to speak: "We for the first time opened our mouths since we came from N Lebanon being now 883 miles from home — We spoke but a very few words & that in a manner sublimely." But their best effort fell on deaf ears; the Shakers moved on.

A couple of days later the men lodged overnight just west of Bulls Gap, Tennessee, where they were excited to view a new map of the United States. This allowed them to assess their location. Nearly a thousand miles from home and further south than any of them had been in their lives, they determined it was time to turn northwest for Kentucky. As their route took them over a mountain ridge, they were dismayed to see "a vast country present to view — mountains after mountains whole ranges lay in directions fm NE to SW."[50] But at a settlement at Clinch River, Tennessee, an unusual encounter gave Issachar and Benjamin an opportunity to establish an opening by carrying out an uncommon act of humanity, which Issachar would later recall.

[H]ere we found a distressing circumstance. A young man who was traveling... struck an Ax into his knee & was laid out in an old negro cabin, and there lay & rotted. He died that night... & it was a real horrid sight, his dung that he lay in nearly half covered his rump, and both his legs were rotten, and corruption & dung were his bedfellows & no mortal to pay any attention to him. So E. Benjamin & I concluded we would lay him out, so we went to the landlady & got a sheet and went at it. We got a tub of water & washed him and laid him out in the best manner we could, but we had to lay him out cross leg'd for we could not straiten his legs. But the people were awfully struck with this deed of humanity & were desirous to have us stay & preach the next day at his funeral, but we told them we must go on.[51]

Benjamin's journal records that this victim of a chance accident along the road was a wealthy young man who had come west from North Carolina against the wishes of his family.[52] Nearly two months into a tedious journey in an unknown wilderness among complete strangers and a thousand miles from their own families, Issachar and his companions must have felt deep empathy for the plight of this young man, who suffered horribly and perished from a random mishap with a common tool that any man on the frontier might expect to handle daily. The people at the Clinch River settlement were so deeply impressed by the compassion of Issachar and Benjamin that they invited the Shakers to preach; it was such actions that helped the Shakers overcome the suspicion of strangers.[53]

The trio crossed the Cumberland Gap on February 25 and headed into Kentucky (figure 4.2). Having left the bitter winter weather behind, the wayfarers faced rain, sleet, and swollen rivers as they moved towards the terminus of the Wilderness Road at Crab Orchard, less than fifty miles south of Lexington, Kentucky. Near the Rockcastle River, the men were appalled when they came upon a carving on a tree marking the spot where a man had been murdered some years before. For Issachar Bates, with his pattern of empathy for men that succumbed to mishaps alone in the forest, this moment was particularly horrifying.

[W]e were informed of the murder of Joseph Lankford . . . We were told that we might see the spot where he was killed. It was written on a tree by Rock Castle River. I expected to see some horrid expression written on such an occasion, but behold when we came to view it this was all that was written — Lankford's defeat. My soul and my flesh shuddered. Is the world that we have got into, one that murder is nothing but a defeat? I will here for the first time expose my horrid feelings. I thought if I was back at Watervliet and would have 24 hours to see my friends and then be laid in their burying yard it would be a paradise to me compared with what I had to go through . . . All these feelings I kept to myself.[54]

4.2 *"Cumberland Gap," after Harry Fenn, 1872. (Library of Congress.)*

The real enormity of the group's task struck Issachar at Rockcastle River, perhaps for the first time. Carried by his newfound zeal to this alien place, he realized that he and his Shaker friends could easily die here, whether by mischance or treachery, and their fate remain unknown to their loved ones back in the eastern Shaker communities. Still, it was in Issachar's nature to conceal his deep fears and to use humor to sustain them all through particularly difficult periods. Losing their path deep in the desolate mountains one day, the men simply halted, exhausted and discouraged. Ohio Shaker Moses Eastwood, lifelong resident of the village of Watervliet, Ohio, where Issachar would eventually preside, later recorded what happened: "They came to a halt and seemed hardly to know which way to go, and had not any particular place to go that he (Issachar) uttered the following prayer: 'O Lord here we go to and fro up and down through the earth ding-split Devil like. If we had our just desserts we would not be here nor no where else.'"[55] The men started to laugh. Suddenly their situation seemed less bleak. As Eastwood notes, "This stirred up their feelings and they proceeded on their journey."

When the group reached Crab Orchard and the end of the Wilderness Road, things began looking up almost immediately. They found lodging at a "decent Methodist house," where they paid a servant to do a thorough washing of their clothes and were refreshed by several good meals. Best of all, they learned from two young women in the household that revivals were under way

4.3 *"Camp-Meeting," Kennedy & Lucas Lithography, 1829. (Library of Congress.)*

at the nearby settlement of Paint Lick (near present-day Berea, Kentucky). On the next day, a Sunday, the Shakers accompanied the women to the meeting of a congregation of dissenting Presbyterians. There they encountered the preacher Mathew Houston, one of several men who would become crucial to the Shaker enterprise in the West and would soon be counted among Issachar's closest friends:

> We found Mathew preaching, pounding at old Esau. After he was through the young women got word to him and he opened the way for us to speak, but we remained silent . . . Next day we went and visited Matthew . . . He told us he was very young in the light, only two weeks old and that he wanted instruction, but told us at Caneridge they knew more about these things . . . The whole family were full of kindness and we blessed them. We tarried in that neighborhood about a week.[56]

Almost immediately, the Shaker wayfarers were charmed by Mathew Houston and his family, who seemed to be kindred spirits. Houston was a well-educated and prosperous Virginia-born Presbyterian minister.[57] Thirty-five years old, blond and handsome, he was a large and imposing man, but affable.[58] His wife, Peggy, was a vivacious and attractive brunette, who took pride in her family's appearance and made sure that the entire Houston

4.4 *Cane Ridge Meeting House, Paris, Kentucky. Historic American Buildings Survey, 1934. (Library of Congress.)*

household—which included two small sons and a mulatto "servant" named Isaac Newton—was among the most fashionably dressed on the Kentucky frontier. An effective preacher with a strong following, Houston had been in the thick of revival activity in Kentucky for several years (figure 4.3), and he had preached to thousands at the massive camp meetings at Cane Ridge in 1801.[59] He was well acquainted with the leading New Light figures in the region, a group of prominent former Presbyterian ministers and leaders in the recent revivals, who in 1803 had seceded as a group from Kentucky's Presbyterian synod to establish an entirely separate church institution.[60] Just before the Shakers' arrival at Paint Lick, Mathew Houston had openly declared his allegiance with this group of New Light clergy.[61] By gaining Houston as a friend and ally, the Shaker missionaries were able to orient themselves to the quickly shifting religious currents in the region. And through Houston, the Shakers secured a favorable introduction to Barton W. Stone, presiding minister over the New Light congregation at Cane Ridge, Kentucky, a location virtually synonymous with the Kentucky revivals and their associated fantastic spiritual events (figure 4.4).

> And then we went to Cane Ridge where we were kindly received generally. Barton Stone their leader took us to his own house where we had

much conversation with him and a number more. They sucked in our light as greedily as ever an ox drank water and all wondered where they had been that they had not seen these things before . . . But there were something yet behind the curtain (as the world called it). The next news of salvation was this. To gain the kingdom we have to take up the Cross of Christ and enter into the same self-denying path of regeneration which he trod or never go where he is gone. And Satan entered into Barton as soon as he understood this . . . Yet he did not let out his enmity for some time, but still showed friendship and desired us, at least one of us, to attend their next camp meeting, which we agreed to . . . So we tarried a number of days, attended their society meetings, and gathered the feelings of the people in a good degree.[62]

Arriving at Cane Ridge on March 13, the Shakers were hosted by Barton Stone himself for the next three days. Stone was a fiery preacher who had come to Kentucky in 1796 as part of a group of fervent young Presbyterian ministers led by James McGready, a Presbyterian missionary of Scotch-Irish descent who had operated an revivalist-oriented academy for would-be ministers in Guilford County, North Carolina. McGready and his followers had overseen the first stirrings of the great revival movement in Kentucky several years before.[63] In 1805, when the Shakers met Barton Stone, he and several fellow New Light preachers who had been most active in the revivals had recently withdrawn from the main Presbytery of Kentucky, due to theological disputes. Stone had established his home and congregation at Cane Ridge, some twenty-five miles northeast of Kentucky's largest town of Lexington. There, some of the most frenzied revival scenes had unfolded, with hundreds of people engulfed in jerking, barking, speaking in tongues, and other riotous actions.[64]

Once at Cane Ridge, where a huge log meeting house dominated the revival grounds, Issachar and Benjamin plunged into spirited debate with Stone and other men of the congregation, talking into the wee hours each night.[65] For the first time since the journey began, the Shakers read aloud the letters written by the Shaker Ministry at New Lebanon to introduce the details of the Shaker message and the trio's mission. Stone was initially enthusiastic, until he realized that, for the Shakers, rejection of sin meant that married couples had to agree to renounce all sexual relations. Still, others in Stone's congregation were deeply persuaded by the Shakers. The missionaries agreed that they would try to return to Cane Ridge to preach at a series of camp meetings later in the spring. Stone told them about them about the four other "New Light" preachers that had left the main Presbyterian synod the previous year, men that the Shakers could also expect to be receptive to hearing their testimony. Two of these preachers, John Thompson and Richard McNemar, had congregations in southwestern Ohio, just north of Cincinnati. For the Shakers, the next logical step was to seek out these two and assess whether or not either of them might prove to be a useful ally in the work of introducing the Shaker message to the region. To that end, the Shaker missionaries headed for an Ohio River crossing at Cincinnati.

> *There was no part of the Country that I had travelled, East, West, North, or South, but what had cost me great tribulation . . . But we trusted only on the mercy and protection of God, for there was no other prospect in view, & we were in his work.*[66]

Although less than four years into his new Shaker life, Issachar Bates had already journeyed farther and witnessed more remarkable scenes than he could have ever imagined. Though he rode to New Lebanon in 1801 seeking to find a home with the Shakers for himself and his family, he ironically set them all on a path that would separate them and alter their family existence forever. From the beginning of his Shaker experience, Issachar allowed the Church to make full use of his singular personal qualities — his gift for preaching, his knack for persuading unbelievers, his singing talent, his hardy constitution that suited him for wilderness travel and physical work. Thus he found himself in March 1805 on America's dangerous western frontier, a forty-seven year old man partnered with new companions, having traveled a thousand miles, charged with carrying a radical new spiritual message into a tumultuous and seemingly degenerate alien region. Ohio lay just ahead, with the prospect of new friends and allies to be gained.

CHAPTER 5

"Like God's Hunters"

SEEKING KINDRED IN THE WEST

*We went about the work that we were sent into this new world to accomplish
… which work we inured ourselves to like God's hunters and went through
this wild wooden world by day and by night, hunting up every soul that
God had been preparing for eternal life. — Issachar Bates*

The three Shaker missionaries had come safely through the Wilderness Road and across Kentucky, and their quest for receptive audiences for their message was leading them toward southwestern Ohio. They faced impossible odds. They were alien to the region, marked as such by their accents and clothing. They carried money for their expenses, but this was risky given the dangers of theft while traveling. They knew no one, and relied upon the mercy of strangers. For months they had had little sense of where their next meal would come from or where their next night's sleep would be. And they sought to convince people of a set of radical ideas that were murky at best, already derided and misconstrued, whose only written expression lay in a single letter from the New Lebanon Ministry that they carried with them.

During the first several months that Issachar Bates spent in the West, his attention focused upon the community of dissenting Presbyterian "New Lights" centered at Turtle Creek, Ohio, in Warren County just north of Cincinnati. Though he and his companions had traveled over a thousand miles, Issachar found himself in a setting not unlike other places where he had lived — crowded cabin dwellings scattered through a forest, large families, pregnant mothers, fussy children, endless work, dirt, and disorder. Of the three missionaries, only Issachar knew firsthand what it was like to attempt to earn a living for a growing family in a wooded frontier settlement. The missionaries were introducing a revolutionary message to this community, namely, that the millennium had arrived and they must "take up the cross," forsake the marriage bed, and enter into a new sinless life. Issachar understood the full impact of that demand more directly than his companions. Only he had felt firsthand the anger and dismay that this conviction brought to a spouse and family.

Gaining converts in the first months was laborious, and the opposition great. Along the way they encountered colorful characters and witnessed memorable events. One man in particular, Richard McNemar, was most instrumental in creating the potential for a new western Shaker family. No other person was more crucial to the missionaries' first months in the West, and he looms large in the missionaries' accounts of the period. The friendship that Issachar and the missionaries forged with Richard during this time would sustain the men through the rest of their lives.

> ⁓ *Since we left the State of N. York, we have seen the face of no mortal, that we have any knowledge of ever seeing before in the World . . . We are all bless'd with a good degree of bodily health, and are not wholly left destitute of spiritual consolation.*[1]

Benjamin Seth Youngs' journal records that the night before the Shaker trio crossed the Ohio River at Cincinnati, Issachar Bates was unable to sleep and rose in the middle of the night to walk about restlessly in the road.[2] Exactly what plagued him in the night is left unsaid; perhaps he was lonely for his wife and children or unsettled about the spiritual confrontations yet to come. After entering Ohio on March 19, the group located John Thompson, who initially mistook them for Quakers. Although dubious after learning they were Shakers, because he had read a derogatory New York newspaper article about Shakers, Thompson took the men into his household for the night. A midweek meeting was held that evening, but the Shakers saw no opportunity for sharing their testimony. They parted the next day on friendly terms, and Thompson informed them how to locate Richard McNemar's congregation at the Turtle Creek settlement, just west of present-day Lebanon, Ohio. Specifically, Thompson urged the Shakers to present themselves at the home of Malcolm Worley, a devout New Light and one of the wealthier members of the Turtle Creek congregation, whose frame house would be relatively easy to locate.[3]

> And on the 22nd day of March 1805 we arrived at Malcolm Worley's, where we found the first rest for the soles of our feet, having traveled 1233 miles in two months and twenty-two days. There we were received with the greatest kindness. Altho' utter strangers before, yet good Malcolm soon knew us, for he said that his heavenly Father had promised to send help from Zion. "And I am glad," said he, "that you are come." . . . We had much conversation that evening with him and Peggy his wife. And then he put us to bed and told us he would hear more of this tomorrow.[4]

Malcolm Worley was part of a large family originally from Virginia. Like many settlers in the region, he had migrated to Ohio by way of Kentucky. In

1805 Worley was in his early forties, and he had been active in Presbyterian and New Light revival circles for several years. He was a member of the New Light congregation at Turtle Creek, which the Shakers had learned of from Barton Stone and over which Stone's fellow New Light minister Richard McNemar presided, Worley was an eloquent and devout man, and Stone had issued him his own preaching credential in March 1804.[5] A prosperous farmer with five children,[6] Worley had settled in Warren County, Ohio, not long before, possibly following McNemar to the area. His frame house in the fairly new settlement of Turtle Creek was considered one of the area's finer homes. He was a widower, and he had recently remarried young Peggy Montfort, more than twenty years his junior, in October 1804.[7] When the Shakers arrived in March 1805, Peggy was several months pregnant and was being regularly seized by "the jerks," a reference to the sometimes violent involuntary motions often experienced by people under deep religious conviction in the New Light revival settings. This was a matter of some concern.[8]

Although the Shaker missionaries arrived unannounced at Worley's home, he received them cordially and immediately entered into deep spiritual discussions with them. He contended that he recognized the three men from a recent premonition of their arrival. The Shakers were given a meal, and the group talked until late at night. Indeed, an Ohio Shaker recounted later that Malcolm "kept Issachar up till 2 o'clock in the morning," so eager was he to learn of the Shakers' mission.[9] Because Worley's spiritual outlook was "singular from other people" whom the Shakers had met, the missionaries were optimistic.[10] Worley offered the three travelers tight sleeping quarters of one bed in his crowded household,[11] and the following day, he led them to the log house of Richard McNemar, a half mile away. Because McNemar was the minister for virtually all of the Turtle Creek community, the Shakers needed to gauge his goodwill before they tried to "open their testimony" with any of the local residents.

⁓ *[W]ent half a mile E to McNemars, a mannered man of about 35 who was brought from the back parts of Pennsylvania about 14 years ago ... In the course of the day we conversed with him but not with much freedom as he felt in a manner determined to still build on something of his own ... At abt 3 we eat dinner & at 9 we eat supper & at abt 10 went to all 3 in 1 bed.*[12]

Richard McNemar was thirty-four years old and a native of central Pennsylvania. As a teenager he had traveled down the Ohio River to Kentucky with a group of Presbyterian missionaries. In the early 1790s he boarded at a small academy on the Elkhorn River west of Lexington, where he undertook classical studies in preparation for the ministry. There he met Malcolm Worley, and the two became friends. In 1792 Richard moved to the vicinity of Cane Ridge, Kentucky, which placed him in the midst of the pioneer preachers who would become the key instigators of the coming revivals. There he met and married his wife, Jenny Luckie. After his Presbyterian ordination in 1798, he became more active in church affairs in the region. Although the church he pastored in Cabin Creek, Kentucky, not far from the Ohio River southeast of Cincinnati, was small, his fame as a preacher spread through the region, and he became a leading figure in the revivals at Cane Ridge, along with Barton Stone. It was McNemar who led the dissension of leading New Lights from the main body of the Presbyterian Church in 1803 to form a new and separate "Presbytery." And it was McNemar who instigated the dissolution of the new Presbytery in favor of a bold approach — namely, for congregations to simply call themselves "Christian" and to eschew further sectarian designations. In 1802 McNemar moved his family to Turtle Creek, Ohio, to take over a small church recently vacated by James Kemper, a prominent Cincinnati-area Presbyterian minister. There he was reasonably close to siblings and in-laws, some of whom were leading citizens of Lebanon and other nearby communities.[13]

Undeniably a popular figure, Richard McNemar was also a conundrum. Although he had lived his whole life in frontier areas, he harbored interests and proclivities that set him well apart from his neighbors. McNemar was deeply intellectual, scholarly to the core. In his brief period of formal schooling he mastered Latin, Greek, and Hebrew. He composed elaborate poetry and hymns, and he held exhaustive knowledge of the Bible. A somber and taciturn introvert, inclined to use Latin even in his own diary, McNemar also posessed a wry wit, which he generally reserved for his personal writings. Unbeknownst to the Shakers when they arrived, McNemar held an active interest in printmaking. As a scholar, he valued the printed word. He recognized the emergence of Cincinnati as a center for printing in the region and was drawn to printing as a potential new trade, should his prospects as a preacher diminish.[14] When he met the Shakers, Richard was cautious but hospitable. He said that he would not stand in the way of the missionaries' efforts to share their testimony with the Turtle Creek congregants and opened his two-story log home to the trio for the night, where they again all shared a bed.[15] Issachar recalled:

And the next day which was Sabbath we went to meeting with him. He preached much to our satisfaction. After he got through I asked liberty to speak a few words, which was granted. I spake but short, after which Benjamin came forward and spake and read the letter which was sent from the Church, for he was our reader and chief clerk, after which a few favorable expressions were made by Samuel Rollins and others . . . The said Samuel was called on to pray . . . "We thank thee O God that thou hast send a Chariot of fire from the east drawn by three white horses to bring the everlasting gospel to this land."[16]

In just a few days, the three comrades had met kindred spirits, and Issachar had preached to a church congregation. The Shaker missionaries seemed to be making a promising start at Turtle Creek. They occupied their time visiting from house to house in the settlement, but a second visit with Richard McNemar just a few days later brought distressing developments that threatened to derail their efforts entirely.

We returned . . . to McNemars — he receivd us kindly — but in the course of our conversation which lasted till about 2 at night (though he had most of the talk himself) he showed a bitter spirit, bringing bitter & philosophical invictives against any & every sort of order which might be in the church &c. His spirit was dark & distressing . . . In the morning every thing appeared very dark just as if the gospel never could find its way among men & has very much felt to be the cost whereon we come at McNemar's . . . his determination appeared to be to shut out . . .[17]

The Shakers were terribly discouraged at Richard's abrupt shift in demeanor, perhaps even more so because of the euphoria of their initial enthusiastic reception. The trio faced a dilemma. They had promised to return to Cane Ridge to preach at Barton Stone's early April revival, so they determined that Issachar would return to Cane Ridge alone, leaving John and Benjamin to persist at Turtle Creek and try to regain Richard's favor. Of the three, Issachar was best suited for the journey, and he was also the most effective preacher in lively revival settings. On March 27, Issachar set out alone for Kentucky, parting from his friends for the first time in months. His reception at Cane Ridge was mixed and his presence provocative.

I arrived at Barton Stone's on Saturday night . . . I was received with outward kindness and a number of people felt very friendly. But the preachers were struck with great fear and concluded that if I was permitted to preach that it would throw the people into confusion . . . Stone told them to let no man deceive them about the coming of Christ, for they would all know him when he came, for every eye would see him in the clouds and they would see the graves opening and the bones rising and the saints would rise and meet the Lord in the air . . . Thus they went on till they were covered with death and even the woods around us appeared to be in mourning.[18]

Barton Stone and the other ministers at Cane Ridge were preaching to crowds that expected the "second coming" of Jesus Christ to occur imminently in literal form, as a divine being descending from the sky. Shaker teaching on this point was quite different, namely, that the second appearing of Christ prophesied in the Bible had already occurred as the manifestation of the "Christ spirit" in Ann Lee some years before.[19] Stone tried to counter Issachar Bates's potential influence that day by emphasizing the points on which Shaker and New Light theology diverged, exhorting people to resist the Shakers' lies. But as Issachar sat by and listened, he deliberately provoked Stone. As Stone declared dramatically that God's chosen "would see the graves opening and the bones rising," Issachar couldn't resist a sly rejoinder, as recorded by a later Ohio Shaker who annotated Issachar's account of the episode: "[R]ight here he said to himself but loud enough for a group of preachers nearby to hear him, 'resurrection of dog turds!' Then they sent a few volleys of hot shot upon him from off the ends of their tin guns. But he only replied, 'the dogs eat Jezebel!'"[20]

With behavior like that, it is no wonder that Issachar Bates attracted attention at revival meetings! In his stage-whispered retort, the reference to Jezebel, the pagan queen who permitted idol worship in Israel, illuminates the complexity of Issachar's wit. Jezebel's idolatry and betrayal of Israel was punished by her execution and the throwing of her body to wild dogs, who afterwards left their excrement scattered across the ground. Thus Issachar's short and blunt remarks spoke volumes. Believing Stone and his congregation to be deeply misguided and even "anti-Christian," Issachar was comparing them all to modern-day Jezebels. Such conduct among the volatile Kentucky preachers placed Issachar on the margins and helps to explain some of the animus that developed against the Shakers. Still, Issachar's new friend and ally Mathew Houston was present on that occasion. He himself took the preaching stand to encourage the people to give Issachar a chance to speak, which was finally granted.

Then I mounted a large log in front of the stand and began to speak. And although the preachers and many others went to their horses to get out of the way of hearing, yet when I began to speak they all returned and all paid good attention. I spake about an hour. The subject I was upon was to show the difference between the spirit and the letter, and when I got through and dismissed they began the controversy. One cried, "spirit, spirit, all spirit." And another cried "I bless God for the spirit for it is all that will do us any good." And so the multitude were completely divided. And Oh! Could I relate the dreams and visions that were related to me at that time — And all convincing them that the Shakers were right & they would own that it was so. But there was that abominable stone bridge that they were afraid to cross, that Bull in the Gap that would not go in himself nor suffer them to go in that were ready to enter . . . But I returned again to Ohio on foot and alone and arrived safe again to the brethren and found the work of God going on. A many had confessed their sins and become living souls and the Devil was mad about it.[21]

Issachar responded adeptly to the opposition at Cane Ridge. Instead of denouncing Stone and his colleagues outright, he preached on the New Testament injunction to hold spiritual insight above institutionalized or codified doctrine. In so doing, he was harking back to the first followers of Christ, who had used the inspired teachings of Jesus to free them from adherence to hidebound Jewish law. This would have been a potent argument for a frontier revival crowd, for whom the revival setting itself offered a needed corrective to the doctrinal strictures of America's large, established church institutions. By invoking the "spirit versus letter" controversy, Issachar was casting Barton Stone and his followers in the role of hidebound and rigid religious authorities with no spiritual vitality — perhaps unfair, but effective nonetheless. And as Issachar contended with other preachers in the region, he began to develop humor as a tactic, such as creating comical wordplay using the names of his opponents and the place names of the region as a way of ridiculing them. Before Issachar left Cane Ridge, people began flocking to him to relate visions they interpreted as having positive bearing on the truth of the Shaker gospel.

Notwithstanding Issachar's confrontational demeanor at Cane Ridge, Mathew Houston seems to have been won over by this point in time. He was already planning to take Issachar and his companions to more preaching appointments in Kentucky. Barton Stone, however, dreaded the Shakers' further work in the region and, specifically, their growing influence on his friend Richard McNemar. He gave Issachar a letter to deliver to Richard, expressing his affection for Richard and sharing news of ongoing New Light evangelism efforts. But the letter also contained a passage written in Latin — which Issachar was unable to understand — in which Stone expressed dismay over the Shakers' growing influence.[22]

When Issachar Bates returned to Turtle Creek, he found things progressing well in his absence. On the day he had left for Cane Ridge, Malcolm Worley and his wife had both confessed their sins, marking the Shakers' first conversions in the West.[23] Benjamin and John had continued circulating among the different households and had gained confessions from six or eight more people, including Malcolm Worley's African-American servant, Anna Middleton, and an Irish immigrant, Cornelius Campbell.[24] Soon after Issachar's return, the group gathered at the Turtle Creek meeting house to hear Sunday preaching by Richard McNemar before an assembled crowd of three hundred, including visitors from communities several miles distant. Richard's demeanor was much altered from his recent hostility, and he confessed to the congregation that he was uncertain about how to counsel them with respect to the Shakers. He indicated that because previous divine "dispensations" had "appeared to turn things upside down," he dared not deny the seemingly revolutionary testimony of the Shakers. In making those remarks, Richard was probably unaware that Ann Lee had been famously quoted as saying that the Shakers were "the people who turn the world upside down."[25] But such remarks would have nonetheless resonated with his audience, people who had both witnessed and participated in America's revolutionary and frontier expansion periods.[26] His listeners also plainly perceived a change in him: "It was plain in all his discourse that an overture was taking place which was according to his faith — many people were doubtless unexpected struck at his sermon & testimony."[27]

After Richard McNemar's Sabbath-day revelation, the Shakers' daily work with the Turtle Creek people became more frenetic. Nearly every day the men walked miles, passing from one cabin to another, testifying, counseling, and hearing confessions. They often split up to cover more ground, with Issachar and Benjamin preferring to go as a pair and John Meacham going out alone or with another convert. Soon the Shakers sought out one of the area's earliest pioneer families, the Bedles, who had come from New Jersey in about 1795 to establish Bedle's Station as a fortified outpost north of Cincinnati — the location around which the Turtle Creek community had been established. The first westerners recorded as confessing their sins to Issachar came from this important family.

During the Shakers' visits, people frequently were overcome by "the jerks." At one house, a young woman holding a baby began to jerk so violently that onlookers took the baby from her arms lest it be hurt, and the jerks grew more extreme as the Shakers spoke as "every solemn sentence appeared to bring them on more violently."[28] Sometimes the jerking was so violent that the missionaries grew concerned, such as one day while Issachar spoke to the Doyle family: "[T]he woman while sitting with her back towards the wall was very violently taken with the jerks, chiefly in her head; & it naturally appeared as if her head would come off or by her every jerk dashed to pieces against the wall: probably there was not between her head & the wall more room than to put the blade of a knife!"[29]

Yet not all households met the missionaries with enthusiasm. Because the Shaker testimony condemned "the works of the flesh" — that is, sexual intercourse — as a sin that any convert must renounce, many were naturally hostile. As the weeks passed, preachers in the surrounding area began loudly denouncing the Shakers from the pulpit, and some of the salacious rumors circulated by Shaker detractors in the East were repeated. Consequently, the missionaries began to encounter hostility on their daily visits. Some people threatened to kill them. The missionaries wrote to New Lebanon that, "there is a number of people in this place, who if then were permitted, would as willingly open our veins as they would eat bread when hungry."[30] Benjamin recorded that occupants of one house "immediately fell on us with violent hands," and the children in the family "ran out of the house bawling as they went — their noise might have been heard a quarter if not half a mile."[31] Nearly thirty years later, Benjamin — by then an elder at South Union in Kentucky — would regale a group of Shakers with a story from the spring of 1805, when he and Issachar visited the Miller family, where John Miller was receptive but his wife Susan "Sooky" Miller was not.

> The case was that Susan's husband John had believed, but Sooky had no notion to do so. Elder I[ssachar] and B[enjamin] went one day to see the family and John was absent. Elder I went into the house and Sooky met him at the door, with fury seized him and pitched him out of the house headlong. Elder B slipped in slyly while she was at work with Elder I, and having gotten him out she turned after Elder B and chased him round the room and finally caught him and flung him on to the bed in a hurry, to spring again on Elder Issachar who by that time had got into the house. But they got possession and she gave up & before long John came home and matters went well. Sooky finally cooled down and became a good believer.[32]

The Shaker testimony to forsake sexual relations was all the more awkward for the missionaries because so many women among the families at the Turtle Creek settlement were pregnant, families lived in close quarters, and married couples who converted had little choice but to continue to both live and sleep together. Still, the Shaker missionaries found Richard McNemar and his congregants to be devout people, many of whom already felt a conviction against sexual relations. For Malcolm Worley, whose young wife, Peggy, was suffering from a difficult pregnancy when the missionaries arrived, the Shaker injunction to "bear the cross" and reject sexual relations amounted to a welcome release that liberated his wife from further suffering.[33] Richard McNemar and his wife, Jenny, who was also pregnant, expressed similar views when she gave birth on April 12: "This day McN[emar's] wife delivered . . . & immediately after broke out in shouting & crying God has delivered me & now thanks to his name the way has been opened that we shall no more live after the flesh! Ric[har]d cried with tears Amen!"[34]

Issachar's personal experience likely made him the best equipped of the three missionaries to counsel new converts facing the difficulty of reconciling Shaker life with family life. Of the missionaries, only Issachar was a husband, who had been forced to turn away from conjugal relations. Issachar alone had had the experience of coming home to announce his conversion to a skeptical wife. And only Issachar was a father, who had struggled with what becoming a Shaker might mean to his livelihood and to the welfare of his children. The people of Turtle Creek—where most households were crowded, lively, and filled with children—may well have identified more closely with Issachar and found his testimony, as a man who had forsaken his own large loving family to carry the Shaker gospel to the West, all the more compelling. In May 1805 a boy was born to the recently converted Edith Dennis, a young woman who was part of the Bedle family—and was given the name Issachar.[35]

As spring continued, the bond strengthened between the Shaker missionaries and Richard McNemar. They had slept in his home, preached at his stand, and witnessed the delivery of his last child. These three relatively unschooled men had boldly challenged his interpretation of the Bible—notwithstanding his erudite knowledge of Latin, Greek, and Hebrew. Though Richard had not yet made his own decision to convert, he clearly interpreted the Shakers' work as the affirmation of a spiritual transformation he had sought for himself and his congregation.

When you first came to my house I thought you were very bold, to come & tell us that we had never had the gospel—but strangely by some of my notes I recollect that last summer I told J Thompson that we had not the gospel—our feet were only shod with the preparation of it!—I also thought that you were 3 stupid sort of Quakers . . . But I soon found that you had verily Supplanted me & I had nothing to stand on—& the building which we were trying to erect you had already created & therefore you must increase but I must decrease.[36]

The deeply intellectual Richard was not given to sudden emotional impulses. What he required was justification of the correctness of Shaker doctrine, based on his own erudite understanding. Once he found that justification, he expressed it in terms that were both persuasive and astonishingly simple:

> [S]ome opposers have come & said how can it be that you should be carried away with such delusion: why them men are Shakers! I traced the Scriptures, "I will Shake terribly the earth": Who? Why God! Therefore He is a Shaker!—And battles of Shaking—& again, I will Shake all nations. Who? Why God: therefore God is a Shaker! And if I am Shaken or are made to Shake others, surely then I shall be a Shaker—thus soon I found that the horrid tang of Shaker was lost![37]

Richard McNemar's growing friendship with Issachar Bates and Benjamin Seth Youngs was also a factor in his conversion. A private and introverted man, he was able to confide in them. As more and more of his congregants converted, Richard poured out to Issachar and Benjamin his anxieties over New Light preachers, who came to harangue him.[38] But he could also relax and enjoy himself with Issachar and Benjamin. One day while walking to visit a Turtle Creek family, the three men fell into talking and ended up whiling away most of the day together in the woods, simply enjoying themselves: "[W]e tarried by the way in the woods till near Sun Set & had the happiness to have a good degree of fellowship & right understanding together."[39] It is no wonder, then, that when Richard decided to formalize his union with the Shakers by confessing his sins, he did so to both Issachar and Benjamin together.[40]

Richard's conversion drew other prominent New Light preachers from throughout the region known as "Miamia" to challenge Richard openly.[41] A prolonged "sacramental meeting" held in April near Turtle Creek brought John Thompson, Richard's one-time colleague, whose preaching electrified the crowd to denounce the Shakers. Issachar later reconstructed Thompson's words and added his own reflections:

> And now these new Eastern men had come to tell us that Christ had made his second appearance. Pause. "But they are liars, they are liars, they are liars!" I will venture to say that the tumult at Ephesus was no greater than was at this place for about half an hour ... Many had come from a great

distance to hear & see what was going on. The whole country seemed in uproar & the very air & woods ringing with the appalling sound of false prophets! Seducers! Deceivers, liars! Wolves in sheeps clothing! Parting man & Wife! Breaking up families & churches, &c, &c.[42]

Amid such uproar, the missionaries were protective toward their new converts, duly concerned that they could be swayed by such tumultuous scenes. Issachar wrote, "I went around and hunted up our little ones and found that they stood strong through the storm . . . through it all the little innocent lambs kept close to their Shepherd & came safe." Even more inspiring, at that April meeting, despite Thompson's denunciation, several families attending from a settlement thirty miles away called Beaver Creek near Dayton, Ohio, were drawn to the Shaker message and invited the missionaries to visit. These families, members of a New Light congregation called Beulah, would become an important focus for the Shakers in the coming years.

In the spring and summer of 1805, with the conversion of more prominent citizens in the Turtle Creek vicinity, such as physician Calvin Morrell from nearby Middletown, the Shakers' prospects continued to improve. Many converts reported dreams and visions involving the Shakers, which also validated the work,[43] and the Shakers recorded one such vision involving Issachar that came from the wife of Calvin Morrell:

> In the course of the evening he related the following remarkable dream from his wife which was seen about the time we first came to Miamia — "I dreampt the time had come for the 12 manner of fruits to be eaten, spoken of in the scriptures — the first was pears of the most beautiful & delicious kind — I saw a man Shake the tree while R. McN held a basket — who also went & dealt them out among the people! — When Is[sachar] was at Morrells she knew him to be the very person both by his dress & appearance![44]

As spring turned to summer, the frenetic pace of the Shakers' efforts slowed somewhat. Area residents began their farm work and had less time to engage in religious debates. Still staying in the Worley's large household, the Shakers shouldered their fair share of seasonal work. Requests for preaching came from converts' friends and relatives living in neighboring areas. Mathew Houston in Kentucky, who had stayed in touch with the Shakers, requested that they return to preach to his congregation.

The three missionaries had not yet introduced the most iconic Shaker practice to the new converts. The first worship meeting to include dancing is recorded on May 23.[45] By early June the Turtle Creek congregation regularly engaged in Shaker-style worship, with "laboring" (dancing) and the singing of songs and hymns introduced by the Shakers themselves or perhaps written by Issachar Bates. Because singing initiated the dance, Issachar's role in the worship was increasingly important. As Benjamin recorded: "Is[sachar] sung a labouring song & most of the believers went forth in the labors."[46] By early summer the Shakers needed helping hands in their work—more missionaries and more singers—so they wrote to New Lebanon suggesting not only that the Ministry send more people to Ohio to help with the work of evangelism but also that the Ministry consider establishing a settlement in Ohio. Recognizing the complexity of such an undertaking, the missionaries included in their letter detailed descriptions of the land and how to purchase it, the local economy, and the livelihoods of converts:

> The face of the Country in the main both in Kentucky and here is very beautiful being neither Mountainous and broken nor yet of a dead level ... it is heavily timbered, but when it is cleared off, the land is free from stone and therefore easy to till and brings forth in great abundance. A great deal of this land remains untaken up; it is laid out in Sections a mile square and is sold by certain men appointed by Congress; The best of it is Sold at 3 Dollars an acre ... Those that purchase take a quarter, a half, or a whole Section or a number of Sections as they choose.
>
> Those that believe are neither very rich nor very poor, Some of them have good farms and some have no land ... The Country is natural to grass and affords a plenty of Milk and butter.
>
> The general price of wheat is two thirds of a Dollar a bushel, and corn a quarter of a Dollar; but in Kentucky one may purchase as much corn as he will at 6 bushels for a Dollar, and 2 bushels of wheat for a Dollar; but all imported goods are high.
>
> We have felt a desire that if it should be thought best, that some of the brethren might come and settle some where in this Western country.
>
> Malcolm Worley and Richard M'Nemar both live on one half Section which is very good land and a beautiful place. Malcolm's quarter is free from all encumberance and is brought into middling good order, Richard has paid for his but one fourth part and as he is unable to pay for the remainder he wishes to have it taken off his hands; about 300 Dollars is yet behind, all to be paid within two years from this time; he feels loathe that it should fall in to the hands of the world, because when he settled upon it which was last summer he believes that he had a special gift of feeling that

God would begin to set up his church on this spot of ground; but in what manner he could not tell. Malcolm also has had the same feeling.[47]

The missionaries had in fact written several times to the Ministry, but because they had received no replies, they did not know whether their letters had reached New Lebanon. Throughout the latest letter the men asserted that they missed their New York community but were creating the prospect of a new community in the West: "[Y]et we have found a number of people here that feel near and dear, they have several times, gone forth in the worship of God; in some measure according to the order of the Gospel; and they begin to feel more and more like brethren & Sisters." And they made it plain that theirs was a daunting task for three individuals: "We some times feel ourselves under as great a burden as we are able to bear, and have as much tribulation as we are able to endure." Because they hoped that the Ministry would send more people to assist in the work, they ended their letter with a description of the travel route between Pittsburg and Cincinnati via the Ohio River, noting that in contrast to their own route over the Wilderness Road, this way "would probably be easier quicker, & cheaper than any other." In a postscript, John Meacham specifically asked that the Ministry consider dispatching Daniel Mosley to join them, a Shaker brother whom the Ministry had very nearly included in the initial missionary party. Alluding to the importance of singing in training the converts in methods of Shaker worship, John also noted that having more singers, so that the full responsibility for leading the dances did not rest on Issachar, "would be very profitable."

The Shaker trio was pleased to finally receive a letter from New Lebanon later in June. Issachar must have been especially happy, because that letter contained a brief but important message about his family at Watervliet, New York: "Issachar's family is well and are comfortably provided for in his absence & Levina was very glad to receive his letter."[48] Several points are apparent even from such a brief passage. Notwithstanding the end of their normal marital relationship, Issachar Bates and his wife continued to care for one another. By permitting Lovina Bates to receive a personal letter and by conveying her sentiments to her husband, the Shaker Ministry indicated that they continued to recognize and respect Issachar's personal attachment to his wife and children. The assurance to Issachar that his family was being comfortably provided for underscores the fluidity of Shaker life at that date, even in the relatively settled New York communities. A full "joint interest"—or formal arrangement for communalism—had yet to be implemented, and many biological families still resided together and provided for their own living. As head of his family,

Issachar must have continued to harbor a sense of responsibility for their welfare. Finally, the message implies that Issachar's stay in the West was intended to be temporary and that he was expecting to return to Watervliet, New York, where he would again reside with his family and play a role in providing for them. Although the three missionaries had stressed in their correspondence that the amount of work in Ohio precluded any of them from returning to New York — "It does not appear to us as if any one of us could at present be spared to return back"[49] — they imply that more brethren arriving to augment their numbers might enable one of them to return.

The Ministry chose three men to assist with the work in the West: "In the latter part of July we had a strong recruit — Elder David Darrow, Daniel Mosley, and Solomon King came from the East to help in the work of God, and we received them with great joy. For truly the harvest was great and the laborers were few."[50] All three men were longtime faithful brethren, whose experience with the Shakers dated back to Ann Lee's lifetime. Fifty-five-year-old Darrow had been among Ann Lee's first converts in 1780 and had given his farmland to help form the Shaker community at New Lebanon.[51] As first elder of New Lebanon's Church Family since 1792, Darrow was an important leader in Shaker society.[52] Like Issachar Bates, he was a war veteran who came to the Shakers as a married man with children.[53] As a leading Shaker elder for more than ten years, he was to assume leadership of the work in Ohio and guide the efforts to establish a permanent settlement among the new converts. Daniel Moseley was also middle-aged, but unmarried. He had embraced the faith in 1780 as a young man of twenty along with his mother, Mary Moseley, who had been a companion of Ann Lee.[54] Daniel was a blacksmith by trade, and he could also sing. The missionaries had requested him by name, believing him to be a good choice for the western labors.[55] Solomon King, a much younger man, born in 1775, had been a small child when his family converted, and he had grown up in the New Lebanon Shaker community.[56] The arrival of this additional group, including a Shaker elder of Darrow's stature, signaled both to the original missionaries and the new converts alike that western initiative was transforming into a permanent expansion.

The three newcomers traveled to Ohio in a covered wagon "loaded with articles of clothing for themselves and the three brethren already there."[57] They joined the missionaries at Malcolm Worley's house and settled into a pattern of preaching trips in the area. But with the six Shakers now crowding in with Worley's large family, the men realized that they needed to acquire some land and build a dwelling house of their own. Ideally, the eastern Shakers would establish a residence on land within the Turtle Creek settlement, where they could live among the converted families and gradually work to establish a full-fledged community. They had already erected a large open-air "stand," or platform of split logs, on a portion of Malcolm Worley's land where it adjoined Richard's land to the east.[58] Many of the converts lived less than a mile from that spot, and even those who lived farther away were contemplating moving closer, as the stand soon came to represent the center of the fledgling Shaker community. Benjamin recorded: "A general feeling seems to prevail among almost all those who have faith & live at any great distance from the stand in Turtle Creek, to move nearer to it."[59] So the Shakers looked for available land adjacent to Malcolm or Richard's property. They learned that the owner of a quarter-section of land next to Malcolm's land on the south side could be acquired for $1,640 from a truculent owner who wished to quit the neighborhood and its Shakers and their peculiar practices. Additionally, there was the possibility of acquiring more land west of Malcolm's acreage. However, the New Lebanon Ministry would need to be fully apprised of the details before approving such large expenditures, and communicating by post was unreliable. Thus it was decided that Issachar should return to New Lebanon where he could report the state of proselytizing efforts in the West and explain the options for acquiring land — and return to the West when his work was done:

> [W]e expect that brother Issachar will set out tomorrow . . . In respect to brother Issachar's returning again to this country, we would inform you that if he could possibly be spared from his family & there should be the gift for him to return it would be much to our satisfaction to have him return as soon as may be. We feel that he has had & still might have a very profitable gift to the people here; this is felt by the people insomuch that if he should not return it would be a matter of serious grief to many of them as well as disagreeable to us.[60]

Likely Issachar was considered the logical choice to return east. As a strong man accustomed to difficult situations, travel, and isolation, Issachar was well equipped to make the journey alone, and the Ministry was undoubtedly aware that they had asked a lot of Issachar to remain separated from his wife and children, several of whom were still very young. When he departed for New York on September 26, carrying a packet of important letters that included the first letters written by Richard and Jenny McNemar to their new Shaker friends in the East, and armed with instructions for best presenting the needs of the growing western community, Issachar was acutely conscious of embarking on an important errand. And he may also have regarded his journey as the homeward leg of a long western adventure that was soon coming to an end. Unbeknownst to him, the Shaker leaders in Ohio hoped for many reasons that he would be allowed to return. Many of the new converts were already so devoted to Issachar that the Shakers may have feared that their convictions would lapse should the Ministry decide to keep Issachar in the East.

It was during this journey back to New Lebanon that Issachar confronted an unanticipated problem and challenge to his own faith, both recorded in a droll account that reveals his storyteller's knack of portraying his inner thoughts:

> And so on the 26th of September I started on foot and alone from Chillicothe. Now I felt that zeal that I bid defiance to all powers, but the power of God. No pain could touch me, but I could order it hence, for I was on the King's business. But when I got near Bethlehem, within about 200 miles of Lebanon, a pain darted through my left foot as sharp as knife work, & it was too much for me, it swelled very fast & turned purple, but I travelled till night, in great pain . . . in the morning could not get my foot into my shoe, stuck my toes in as far as I could and went limping along and then I went to contriving. I will stop and get a moccasin made. Well then, I cannot stand to walk, I will buy a horse. I can pay $26 Dollars and get trusted for the rest till I return. Well that will never do, for I cannot bear my foot to hang down. But this will do, I will stop and hire a man to take me in a wagon, and the Church will pay him when we get there. That will do. All at once a voice whispered, "Where is thy faith?" I answered with real unbelief, <u>faith</u>, I should just as quick think of asking for my leg to be cured, if both bones were broken off. Again came the whisper, "Whatsoever you shall ask the Father in my name, it shall be done." Now I cannot describe my feelings . . . and in a moment a pain darted up my thigh, and it was all over, my foot was as well as ever . . . I put on my shoe and started a song & ran 2 or 3 miles. And I suppose the people that saw me took me to be a crazy man, but I did not care for that.[61]

Later Shaker writers have noted Issachar's victory over his foot injury during his solitary 770-mile trek to New York as one rare example of a "healing gift."[62] Certainly it was a critical experience for Issachar Bates. Instead of calling upon his faith to sustain him through a physically painful episode, he instead began desperately contriving other solutions before finally interpreting the situation as a spiritual test. Like many formative moments earlier in Issachar's life, this one also occurred when he was alone, out of doors, and journeying.

After arriving at New Lebanon, Issachar Bates conferred with the Ministry and elders over the situation in the West.[63] Doubtless, he recounted death threats and ruffians who rushed upon them while preaching, brandishing clubs. (Unbeknownst to Issachar, the open-air worship stand had been destroyed by arsonists the night after he departed for New Lebanon.[64]) Regarding Turtle Creek's geographic setting and available land, Issachar was able to paint a rich picture, all the more so because of his own familiarity with settlements being literally carved from the frontier. A letter from David Meacham, Trustee of the Church, reveals that Issachar's task met with success: the decision to purchase land that would provide a basis for a permanent home and a plan to send Shaker sisters soon to join the brethren.

> We on the 17th of instant October rec'd your kind letter (by Issachar)
> . . . we rejoice and are comforted by the content thereof, together with
> the clear opening and communication to us by Issachar of the increasing
> work and power of God in those parts . . . We fully agree with you that it
> is really necessary for you to have a habitation of your own . . . We also
> feel full union . . . with your proposal of purchasing that quarter section of
> Timothy Sewell; as we with you consider this to be a point of wisdom to
> take all due advantage in such matters. We shall gladly send a sufficiency
> of money as soon as we have a safe opportunity, we judge that you may
> safely engage the money by the first of June next . . . You signify that some
> of our Sisters may be helpful with you in your labour. We expect that
> there will be a gift for some to go from here. Perhaps they may arrive there
> by the first of June next. They will need house room as well as household
> furniture bedding, &c. We desire that you inform us by letter whether or
> how those things can be purchased there, or whether there must be some
> necessary things carried from here.[65]

As first Deacon and Trustee, David Meacham oversaw financial matters for the Church, such as major property purchases.[66] It fell to him to consider the practical details of the Shakers' expansion to the west — not only choosing property, but considering how safely to convey money for the purchase, amass building materials for a house, and set up a well-supplied functioning household, all in a frontier area. Because Meacham indicates that money for the property purchase could not be expected until the coming June, when it could be carried west with a group of Shaker brethren and sisters,[67] possibly also bringing a load of household supplies, it can be inferred that the Ministry did not initially intend to send Issachar back to Ohio. However, before this letter was sent, further discussions with Issachar altered the Ministry's thinking.

> Since writing the above it is concluded that Issachar should return there;
> we think that he may arrive by the last of December next. We propose

to send [the money] by him. Also we think it proper to inform you that we understand by Issachar that there is a piece of broken land lying joining on the west side of Malcom's land on which there is a small stream of water, as well as some useful stones which will be necessary for building . . . we are willing that you should purchase for us so much as will secure the privilege of water works, and stone . . . the deeds may be given to me.

Evidently Issachar persuaded the Ministry to ponder a bigger picture. Acquiring the nearby "broken" land, in addition to the quarter-section already under consideration, would give the Shakers a mill site and stone for building foundations. Clearly the outlines of a future community were beginning to take shape. Deciding to send Issachar back to Ohio immediately with the money to purchase land accelerated the eastern Shakers' plans for establishing a permanent seat in the West.

The question of whether Issachar Bates sought a return to Ohio at that juncture is an important one, as it has bearing on how he perceived his role in the Shaker world and how he himself wanted to live his life. In writing about this period nearly thirty years later, Issachar would state unambiguously that he was sent home to get money to purchase land, implying that his return to Ohio was never in question. But correspondence written at the time suggests that the Ministry only came to that decision after taking into account a bigger land purchase than originally intended. Perhaps Issachar wished to return to Ohio and proposed the additional land purchase with the hope that the Ministry would realize he should go back to help the brethren execute those transactions and commence building. Perhaps the Ministry also took into account the concerns expressed by David Darrow and the other Shakers in Ohio that the loss of Issachar would cause "serious grief" among the new converts. By now, Issachar may have believed that he belonged in the West. For most of his forty-seven years, Issachar had lived in frontier settings where communities were still emerging. As a young adult he had sought moves into frontier areas, both for the economic opportunities and the relative freedom such moves afforded. Converting to the Shakers and moving himself and his family to Watervliet, New York, had been the first time in Issachar's life that his movements took him *toward* — not away from — a relatively settled area. But while his wife and children made a comfortable home among the Shakers at Watervliet, Issachar himself continued on to new frontiers, first through extended preaching travels in the region, and later when he was dispatched west. Whether Issachar preferred returning to the West over remaining closer to his wife, children, and other family members is unknown, but it is probable that he did. Ironically, bringing himself and his family into Shaker "order" gave Issachar a measure of personal freedom that deeply suited his peripatetic nature. With the knowledge that his family would continue to remain comfortably ensconced at Watervliet, where Lovina lived among her children and her in-laws and did not lack for the basic necessities of life, Issachar likely had little desire to remain with them. He had new friends and companions, and he was helping build a community in America's latest frontier region. Best of all, he had endless new audiences for preaching the Shaker gospel, which he clearly excelled at doing.

Yet the prospect of returning Issachar Bates to Ohio — a relatively new convert who had a young and growing family among the Shakers at Watervliet — was not something the Ministry undertook lightly, however effective a preacher he might be and however well suited to frontier life. That Shakers forced the breakup of families was a common critique among detractors, and the Ministry may have preferred to avoid providing an example of just this practice in the family of one of their leading preachers. The Ministry had already demonstrated a commitment to keeping Issachar's family comfortably situated, and Issachar must have taken some comfort in seeing this for himself. About the time he departed for Ohio on November 18th, a new building project was under way at Watervliet: a group of workers that included several young men from New Lebanon were "engaged in building a house for Issachar Bates's family," which was virtually completed by December 13.[68] If Issachar harbored any misgivings over returning to Ohio, having Lovina and the children even more securely settled in their own house may have mitigated them. And being able to report their well-being would also have helped to counteract any perception by the new western converts, for whom Issachar had already exhibited paternal impulses, that Issachar was indifferent to his own biological family's needs.

Issachar spent the latter portion of his one-month stay in New York at the Watervliet community visiting Lovina, his children, and his extended family there.[69] Details of his visit are unrecorded, but he surely spoke to Lovina and learned how she and the children were faring. Whether they treated this visit with the gravity it deserved is unknown, but in fact Issachar and Lovina never saw one another again.

When Issachar left New Lebanon and Watervliet on November 18 to walk back to Ohio alone, carrying nearly two thousand dollars for a major land purchase, he probably again felt the gravity of being "on the King's business." Apparently the Shaker Ministry not only trusted Issachar implicitly (such a large amount of money might have been a temptation to some) but also were confident in his ability to guard the money during the journey, no mean feat in the rough traveling conditions of the day. Benjamin Seth Youngs, who was obviously delighted at the decision of the Ministry to return Issachar to Ohio, recorded his friend's safe arrival back at Turtle Creek on December 11: "I was glad at the returning of Issachar to this Country, my brother, my right hand, my companion & fellow laborer in the vineyard of the Gospel. Without him I feel alone, having no one likeminded with me in all things."[70]

Coincidentally, just as Issachar's departure more than two months before had been followed by an episode of persecution later that same night, likewise the Shakers were targeted for more harassment the night after Issachar's return. This time, as the men sat talking by the fire at Malcolm Worley's, they "were surprised by a set of ruffians who (it appear'd) with clubs broke in two sashes of the windows & 13 panes of glass."[71] This was hardly a surprise to Issachar, and he learned that his friends had been suffering a range of abuse in his absence: "I found those who rejected the gospel in the same employment in which I left them, breaking glass windows, cutting down orchards, throwing down fences, burning buildings, &c, &c. But found those who had accepted the gospel and had confessed their sins joyful, comfortable, and strong in the Lord and in the power of his might. And I verily believed I feared not all the Western world."[72]

■ Issachar Bates had returned willingly to rejoin his Shaker brethren and the growing spiritual family of western converts in this "land of daily persecution."[73] Where before he had arrived a complete stranger in an unfamiliar place some nine months before, he now was greeted as a brother and friend returning home. In a short time, Issachar and his companions had begun a bold expansion of the Shakers' spiritual family in this frontier region of Ohio and Kentucky. Their presence and their preaching was shaping the religious climate of the entire area, as evidenced by the crowds they drew, the confessions they administered, and the persecution they received. They had established spiritual allies across 150 miles and confronted the leading preachers of the region, contending with increasing antagonism. But they now counted one of the foremost of these leading preachers — Richard McNemar — among their closest friends. Richard's conversion was probably the pivotal incident in an eventful nine months, and it would not be an exaggeration to say that his long-term impact on the evolution of the Shaker West would rival that of the missionaries themselves. Turtle Creek now loomed large in the religious landscape of the region as a place engulfed in momentous events: "[I]ndeed the attraction of people in all parts far & near appears very much to center at the Miamia, as though something very extraordinary was there — either the work of God of or great delusion."[74]

With Issachar's return to Turtle Creek, bringing money and instructions for building a permanent Shaker settlement and a complex community, soon to include eastern Shaker sisters as well as brothers, he ceased to be simply a sojourner in the West, a missionary dispatched by the parent Church. Rather, the West was now his home. Issachar could not have known that nearly twenty-five years would pass before he was able again to visit his old home at Watervliet or his friends at New Lebanon. He would spend the rest of his long and productive middle-age years building up the Shaker enterprise in the West.

CHAPTER 6

"Thorns and thistles did abound"

THE GROWTH OF THE SHAKER WEST

Moved on at God's command, Till they reached this western land,
Where a wilderness they found, Thorns and thistles did abound.
—Sally Eades, "New Year's Hymn"

As 1806 began, Issachar Bates and the other eastern Shakers were optimistic about the prospects of Shakerism's expansion into the western frontier of the new country. During worship with the "young believers"— the term given to the new western converts—on Christmas Day, they had all experienced prophetic signs of the gospel's increase, "particularly towards the South and West."[1] Rumors circulated that a mob was being raised to drive the "old believers"[2]—the term used for the three original Shaker missionaries who had arrived in March 1805, along with the three additional easterners who joined them from New Lebanon that summer—out of Ohio and back where they came from. But at the same time, the Shakers took persecution as a sign that they were doing God's work in challenging the sects of the area. With a strong base of young believers in Richard McNemar's Turtle Creek congregation, allies in other places, financial and material support from the eastern Ministry, and a promise of still more easterners arriving to help with the work, Issachar and his fellow old believers had every reason to be confident. For Issachar, the next several years were an exciting period of near constant travel and creative endeavor, punctuated by danger and by encounters with colorful figures, as he poured his whole self into building up the spiritual edifice of Shakerism in the region.

Between the Miamis
The table is spread[3]

With the money Issachar Bates had brought back from New Lebanon at the end of 1805, the six old believers in Ohio set about purchasing the southwest quadrant of Section 24 in Turtle Creek Township of Warren County, about three miles west of the county seat at Lebanon (figure 6.1).[4] They felt fortunate to acquire land that was adjacent to that of Malcom Worley, their first Turtle Creek convert, virtually at the center of the Turtle Creek neighborhood, and in an area of great agricultural potential. As one early-nineteenth-century ge-

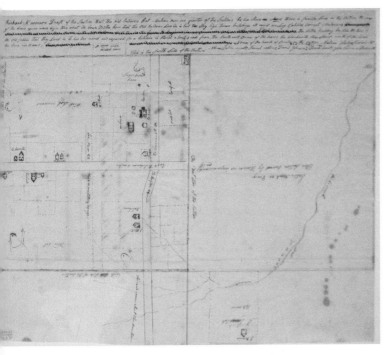

6.1

*"Section that the
Old Believers Bot,"
circa 1807.
(Courtesy of
the Shaker
Museum|Mount
Lebanon,
New Lebanon,
New York)*

ographer and western traveler put it, "The country between the two rivers
Miamis is said to be one of the most fertile in America."[5] The purchased land
was registered in the name of David Meacham, Deacon and Trustee of the
United Society. During the early months of 1806, the old believers prepared
to build themselves a house, conscious of the need to withdraw from living
in close quarters with the Worley family. A letter written to New Lebanon in
March reported progress on a two-story frame house, thirty feet by forty feet,
with chimneys at each end, whose interior floorplan would be "something in
the form of the East house at New Lebanon."[6] The spacious house, they said,
would allow them to accommodate the eastern Shakers whose arrival they expected later that year, as well as the many inquirers who came to Turtle Creek.
They wrote of using the winter months for preparing shingles and clapboard
siding for the house.

Meanwhile, the old believers' influence over the Turtle Creek converts
continued to broaden. The male converts wanted to mimic the dress of the
old believers, whose garb appeared quaint and old-fashioned, somewhat like
the traditional dress of Quakers.

> They say they want no other manner, form, or colors than was first sent
> to them from the Mount — even from the crown of their hats to the soles

of their shoes — They say that the outward dress that the first Brethren appeared in was as great pleasing to them as their word & testimony. It witnessed to them that they were the true followers of Christ — & had forsaken the course & fashions of the world.[7]

Some converts assumed new names to match names of prominent eastern Shakers, such as Asenath Edie, who adopted "Asenath" to match the name of a popular young eldress at New Lebanon. So eager were the converts to learn about Ann Lee and the struggles of the first Shakers that the old believers wrote home for clarification to make sure they had their facts straight.[8] Babies continued to be born to women who had been pregnant at the time of their conversions, and several of these infants bore names matching those of eastern Shakers or of the missionaries themselves. A baby Issachar had been born to the Dennis family the previous spring, and in January 1806, a second baby Issachar was born to the Abels, another Turtle Creek family. In December 1805 and January 1806, the Rollins and Edie families both chose the name "Lovina" for new girl babies, possibly to honor Issachar Bates's wife.

But Issachar Bates was probably too busy in 1806 to take much note of such things. Most of his time was spent in travel, revisiting people who had heard the Shaker gospel during 1805 and carrying the gospel to new audiences. The old believers were determined to cast a wide net to expand their growing flock of Shaker converts, a task that had begun the previous year with Issachar's return to Cane Ridge and with the missionaries' continued contact with Mathew Houston and his congregation in Paint Lick, Kentucky. Some of the Turtle Creek converts had also provided introductions to relatives and friends living in other areas. In June 1805 Richard McNemar had led the Shakers to the Dunlavy and Knox families in Adams County, Ohio, southeast of Turtle Creek. The sisters of Richard and his wife were married to John Dunlavy and John Knox (respectively), prominent landowners in a settlement called Eagle Creek.[9] There Benjamin and Issachar had spent time preaching in the summer of 1805, and John and Cassia Dunlavy had confessed their sins. The beginning of 1806 found Issachar together with Richard, visiting among the Dunlavys, Knoxes and other Eagle Creek families that were being drawn to Shakerism, before going on to Cabin Creek, Kentucky, Richard's home for several years, where they preached among Richard's in-laws and former associates.[10] While in Kentucky, they returned to Paint Lick to visit Mathew Houston and his family, who confessed their sins that February with several other families in Houston's New Light congregation.[11] Eventually, word of mouth, along with Richard's longstanding familiarity with this region of Kentucky, led the men to the small settlement of Shawnee Run in Mercer County, where they found a very receptive audience.

> ∼ *The land is trembling, one denomination dashing against another & breaking one another to pieces with preaching, letters, & pamphlets — & respecting the testimony one preacher running to meet another preacher, & one post to meet another post, to bring the king of Babylon word that the city is taken at one end — & all in confusion — these are the signs of the times.*[12]

By April Issachar Bates was back at Turtle Creek, where he and other Shakers attended the nearby annual "sacramental meeting" presided over by New Light preacher John Thompson, Richard McNemar's former colleague. It was at the sacramental meeting the previous April that the Shaker missionaries and their new converts had withstood a bitter diatribe from Thompson and other hostile New Lights. This year, in the face of the Shakers' obvious success in establishing a foothold at Turtle Creek, neither they nor their converts were intimidated. Benjamin wrote of Thompson's preaching: "The same kind of old stuff."[13] But some of the New Lights from the Beulah congregation at Beaver Creek near Dayton, who had come for Thompson's sacramental meeting, stayed to hear the Shaker preaching, and at the end of April, Issachar and Benjamin returned to Beaver Creek at their invitation, where they heard several confessions and led the people in Shaker dancing. Issachar would return there many times in the next several years — together with Richard, Benjamin, or others — hearing more confessions and advising the people on how to integrate the Shaker gospel into their lives. Little did Issachar know that this Beaver Creek settlement would ultimately be the site of his longest continuous home in the Shaker West, where some twenty years in the future he would preside as elder over a small Shaker community.

> ∼ *In the month of June, 1806, we had another blessed recruit, From the church in the East. Viz — Peter Pease, Samuel Turner, Constant Mosley, Eldress Ruth Farrington, Lucy Smith, Ruth Darrow, Molly Goodrich, Martha Sanford, & Prudence Farrington. This made us feel strong . . . After we moved into our new house we gathered in a few young believers in with us which formed a kind of Church order. This I called my home and it was a good one too; yet, I did not enjoy it but a short part of the time. For I was travelling the western world, from side to side and almost from end to end; Sometimes with my peculiar friend and fellow traveler, little Benjamin, (for by this title he was*

known thro' out the country, & generally mentioned in terms of respect by friend & foe).[14]

The six old believers at Turtle Creek were delighted when another arrival more than doubled their numbers. Nine eastern Shakers, including six women, had set out for Ohio in a pair of covered wagons. They followed roads west across Pennsylvania and into Ohio, recommended by the Ohio Shakers as preferable to the Wilderness Road through Kentucky. But the journey was arduous for wagons loaded down with furniture, household goods, and clothing. Issachar, together with westerners Malcom Worley and Calvin Morrell, were obliged to meet the group at Chillicothe in south-central Ohio to help bring the wagons across the narrow track that then sufficed for a road. Ruth Darrow, daughter of David Darrow and one of the six eastern sisters wrote, "Issachar and Calvin went on before us with their axes cutting new roads and making bridges for it was a continual swamp for three days after they met us."[15] Issachar and the other Shaker brethren brought the first eastern sisters to the West through the sheer force of their will. These six women were all longstanding Shakers well-respected in the eastern communities.[16] Ruth Farrington had served alongside David Darrow as Eldress of New Lebanon's First Family from 1796 until Darrow's departure for Ohio the previous summer,[17] and New Lebanon's transfer to Ohio of both the First Family Elder and Eldress signaled the Church's deep commitment to — and confidence in — the ongoing western expansion. All of the women were healthy and mature adults who had been Shakers for most of their lives. Two were in their forties. Ruth Darrow was the youngest at twenty-five.[18] The prospect of eastern Shaker women enduring dangerous traveling conditions and trading life in comfortable established villages for a meager existence in a rough frontier settlement was something the western converts hardly expected, but the women, especially, longed for. In her letter addressed to eastern sisters the previous September, Jenny McNemar had spoken for most of the western women when she declared how much she yearned to meet other Shaker sisters.[19] During Issachar's fall 1805 visit to New Lebanon, he had urged the Ministry to send women to help teach and counsel the female converts in both spiritual matters and the practical aspects of Shaker life, such as dress and collective childcare. That he was addressing a profound need in the community cannot be much doubted. The young believers' first glimpse of eastern Shaker women was overwhelming; most wept and some collapsed to the floor.[20]

With their numbers augmented by women, Issachar Bates wrote that the old believers could form a "Church order." By this he meant that the believers could establish a household spatially organized for genders to eat and worship side-by-side, but sleep and work separately, with daily activities governed by the dual authority of David Darrow and Ruth Farrington. In their spacious frame "house of David" constructed on their own land, the old believers sought to institute a household that would serve as a model for the young believers, who still remained scattered around Turtle Creek in their own cabins and small houses.[21] The several youthful converts who were selected to join the old believers as part of this initial "Church order" household included twenty-three-year-old Edith Dennis (who had given birth to the baby Issachar in May 1805), Edith's twenty-year-old sister Eunice Bedle, and Berachah Dennis, a young man.[22] Why such youthful people among the many likely Ohio converts were selected to live alongside the seasoned old believers is not clear. However, the zeal of Edith and Eunice is apparent; they are noted as being particularly active in leading other worshippers in dance: "At noon the believers met at the Stand — Is[sachar] and Daniel preached . . . beautiful exercises of running round in a body 20 or 30 believers for the space of half an hour — Edith D. & Eunice B. began it first . . . with wonderful swiftness and solemnity."[23]

As Issachar Bates's second year in the West drew to a close, Turtle Creek was slowly evolving into an orderly Shaker settlement, and his preaching had yielded scores of converts scattered from Dayton, Ohio, to the north to Eagle Creek, Ohio, to the southeast, to Paint Lick and Shawnee Run, Kentucky, to the south. In a relatively short time, Issachar and Benjamin had become well known regionally and, among some, almost revered. In November 1806, a large group of Kentucky converts traveled by wagon to visit Turtle Creek, carrying gifts of tobacco, cotton, wool, cider, and various foodstuffs. Unable to contain their devotion to the old believers during three days of exuberant meetings, the visitors insisted during one worship session that they be permitted to kiss the feet of each eastern Shaker brother, beginning with Issachar and Benjamin:

> This evening, after laboring & singing a long time . . . Henry Bonta after much entreaty had the privilege of satisfying his feelings to kiss the feet of all the Brethren who came from New Lebanon — Accordingly, while they were sitting in a rank 8 in number he began at Benjamin & Issachar & went thro pulling off their shoes & kissing all their feet — William Gordon also followed & then Henry returned repeated the operation putting on their shoes again — Then they renewed the meeting in songs & dances, strong, powerful & comfortable.[24]

While pleased to see such zeal manifested in these young believers from Kentucky, Issachar was also dismayed when during worship the next evening some of the young women, freed of their inhibitions during spiritual exercises, heckled Mathew Houston, now one of Issachar's closest new western friends:

> In the evening the Ky sisters being much engaged in singing, dancing in thankfulness — One of the sisters said to Mathew the P. Minister see the disorder. He got on a chest & called several times for Order, they heeded it not.
>
> The great Presbyterian Minister humbled — Ann Bruner under exercises came to Mathew taking him by the hand invited him to come down — immediately he sat down on the floor, then asked if he was not low enough? She told him again get down! He then prostrated on the floor — She took a candle & held it to his face & asked him if he loved the light? Sally Shields who continued bowing & jerking — came to him inviting him to preach a Sermon — he said he had not studied it — & moreover said he was never so ill treated in his life. He got up & they still under exercise got him in a corner — bowing around him in derision honoring him asking for a sermon — He begging time to study it &c. After sufficiently humbling the Presbyterian the meeting continued with power for some time before closing.[25]

This incident reveals part of Shakerism's appeal for the less educated frontier settlers. The combination of an emphasis on the spiritual equality of all people and the rejection of institutionalized churches and their clergy was profoundly empowering to people who chafed at social restrictions and resented mandatory deference to people of higher social classes. The old believers realized the delicacy of their task — how to encourage spiritual freedom but at the same time create an orderly social environment. The day after Mathew's "humbling," both Issachar and Mathew preached "with great and singular satisfaction to old and young," and when the Kentucky visitors departed, the same sisters who had behaved with such abandon were "all in perfect uniform in the order of Believers from head to foot neat, clean & exemplary, as if they had had a privilege for years." As they traveled home to Kentucky, they stayed overnight at an inn by the Ohio River, where they worshiped in an upper room and "[t]heir singing was plainly heard in the streets of Cincinnati on the opposite side of the River."[26]

> ⌇ While walking from Worleys to the Society meeting B had some special feelings about the Indians & communicates the same to Is — It will be nothing

6.2

Ten-s qúat-a-way, The Open Door, Known as The Prophet, Brother of Tecumseh, *by George Catlin.* *(Smithsonian American Art Museum.)*

strange if the Ohio Indians should see & believe — none had such feelings before.[27]

During their quiet interludes on the trail together while journeying from place to place, Issachar Bates and his companions talked about the places where they might preach and the audiences they might persuade with the Shaker gospel. As early as the spring of 1805 they had heard rumors of a religious revival among the Indians of the region and had talked of carrying the Shaker message to them.[28] At the time the Shakers arrived in Ohio, many of the Shawnee and allied tribes inhabited a region west of a north-south treaty line established at Greenville, Ohio, near the headwaters of the White River in neighboring Indiana Territory. It was there in about 1805 that a Shawnee named Lalawethika, the younger brother of Tecumseh, had endured a series of disturbing religious visions that plainly illustrated to him the consequences for various wicked behaviors. As a result, he renounced alcohol and began a vigorous program of charismatic preaching among the Indians. He adopted a new name, Tenskwatawa, meaning "the open door," and began urging the Shawnee to purify themselves of all practices adopted from white Americans and embark on a spiritual revival. To most, he became known as "the Prophet" (figure 6.2). About 1806 he moved with his brother Tecumseh and a very large group of followers back into Ohio to a settlement near Greenville, where the treaty expelling the Shawnee had been conducted in 1795.[29]

News of the Shawnee presence and the rise of a new Indian "Prophet" generated concern in the white settlements of the Miami region. Government officials grew worried when they heard that Tenskwatawa was conducting a purge of "witches" among the Shawnee, including some Indians influenced by Christian missionaries.[30] New tensions developed between the Shawnee at Greenville and nearby Ohio settlers. Tenskwatawa, who seemed intent on spreading his religious message of return to Indian culture and rejection of white influence, drew representatives from many tribes, who came to Greenville to hear him.

It was in the midst of these gathering concerns that the Shakers of Turtle Creek decided in mid-March 1807 to send a delegation to speak with the Shawnee Prophet. With only a general idea of where to find his settlement, which they believed lay a few days' ride to the northwest, Richard McNemar, Benjamin Seth Youngs, and David Darrow "set out like Abram of old not knowing whether we went but gathering . . . that the people lay somewhere to the North & that it was our Duty to find them."[31] Guided on the way by Indians and French traders they encountered, they found the Shawnee village near the old fort at Greenville and there spent several days visiting with the Prophet—introduced to the Shakers as "Lallawasheka," a name meaning "great voice"—and with Tecumseh and several other chiefs.[32] Fortunately, two of the Indians present—Peter Cornstalk and George Bluejacket—were able to interpret, facilitating a series of conversations with the Prophet and others. The men were awestruck by the Indians' enormous timbered "meeting house" built for worship, 150 feet long. All preachers themselves, and familiar with the challenges of outdoor speech-making to scattered crowds, the Shakers were particularly amazed at the vocal delivery of one of the Indian orators, identified as a cousin of Lallawasheka: "Ten thousand people might have distinctly understood him & his voice might have been heard over the plains for the distance of at least two miles."[33]

Later that spring three of the Shaker converts from Beaver Creek went to Greenville and had further conversations with the Prophet and his people.[34] At the end of May, some twenty-five Indians, including Tecumseh (figure 6.3) and the aged Chief Bluejacket, along with interpreter Peter Cornstalk, arrived at Turtle Creek, guided there by the Beaver Creek Shakers. During their stay, they witnessed Shaker worship and preaching, and a crowd of several hundred assembled, "for the country round about seemed all in a commotion about the Indians—not knowing what these things meant."[35] The Shakers' obvious kindness and generosity to the Indians provided another rationale for local opposition against the Turtle Creek settlement.[36]

The Shakers' Ohio neighbors were not the only ones to worry about the emerging relationship between the Shakers and the Indians. When Mother

6.3
Tecumseh full-length portrait, *drawn by F. Brigden. (Courtesy of the Ohio Historical Society.)*

Lucy Wright, the Shakers' principal authority at the New Lebanon Ministry, received David Darrow's report of their initial visit, she was openly dismayed: "[S]ince I have heard of your going after the Indians, I have felt some tribulations on that account though I do not know the cause of your going & therefore cannot judge whether you went in the gift of God or not, or whether it would not be better to have sent some of the young believers than to have gone yourself I leave you to judge — but this I know that as you are the first in your order your Gift is to bear & suffer the most for the increase of the Gospel."[37]

Part of Mother Lucy's worry was that David Darrow himself, the senior Shaker in the West, had gone to the Shawnee settlement, a seemingly risky move in the face of reports of Indian atrocities that the eastern Shakers had surely read. Thus the New Lebanon Ministry suggested that if anyone was to go to speak to the Indians, it might better be the young believers, who were keen to preach the gospel. And the New Lebanon Ministry was clearly appalled at the prospect of Indians coming to live among the young believers at Turtle Creek and elsewhere, and a letter to Darrow plainly tried to quell any aspirations of converting the Indians:

> We believe it [preaching to the Indians] ought to be done by some of the young believers, that . . . have not much gift in relation to white people

and then leave them to act for themselves, & by no means gather them, for they are Indians & will remain so, therefore cannot be brought into the order of white people, but must be saved in their own order & Nation, we believe that God is able to raise up them of their own Nation that will be able to lead & protect them . . . therefore we believe it to be wisdom not to meddle much with them.[38]

However, the Shakers at Turtle Creek continued during the summer of 1807 to pursue their newfound friendship with the Shawnee, unaware of Mother Lucy's concern. In August, Issachar Bates and Richard McNemar made yet another visit to Greenville.[39] The route took them through a prairie covered with ancient Indian earthworks: "all these mounds & the prospects around them are great marks of antiquity & are very striking to the eye."[40] At Greenville, Issachar met Tenskwatawa, saw the enormous Indian meeting house firsthand, and witnessed a worship assembly that continued overnight with singing and dancing.[41]

Soon after this visit, a group of fifty Indians returned to Turtle Creek, arriving on August 28,[42] much to the consternation of the local militia: "We are threatened with being put to the swords point for showing charity to the poor Indians. This threat is from one Saml Trousdale, a Militia captain," declared David Darrow in a letter to New Lebanon.[43] Nonetheless, Issachar Bates, Richard, and Benjamin jointly composed a long letter to the Prophet in which they summarized the opening of the Shaker gospel in America.[44] In that letter, recorded in Issachar's handwriting and entrusted to Tecumseh to deliver to his brother, they expressed strong empathy for the Shawnee in light of the derision directed toward their spiritual reawakening by white detractors, noted that the Shakers had experienced similar frustrations, and took the opportunity to give the Indians a Biblical orientation to the Shakers' worship practices:

> Brothers, we do not think strange if some people call the work of the good-spirit which is among you foolishness and nonsense. It is because they do not understand it. So they say of the work among us. They . . . say our good people who have confessed & put away their sins ought not to dance & rejoice before the great spirit. But we tell them that the good people did so more than three thousand years ago, when they got away from Egypt a country of wicked people & went to a place where the prophets of the great spirit told them. But after awhile them good people did wicked, & then the wicked people stole Dancing away from them. But the good spirit spake by his prophets & said that in the last days, when the day of judgment would come on the wicked, then the good people

should rejoice again in the Dance, both young men & old together, & the good prophets wrote it down more than two thousand years ago, that the good people might see it. If the Interpreter has a Bible, he may find these things in Exodus 15.20 & in the book of Jeremiah 31.14 & in many other places. But brothers, what is the reason that the wicked people do not believe when they see a good people that will not cheat, nor lie, nor drink whiskey, nor quarrel, nor fight, nor do any bad thing to any one? The only reason why they do not believe the work of the good spirit is because they want to be wicked.

We say that the great spirit has raised up prophets of your own, as he had promised long ago. But there are a great many good chiefs and great men, and peacable citizens who love and observe the laws of the country, and want to live in peace, and such are willing that you should be good, and serve the great spirit in your own manner, without being taught by ministers sent from the white people. Brothers, we are still glad to see you, and if a few of you should come down this fall with young George Bluejacket, we will love to talk with you again, but we think it not best for many to come.

Awareness of both local resistance to the Shakers' Indian outreach and the objections expressed by Mother Lucy are strongly implied in Issachar's letter. A second letter signed by David Darrow and sent to the Prophet at the same time notes that the Shakers' chief preachers — probably meaning Issachar Bates, Richard McNemar, and Benjamin Seth Youngs — would shortly be leaving for engagements elsewhere: "Our prophets are going a long journey over the Ohio & Kentucky Rivers to see many people who mean to be good, & they expect to be gone eight or ten weeks from this time, & our people cannot talk any more with you till they return."[45] Perhaps in light of Mother Lucy's reluctance for the Turtle Creek Shakers to get too deeply involved with the Indians, Darrow was trying to ensure that their acquaintance with Tenskwatawa did not intensify any further.

In fact, David Darrow did have another mission in mind for Issachar Bates and Richard McNemar. Later in September, these two together departed for a journey to south-central Kentucky and northern Tennessee, areas that had not yet been visited by the Shakers.[46] As they journeyed south, they were joined by Mathew Houston. The group hoped to reach a district known as Cumberland, in the vicinity of the Cumberland River and its tributaries that formed the watershed of the Tennessee–Kentucky borderlands:

Issachar and Richard . . . with Mathew Houston set out for Cumberland — but after leaving the furthermost believers in that State . . . they went 105 miles still on S. West, towards Cumberland, where they found a people in what is called the Barrens, who were prepared for the Gospel.

Here they Staid and made labors from the 17th of October till the 20th of November: in which time about 25 opened their minds — Among these is one John Rankin; formerly a Presbyterian preacher — a man of abilities & note, and one of the subjects of the late revival . . . The brethren felt a great opening while they were there and this is the only reason why they did not go to Cumberland . . . Observe, Cumberland is not a county, but a kind of district containing many counties in the State of Tennessee . . . These Barrens above mentioned, are very extensive plains in the S. west part of Kentucky, divided into counties and inhabited. Some part of the Barrens are covered with a kind of oak Shrub and resembling the pine plains between Albany and Watervliet — and some parts are covered with groves of different kinds of timber. But no pine — The country round the waters is thickly timbered, the Soil of the Barrens is rich and fertile — The waters are very excellent, and the country is beautiful in nature. — The counties where those have opened their minds are Warren and Logan, and the place where John Rankin lives is called Gasper.[47]

The area known as the "Barrens" was sparsely populated but agriculturally promising, and even more promising spiritually. Issachar, Richard, and Mathew found such receptive audiences in Logan and Warren counties in south-central Kentucky that they never reached the Cumberland region that was their primary goal. The response from John Rankin's congregation — a group of New Lights who had been active in the recent revivals and were looking to resume that spiritual intensity — at a settlement called Gasper River was especially enthusiastic. During about a month of intensive visiting and preaching, Issachar and his companions heard the confessions of many new believers, ranging from the distinguished preacher himself to many local settlers, their extended families, and their slaves. The Eades family, who would become prominent members of the Shaker community at Gasper, was typical in having confessions across two adult generations, along with household mulatto slaves. Members of the McComb family who confessed were intermarried with the Eades family and also had kin in the Ohio River settlement of Red Banks, Kentucky, some one hundred miles away, where the Shakers would be dispatched in a few months.[48]

➤ *Sometimes I travelled with Richard, sometimes with Malcham, Sometimes with John Dunlavy, some times with Mathew H, and sometimes with a part or all of them, and gone from one to two or three months at a time, and once, nine months, rushing & wading thro' many parts of Ohio, Kentucky, Tennessee, Indiana, & Illinois.*

From the year 1806 till 1811, it will be in vain for me to undertake to state any particular dates for it was every time and every where, every how and every place. However, this was my consolation. The above mentioned brethren who were my companions in tribulation, were strong & faithful.[49]

More than anything else during the first five or six full years in the West, Issachar Bates was a creature of the road. Having decided to widen their circle well beyond Turtle Creek, the leading Shakers in Ohio needed to keep evangelists actively moving through the region. As openings for the Shaker message were established and conversions began in various places, the need for travel to those places did not subside; rather, it intensified. The Shakers were all too aware of the vulnerability of new converts. David Darrow wrote that no man would sow crops in the wilderness then go off and leave them unfenced and untended, and "[s]o it is in the gospel."[50] Once a group of young believers was established, it had to be nurtured carefully, which necessitated regular and frequent visits. Persecution from community, personal misgivings, family pressures, inability to adhere to the practical demands of the Shaker faith — these and more might provide justification for backsliding. As the Shakers' efforts yielded converts across a nearly three-hundred-mile wide expanse, regular visits meant that some of the old believers together with some of the more stalwart and dependable young believers were almost continuously on the road. When writing his autobiography in 1832, Issachar Bates looked back on the period of 1806 to 1811 as a virtual blur of constant movement. And indeed it was. But this life of perpetual travel meant that Issachar Bates was perceived by many young believers — rightly or wrongly, by virtue of being a messenger — as one of the authors of their new faith. His presence during initial conversions and his subsequent visits to multiple areas of concentrated evangelism — Paint Lick, Eagle Creek, Beaver Creek, Shawnee Run, Gasper River, Red Banks — gave Issachar the opportunity to forge lasting relationships across the western Shaker world. Years later, he would still be seen as a "father" figure by Shakers from one end of the West to the other.

We are Sensible that not all of any of us have fully got rid of that soft delicate & retired manner of sense, or in other words that Neat complete and orderly way & Feeling in which we have lived in the Church — So that the ways & Methods of the People in the Wilderness appear the more raw

& uncultivated ... & our Present time of trial & Bodily separation from the church is rendered the more Severe. We have not yet become fully seasoned to hardships, our feelings and abilities are not so prepared & adapted to the rough & rugged manners that are abroad in the world.[51]

Issachar Bates was unique among the old believers in that he arrived in the West well accustomed to frontier conditions. Together with Benjamin Seth Youngs, he had become inured to itinerant rural preaching during his early years of Shaker life. But for the other old believers, adapting to the frontier was a struggle, because it differed so sharply from their orderly existence as eastern Shakers. Most old believers were less effective at "pioneer work," namely, mingling with the rough masses and eliciting initial conversions. But they could help nurture converts during the many subsequent visits undertaken. And traveling the long trails and byways of Kentucky and Ohio with other old believers gave Issachar many unforgettable interludes for conversation, fellowship, and sharing of confidences.

I learned something from all my companions with whom I traveled. And from my beloved Elder John M . . . I learned much good. Let me never forget him! With him, with Father David, and all the eastern Elders I have traveled more or less, in visiting believers, and I was always learning something of them. Tho' they were not much called into the pioneer work in which we, (little Benjamin, myself & others) were, yet, they were our strength and our support; and may they be blessed, both male and female forever.[52]

Issachar Bates seldom traveled alone during this period. Many of the journeys were in company with some of the strongest of the young believers, others were with various old believers. Those Shakers with the strongest skills at "pioneer work" included a relatively small set of men: Issachar Bates and Benjamin Seth Youngs among the old believers and Richard McNemar, Mathew Houston, Malcolm Worley, and John Dunlavy among the young. It is worth nothing that the latter four were already well-known preachers in the region when they came to Shakerism, already familiar with the camp-meeting revivals of the region.

Then I took John Dunlavy (leaving Mathew H & Samuel Sering to guard the people) & went to the Red Bank, where we had some strange movements. A large body of people assembled, at the house of John McComb.[53]

In January of 1808, Issachar Bates led a group back to Gasper River to visit the new converts there. While there, they decided to journey up to Red Banks, Kentucky, on the Ohio River. This was new territory for the Shakers, but they were confident of a cordial reception by the family of John McComb, whose kin were among the new converts at Gasper. A multitude of local people gathered to hear the traveling Shaker preachers. There Issachar had an unusual encounter with the wife of a prominent Kentucky politician:

John preached first; and while he was speaking I noticed a very nice look-ing woman dressed in black silk, who paid uncommon attention to what was said. After he was thro' I arose & spake, confirming what had been said and adding more. And as soon as I ceased speaking, this woman stepped up to me & took me by the hand and said "Come thou blessed man of God, I want you should go with me," And she held her clinch and led me thro' the crowd about twenty rods from them and stopped: "Now," said she, "I want you should lift your hands with me to Heaven, and give thanks to God, that I have lived to hear the everlasting Gospel." I com-plied. "Now," said she, "I will confess my sins." And at it she went; and O! the beauty & honesty of that woman's soul! And after she was thro', she called to her little son (who had been standing afar off wondering what had befallen his Mother), and said, "Washington, Come here my son and see Jesus Christ"! So he came on, & took me by the hand, and I said, you may see a servant of Jesus Christ, but I felt awfully mortified.
When I come to find out with whom I had been dealing, behold it was General Posey's lady! He was then in the assembly at Frankfort: he was afterwards governor of Indiana. But when he returned home, and found the state his wife was in, he was in great distress, but behaved himself well. And they settled the matter on this wise; that she would live with him, only she would have a room & a bed to herself & never more sleep with him. And so it stood ever since; for she is a real daughter of Abraham.[54]

The typical frontier assemblies that the Shakers addressed seldom in-cluded handsome women dressed in fine silk. Issachar Bates was struck by this woman's appearance even before she approached him, and he was prob-ably too surprised to protest when she took him by the hand in front of the entire crowd and began to lead him away. Some hundred yards gave them privacy, though her little son followed along after them. For Issachar, being approached in the midst of a worship meeting by a "world's person" (as the Shakers commonly referred to non-Shakers they confronted) who wished to confess on the spot was not unheard of. But such a response from a woman of obvious wealth, beauty, and social standing was extraordinary indeed. More remarkable still was the spiritual depth and sincerity of her confession, impressing Issachar as few individual confessions ever did. He was embarrassed when the woman introduced him to her son Washington as "Jesus Christ." But he was shocked when the woman introduced herself as Mary Posey, the wife of General Thomas Posey, an elected official who had recently run for governor in the state of Kentucky.

To Issachar Bates, the name of Thomas Posey was familiar and venerable. A Virginia native and a friend of George Washington, Posey had been an officer in the Revolutionary War, present at some of the same engagements as fifer Issachar Bates.[55] In the 1790s, Posey had re-entered the army as a brigadier general and served with Anthony Wayne in the campaigns against the Indians of the Northwest. Mary Thornton Posey, a wealthy widow from Virginia gentry, was his second wife. By 1804 they had purchased a large piece of land a few miles from Red Banks, Kentucky, where they established an estate called Longview.[56]

Issachar Bates's account of Mary Posey's confession is a rare example of the Shakers attracting a person of elite social standing and even moderate fame. His claim of Mary Posey's spiritual commitment to the Shakers is impossible to verify independently, though it is quite plausible. Certainly, their meeting could have taken place. Around 1808, Thomas Posey was spending most of his time in Frankfort, the state capital, leaving his wife, who was then fifty-two, at their Red Bank estate with their nine-year-old son, Washington.[57] Mary was known for her attraction to evangelical religion, and even for her tendency to seek out charismatic traveling preachers. Her friends noted that she "took the side of religion." Thomas Posey's contemporary biographer depicts Mary as sympathetic to public conversion experiences. Mary Posey's striking appearance is also reflected in the historical record. A friend of the Posey's describe her as "a beauty in her youth," who in middle-age was "a fine and stately person."[58]

Perhaps the most intriguing aspect of Issachar Bates's account of his meeting with Mary Posey is his claim that she and her famous husband arrived at an arrangement whereby she would live a celibate life in their household. Issachar's record of their meeting was written down in 1832, yet he refers to her in present tense, implying that he maintained contact with her and was still aware of her adherence to certain Shaker principles. The only evidence of a subsequent meeting with Mary Posey, however, is a notation that Issachar and other Shakers visited the home of John Posey on May 28, 1808, a few months after their first visit to Red Banks. John Posey was Mary's adult stepson, to whom she was very close, who lived with his wife Lucy on a farm a few miles west of Red Banks. This visit provided a likely opportunity for the Shakers to meet Mary again and to counsel her on her new faith. In fact, Issachar's assertion of Mary's devotion to Shaker tenets is not contradicted by anything in the historical record. Thomas Posey's biographer notes that the couple spent most of their time apart until 1810, due to his political career, and from 1810 to the end of his life in 1818 they lived almost entirely apart, with Mary spending most of her time in her children's households. She left behind some correspondence, which portrays her as entirely happy and very involved in the life of her children and grandchildren.[59] Like the believing woman of the Gospel of Luke, who boldly declared she deserved to be healed by Jesus on the Sabbath because she was a "daughter of Abraham," perhaps Mary Posey impressed upon Issachar Bates—who called her a "daughter of Abraham"—that she deserved the Shaker gospel, though her elite social standing prohibited her from living among the Shakers.

The Shakers gained about two dozen converts in in Red Banks in 1808, and they expanded their efforts still further—though not without resistance. Issachar Bates relates an encounter with a mob in nearby Indiana Territory in the fall of that year:

> Soon after we arrived & began visiting, a mob of 12 came upon us on horse back, with ropes to bind us, headed by another John Thompson.[60] He stepped up to me & said, "Come, prepare yourselves to move." "Move where," said I. "Out of this country," said he, "for you ruined a fine neighborhood & now we intend to fix you. Your hats are too big, we shall have a part of them off and your coats are too long, we shall have a part of them off. And seeing you will have nothing to do with women, we will fix you, so that you will not be able to perform." "Well," said I, "have you any precept?" "Yes, precept enough for you." "Well you must show it." "D—d you, get on your horses, for you shall go." "Well I will tell you up and down, we shall not go with a mob." Then John Hadden spoke: "If you don't go & get your horses, I will get them, for you shall go. So where are they?" "They are in William Berry's stable . . . But if you get them we shall not get onto them." "Well then we will put you on." "Well then we will get off again." "Well then we will tie you on." "Well, you will have a hard job of it, before you get thro." And by this time, all the rest of the mob were laughing, and said, "Come let us go." So they started; but John Thompson looked back & let off these words, "If you ain't gone before Saturday night, I'll be d—d if you don't go dead or alive."[61]

This account exhibits Issachar Bates's use of droll humor as a strategy to cope with persecutors. Refusing to be intimidated, Issachar enlisted the aid of local authorities "who stilled them very quick" when the men returned to carry out their threats. But Issachar also writes that he experienced the worst harassment in the midst of worship meetings, because detractors perceived that he used music and dance to ensnare susceptible onlookers.

> Now this was the cause of a great deal of my persecution.[62] As I was a singer, it always fell to my lot to sing the first laboring song, in breaking the way to worship God in the dance. And whenever they broke thro' into the mortifying work, they were generally exercised with the power and gifts of God. And this, however solemn, would stir up the enemies of the cross, in particular at me, as being the cause of this strange work. But I always escaped their hands, & my life has been given me for a prey unto this day.[63]

Even amid the excitement and color of his fast-paced life in the West, Issachar also brooded on his wife and children. A lengthy postscript added to a letter he wrote to his friend Seth Youngs Wells in December 1808 reveals his inner conflict over his life in the west, as well as his lingering affectionate concern for his wife, Lovina: "Sister Levina . . . I have a few lines for you by your self . . . I want that you should send me word positively that you are glad that I am in this country and that you wish me to stay as long as God has any work for me to do. Every sensation of my soul is stretched toward the west. I cannot look toward the east at present."[64] Issachar needed reassurance. Even though he clearly had no intention of returning east anytime soon, he still harbored misgivings that his life in the West was inflicting unhappiness upon Lovina. He needed an unambiguous guarantee, from her own pen, that she did not begrudge him the life on the western frontier that he so plainly reveled in. Seldom has a Shaker's loving concern for the feelings of his spouse been so candidly recorded. He ended the message, "I want you to be strong, I want you to be comfortable . . . I want you to be saved with a great salvation. I hope to have the best news from you that ever I did and shall comfort myself with this. Farewell in love . . . Issachar."

Music and poetry likely offered welcome distractions whenever Issachar's thoughts turned to his wife and family. Music was a vital part of his life during this period of constant travel evangelism and visiting of young believers. Already a poet whose published work reflected inspiration drawn from the experience of travel, Issachar continued to use his journeys to generate lyrics and tunes for new hymns.[65] Hymns were essential features of Shaker frontier worship because the lyrics helped to transmit the tenets of Shaker doctrine, which was still evolving and just beginning to take written form.[66] Ironically, both Issachar and his friend Benjamin were deeply involved during these years in articulating Shaker doctrine—Benjamin through his role as lead author of *The Testimony of Christ's Second Appearing*, the first published expostulation of Shaker theology,[67] and Issachar through the authorship of long doctrinal and spiritual hymns. Indeed, although Benjamin's volume was a deservedly celebrated achievement, the hymns being written in this period by Issachar and Richard McNemar, the other chief early hymn writer in the West, were of equal or even greater influence as instructional tools. Relatively few young believers would have had access to a printed work such as Benjamin's *Testimony*. But multiple hymns were sung and taught at worship meetings, creating obvious opportunities to explain and reinforce Shaker doctrine and inculcate converts in Shaker values and practices. As a letter from Ohio to New Lebanon remarked, "our songs are great conviction and strength to the people."[68] Although Issachar Bates is not remembered as one of Shakerism's learned theologians, he was nonetheless deeply influential in articulating Shaker doctrine and spirituality in ways that were perhaps more appealing and palatable to the average person than weighty theological tomes.

One of Issachar Bates's influential hymns from this period is "Great Shaker" (see appendix 2). Its text takes on a key distinguishing feature of Shaker theology—namely, the dual-gendered nature of God—and lays out a radical argument that the child Jesus was the first Shaker, all in a metrically complex pattern unusual in Shaker hymnody. In its verses can be seen an early explication of "Mother wisdom" being personified as the female half of God, along with the characterization of Jesus' death as the "murder" of "this shaker." Another verse names "Anna" Lee as the revelator of Shaker doctrine and even alludes to her early period in a Quaker congregation. The complex text must have held wide appeal, because it can be found reproduced in dozens of unique manuscript hymnals compiled by western and eastern Shakers alike.[69]

Many of Issachar hymns from this period were included in the Shakers' first printed hymn book, *Millennial Praises*, published at Hancock, Massachusetts, in 1812. The idea to publish a hymn book was a direct consequence of the Shakers' western expansion.[70] Becoming more active in frontier camp-meeting settings highlighted the utility of hymns as tools to teach Shaker doctrine and of hymn-singing to generate atmospheres of shared camaraderie with potential converts. Richard McNemar was, if possible, an even more avid poet than Issachar and equally devoted to generating a foundational repertoire of hymns reflecting the full range of Shaker doctrine and spirituality. Starting in 1807, correspondence from the West commonly contained hymns, which encouraged eastern Shakers to compose hymns, too. The church at New Lebanon soon decided to compile and print a hymnal, because scribes could not copy hymns fast enough to satisfy believers. At least 94 of the 140 hymns in *Millennial Praises* were composed in the West; of those, about 70 were composed by Richard McNemar alone, and another dozen were composed by Issachar. In one of those, "Spiritual Wine," Issachar uses drunkenness as a metaphor for spiritual liberation of Shakerism. In another, "Old Adam Disturbed," he scrutinizes the Shaker attitude toward marriage. Another, "Gospel Sound," apparently draws from his own conversion experience of initial relief at the confession of "secret sins," followed by a protracted period of adjustment to the new life of renunciation of sin and withstanding of persecution: "But Oh, alas! How soon we found / We were not free from Satan's ground! / We had our battles yet to fight / Against the flesh with all our might." Issachar incorporates some Shaker history in "The Gospel Commencement," telling of the arrival of the Shaker message from England and subsequent spread. And in "The Journey to Canaan," he uses the story of the Israelites' biblical wanderings in the wilderness to parallel the actual wilderness journeys that he and many on the frontier experienced as a fact of life. One of his most interesting early hymn texts, "Rights of Conscience," uses a narration of George Washington's heroic deeds as a starting point to assert that the Shaker message is a fulfillment of the Revolution's true cause, the securing of "rights of conscience" for all Americans. It is a hymn in which Issachar clarifies his continued patriotism, and he probably used it to appeal to the many patriots and veterans in his crowds of listeners.

One hymn by Issachar Bates that effectively captures the often frenetic journeying of the years from 1806 to 1810 is called "No Escape from Judgment" (see appendix 2). In ten rollicking stanzas laced liberally with puns and regional place names, it takes the singer/reader on a headlong journey through the early western frontier of Shakerism, depicting the Shaker gospel as relentlessly chasing down the foes that would dare to combat it, with the clear message that naysayers can run, but they cannot hide:

> Your Mad River flight Has not been out of sight
> Nor your Stantown battery of scorn,
> Your White Water plot will burn you so hot,
> You will wish you had never been born.
> Your Springfield stronghold With her warriors so bold
> In regions of darkness are cast

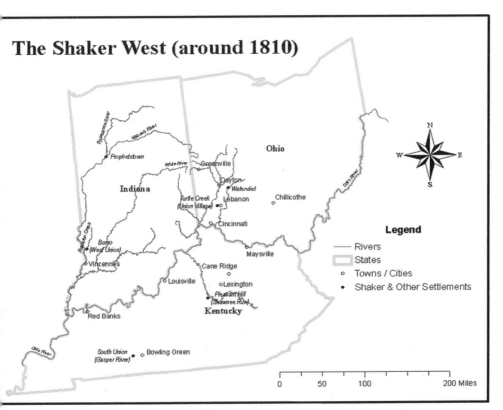

The Shaker West (around 1810)

6.4 *The Shaker West, around 1810. By 1810 five Shaker settlements had been established in the "West." This map reflects locations where the Shakers interacted with Indians, including Greenville, Ohio, and Prophetstown, on the Wabash River in Indiana Territory, as well as other communities frequented by Shakers. (Map by Carol Medlicott and Hongmei Wang.)*

You may fortify Caneridge And lay Stone for your bridge
But your mortar's untempered at last.

If Kentucky grows too hot You may hunt another spot
For a season to cover your sins
But it is a poor relief To be running like a thief
With a conscience tormented within
You may go to the Wabash To find ease to the flesh
But Busrow is all in a flame
You may flee to Elk or Duck Or tarry in Kentuck
But the gospel will bring you to shame.[71]

By now there were many locations in the region demanding the Shakers' attention (figure 6.4) During the brief interludes in the years leading up to

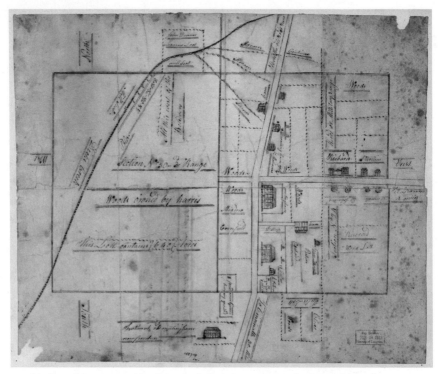

6.5 *"A plan of the section of land on which the believers live in the State of Ohio,"* circa 1810. (*Library of Congress.*)

1811 when Issachar was not traveling, he returned to the place he considered his western home, namely the "house of David," built for the family of old believers at Turtle Creek. There he joined in with whatever work was most pressing—surveying, building, preparing fields, or planting. Possessing some skills as a gardener and nurseryman, he began planning orchards of nut trees at Turtle Creek and proudly showed his newly planted pecan trees to William Deming and Eliab Harlow, two visitors from New Lebanon, in July of 1810.[72]

As the Shakers expanded their property holdings at Turtle Creek (figure 6.5), they began to build more structures, diversify their agricultural initiatives, and produce manufactured and farm-related items to sell. But the prosperity of the Turtle Creek community and its obvious aspirations for spiritual and temporal growth made it an easy target for abuse. In the summer of 1809, Issachar was home for most of August, in between journeys to central Ohio and to the Wabash River region. During that month, the old believers' dwelling at Turtle Creek experienced a break-in by robbers. Issachar had arrived home just that night, carrying a large amount of money. His role in the story of the robbery attempt was recorded many years later by an Ohio Shaker:

> Issachar Bates was expected home from Cincinnati where he had gone to draw from three to four hundred dollars from the bank. He was on horseback coming home, had passed through Lebanon and west of town some distance. On the road his horse stopped, and would not go another step forward. Finally Issachar thinking the horse might know more than himself dropped the bridle loose, and the horse instantly turned into the woods for home. There was a misty rain and the night was dark.
>
> No one in the family knew when Issachar arrived. In the house and tired, he noticed a vacated bed nearer than his own room, and crept therein with his money.
>
> He awoke at the crash of the front door falling in (broken by fence rails) and the clock striking 12. Money was his thought, and he scattered what he had brought amongst the straw in his bed tick, then turned on his face and went to hard snoring (in pretence). The robbers with torches in hand went to Issachar's room and swearing about old Bates being so late.
>
> Issachar's money was saved. The robbers having searched the drawers of the house, the chests, the trunks, and the brethren's pockets amassed six dollars.[73]

This account implies that the robbers were expecting Issachar's return, aware that he would be carrying money. Richard McNemar, who was also home the night of the robbery, observed the confusion that ensued when a young Shaker threw a chair down the stairs to obstruct the robbers' rampage through the house. Stimulated, Richard immediately sat down and wrote a poem about the incident, which was read at meeting the next morning.[74]

By 1810, the settlement at Shawnee Run had been launched by sending a team of old believers to serve as elders. A preliminary covenant had been executed there to move the believers from their private family units into collective dwellings under the Shaker plan for communitarianism known as "joint interest." David Darrow was contemplating a similar launch of other communities in Indiana Territory and at Gasper River, but Turtle Creek itself had not yet been brought into "gospel order" (i.e., spiritual order) under the economic joint interest. So in the spring of 1810, that process began with the implementation of a covenant for the members of Darrow's small family. In reality, that family had been functioning as a "Church order" since moving into its newly built dwelling house nearly four years before, but the old believers and others who made up the family had no covenant to formally bind them together and order their temporal and spiritual relationships. Having one would provide a model for the young believers and a stimulus to establish more collective families. This covenant asserted the family's intention to live under the spiritual care of David Darrow on the premises purchased by the church, and it pledged signatories' mutual support of one another. It is a document remarkably vague as to management of collective assets. It stipulates only that signatories not bring any debts against the family and that signatories be free to withdraw any property they bring in with them if they leave the family to reside in another family. This covenant is the only one ever signed by Issachar Bates during his thirty-year residence in the West, a point that would rear its head more than twenty years later, when he and Richard McNemar together labored over the revision of a covenant document for the village of Watervliet, Ohio.

> *I have now literally run a long crooked race . . . I traveled 38,000 miles and most of it on foot. Since that time . . . I have heard the first confession of sins from the mouth of about 1100 persons. And in that time I have been mobbed and persecuted in every place and been called by almost every base name that could be thought of and my life threatened as often as any dog's life. In Ohio they called me "Bellwether." In Kentucky they called me "Old Rough and Ready." They have called me any name but Issachar Bates. But I have never regarded it, for it was what I expected from this generation. In all this time I have a good conscience, for I know that I have never wronged one of my persecutors and that has been my comfort and peace. And also on the other hand I have been filled with joy and comfort whenever I visited the different societies where they had been honestly taking up the cross. To see them filled with the power and gifts of God, this made ample amends for all my persecution.*[75]

Because of Issachar Bates's travels and labors from 1806 to 1810, Shakerism advanced farther than ever throughout the western frontier, beginning to push even to the very margins of settled country in western Indiana Territory. Along the way, Issachar had encountered some of the region's most intriguing characters — fiery preachers and Indian warriors, an aristocratic general's wife and a Shawnee shaman. He had withstood persecution and helped lay the foundations of what would become the largest Shaker communities in the West — Turtle Creek, Shawnee Run, and Gasper River (later called Union Village, Pleasant Hill, and South Union, respectively) — along with the community that would eventually become his longest-running western home,

Beaver Creek (later called Watervliet), Ohio. Issachar's challenges in these years forced him to draw deeply from his personal resources—preaching, songwriting, humor, and sheer persistence to stay on the trail day after day as he journeyed from one end of the region to the other. But in Issachar's own words, "This work it has begun / And has gather'd one by one / Till Zion's foundation is laid."[76]

CHAPTER 7

"What trials yet before us lay"

TRIBULATION ON THE WABASH

Each furnished with his staff and knapsack, And some provisions for the way
We ventured on without conceiving, What trials yet before us lay.
— Issachar Bates, "A Winter Journey to Busroe"

The summer of 1808 found Issachar Bates and his "fellow travelers" venturing even further west to the very edge of white settlement in Indiana Territory, over two hundred miles from Turtle Creek. A lively cluster of local families along Busseron Creek, a small but navigable tributary of the Wabash River just north of the territorial capital of Vincennes in Knox County, would form the nucleus of the westernmost Shaker outpost. Here the Shakers got a rocky start. Strong resistance from local preachers necessitated several difficult journeys by Issachar and others to keep the converts' zeal from flagging. And in 1811, Issachar was sent to temporarily assist four select individuals from Turtle Creek who had taken charge of the "Busro" society as its first presiding elders. Once there, he faced conditions as challenging as any he had ever experienced. In addition to the disease-ridden climate, the believers' land lay at the margin of the settled area, with the Shawnee and other tribes dominating the adjacent regions. While the Shakers at Busro labored to establish a productive community, they were literally thrown off-balance by the New Madrid earthquakes and soon even more terrified to find themselves in the crosshairs of the coming war between the Americans and the British.

Issachar and his company went still further . . . About 70 opened their minds at one place among which number are three able preachers. This is on the Wabash River in the Indiani territory . . . about 160 miles in a west direction from where we live but we know of no road to this place only round about through Kentucky. Issachar went first to Mercer County in Kentucky 144 miles in a south direction from here, thence 130 miles southwest to Gasper in Logan County, thence 100 miles bearing a little west of north to the Red Banks . . . then crossed the Ohio and traveled 85 miles due north to the Wabash in Knox County in the Indiani Territory.[1]

For two and a half years, Issachar Bates and his preacher companions had moved almost constantly through the region. As people "opened their minds" in one place, they commonly told the Shakers of receptive kin and friends elsewhere. Thus had Issachar Bates been led to Red Banks, Kentucky, first in February 1808 and then — along with Mathew Houston, John Dunlavy, Malcolm Worley, and James Hodge — again in May. During the latter visit, the group decided to press north to seek a New Light preacher named Robert Houston, who was probably Mathew's elder brother.[2] Like Mathew, Robert Houston was born in Virginia in the late 1760s, had migrated to Kentucky, and had broken away from the Presbyterian Church in 1803 at the same time as had so many associates of Barton Stone and Richard McNemar, including Mathew Houston. By 1806 Robert Houston had moved to frontier Indiana Territory near Vincennes, the territorial capital.[3]

Red Banks, Kentucky, lay on a looping meander of the Ohio River directly adjacent to Indiana Territory. It was also very close to areas of Indian activity just to the west in southern Illinois Territory, where the Shawnee traveled seasonally for hunting and salt supply. Sixty miles due north lay Vincennes, a thriving frontier town on the Wabash River founded by the French in 1732, which had been a key western military outpost since the Revolutionary War. Since Vincennes had been named capital of Indiana Territory in 1800, military authorities in the region had worked to establish overland trails, or "traces," linking it with other population centers. Some of these integrated older Indian or animal trails, such as the Buffalo Trace, surveyed in 1805 between the falls of the Ohio at Louisville and Vincennes to the west. About the same time, Vincennes residents had also petitioned the U.S. government to support the development of a trace between Vincennes and Red Banks, and this led to the establishment of forts, taverns, and ferry crossings along the route. In 1807, soldiers from Vincennes were ordered to patrol the Red Banks Trail to discourage Indians from interfering with white travelers.[4]

The decision of the Shakers to push north from Red Banks to seek Robert Houston may well have been influenced by the fact that the Red Banks Trail had been so recently secured. In any case, they located Robert Houston, together with other leading members of a thriving New Lights congregation a short distance north of Vincennes living around Busseron Creek, a navigable tributary of the Wabash River. Its name derived from Francois Busseron, a leading French citizen of eighteenth-century Vincennes.[5] "Busseron" was applied to both the creek and the extreme northern part of Knox County in which Vincennes was situated, and its Anglicization reflected a range of spellings — from Busserow to Busro.

↝ *Then from the Red Banks we crossed the Ohio into Indiana, went to Busroe Creek on the Wabash, and in that place and in the borders of Illinois we tarried three weeks, preaching, singing and dancing: for here were a people waiting for us and they were very swift to hear, and before we left that place there were seventy persons that confessed their sins, & we left them all rejoicing.*[6]

In 1808 Vincennes was a thriving city of about three thousand people.[7] With nearly a century of European settlement, it far outstripped the cultural sophistication of most frontier outposts. A university was already established, as well as a subscription library. The territorial governor, William Henry Harrison, lived in a gracious mansion called Grouseland, an architectural gem (figure 7.1). The population of the area reflected the frontier melting pot at its most extreme. French, Spanish, Anglo-American, African-American, and Indian all mingled in the region. The Shakers were aware of this immediately. One of their first meetings in the area drew "a blessed assembly of people, white, yellow, & black."[8] Intermarriage was common, producing the "Wabash creole" that some were beginning to recognize as a singular "breed" of Americans.[9] French Catholicism mingled with Baptist and New Light preachers, along with circuit-riding Methodists, to produce a diverse religious environment.

> Now this wonderful movement was so great and this being only a Territory, I did not know whether there was any government over the devil at all, so I told the Brethren I determined to call & see the Governor & know the worst. So we called at his house in Vincennes. His wife told us, he had rode out, "but I think you will meet him," and we did, & said to him, "Governor Harrison, we have been up to Busro, preaching our faith, & a number have embraced it, & we want to know if there are any kind of laws in this Territory to protect them?" "The same law" said he, "that there is in any of the United States. You have a right to preach your faith, & any have a right to embrace it. So you need not be uneasy. I will protect you." And he has always been up to his word, for we soon had to come to a proof of it.[10]

Because Indiana was still only a territory, Issachar Bates and the other Shaker evangelists wondered whether their missionary efforts might lack the legal protections offered by the U.S. Constitution. Yet Issachar was brash to confront Governor Harrison directly. That he did so — and that this initial meeting was the foundation for a long productive relationship between Harrison

7.1 *Issachar Bates visited William Henry Harrison, governor of Indiana Territory, at his mansion, Grouseland, in Vincennes. (Photo by author.)*

and the Shakers—testifies to one of Issachar's known traits, namely an un-canny ability to relate to people of any social class, from elite gentlemen to the basest scoundrel.[11] A personal guarantee from Harrison was reassuring, and the Shakers departed Indiana that June confident they had made a good beginning.

Autumn of 1808 found Issachar back in the Wabash region with Mathew Houston and Malcolm Worley a second time. During October and Novem-ber, they moved back and forth among the Busro converts and those at Red Banks and further south at Gasper River.[12] Their greatest concern for the Busro converts was their susceptibility to aggressive overtures by Peter Cart-wright, the chief Methodist evangelist of the area. Cartwright had learned that the Shakers claimed "the millennium was unfolding right then and there in the mud and swamps of Busro, Indiana," and he traveled there expressly to "battle" the Shakers.[13] As 1808 closed, the Shakers were fearful of losing the gains they had made there.

The sixteenth day of January,
Thru stormy rains, thru ice and snow,

From Turtle Creek we took our journey,
To see the brethren at Busro.
Near sev'nty miles we had to travel,
Before we left the settlement;
A howling wilderness before us,
A thousand furlongs in extent.[14]

By January 1809, the situation at Busro was believed to be dire. "Father" David Darrow at Turtle Creek valued the efforts put into the Wabash region too highly to permit failure and dispatched Issachar and Benjamin, together with Richard McNemar to make up a threesome. Rather than take the circuitous route through Kentucky, the men decided to attempt the journey along a newly blazed route leading from Cincinnati to Vincennes directly across the wilderness of southern Indiana Territory. The crossing was risky. There were many Indian settlements along the rivers in that area where, not many years before, Moravian missionaries had suffered appalling torture. White settlers were few and far between, so finding inns and provisions for travel by horse was not an option. Weather conditions were not conducive to foot travel. But the men were confident they could make it through. They packed knapsacks with a five-day food supply and set out.

The hoped-for five-day walk to Busro turned into a sixteen-day nightmare during which the three Shakers nearly died of hunger and exposure. A description of the ordeal written by Joseph Allen, one of the old believers at Turtle Creek, soon after their return that spring deserves to be read in full.

I send a little poem, compos'd on the journey of Benjamin, Issachar, and Richard, to the Wabash River in the Indiana Territory, about 230 miles west of this place. For the better understanding of which, it is proper to observe, that the circumstances of the believers at Busro indispensably required a visit at that inclement season of the year. That in consequence of a remarkable flood, and the want of ferries in the wilderness, it was deemed wholly impracticable to go thru with horses; therefore the only alternative that remained was to perform the journey on foot, and carry provision sufficient to subsist on, thru the uninhabited wilderness. They were conveyed with a couple of horses to Whitewater, about 35 miles; thence their way lay down the Ohio river, from which the creeks that empty into it had been so backed up and frozen over, and the water fallen from the ice, that they had to travel for miles on broken ice: some of those creeks they cross'd on broken ice; others being open, they waded the water, which was excessively cold. Locry was the last of these streams;

where they were detained one day, in consequence of high water, from rain, which had fallen the day before. Here they left the inhabitants, and the backwaters of Ohio, and steered thru the woods to a new road, which was cut last summer, from Post Vincent on the Wabash, and terminated on Locry, seven miles above the settlement; which road they followed thru the rest of the wilderness. The brethren returned by the same route, thru many scenes of difficulty, especially in passing rivers, creeks, and overflowed lands; some of which they had to wade for miles and particular parts of which were impassable by any other way than by poling themselves along upon old logs, which they found afloat. However, they arrived home in safety, March 29th, and are now in good health. And we are all much satisfied with their journey, and the good account we have received from the believers at Busro.[15]

As the journey began, some of the most miserable winter weather imaginable descended on the area — heavy snow and bitter cold, followed by sleet and rain. The men began by following the well-populated Ohio River route out of Cincinnati, as far as the mouth of Laughery (Locry) Creek, near present-day Aurora, Indiana. Finally they turned away from the river, hoping to find the "new and unfrequented road"[16] leading from Cincinnati to Vincennes. They were probably seeking the route first blazed by a Captain E. Kibbey in 1799, but which had not been fully laid out for several years.[17] But the men found little evidence of a route of any kind. The area today remains a complex watershed, encompassing multiple branches of several rivers, together with countless creeks. In the winter of 1809, the weather had brought most of the rivers out of their banks, forming vast expanses of icy standing water, a "horrid watery world," as Issachar would later write.

But even in these desolate surroundings, music enlivened the Shakers. At one point, desperate to find high ground to survey the landscape and search for a way through, the men ascended a hill and were relieved to see they had made more progress than they thought:

> After having, with much difficulty, danger, and fatigue, succeeded in crossing a very wide extended branch of the river Locry, they rested from midnight till morning; and then resumed their course and traveled till they reached the summit of a hill; at which place they halted, and Br. Issachar received and sung the above tune. And they united in the dance, thanking God in their hearts, for the preservation of their lives & their health and strength. The sufferings they endured on this journey are briefly sketched in a poem.[18]

Singing and dancing together probably warmed them and revived their spirits (see appendix 2, "Given by Inspiration"). But many miserable days still remained, during which the men grew lost. They tried to fashion rafts with floating logs, as well as snowshoes, all in hopes of crossing the icy quagmire, but they only succeeded in soaking themselves and contracting frostbite. Their food ran out, and they were forced to eat carrion that they found in the woods. Finally, they found a settler's cabin, where they were given shelter and a much-needed meal. Neither the sixteen-stanza ballad that Issachar composed to commemorate the journey nor any other writings about the event note the fact that Issachar passed his fifty-first birthday toward the ordeal's end. Nor is any mention made of what the men specifically accomplished upon reaching Busro.

The winter trip across the frigid Indiana wilderness did generate one lasting achievement in the form of Issachar's ballad, usually referred to as "Journey to Busro" or "Winter Journey to Busro." Sent to the East only a few months after the journey's end, the ballad was copied widely across the Shaker world for the next several decades and integrated into hymn books, journals, and other writings. When Benjamin Seth Youngs visited Enfield, Connecticut, almost twenty years later, in 1827, he reminisced about the journey and sang the ballad so others could learn it. Because Issachar's ballad immortalized the "journey to Busro," the Shaker experience in Indiana remained a vivid and lasting story for Shakers everywhere, even for those Shakers who lived far from the West. References to it can be found throughout Shaker writings about the West, and Issachar's harrowing wintertime "Journey to Busro" became a motif in Shaker culture for the entire initiative of western expansion.

Throughout 1809 and 1810, Issachar Bates and other Shakers from Turtle Creek and elsewhere traveled back and forth to Busro, continuing to shore up the converts and assess the prospects for establishing a full-fledged community there.[19] The hardships of the wilderness route across Indiana Territory did not abate. During an eleven-day trek in 1810, the Shakers saw bears, wolf, and "panthers" — probably mountain lion — fashioned Indian-style brush shelters, and struggled to avoid quicksand, which nearly swallowed Benjamin Seth Youngs and his horse.[20] But the many trips were necessary if a community was to be launched. Other groups of believers were urged to move to the Indiana location to form a consolidated group, specifically the converts from Red Banks, Kentucky, and a large group from a settlement called Eagle Creek in Adams County, Ohio, southeast of Cincinnati.

By the middle of 1810 the Busro settlement was making a promising start, with many ardent families and nearly a thousand acres of land. Governor

Harrison remained aware of the Shakers' presence and continued to interact with them. Harrison's correspondence with the Secretary of War in May 1810 demonstrates that he hoped to use the Shakers — and Issachar Bates specifically — as emissaries to the Shawnee Prophet Tenskwatawa, who had moved his base from western Ohio to the village of Prophetstown on the upper Wabash, coincidentally about the time that the Shakers first began to gather converts near Vincennes.

> I have also sent for the leading member of the Shaker Society (a religious sect of very extraordinary principles which you may have heard of) who resides about 20 miles from this place, with the intention of prevailing upon him to take a speech to the Prophet. This scoundrel (the Prophet) affects to follow the Shaker principles in everything but the vow of celebacy, and the above mentioned leader has assured me that he believes the Prophet to be under the same divine inspiration that he himself is (a circumstance by no means improbable) but that for reasons growing out of his situation as a savage he was still permitted with his Indian followers to cohabit with women.[21]

Harrison implies that he has been well apprised of the Shakers' interactions with the "religious Shawnee." Though Issachar Bates is not named in his passage, he was the only "leading member" among the Shakers known to Harrison who was also personally familiar with Tenskwatawa. The confident manner of this Shaker leader, as characterized by Harrison, is entirely consistent with Issachar Bates. Whether or not Issachar ever consented to deliver a message to the Shawnee on Harrison's behalf, the exchange confirms the governor was in ongoing dialogue with the Shakers themselves.[22]

But although the Shakers had made an excellent impression on Governor Harrison, others in the region were not so welcoming. As a consequence of the Shaker missionaries' success and the arrival of more Shaker converts from Red Banks, Kentucky, to swell the growing ranks, the voices of detractors grew louder. In October 1810, the *Vincennes Western Sun*, devoted most of an issue to an extensive article denouncing Shakerism by Colonel James Smith, a respected veteran from near Cane Ridge, Kentucky, who had become hostile toward the Shakers upon the conversion of his son and grandchildren.[23]

Meanwhile, the converts at Busro were enthusiastic but lacked leadership. Issachar Bates and others made periodic visits, but the prospect of ensuring a living for such a large community was increasingly problematic. Benjamin Seth Youngs, who was at Busro during the fall of 1810, observed, "It is difficult here to get anything accomplished, here everything is in confusion — no lead, no order, every thing behind hand — vast fields of corn lie untouched, winter close at hand, no preparations to meet it."[24] Clearly it was necessary for the Busro people to have a "lead," namely, a set of authority figures drawn from the ranks of the "old believers" in the West.

Early in 1811 Father David Darrow at Turtle Creek decided to finally launch a permanent community at Busro by formally resettling a group of Eagle Creek believers there, along with a four-person team of elders from Turtle Creek. Orchestration came from Darrow and his female counterpart, Ruth Farrington, with considerable input from Mother Lucy Wright at New Lebanon, who urged the elevation of two Ohio converts into leadership positions to help launch the Busro community: "Respecting Archibald and Ruth going to Busro we have no objection if you feel the Gift for their protection and we think they would feel the most comfortable to have some of the young believers that live in your family to go with them. Are they not old enough in their faith to do good? Yea, Mother answers, they are."[25]

Ruth Darrow was already somewhat known to the Busro people, having visited the site briefly in late in 1809.[26] Archibald Meacham was probably known only to those few Busro converts who visited Turtle Creek in the autumn of 1809.[27] But the appointment of Elder Archibald and Eldress Ruth was shrewd and deliberate on Darrow's part. Like his elder brother John Meacham, who had come west as one of the missionaries in 1805, Archibald was also a son of Joseph Meacham, Ann Lee's first American convert. As such, he represented to the frontier people of Busro a physical link to Shakerism's founding generation. Now thirty-one, Ruth Darrow was the daughter of David Darrow. She had been a Shaker all her life, as her parents had converted when she was an infant. To the Busro converts, Ruth represented a direct link to the authority of "Father David" at Turtle Creek. The two young believers appointed as "helps" to Archibald and Ruth were James Hodge and Edith "Salome" Dennis.[28] Edith Dennis was a member of the Bedle family, pioneers in southwestern Ohio since the 1790s. She had confessed her sins at Turtle Creek in 1805, and her inclusion in the household of the old believers in 1806 signaled that David Darrow was probably anticipating placing her in leadership eventually. She and Issachar Bates had already begun to develop a close bond.[29] She had taken the name Salome, possibly as namesake to a prominent eastern Shaker sister, Salome Spencer, or to a New Testament figure.[30] James Hodge was a thirty-year-old native of North Carolina, who had confessed his sins somewhere in Kentucky in 1807.[31] Thereafter he traveled often with the Shakers on preaching journeys. Hodge's selection as Archibald Meacham's "second" suggests that Darrow must have regarded him as both zealous and highly trustworthy,[32] considering the number of prominent converts who had been with the Shakers much longer.

〜 *Elder Archibald Meacham, Eldress Ruth Darrow, James Hodge, and Salome Dennis were gone to Buserow, and I must follow them . . . to this Wabash World, where I am now called to make my home.*[33]

Issachar arrived back at Turtle Creek in late March 1811. He had been in Kentucky for several months, helping the new settlements in Mercer and Logan Counties. He had last been at Busro seven months before, in August 1810.[34] There had been other trips, too; none as harrowing as the 1809 winter journey, but each fraught with some hardship. Issachar was dismayed to learn that David Darrow wished him to return to Busro yet again, trailing the group that had just left Turtle Creek on March 20 with the intent of joining the believers en route from Eagle Creek in Adams County. Because Issachar was reasonably familiar with Busro, his reluctance to return there is surprising until one looks more carefully at his own explanation. Having spent time among all the converts that Darrow was now trying to cobble together into a cohesive community on the Busro prairie—not only those from the local area, but also the people from Red Bank, Kentucky, and from Eagle Creek, Ohio—Issachar was pessimistic. He expressed this view to Father David:

> Father wrote to me and requested . . . who would be a suitable person to take the lead of that society at Busro. The answer I returned was these very words—"it will take the wisest man on earth to lead that society," and this was all I said. But now I will give my reasons why I thought so. Now the Busro society of themselves were a mixed multitude—White, Yellow, and Black, add to this the Eagle Creek & Red Bank believers all to be gathered there to mix with them, and the country though beautiful to look at was naturally sickly, and right on the very margin of a frontier. Scarce a human north of them but Indians, and war just at hand.[35]

Yet Issachar's familiarity with the different people being gathered at Busro may have been a main reason that David Darrow chose to send him back there. Other reasons were obvious—among the old believers Issachar was by far the best adapted to frontier life. He had also already made the acquaintance of the territorial governor at Vincennes, whom the Shakers wished to have as an ally. This likely was a crucial factor indeed, in Darrow's thinking, as the mob violence that the Turtle Creek Shakers had experienced just a few months before had highlighted the importance of cultivating friendships with local political authorities. On a purely practical level, Darrow needed Issachar to escort one of the Eagle Creek believers, sixty-year-old John Knox, whose family was already enroute to Busro. Knox himself had stayed behind to liquidate property. Darrow probably intended that the pair follow the newer road between Cincinnati and Vincennes through southern Indiana Territory. Though the shortest route, it was still considered too difficult for all but the hardiest travelers. It was certainly a route that Issachar already knew and hated, having nearly died of hunger and exposure along it two years before. Frustrated at the assignment, Issachar wrote, "Water, water, & no bridges for hundreds of miles wading, fording & swimming, great waters . . . How many times have I plunged thro' that doleful track 240 miles! & 150 of it without a Cabin! & the most difficult waters that ever run above ground." To make matters worse, Knox had a quantity of cash to carry with him, intended to become part of the new community's assets.[36]

> As tho' this was not enough to crush me, I asked Father who was to go with me. He told me it was aged John Knox, an infirm man who had 250 dollars of money to take along. His son had guarded that far with his rifle . . . And now I must guard that poor old man with his money 240 miles through that wild wicked part of the world with no other weapon but my faith. It was about as heavy to me as death, and there was no one on earth that I could blame for it all, only reflect on my hard fortune . . . But when Father found how heavy it went with me he told me that if I would go and make a good long visit and help to gather the people to Elder Archibald then I might return. This took off a great load . . . I started with good old brother John Knox, and had the honor to guard him with $250 of money in the time of the robbers, and I felt like cursing it all the way, for my soul was in trouble enough without that filthy stuff. But through much tribulation we arrived safely.

Clearly, Issachar must have protested his assigned task of returning to the Indiana frontier so strenuously that Darrow relented and told him he need only stay a short time, an act that suggests both affection for Issachar and confidence in his abilities.[37] He did not want to force Issachar to do something onerous, but he also realized that the believers at Busro might be more easily reconciled to the leadership of Archibald Meacham — a relative stranger — if Issachar spent some time there to ease the initial transition into the new settlement. It is also likely that Darrow realized the drawbacks of Issachar remaining permanently in Indiana. A year earlier, Darrow had written in a letter to New Lebanon that certain men, including Issachar, were so valuable as evangelists that they should not be committed to any single community for a long period: "Benjamin, Issachar Richard & such ones as have a gift in word & doctrine to the world — must not be bound to any People Steady — but must be ready to go when the gift comes."[38] Still, defying Father David weighed on Issachar's conscience. Obedience to one's lead — namely, the hierarchical authority of the Church — was utterly crucial to Shaker life. Even though fighting Father David so hard on this point ultimately brought Issachar what he wanted — an assurance that he didn't have to stay in Indiana — it also caused him acute remorse and the nagging fear that, as he would write, his "soul was in trouble."

> *The 23rd of April I set out for the Wabash, arrived there on the 29th, found Archibald, James, Ruth and Salome ... They received me thankfully and freely opened the door for my gift. Surely (said I) here is work enough for us all.*[39]

Issachar Bates's exact role at Busro may not have been clear to the newly appointed elders. Mother Lucy Wright in New Lebanon had made it clear to David Darrow that she wished young believers to share in the leadership at Busro as "seconds" to old believers Archibald Meacham and Ruth Darrow. Issachar had been far away in Kentucky during the planning of Busro's launch, and Archibald and Ruth may not have realized that David Darrow intended for Issachar to follow them to Busro. By 1811 Shaker gospel order dictated that leadership be vested in a team of four — male and female "leads" as elder and eldress and male and female "seconds" as "elder brother" and "elder sister." It would have been important to underscore gospel order at every turn for the motley inhabitants at Busro. Archibald and Ruth may have regarded Issachar's presence as awkward because he held no clear role in that hierarchy. Also, Archibald may have seen Issachar's arrival as a slight, a sign that David Darrow lacked full confidence in his abilities to "gather the people." Issachar's remark in his December 1811 letter to a New Lebanon deacon that the elders at Busro "freely opened the door for my gift," when it was pointed out that there was enough work for everybody, may have been his way of saying, without open criticism, that the elders were not quite certain they wanted him there.

> Then all hands went to work building cabins, fencing fields and preparing to build mills. The Eagle Creek and Red Bank believers came on, and we were pretty strong in number.[40]

For the new hands at Busro, the landscape along the Wabash River must have seemed exotic indeed. Busseron Creek, like other tributaries of the

7.2 *The luxuriant flora and fauna along the Wabash River and its tributaries drew the attention of early nineteenth-century naturalists. After Karl Bodmer, Swiss, 1809–1893; Sigismond Himely, engraver,* Mouth of the Fox River (Indiana), *aquatint, etching and roulette on paper. (Joslyn Art Museum, Omaha, Nebraska, Gift of the Enron Art Foundation, 1986.49.517.5.)*

Wabash, met the river in a lush bayou of standing water, towering trees, luxuriant undergrowth, and colorful bird life (figure 7.2). Beyond the bayous stretched prairie grass, which the Shakers at Busro set about transforming into productive farmland. They shared the terrain not only with the teeming wildlife but also with the indigenous inhabitants, who came among them in great numbers in the first few months after Issachar's arrival. For the transplanted Ohio converts, newcomers both to the prairie environment and to living so close to Indians, Busro was an alien world. The account of William Redmon, then an adolescent convert from Eagle Creek, deserves to be read in detail, as it brilliantly portrays the Busro Shakers' environment in 1811 when Issachar Bates arrived there for his first long stay:

> Prairies I had never seen before; some as level as the Ocean with nothing, only the ethereal Blue, to bound the sight, the prairies covered with a <u>thick coat</u> of Grass . . . Here for weeks & months, the Indians were our nearest neighbors, enjoying themselves in hunting, fishing, horse races, running foot races, wrestling, jumping, &c &c. Also at the same

time keeping up a little domestic Commerce, having for barter deer-skins dressed & raw, moccasins, some of them tastefully wrought with porcupine Quills, and other articles peculiar to them. At that time they were perfectly innocent & harmless. When Melon Time & the fruit season came on,[41] they came down the Wabash by the hundreds to enjoy the Good things of the land: Canoe loads of these copper-colored semi-barbarian Brethren came down the Wabash River and encamped in our neighborhood. The Males in a perfect state of nudity, excepting the figleaf-locality, their whole bodies greased & painted to the very nose: And yet they were a very modest well-behaved people; especially the squaws, also were decently clad in cloth-coat and calico frock: When the infant was nursed, he was introduced under it, mostly out of sight. These Sons of the forest enjoyed the Melon season to the Nines; visiting the saints daily from house to house, feasting on melons and anything else they could get; never refusing to eat, at all times and hours: Begging was now the Mode: Melons they considered as water, not to be paid for. As the season passed away, they gradually moved off West & North, into their accustomed Winter Quarters, where Wild Game were more abundant.

In singing & dancing the males exclusively excelled all people: their exercises were peculiar, the accented notes were touched, not with a fantastic toe, but with a laborious active motion, accompanied in beating time, with the hands, the rattling of Bear's claws, Deer's hoofs, stones in a gourd & a one-stick Drum &c &c. This feast dance terminates in the War Dance, the Indians being painted in a most hideous manner; exercising vehemently & vociferating & screeching like so many panthers & demons; at the same time wielding their war clubs and hatchets: Some thot' these were Religious Dances, but aged John Slover said they might have religion, but it was of the same kind as practiced when they had him at the stake to be burnt, and some were now engaged who were present at that awful scene! Slover moved his all on the next Monday toward South Union.

Of the inhabitants of the Wabash Country I must say a word; the Males were clad in buckskin pants suspended by a leather thong; shirts if they had any, were French check, with a coarse Blanket Chappeau; the Coronet a Raccoon's cap. This habiliament was well calculated to shield their bodies, from the everlasting piercing winds of the Prairies. You must recollect that these inhabitants were on the extreme frontier of Indiana Territory; only one family between them & St. Louis, Missouri, and that was killed by Indians the first winter after our arrival. The Prairies, rivers, ponds, bayous, &c. abounded with birds, fishes, fowls, & game of all kinds peculiar to that country: Wild geese, swans, pelicans, brants, cranes, ducks &c. Fishes astonishingly plenty, of strange kinds & uncommon in size. Among the numerous birds, Paroquets as mischievous as beautiful; Black Birds by millions; Prairy Hens by thousands, they rose from the fields as a cloud making a noise like thunder. But I must not be tedious for it would require a Book to hint at all the peculiarities of this New World, as seen by my juvenile eyes.[42]

A few things about this extraordinary narrative merit comment. Redmon was clearly fascinated by the Indians, whom he does not denigrate in his account. Although his boyhood home had been rural southern Ohio, its landscape and people were genteel compared to the prairies of far western Indiana territory, something reflected in his observations of the wildlife and of the Busro converts' rough "habiliament," or attire. Redmon's own experience with the sometimes riotous Shaker dancing make his observations of Indian dancing all the more potent. And his account of the reaction of one particular Busro inhabitant — "aged John Slover," who had heard the Shakers preach at Red Banks, Kentucky, and had confessed his sins to Issachar Bates in 1808 before relocating to Busro with his son and other family members later on[43] — offers a rare glimpse of a frontier character whose exploits achieved renown later in the nineteenth century.

In fact, the same John Slover who had been drawn to the Shaker gospel from the preaching of Issachar Bates had as a child about 1760 been famously captured by the Shawnee and held for several years, during which he became fluent in Indian languages. Later, he was a scout for the ill-fated Crawford Expedition, a 1782 campaign against the Ohio tribes. Captured along with other expedition members, Slover endured brutal torture and narrowly escaped death, being the only one of the party to return alive, coming safely to Wheeling on the Ohio River after a harrowing flight across the Ohio wilderness, riding naked on a stolen Indian horse. Later in Pittsburg he told others of his ordeal, before moving on with his life.[44] Much later, Slover's story was integrated into a sensational volume titled *Indian Atrocities: Narratives of Perils and Sufferings of Dr. Knight and John Slover Among the Indians During the Revolutionary War*, published in Cincinnati in 1867. It contains Slover's first-person account of the time when, in the words he used at Busro in 1811, "they had him at the stake to be burnt":

> I was tied to the post, as I have already said, and the flame was now kindled. The day was clear, not a cloud to be seen. If there were clouds low

in the horizon, the sides of the house prevented me from seeing then, but I heard no thunder, or observed any sign of approaching rain; just as the fire of one pile began to blaze, the wind rose, from the time they began to kindle the fire and tie me to the post, until the wind began to blow, was about fifteen minutes. The wind blew a hurricane, and the rain followed in less than three minutes. The rain fell violent; and the fire, though it began to blaze considerably, was instantly extinguished. The rain lasted about a quarter of an hour. When it was over, the savages stood amazed and were a long time silent.[45]

It must have been remarkable for the Busro Shakers to have in their midst the John Slover who had lived part of his life among the Indians, still knew some Indian language, and could recount to his fellow believers a seemingly miraculous deliverance from a brutal death during a scene not unlike the ones they were now witnessing with their Indian neighbors. Young Redmon's recollections depict a Slover who remains wary of the Indians, who is unsettled when the scene begins to evoke memories of his past ordeal, and who imagines that some of the Indians present were among his torturers some thirty years before. So shaken was Slover that he soon left Busro for the comparatively safer setting of Gasper River, Kentucky, even though his family members remained. For Issachar Bates, who had gone with Richard McNemar to visit the Shawnee in Greenville, Ohio, in one of a series of attempted Shaker overtures to the Shawnee that had ended "with our persecutors at our heels,"[46] Slover's stories would have been sobering indeed. The previous summer when Issachar had been at Busro for a visit of several weeks, Tecumseh himself had passed through the converts' land on his way to a contentious meeting with Governor Harrison in Vincennes, and other Indians — perhaps including Tecumseh's brother, the Prophet Tenskwatawa — attended Shaker worship.[47] Now Issachar was back at Busro again, and the Indian activity had not abated. With more than six years' experience in the region, journeying across areas where Indians still lived and where relationships with white settlers could deteriorate at any time, Issachar may himself have felt uncomfortable at Busro, where the presence of Indians was a part of life.

[I]n the month of September Elder Archibald, Eldress Ruth, James Hodge, and Salome went on a visit to Union Village [and] left me with Brother Joseph Allen to take care of matters. And I feeling zealous to have things move fast I was day after day in the Busero Creek cleaning out old logs to make a place for a mill dam. And also I was three days stocking wheat in the sun without a hat. And soon after this I was taken very sick and my distress was mostly in my head. But in about three weeks I got about again, but never have got over it to this day.[48]

In any case, Issachar Bates, along with another old believer, Joseph Allen, remained at Busro and continued leading the work of building and harvesting the first season's crops. Among the two dozen old believers then in the West, Allen was a "mechanic" from the small Shaker community at Tyringham, Massachusetts, who had traveled west alone in 1809 specifically to help with building projects in the new communities.[49] Issachar was eager to move the work along as quickly as possible, but was taken ill. From the conditions he mentions, he could have suffered heat stroke. But given the time of year and the circumstances, it is quite likely that he contracted malaria, later to become the scourge of the Busro Shakers.

In the early nineteenth century, malaria was all too familiar to the early white settlers of humid low-lying areas of the North American interior.[50] It went under many colloquial names—"fever and ague," "chills and fever," "autumnal fever," and "tertian," or "three-day," fever.[51] We know today that types of malaria include the *malariae*, which is associated with the autumn season, the more deadly *falciparum* associated with tropical and subtropical latitudes and also autumnal, and the more geographically widespread and less deadly *vivax*, associated with spring and summer. Of the three, scholars believe the *vivax*, which typically presented as a three-day cycle of chills and fever, to have been the most prevalent in the low-lying riparian lands of the North American frontier.[52] But pioneer accounts persistently note outbreaks in early autumn, pointing to the presence of the other types also.

Typically, malaria attacked white settlers in the first years after arrival in a susceptible part of the humid trans-Appalachian West, usually manifesting itself in the late summer or early fall. Mosquito carriers stay close to still water, and they would multiply rapidly as settlers felled trees and introduced more sunlight into the bayous and other areas of standing water, and then invariably attack the humans working in such conditions. The mosquitoes would also quickly adapt to pioneer settlements, taking advantage of water troughs, wells, and cisterns—which brought them in closer proximity to their new food source. Later, as settlers' livestock multiplied, the mosquitoes typically began to rely less on humans, preferring farm animals. At the same time, continued improvement to land would eliminate mosquito habitat.[53] Consequently, pioneers customarily experienced malaria as a malady of the opening years of a settlement, diminishing in intensity as the years passed but continuing to vex past victims with periodic relapses.

7.3 *Busseron Creek today, near its confluence with the Wabash and at the former site of the Shaker mill. (Photo by author.)*

Along the oppressive tributaries and bayous of the Wabash River country, a newly arrived settler working "day after day in Busseron Creek cleaning out old logs" could scarcely have avoided contracting malaria (figure 7.3). Symptoms would have included "skull-splitting headache," and relapses could have occurred for many years. By his own account, Issachar Bates's illness, which he never "got over," seems to fit this description. Moreover, he notes in a letter written later that year that not only was he "down with the fever" in early September, but more than forty people among the newly arrived Eagle Creek brethren at Busro were stricken at the same time, a pattern that also fits malaria.[54]

Besides struggling with illness and dealing with Indians as their near neighbors, the Busro Shakers were in the midst of mounting hostilities between the tribes and the local military authorities, which Bates addressed at some length in December of 1811:

> Indians began to gather in from the different tribes. We being on the outmost of the frontier, they encamped nigh to us, waiting for the different tribes to collect, which took them about two weeks; then Tecumseh,

their head chief came and led them to Vincennes . . . saying to the people "Look, see our squaws and children. We do not go to war so; we only came here because the governor sent for us." Yet notwithstanding all this, the people moved into forts, and into towns, bag and baggage all around us . . . I would just observe that a number of leading men in the Territory were sorely tried with the manner in which things were conducted. The governor had light horse and three or four hundred footmen together for a week or ten days to guard the town against this unprepared company of Indians, squaws, and children. After all this parade was over, and every voice from the Indians was peace . . . the governor sent them away with a party of men hard at their heels to keep them from pilfering from the inhabitants. But this was like setting the dog to watch the butter for they did more mischief in one night than the Indians had done all summer . . . The matter was now settled. The governor receives liberty from the president to manage all these things according to his wisdom . . . War! War! War! The militia is drafted, the Believers with the rest. Tribulation is our portion day and night.[55]

Historians' accounts confirm the substance of Issachar Bates's observations. Since the angry confrontation between Governor Harrison and Tecumseh the previous summer, Tecumseh and his brother Tenskwatawa had been rallying the tribes throughout the region to join in a massive resistance against American expansion, and they were receiving advice from the British. Harrison and Tecumseh each seemed to expect a military confrontation by the summer of 1811.[56] But Tecumseh traveled to Vincennes with an entourage of women and children, arguing unconvincingly that the fifty canoes filled with warriors had followed along unbidden. For his part, Harrison had fortified Vincennes with hundreds of additional troops to intimidate the Indians, and in the early fall began moving north to build a fort closer to the Indians' main concentration at Prophetstown.[57]

The governor's army was expected on every day . . . And to mingle my vinegar with gall, some of the wicked Potawatomies came by night and stole our teams from the mill ground — four of the best horses among the Believers . . . This loss, which was about 500 dollars, was gained on another quarter for it cooled the prejudice of the world concerning our friendship with the Indians. I would just observe that this is a trick which these wicked Potawatomies have carried on for several years, to follow the Prophet's party and steal that it might be fathered[58] on them that did it not. . . . The 17th, the Army began to come on. One company of light horse and two companies of riflemen encamped near us. The contractor made use of our shop in the dooryard for a storehouse, and had a slaughter yard back of it. There it was drums and fifes — blood and whiskey — alas! alas![59]

The loss of four valuable horses was indeed galling but not unusual, and the Busro Shakers were not alone in suffering theft at the hands of Indians. Throughout the lower Wabash, settlers were reporting their losses to Governor Harrison, who used the incidents to help justify his mounting campaign north toward Prophetstown.[60] The Shakers now appeared to be victims, too, countering the impression among the settlers that they were Indian sympathizers. But privately Issachar Bates was inclined to give Tenskwatawa's people the benefit of the doubt and to single out a separate group of Indians as culpable in the thefts. His reaction may have been colored by the Shakers' many efforts to reach out to the Prophet over the past several years, or it may have been based on previous observations. In any case, the army's escalating preparations for war with the Indians brought them to the Shakers' doorstep. For Issachar, the gathering troops with all their weapons and accoutrements, "drums and fifes — blood and whiskey" — must have taken him back to his own youthful days in the Army, when he not only led troops with his fife but also developed his fondness for whiskey. His comments suggest these were uncomfortable memories.

About the 26th the whole army came on with the governor and encamped in this place. — Note: in this army there were 500 regular troops from New England, commanded by Col. Boyd from Boston — There the kind hand of God in his providence was stretched out a little to help us. These people testified they were acquainted with the Shakers at the eastward . . . Col. Boyd bore a public testimony at Vincennes, and at other places, that the Shakers at the eastward were the best people on earth. This blunted the edge of every weapon that was formed against us. He appeared to be as glad to see us as tho' we were his natural kin. There was also a Col. Davis from Kentucky who commanded the troops of horse. He was acquainted with the believers there and was very friendly. He being a lawyer, Joseph Allen being acquainted with him [we] went to him for counsel. For at 12 o'clock all the Brethren on the muster role were ordered to join the army. We went to the Gov. according to his counsel and told him what we could do and what we could not. The Gov. replied that he knew our faith and that the matter might rest until he returned and that he would assist us in a petition to the assembly to be released.[61]

Still, Issachar had to admit that the assembling army brought about favorable developments for the Busro Shakers. One arriving officer was not only a New Englander, he also knew and admired Shakers in the East. From their accents and mannerisms he may have recognized the two stand-ins for the Busro elders, Issachar Bates and Joseph Allen, as fellow natives of Massachusetts and Issachar as a former soldier. The good reputation of Kentucky Shakers similarly paved the way for a cordial friendship with another arriving officer, who counseled the Busro Shakers on gaining an exemption from military service. Although he already had formed an acquaintance with Governor Harrison, Issachar would have welcomed the support from these officers.

Three of the Busro elders returned late in October, and Issachar Bates returned to Turtle Creek (by then called Union Village), believing that his Indiana interlude was over. But while there, he had the opportunity to explain to David Darrow the complexities and perils of the Shakers' life on the Wabash in a way that Archibald Meacham, who had missed many critical events and who had little acquaintance with Governor Harrison, had been unable to do. Darrow gave him leave to write a full account for the New Lebanon Ministry, which Issachar prepared in a letter to Deacon Richard Spiers. He closed the letter with the remark, "[T]he Indians are now stirred up and the frontier left without defense, which is very distressing to the believers on the Wabash."[62] It was clear to Darrow that, with war looming and the security of the Wabash region uncertain, the Busro settlement still needed Issachar's insight and experience. Issachar was not pleased: "But alas, I soon found that I had got to make Busroe my home . . . So in the winter I started with James Hodge and plunged through that horrid watery world once more, still approaching nearer & nearer the place of bloody war."[63]

When Issachar Bates arrived back at Busro, he was immediately met by another seeming calamity—the great earthquakes of 1811 and 1812 along the New Madrid fault. The earthquake event, which extended over several months, had its epicenter more than two hundred miles southwest of the Busro, near the junction of the Ohio and Mississippi Rivers. But because the sedimentary soils of the Mississippi-Ohio-Wabash watershed region conducted the earthquake's energy efficiently, the shaking felt at Busro from the strongest earthquake on February 9, 1812, was probably in the range of 6.0 to 6.9 on today's Richter Scale.[64] In fact, the earthquakes were felt as far away as southern Ohio. (Issachar had been at Turtle Creek for the first of the series, on December 16; what he described as "four strong shocks of an earthquake, or rather a reeling of the earth," was strong enough to frighten people out of their houses in nearby Lebanon, Ohio.[65]) At the Kentucky Shaker settlements, chimneys were knocked down, perhaps some of the same chimneys that Issachar Bates had worked to help build a few years earlier. The Busro Shakers reported no material damage to their rough log structures, but the people were frightened. Buildings in Vincennes had been damaged, and the Shakers heard of freakish effects of the shaking. One Busro believer wrote, "From correct information, we learn that the shaking occurs almost daily in New Madrid . . . Large chasms can be seen in many directions . . . a mile or more in length, from which muddy waters and sulphureous vapors sometimes issue most frightfully and almost strong enough to suffocate the inhabitants."[66]

For Issachar Bates, who had witnessed unusual natural phenomena immediately before the outbreak of the Revolutionary War, the earthquakes may have appeared to be a supernatural extension of the political upheavals clearly under way in the region. Settlers throughout the area imputed spiritual meaning to the earthquakes, and many were frightened into churches. Issachar refers jokingly to the "earthquake Baptists" of the area, when he writes how he teased a local Baptist minister: "I told him I expected he would need dipping again before these earthquakes were over . . . and he was a little miffed."[67] Many of the Shakers believed that the earthquakes were a sign of the spiritual "shaking" that they themselves were imposing upon the region. One of the old believers back in Ohio composed a hymn called "The Earthquake," which included the line "dwelling houses crack for joy," a reference to the physical impact of the shaking.[68] Issachar's hymn from this period, called "The Great Shaker" (see appendix 2), and its opening allusion to God, "the great Shaker of heaven and earth," may reflect his belief in the earthquake's divine origin.

The ministries of both Union Village and New Lebanon were well aware of the difficult conditions facing the Busro believers. Though communication from Busro was sparse, the events around Vincennes relating to the coming war with Great Britain were well reported in newspapers. That news, together with Issachar Bates's thorough reporting throughout the summer and fall of 1812, helped guide the ministries in the counsel they sent to Busro. One chief concern was that the Shakers might be harassed or even harmed because of their refusal to fight. Deacon Richard Spier of New Lebanon wrote to encourage them that the worst likely would not happen: "For any to threaten that they will kill you if the Indians do not or that they will show you Indian play, act the civil murderer, & impute it to the savage betrays a disposition that good heaven cannot long indulge on the civilized soil of America."[69] But he also acknowledged the great fear that Busro families were feeling, and he recommended that, at least temporarily, children be permitted to stay close to their parents, although this was contrary to normal organization within

Shaker communities: "A child comes very near to the feelings of some parents especially in times of danger . . . and if all or any are under the apprehension of danger [you] may find it best for children to remain with their parents."[70]

In light of these threats, Issachar Bates conferred with the governor and received a tempting offer for the Shakers to take shelter at Grouseland, Harrison's stately home in Vincennes.

> Governor Harrison made us a fair offer. He told Robert Gill & me that he was going to move right out of his house to Cincinnatia & we might move into it & if that would not hold us all, he would provide tents for the rest & would set 600 men to guard us, & it should not cost us one cent. We thanked him, but told him we could not do it . . . He added, "you will have to do something to secure yourselves, for you are very much exposed; tho' I don't believe that any of the Indians will harm you except the Pottawatomies, and there is no trust to be put in them, and if they would come and kill and scalp your women and children 'twould be all laid to your Elders. Now I have no thought that you are afraid of dying, for if I was as sure of heaven as you are, I should not be afraid of death.[71]

By August 1812, news that Fort Harrison some forty miles to the north was surrounded by Indians was followed by reports of people being killed much closer, only a few miles away. Then the Shakers "got up one morning and found the Indians had been among them — they saw their tracks very plain and thick in the dry sand . . . Round their meeting house, up to Archibald's gate."[72] The army returned — "the believers settlement was their head Quarters to make a stand" — and intended to appropriate the Shakers' entire food supply to feed the soldiers. Clearly, the Shakers had to depart. But moving such a large number of people was no easy task. The shorter "wilderness" route across the southern interior of Indiana Territory was vulnerable to Indian violence,[73] and the believers lacked wagons sufficient to move themselves and their baggage. So they chose to start out by water, sending Issachar Bates by land to Union Village to inform leaders there that the Busro community was enroute. The logistics were complicated. Union Village had to send wagons to help the move, meeting the people along a circuitous route that took them south to Red Bank, Kentucky, further south to the Shaker settlement at Gasper River (now called South Union), east across Kentucky to Pleasant Hill, and finally north to Ohio and Union Village. As Darrow wrote, "Their journey was something similar to the Israelites: around in the wilderness to get to the Promised Land."[74]

Some enter the field, for a short expedition,
and others enlist for a solid campaign,
But all who are faithful until their dismission,
a happy reward for their service will gain.[75]

The pacifist Shakers had employed warfare metaphors in worship and preaching since their beginnings in America. But until the events around Busro on the Wabash in Indiana Territory, no Shakers had ever directly experienced the ravages and devastation of actual warfare. From hopeful beginnings in an environmental setting that was challenging but brimming with potential, the Shakers at Busro suffered expulsion from their settlement and an uncertain future. Drawn far more deeply into the Wabash world than he ever intended, Issachar Bates would continue to be yoked to Busro's fortunes for some time to come.

CHAPTER 8

"And with much animation we lived at Busro"

AN ELDER IN INDIANA

This pleasant situation was view'd with admiration,
and with much animation, we lived at Busro
— "A Lamentation for West Union," 1833

Now all the particulars that took place from 1814 to 1824 while I stayed
at Busro, I shall leave for fireside talk ... Only this much I can state, we
went to work & made a comfortable living as to food & raiment, erected
good buildings & mills & kept a good measure of faith & gospel order.
And in a few years we had things in pretty good condition ... Now after
I have stated a few more circumstances, I shall leave Busro to its fate.
— Issachar Bates

By 1812 Issachar Bates had risen to the occasion at Busro. His acquaintances with both William Henry Harrison and the Shawnee leaders, along with his familiarity with military settings, had uniquely equipped him to help the Busro community navigate "the dangers and troubles of the war."[1] Probably on that basis, Issachar was named among the elders of the new ministry for the Busro community when the believers returned to the Wabash in 1814 and reconstituted the settlement as "West Union." Issachar remained at Busro for nearly ten years, helping transform the community from a sickly group in a straggling collection of rough cabins to a handsome and productive Shaker society. He reveled in applying his musical talents to the community's joys, challenges, and transformative moments. He also forged an acquaintance between the Shakers and another separatist society, the German immigrant followers of George Rapp, who established their settlement of Harmony, Indiana, not far away. But most of Issachar's attention was captivated by the many difficulties of life at Busro — sickness that claimed beloved comrades, conflict among the elders, members who resisted obedience, and separation from friends and family.

Prepare yourselves for war and strife —
Trust not in horses, lands, nor wife

For you must live a pilgrim's life —
a life of self-denial.[2]

The Busro Shakers were now both scattered and economically reduced. Some had stayed at South Union, others at Pleasant Hill. Thirty-five went to Union Village, sick and exhausted, and were installed as a group into the "East house," in that portion of Union Village that had once been Richard McNemar's land.[3] Initially they relied on material support from Union Village. Though their first seasons at Busro had been marred by warfare and sickness, they had been exceptionally productive. Crops, livestock, promising orchards, mills, and fencing all were abandoned. Some valuables, such as window glass and ironware, were buried in hopes of retrieving them later.[4] The Shakers had laid the foundation for producing and marketing spinning wheels at Busro, a shrewd fiscal strategy in an area that produced wool, flax, and cotton. Left behind at Busro were the prepared parts to manufacture over one thousand variously sized spinning wheels.[5] The Shakers wrote, "All these things are left to the tender mercies of the wicked, which is cruel." The estimated monetary loss was over ten thousand dollars.[6]

Instead of staying together with "Archibald's family" at Union Village, Issachar Bates returned to Busro where he spent part of 1813 trying to secure payment from the army for the materials seized for use by the soldiers. As Darrow noted of the army, "Wherever they go, they have the power to take whatever they need, but these have it appraised and give certificate on the quartermaster or treasury." We can assume that Issachar's experience in dealing with the military was needed if the Shakers were to extract any compensation for their abandoned possessions on the Wabash.

Manuscripts reveal that the eastern Shakers were deeply shaken by what had befallen the Busro settlement. No Shakers had ever found themselves literally on the front lines of a bloody war, at real risk of death at the hands of Indians. Easterners were familiar with accounts of Indian atrocities, which had earlier caused Mother Lucy Wright to urge the westerners to be cautious in their Indian overtures in Ohio. Learning of the Busro ordeal, of the losses to that promising group, and of their tenacious retreat to Ohio, eastern Shakers seemed overwhelmed. Indeed, Lucy Wright seems to have taken a particular interest in Busro. And Issachar Bates's role at Busro garnered special attention, as witnessed in this long and earnest letter sent to Archibald Meacham:

We consider you as being between two furious Armies; even as
Lambs among wolves & your courage has held out until the last even
till there was no more encouragement of success short of flight —

Truly ye are warriors indeed — where shall we find any like unto you — There has not exceeded this, nay, not in Israel . . . Therefore you are Mother's children — and are near her heart. Yea she loveth you as her darlings . . .

We received Intelligence by the publick papers concerning the war and the desolations that were prevalent in the Country round about you — how that fort Harrison was besieged by a vast superior force of Savages & the difficulty they were under in sending word or requesting assistance from their friends, by reason of the street watch & guard on the Wabash kept by the Indians who were so greatly exasperated by the destruction of their towns &c — And being sensible that if they could receive any relief, the Armies must again pass through your village — or have their head-quarters there —

O how it made us fear for our beloved Brethren & Sisters — We said to each other with the voice of sympathy, our Brethren & Sisters are in strait places — they are unavoidably in trouble — when or how shall we hear from them — we were impatiently waiting; we watched the post office in season & out of season for Days, weeks, & months to find letters from our friends in the west, but found none — We query'd within ourselves, is the passage shut that no letters can pass? Is our enemies so enraged against believers because they will not bear Arms that they will not suffer communication? Or what can be the matter?

Mother had a gift for us to pray for our Brethren & Sisters in the west, both old & young Believers . . . Mother said, "They are in trouble," we kneeled down & prayed heartily . . . We still kept a look out & after a long time we found some letters — O! how Anxious were we to hear — the family was assembled to hear the contents . . . Brother Issachar is accounted among us as a faithful Minister of the Gospel — He has spared no pains or labour — but has been willing to take the front of the battle in gathering souls in different parts of that Country — And especially at Busrow he has gathered a fine crop & gained a good inheritance there — We were sure he would not spare his life but would do all that lay in his power to help protect the people there.

When we heard that he had again started for Busrow, to gather up the remnant that was left there — We said within ourselves! Does Issachar's Patience yet hold out? Does not his courage & strength fail? Surely God gives him strength & power, equal to his day — according to his promise — And we earnestly desire & pray that God will return him to you again in peace that you may comfort him on our behalf.[7]

Though David Darrow had earlier promised Issachar Bates that he might sojourn at Busro only temporarily, events had proven Issachar to be virtually indispensible to the Busro enterprise. By late 1812, his name was included in correspondence along with Archibald Meacham, Ruth Darrow, and Salome Dennis, implying that he was assuming the formal role of elder. Early in the spring of 1814, plans began for the return to Indiana. Archibald Meacham went to Busro in March with a large group of men and women to assess the site's condition and begin to lay some crops.[8] As the eastern communities wanted to contribute to the effort of reconstructing this westernmost Shaker outpost, the New Lebanon and Union Village ministries arranged a rendezvous in Pittsburg, Pennsylvania, whereby a wagon loaded with supplies for Busro—along with $1,500 in cash—could be conveyed from east to west.

Shortly before the first of June 1814, Issachar Bates traveled to Pittsburg with Solomon King, second elder to David Darrow at Union Village.[9] The meeting between Issachar and the New Lebanon brethren was momentous. It signaled the determination of the central Shaker Ministry to resume efforts in far-off Indiana, and the Ministry's confidence in the undertaking. The eastern societies would not go to the trouble of sending out valuable goods and cash money to support a doomed project. The sheer productivity of the Busro settlement in only two short seasons, against a backdrop of warfare and sickness, had been truly astonishing, and the potential for economic growth on the fertile Wabash lands seemed to warrant the extraordinary efforts expended to help the Busro Shakers resettle. But the June 1814 meeting in Pittsburg is notable for another reason, too. While on that journey to Pittsburg, serendipity brought Issachar Bates and Solomon King together with representatives of another communal society, the followers of German pietist George Rapp, with whom they seemed to hold much in common.

> *Now, Brother Seth, in relation to the Harmonians . . . they purchased a tract of land in the state of Pennsylvania 26 miles northeast from Pittsburgh. There they gathered together and built a town. In the month of June 1814. Elder Solomon and myself visited them. This was the first acquaintance they had with believers . . . They informed us that they had purchased a large tract of land on the Wabash—and intended to move to it that season—which they did—which is about 70 miles below us. We have frequently visited each other and support a good degree of union.[10]*

Just as the Shakers were preparing to return to Busro, the Harmonists (also called "Harmonians")—or followers of Rapp—were planning a move from "Harmony" near Pittsburg to newly purchased land along the Wabash in western Indiana Territory. At precisely the time that Issachar Bates and Solomon King were traveling to Pittsburg, George Rapp was returning with an English-speaking follower from a journey to the Wabash, where they had been arranging their group's land purchase. Exactly where the two parties met is uncertain. Because Issachar writes that he and Solomon "visited" the Harmonists, it is possible they went to Harmony expressly to find them. It is also possible that the two traveling pairs met on the road, since manuscripts confirm that they were bound for Pittsburg at the same time along the same route. Few of the Harmonists spoke English, and neither of the Shakers were known to speak German, but because Rapp counted English-speakers among his followers, the meeting led to a productive exchange, opening what would be a long and fruitful acquaintance between the two groups that would persist for decades, long after both groups vacated Indiana.[11]

By the middle of August 1814, well over two hundred believers once more occupied Busro. One initial order of business was drawing up a covenant to regulate the believers and establish the joint interest. This document, signed by most members in early 1815, drew the community — to be formally named "West Union" — into gospel order under the eldership of Archibald Meacham and Issachar Bates. The signatories were indeed the "mixed multitude" that Issachar Bates had once spoken of. In addition to white Americans, there were many free blacks and multiracial people, as well as several Europeans — a Pole, an Irishman, and at least one German. There was at least one interracially married couple with children. One man of black ancestry also spoke Indian languages, suggesting he may also have had Indian forebears.[12] Thus the latest covenanted Shaker community in America was probably also America's most racially and ethnically diverse group of Shakers.

While the large number of inhabitants made the village at Busro appear robust, a large segment comprised children and adolescents.[13] Neither could "robust" describe the health of Busro's people in the early years after the return. The village repopulated precisely at a time when the people would be most susceptible to malaria — late summer. The Busro diarist who wrote on August 22, "[T]he people were generally well when they landed," observed eight days later, "The fever still goes on with violence."[14] When Eldress Ruth Darrow, a strong healthy woman in her early thirties, succumbed to a wracking case of malaria on September 18, people nearly despaired. Salome Dennis was left to assume the mantle of female eldership, the first "young believer" in the West to be placed in such a position.[15] After news of Eldress Ruth's death reached the East, Issachar Bates — who had paid tribute to her with

8.1 *Hybrid nut trees, likely planted by the Busro Shakers, stand on the prairie at the Busro site today, a last vestige of the once-thriving nut orchards cultivated by the Shakers. (Photo by author.)*

a touching memorial hymn sung at her funeral—received a letter from his friend Seth Youngs Wells expressing shared grief and support:

> [O]ur family Assembled in the Evening and we again Renewed our Prayers and on our knees rehearsed the Sufferings and Afflictions that our poor Brethren and Sisters in that Distant wilderness had gone through . . . The Raging Pestilence again broke out among them distressing fevers brought them low, Grim Death Stalked among them, and alas their beloved Mother was snatched from them . . . We wept and talked till we felt released . . . Dear Brother Issachar, What shall we say more?[16]

However, by the time Issachar received that letter in April 1815 and sat down to prepare a reply, things were looking up at Busro. Whether owing to good weather, good farming outcomes, relief over the end of the war, stability offered by the new covenant, or simply the people's resilience, letters written by the West Union Ministry that April were optimistic. Issachar's letter to Seth Youngs Wells describes a springtime landscape bursting with potential (figure 8.1).

We shall not relate what we suffered through the fall and winter . . . Nay we will forget it—for we have good food and raiment, and no fearful apprehensions of want—but to the contrary a good prospect of crops for this is a goodly land. I can this moment lift mine eyes at this window to the east and survey 10 or 15 miles of a beautiful green grassy plain covered with cattle & sheep in hundreds . . . the most beautiful sight that nature ever exhibited. I can look out at the west window and see more than a hundred acres equally green with wheat oat and barley and a beautiful young orchard of about 800 apple trees the greatest part of which are now shedding their blossoms, and about 600 peach trees with more fruit on the most of them than they can bear, if one fourth part should hang on— and a nursery of (for a guess) 10000 and more than 1000 fit to set. If I go to the south I can walk near a mile on ground that is now in preparation for planting corn. If I go to the north a large field is there—but I will stop. This is only earthly glory, not that I mean to glory in it. Nay I am afraid of it, I am jealous that it is too good for young believers to make a wise use of. For it is in truth the easiest and best place to get a living in that ever I saw—and the devil knew it before we did.[17]

In Issachar's mind, the Busro believers could hardly help but prosper. Despite past suffering, morale that spring seemed good. People enjoyed camaraderie with one another and with their eastern counterparts, through letters, gifts, and exchanged songs. This is evident from a letter written by Eldress Salome to eastern sisters who had sent her the gift of a garment, a special honor indeed. (With the death of Eldress Ruth Darrow, Salome filled her position by default. She would remain first eldress until another old believer, Martha Sanborn, was sent out from Union Village to relieve her the following year, returning Salome to the supporting role of second eldress.) In the same letter Salome expresses an affectionate bond between the Busro elders and two of Issachar Bates's natural children in the East, Polly and Issachar, both of whom had sent songs as gifts. In return, Salome sent some of Busro's songs written by "Big" Issachar. Her letter deserves to be extracted at length, because the voices of western-born women have received comparatively less attention in the growing literature on Shaker women.[18] Salome Dennis was not only a key figure, sharing leadership alongside Issachar at Busro, but the two were also clearly enjoying their deepening friendship during this period.

> I Feel my Self honored that I may have the Privilege, in union with my
> Beloved Elders of taking this method to Return my Cincere thanks to
> You, for the notice you have taken of me, and in Particular for the Beauti-

ful garment you Sent me. O what a pretty thing — Shure Enough What a beauty — I never had so much as Dreamed of this — that the Garment of my Lord and Savior, and of my Blessed Mother, would be presented to me, to put on and wear — my Soul is delighted with it. But but but what — But if I could do with it as Little girls of the world do with a present of their Mother's garment, to have it laid up for them till They grow big Enough to wear it, and so look at it once in a while to see how pretty it looks, But but alas! this will not do! for it is too little Now, or Else I am to big — and yet it was Sent to me to put on and wear, And I must and will do it if it Stagnates all the nasty blood in my flesh . . .

And now what is left of my Paper I must fill up with love and Thanks — I thank you kindly for the "Wedding Garment" Hymn, my kind love and thanks to Polly Bates for her pretty Little token of love, we have got tunes fitted to them — They go sweetly, and as a token of my love in Return, I send on the back of this a Little Hymn Composed by Brother Issachar on the funeral of our beloved Eldress Ruth . . .

The following Hymn was Composed by Big Issachar last August Coming thro' the wilderness to Prepare the way for Elder Archibald & His Company who Came by water, and was learned by those that were on the Ground, and sang to the whole when they arrived, as a welcome salutation. And is sent in part pay for a pretty little song that was sent to me in the name of Little Issachar (a pretty name I wish there was two of them). Big Issachar learned it very quick, and we sing it here, it is Called the Prettyest Thing that Ever Was.[19]

Salome's letter is both revealing and endearing. Her delight over the garment gift is infectious; her disappointment that it is too small is palpable. Perhaps Salome was larger than average in stature. She exhibits a familiar tone toward Polly Bates and "Little" Issachar Bates, perhaps because she had heard their father talk about them. Her charming use of the "big" and "little" nicknames for the Bates father and son reveal her obvious affection for the elder and, by extension, for his son. Her remark that she wishes there were two "Little" Issachars may have been an oblique reference to Issachar Dennis back at Union Village, by now almost nine years old, her kin and possibly her own son. Her letter continues with a description of how the Busro people integrated the song sent by "Little" Issachar into their own worship, including a reference to a young woman's joke about the comparative ugliness of the Busro people: "[B]ut when we Come to bring it along side of their Hymns that they sing here on their battle ground, it is like a nat on the oxes horn. One of our young Sisters observed that Instead of Singing, "I never did feel so pretty before" It would fit her much better to Sing, I never did feel so Ugly before."

The conviviality suggested in Salome's letter is borne out at the same time by Archibald Meacham, who reported the formation of four "families" within the community that "have all come into one Joint Interest in Covenant Relation." The believers, he said, "appear to be more reconciled to the order of the Gospel, so that the Place feels more like being Prepared for the ark of the testimony to Rest than it ever has before."[20] Meacham also provided a description of the unusually zealous worship of the Busro believers:

> I will state the manner of our Meetings. The Center family assembles in the meeting house every evening, the meeting commonly begins by singing an Anthem or a Hymn and then prepare to labour and singers place themselves to sing and sing sometimes two or three songs, and by that time the singing is entirely drowned by the Different Exercises so that the Sound is like mighty thunderings, some Stamping with all their might and Roaring out against the nasty Stinking beast & filthy whore which has made all nations drunk with the wine of her Fornication, Others turning with great power and warring against the flesh and at the Same time a number Speaking with new tongues with such Majestic signs and motions that it makes the powers of darkness tremble yea & the good believers cry out with thankfulness to God for the special notice of God to them, thus the meetings frequently continue with such like Exercises for two hours without any cessation, tho sometimes there is a cessation long enough to partly sing a Hymn when it would begin with more Violence than ever, so that by the time that meeting is closed the people will be as wet with sweat as tho they had been plunged into a River.[21]

Because the rejection of physical desire — or "the flesh" — was such a key part of Shaker theology, early worship necessarily emphasized the repudiation of lust and related sins — greed, envy, and so on. The source of these human frailties was typically materialized as Satan, or "the beast," along with his counterpart the established church institutions, repeatedly characterized by the Shakers as the "whore." Examining early worship at Busro reveals that the "beast" and the "whore" were explicitly blamed for the believers' seemingly endless struggle against sickness. The "battle ground" mentioned by Salome Dennis in her letter of 1815 is a reference to the distinctive worship that appeared to dominate the Busro society for several years, in which the people (who had, after all, witnessed real warfare) mimicked a violent confrontation with the "beast" in an attempt to purge disease from the community. This battle had begun when the Busro believers were staying at Union Village in 1813 and early 1814 and the entire community was suffering sickness and an appalling number of deaths:

> In early times at Union Village they once had a gift which they called the War (spiritual) times. They rose at four o'clock a.m. and had meeting sweet singing and hard dancing to defend themselves against the attacks of the evil one, either through their own passions of a fallen nature or from sickness. It was after the Busro people came and brought the pestilence of their Wabash or army fever that took so many precious ones from their ranks. In these meetings they also labored and prayed for healing gifts for the sick and which in some cases was affected.[22]

Salome's 1815 letter identifies a Busro song that accompanied this exercise, replete with evocative references to "stink" and "smell" typical of pioneer writings about disease, especially in hot, humid areas:

> I will send one verse of Sacred harmony, and this is as much as they can bear to sing at one breathing spell, and then Raise the Seige again, and so Stamp and Roar, and then sing again about the Beast—

> To Virgin Souls he is a foe, But loves a Stinking whore
> With one Consent we bid him go, And Shew his head no more
> Chorus: Ah the beast the nasty beast, His Stink I Cannot bear
> He came from Hell I hate his smell, We will not have him here[23]

For the next several years, many letters from Busro contained references to seasonal sickness. In the early fall of 1815, Issachar Bates suffered from "fevers," probably a malaria relapse.[24] In September 1817, Archibald Meacham noted that the annual struggle with "pestilential fevers" continued: "Pen cannot describe nor tongue express so as to convey a real Sensation of the tribulation and anguish of both soul and body that we have all experienced by reason of those pestilential nasty stinking distempers."[25] Issachar wrote to his friend Benjamin Seth Youngs in November 1818 that the season's "doleful siege" was mostly over, and the sick were on the mend, but, he wrote, "if we do not have tribulation here, I want to go to some place where I can find out what it is."[26] In January 1819, Issachar vented in a letter to the New Lebanon Ministry his irration that reports from Busro seemed invariably to contain bad news:

> For some cause or other it hath been our lot (at West Union) for the most part, to burden our beloved friends in the east with our calamities either by the distresses of war, or sickness, or some other work of the devil, so

that it becomes irksome to write . . . We got along with our affairs tolerable well the season past, and the society were more healthy than they
ever were in this place before, till the middle of August, and then the fever
came on us with fury . . . [T]hen we betook ourselves to prayer, and we
obtained help from God, so that we made war with the destroyer. When
any were violently seized, we would assemble at the meeting house and
labour till they were released, which often took place.[27]

As Issachar's words imply, spiritual warfare remained virtually the only
available weapon against disease at Busro. Issachar singled out Salome's assistance and companionship during this difficult time — "Our good sister
Salome was numbered among the sick although it was only about one week
and the rest of the time she was a zealous helper" — and he expresses relief
(and betrays his impatience with Busro's unruly children at the same time)
that the epidemic caused only one death: "the destroyer got nothing but one
little wicked boy."

Without a doubt, seasonal bouts of malaria and other illnesses plagued
Busro's first several years,[28] but the seemingly constant presence of disease
was just one among several difficulties. Manuscripts also point to a rift between Issachar Bates and Archibald Meacham, which may have stemmed
partly from the fact that Archibald envied Issachar's relative mobility. Even
though, Issachar's principal care as a member of the West Union Ministry had
to be the people of Busro, he nevertheless still undertook a fair number of
journeys. Some of these were to destinations close by, such as the settlement
of Harmonists along the Wabash south of Vincennes. Interested in possibly
consolidating the two groups, the Busro Ministry — generally in the form of
Issachar, Archibald, Salome, and others — made frequent trips to Harmony
during the first several years after the return to Indiana. During these visits
they sang, danced, and spoke with the Harmony leaders, who were not always
sure what to make of them. A letter written to George Rapp in 1816 reports
the visit of the Shakers' "two directors and two women who, by them, live in
adjoining rooms," indicating fairly clearly that the Harmonists were not sure
whether to believe that the Shakers are really celibate.[29] Issachar wrote plea-
surably to Seth Youngs Wells of his discussions on music with Charles Miller,
"their chief singer," who was interested in the original hymns that Issachar
and other Shakers are writing.[30] The Busro elders also agreed to host George
Rapp's daughters Gertrude and Rosina — who may have reminded Issachar
of his own distant daughters — for a period of over a year, so that they could
learn to speak English.[31]

But Issachar Bates also made many trips to Union Village and to South Union in Kentucky, often alone. These trips had various justifications—escorting brethren who needed to travel east, providing guidance to traveling elders unfamiliar with a route, accompanying sick believers seeking medical treatment. Given Issachar's established fondness for mobility, it is reasonable that he would seize every opportunity travel. Going to South Union meant seeing Benjamin Seth Youngs, his closest friend, as well as the other old believers who made up the Ministry there. Travel to Union Village probably afforded opportunity to visit with Richard McNemar and Mathew Houston, both good friends, as well as to receive some spiritual encouragement from Father David Darrow. In the many poems and hymns attributed to Issachar Bates during the 1810s and early 1820s, there is evidence that he took advantage of time at Union Village to write hymn texts, perhaps drawing inspiration from Richard, a fellow poet. One lengthy doctrinal poem by Issachar Bates titled "The Voice of Wisdom or Mother" appears in a formal manuscript layout together with a substantial explanatory essay and a cover page that dates the poem to 1819 and places its origin in Union Village.[32] From the appearance of the work, it may have been intended for printing as a pamphlet, suggesting a collaboration between Issachar and Richard, who retained his interest in the printing profession and in establishing a printing enterprise among the Ohio Shakers.[33] In short, travel from Busro afforded Issachar a wealth of distractions, including many productive ones. It is true that during one period Issachar remained more or less stationery in the Wabash country for about three years, except for visits to the nearby Harmonist settlement, yet he clearly chafed at what, to him, felt like unaccustomed restriction: "[W]hen I traveled from place to place, I thought I was something of a judge of believers getting along—but I have been so long in one spot, and at one thing—labouring, teaching, reproving, suffering, watching, praying, hoping, and waiting for people to get along—that I hardly know what GET ALONG is . . . I am sinking under this burden."[34]

Charged with sharing principal care of the believers at Busro, in contrast to his activities of working among world's people and new converts, Issachar Bates may have been sinking under these responsibilities and inclined to brood over his situation. The gregarious Issachar missed his years of freer movement, of interacting with an ever-shifting array of people. He missed his friends, among both old believers and young believers. He missed his family back East. Receiving songs as gifts from Polly and "Little Issachar" reminded him of all his children. Among the closest of his new western friends, the only one with him at Busro was Salome Dennis. It is clear from her writing that some of Issachar's happiest times were those spent with her and with other Busro believers who enjoyed the sociability of singing and dancing. His yearning to spend time among old friends is evident in one letter sent to "Beloved Benjamin," now the chief elder at South Union:

> I want to see thee and talk with thee — yea I want to set down between thee and E[lder] Joseph before that little open stove, and drink some cider and then walk in and smoke a pipe with E[ldress] Molly and E[ldress] Mercy, and talk a little about simple things, and have it all talked over about New Lebanon and Watervliet and all the good things we could think of, and then go round and see all them pretty children that I once called mine, and see all what ye are about there . . . but I do not expect to get the privilege to come and see you this season.[35]

This short passage speaks volumes about the importance Issachar Bates attached to his circle of friends. He pined for the chance to spend time with Benjamin and the other elders at South Union, all easterners, with whom he could reminisce — and probably gossip — about the New York communities. His letter offers a glimpse into the relaxed after-hours setting of a group of middle-aged Shaker elders and eldresses, men and women with years of shared experiences, taking immense pleasure in simply sitting together by the stove, smoking clay pipes. The "children" Issachar refers to at South Union are the young believers whom he worked to convert more than ten years before and with whom he had spend so many interludes during his roving years before stepping into the Busro ministry. And the "cider" that he plainly relished would have been a fermented drink with some alcoholic content, not a beverage then expressly forbidden among Shakers.[36]

In contrast, Archibald Meacham seldom traveled, and manuscripts portray him in this period as a sober and serious man. His jealousy over Issachar's comparative mobility and his close friendships is plainly expressed to Benjamin Seth Youngs in a letter discussing visits between Busro and South Union:

> Now Dear Brother I do not know but that I have granted all thy requests that thou hast asked, except in relation to Elder Issachar's going to South Union this fall, which thing appeared very difficult in our distressed situation, not only that he has been there twice since I have, and I did not know but that it would justly be my turn next. However, I do not suppose that thou would be so glad to see me there, as thou wouldest Elder Issachar. Notwithstanding, I am fond of union, and am willing to unite

with all good believers on fair equitable terms, so as to keep a good under-standing with Believers in every place.[37]

The bond between Issachar and Benjamin—longtime companions since they were sent out as missionaries together in 1803—was well known to all the old believers. For Archibald, who then lived with Issachar, quite literally in the same room, observing that bond and being unable to enjoy a similar close-ness with anyone must have been vexing. Added to that, it was Issachar—not Archibald—who was the virtual "founder" of Busro, the one who had helped carry the Shaker gospel to the prairies in 1808. Many of the believers at Busro had converted because of Issachar's preaching and had made their first confes-sions to him. The initial justification for sending Issachar to Busro had even been to help "gather" the people to Archibald, an uncomfortable reminder that Archibald lacked the personal charisma to gain acceptance on his own. And Issachar had made it plain to David Darrow that he had never wanted the assignment. Now, years into the enterprise, it was Issachar who enjoyed the people's affections, who had a nickname, who seemed able to travel when he wished. For Archibald, this all may have been hard to take.

The rift between Issachar Bates and Archibald Meacham comes into even sharper focus when considered in the context of the Busro believers' reaction to malaria. Long before the eastern ministry decided to close Busro entirely, there was some consideration of uprooting the community and moving it entirely to a new site. The Busro Shakers had acquired over twelve hundred acres of unimproved land in Illinois along the Embarrass River (also called "Ambrau" in some sources), a tributary on the western side of the Wabash.[38] In December 1819 Archibald Meacham solicited the views of the eastern Min-istry in moving the entire community of West Union to this Illinois land, on the basis of the "sickliness" of the Busro site.[39] Learning of Archibald's plan, Issachar used a trip to Union Village to find opportunity to compose a private letter of his own for the New Lebanon Ministry, detailing his objections to a move:

> [I]t felt to me that Elder Archibald had been soliciting the Ministry, for some counsel in relation to moving from West Union, to Embarrass. And as I was in Kentucky, when the letter was written and sent on. And being satisfied that Eldress Martha, and Salome, were unwilling to move to that place, and the greatest part of the society, unwilling also. And as my own feelings—yea, my faith, and judgment (according to my best understand-ing) have ever been opposed to it. And as I never could feel that the Min-istry at Union Village felt a union with it, it will therefore be a releasement

to my mind, to inform the Ministry at N Lebanon that it was in this manner, that the Ministry at West Union, wrote unto them on that subject. For it is truly mortifying to me, that after so often renewing our resolution to our friends in the east that we were determined to maintain the gospel on that ground, that after all we should turn about and despise the place, because we have been sick there in years that are past or for fear that we shall be sick there again, since there hath no alteration taken place for the worse . . . for it is now going on two years since we have had any sickness to complain of. And if we should leave our ground for the sake of health, it appears to me it would only be fleeing from a Lion to a Bear. For by the form of the country, and our own proof, and experience, hath proved to every understanding, disinterested person, that there is no material difference, as to healthy or sickly, places, within the compass of one hundred miles around us — and for more than that to the west. But if I had not believed that it was the gift of god that called me to West Union, I never should have gone there. For it was the greatest cross that ever came in my way since I confessed my sins. But seeing I did believe it, I have always testified, both in sickness and in health, from the beginning, that I believed that in faithful obedience to the gospel, and by good economy we should overcome, and clean off even the very cause of the sickness — (and I believe that it hath come to pass in a good degree) — and this hath been a uniform testimony from us all (in the Ministry) till about eighteen months ago — and I am sure that I never felt any thing more deathly to my soul from a believer — than to hear it reversed — but I have said enough . . . for I dare not presume to decide any of these matters — but I truly and candidly am labouring to do the best I know.[40]

Issachar's letter suggests that Archibald had taken advantage of Issachar's absence in Kentucky to float an ill-founded proposal to move the Busro believers to the Embarrass River site, against the express wishes not only of Issachar but of the two eldresses and most of the society. The letter paints Issachar's dismay that the New Lebanon ministry should perceive the Busro elders as hypocritical, pledging their commitment to the Busro site while at the same time planning a move elsewhere. From an environmental perspective, Issachar's assessment of the Embarrass site as having no relative advantage shows keen insight, probably accurate. Indeed, because of the association of malaria with land in the first stages of agricultural improvement, the Shakers might have experienced more malaria at Embarrass, not less. By admitting candidly that going to Busro was the most onerous task he had undertaken in his Shaker life, Issachar appeared all the more sincere in his assertion that he believed the Busro site to be a place where the Shakers could yet prevail over the challenges that faced them. At the end of the passage, Issachar insinuates that he feels betrayed and misrepresented by Archibald.

Another perspective on the rift between Issachar Bates and Archibald Meacham can be found in the writings of Busro Shaker William Redmon, who had come among Busro believers in 1811 as a boy (and who would later write such eloquent observations of the prairie, the wildlife, and the Indians). In a set of retrospective remarks about the problems of the Busro community and the reasons for its ultimate demise, he singles out the differing postures of Issachar and Archibald toward combating sickness.

> It was undoubtedly the opinion of some of our leading characters that nothing was wanting but implicit obedience to our Ministry, to make us as healthy as any people in the world. This enthusiasm, however, was entertained only by a few, whose hoary heads could be warped to almost any thing but sound reason. George Legier was of the above opinion. John Hancock, remarkable for many healing gifts, and every other enthusiastic opinion, was an ardent associate of this new theology. Elder Issachar went so far in it one night as to say (after a very sharp meeting and paling of the Prince of the Air out doors) that the air was purified, and that West Union was as healthy as any place in the world. Elder Archibald was not of this opinion, his sound judgment in this matter could not be warped by the most profound theologist of this new divinity.[41]

From Redmon's perspective, the almost elderly Issachar Bates — then about sixty — represented superstition and absurd fanaticism, and drew the other "hoary heads" of the aged and ignorant along with him. The younger Meacham — in his forties — represented rationality. Redmon's allegation that Issachar led the people in a mock outdoor battle against the "Prince of the Air" — a New Testament reference to Satan — rings true, in light of the vigorous "warfare"-style worship so repeatedly described during these malaria-ridden years at Busro. However, Redmon's account is an oversimplification. Issachar's letter to the New Lebanon ministry had declared that he believed both spiritual obedience and good habits of economy together were needed to heal Busro of its ailments. To the extent that good habits of economy included consistent improvements on the landscape, in building, and in farm production, those very actions could be expected — over a few years — to create an improved environment for the inhabitants' health, which did in fact come to pass at Busro.

While he lived at Busro, Issachar Bates remained one of the site's greatest champions. The productivity of the land was undeniable. Although the area experienced periodic crop damage from insect infestation and drought, along with tornado damage to a new barn and several miles of fencing, for the most part each year saw gains. By 1816, the settlement had shown astonishing progress despite being hampered by disease. A traveler identified a remarkably diverse farm operation of cotton, indigo, grain, and potatoes, hundreds of sheep, aggressive local marketing of vegetables, and the finest orchards in the area.[42] Given Issachar's known interest in tree husbandry, exhibited as early as 1810 at Turtle Creek, it is possible that Busro's orchards were his particular inspiration. Against the increasingly sophisticated farm, orchard, mill, and shop production, however, the people still lived in a collection of log buildings. A Shaker apostate who lived briefly at Busro in the early 1820s later published a salacious claim that the Busro elders lived in luxury and maintained a private wine cellar while the people lived in squalor — a certain exaggeration,[43] but one that may have stemmed partly from the elders' efforts to set an example of orderly living in a region where disorder prevailed.

For Issachar, the frontier living conditions reaffirmed the frontier habits of the believers, especially the young men whom Issachar and others were trying to reorient to become obedient and proficient workers. Issachar expressed his frustrations to this regard to his eastern confidant, Seth Youngs Wells:

> I believe that we live on the best and most easy part of all the face of the earth for cultivation — and this makes it far more distressing to me than if we lived on the barrens between Watervliet and Albany — for . . . I behold the natural beauty and extensive production of the land . . . and view the beings that inhabit it, and in particular those who are called to redeem & subdue it. Sprightly and active men, surely one among them all but what can cut off a wood-pecker head with a rifle ball at the distance of six or eight rods, or course a bee through the woods to his hive in a few minutes, but not one among them all (two years ago) that knew how to hang a scythe or use it when it was hung, or how to use any other farming tool except an axe. This fills me sometimes with such tribulation that I can hardly stand still one minute in a place . . . and for all this abundance the people here do not work more than half as many hours as the people do at the eastward — and waste more than four times as much.[44]

As an antidote to the perceived lack of "industry" among the Busro believers, Issachar Bates employed a favorite tactic — song. His hymn "Industry and Economy," written at Busro, became popular among Shakers in West and East alike because it reaffirmed the virtue of diligent habits in Shaker communities. Issachar drew on nature metaphors to remind believers that nature itself ordained all beings to be industrious, so people need not be resentful of the expectations of Shaker life:

> All nature calls for busy hands, For this is heav'n's decree;
> The beast, the bird, the insect stands A monitor to me;
> The little busy artful bee Works ev'ry shining hour,
> And her industry I can see, In ev'ry opening flower.[45]

In spite of Issachar's heavy critique, accounts of Busro from non-Shaker travelers make no mention of an absence of industrious activity. To the contrary, the many published observations of Busro during the years of Issachar Bates's life there indicated a prosperous and orderly community, the people generous and friendly. Thomas Dean, an advocate of the Brotherton Indians in New York State who journeyed up the Wabash in July 1817 seeking land to which that tribe could remove, visited Busro.[46] He observed that the Shakers' daily life there was regulated by the blowing of a trumpet, beginning with a 4 a.m. fanfare summons to the meetinghouse, where a session of dancing and singing ensued.[47] Dean spent three days at Busro, during which he conversed freely with "principal men," enjoyed meals prepared by the sisters, and lodged in a clean private room. The fact that Dean was both a Quaker and devoted to "Indian philanthropy" may have drawn the Shakers at Busro—and probably Issachar Bates in particular—to engage him in conversation. In any case, Dean records a discussion of Tecumseh, the Prophet Tenskwatawa, and the causes of the hostilities of 1811 that likely involved Issachar:

> They spoke of many losses and hardships they have had in consequence of the war, and that they thought Tecumseh and the Prophet had been very much misrepresented . . . that they were in his opinion Christian Indians, opposed to war, and he thought it was an unguarded expression of General Harrison to one of the Pottawottomi chiefs by the name of Winemank that caused the battle at Tippecanoe; that there were not more than 250 men engaged in the battle out of 800 which had assembled at the Prophet's town for the purpose of information, or of religious devotion; that they were well acquainted with the Prophet and believed him to be a peaceable and a good man.[48]

The tenor of the comments Dean recorded virtually ensure that the main speaker was Issachar Bates. No one else then at Busro had such longstanding familiarity with Tecumseh and the Prophet, or had been privy to the interactions between Harrison, Tecumseh, and the other tribes in 1810 and 1811. The exchange also reveals the intensity with which Issachar continued to replay those experiences in his memory, even six years later. The opportunity to discuss his longstanding acquaintances with the Shawnee leaders, reaching all the way back to 1807 when he and others at Turtle Creek first sought out the Prophet's group with the hopes of converting them, must have been profoundly welcome to Issachar.

But Issachar's life at Busro necessarily focused more on the future than on reliving the past. As the cycles of fever diminished at Busro, more of Issachar Bates's attention was drawn to the community's physical expansion. Work began in 1820 on a large brick dwelling. In early 1821, Issachar wrote on behalf of the West Union Ministry to report that Busro's situation had turned prosperous ever since deciding to build the dwelling — a sign of a "special blessing." And although Busro had long been hampered by a lack of building materials, a source for foundation stones was now found.

> We feel as though we have had a very special blessing in relation to this building since we began it . . . we had fine weather for business — the winter here for two or three seasons past appear to be getting longer, colder, drier, and more even, which feels more agreeable than might floods of water. Ye may judge that it hath been dry in this country — we got all the stones for our cellar wall out of the bottom of the great Wabash which was a great favour to us. We got all our stones in the Wabash. We have often thought of the words of the psalmist (while we were rolling out such nice stones, which had been hid where the finger of man could never before touch them), "What ailed thee thou sea, that thou floodest, And thou Jordan that thou was driven back? (Answer) At the presence of the Lord, at the presence of the God of the whole earth." What ailed thee thou Wabash that thou was so dryed up? Because we had a special gift of God to go to building in this place, where God hath placed his name and we took hold of it and God — even God — opened the way, that he might confound and put to silence an unbelieving spirit, that was always crying out that we had nothing here to build with. But we have now found out that we have enough to build with, and that if we do the work, God will provide the stuff.[49]

Characteristically, Issachar sees a divine hand in a natural event — in this case, a dry summer and autumn causing water levels in the river to diminish, thereby uncovering stone that the builders could not have otherwise reached.

The process of construction unfolded slowly over two years, with assistance from two Union Village brethren, but the Union Village Ministry was sympathetic to the comparatively slow process of building at Busro, relative to other western Shaker sites:

> [W]e feel no disposition of casting any blame on the people there on account of their being so far behind other Societies, in the way of building, or on account of their broken and scattered situation in time past. For we think it is or ought to be considered that a considerable part of the difficulties under which they have had to labour have originated from causes which other Societies have not had the painful lot to experience.[50]

By spring 1822 the new dwelling was ready. The family of sixty that moved into this commodious brick, stone, and plaster structure — surely finer than anything they had lived in before — must have been particularly delighted when "Elder Archibald handed out the rules and regulations to be observed therein."[51] But in writing on behalf of the Busro ministry, Issachar asserted that the new dwelling helped create order — which the believers had lacked — and the community would continue to reap the benefits.

> Now in relation to our progress . . . the small increase which we have had in outward accommodations, gives us good reason to hope that a foundation is laid whereby we may begin to increase. For we suppose that all believers know that without order there can be no real increase, and where there is a lack of outward accommodation there will be a lack of order. This has been our painful situation, but in these things we are gaining ground. Our new brick house is well finished off — and a family of sixty people moved into it May 23rd. Likewise, in the young believers order, a new hewed log house was well finished off, and a family gathered into it, the first of this present month. This is a great releasement to us. We seem to know now where our people are — without hunting all the groves, and high places, and under every green tree to find them. And moreover, this seems to encourage them to go on and build more. We are now building a framed meeting house — 50 by 40. The materials are mostly on the ground, and the workmen are now framing it . . . we can have meeting in it the coming fall and winter.[52]

In short, it seemed that the Busro believers were on a roll. Material life at Busro was growing increasingly prosperous. Issachar Bates was particularly pleased to report their luck in cotton and flax production, declaring, "We have raised as good a crop of Flax on this prairie the season past, as ever we saw grow out of the earth" and that "we also raised a good crop of cotton perhaps

100 weight—this makes our good sisters look pleasant." In the spring of 1822 Issachar was able to show off the progress made at Busro to his good friends from South Union, when Benjamin Seth Youngs and the rest of the South Union Ministry came for a two-week visit that combined socializing with selecting newborn calves to take back to South Union in hopes of starting a cattle business.[53] With the river unusually high that spring, the visitors experienced one of Busro's infamous problems—floods—firsthand. Issachar and Salome toured the visitors around most of the Busro community by boat, poling their way through swollen bayous.[54]

A visit to Busro from the Union Village ministry later in 1822 must have given Issachar considerable pleasure because it afforded him the opportunity of exhibiting Busro's progress to Father David Darrow himself, who had extended endless patience to both Issachar and to Busro more generally. Darrow was duly impressed with what he observed (figure 8.2).

> And as to the old Busroe fever, which there has been so much talk about heretofore, we found but little of it there: but we found a large brick house on Busroe plains well finished off, and occupied by a large family of good believers; with which both them and us were much better pleased with. Also they had a meeting-house framed, ready for raising after harvest and they were in strong hopes that they should get it up and enclosed this fall and enough done to it, so that they might be able to have their public meetings in it before long. Their old log meeting house is getting entirely too small for public meetings; since they are beginning to have some increase of young believers.[55]

As the Union Village Ministry concluded its visit, Darrow decided that the group should travel on to South Union instead of returning to Ohio immediately. Issachar was designated to accompany them as their guide, since the Union Village group was unsure of the route. This change of plans brought about an unanticipated pleasure: a spontaneous "reunion" of most of the old believers then in the West. A South Union journal records the event.

> Also on the 25th of July we had a visit from the Ministry of Union Village. Brother Issachar came with them from West Union where they had likewise staid 15 days. In the mean time . . . we had also a visit of the Ministry from Pleasant Hill—i.e., part of them (Elder Samuel, Eldress Anna and a young brother & Sister). This was the first and only time that so many old believers who came from the East have happened to be together in one place from all the different societies in the western country since those

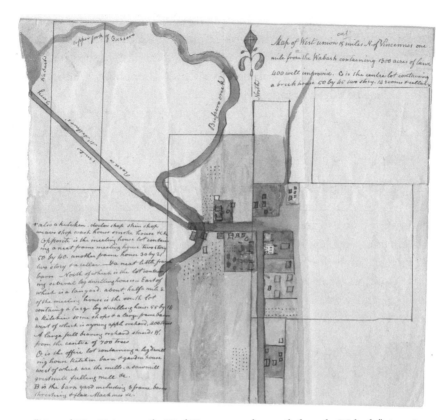

8.2 *"Map of West Union 15 miles N of Vincennes and one mile from the Wabash," circa 1825, attributed to Richard McNemar. This map was likely intended to exhibit the improvements at the Busro site for the distant Shaker Ministries in Ohio or New York. (Courtesy of the Western Reserve Historical Society.)*

societies were established. All this you may be sure made it a good visit to us. All the old believers (except 4) were here together. We were blessed with a plenty & we were all thankful and joyful.[56]

The enjoyable interlude could not last. Issachar Bates returned to Busro to face sad and difficult times. Martha Sanborn, who had succeeded Ruth Darrow as principal eldress, was suffering with breast cancer, which was both excruciating and debilitating. Issachar escorted her to Union Village in hopes of finding better medical care for her,[57] but her condition deteriorated and she died painfully in the fall of 1823, ironically while Archibald Meacham was suffering himself from a 3-day relapse of his malaria. Issachar paid tribute to Martha in the hymn he wrote for her funeral. But perhaps even more heartbreaking for Issachar was that Busro received word in October 1823 that

Polly Bates, Issachar's thirty-five-year-old daughter at Watervliet, New York, had died of a lingering battle with tuberculosis.[58] Issachar had last seen her about eighteen years earlier. Since then what communication they are known to have shared was indirect, through songs and other oblique messages exchanged between their two communities.

> *But God is my witness that I bore it with all the patience I had, and that I did them all the good I was able to, and did all the work I was able to do.*[59]

On January 29, 1824, Issachar Bates set out alone from Busro for a visit to Union Village.[60] Perhaps as he traveled he reflected back on another January journey between the two sites, the harrowing trip of 1809 with Richard McNemar and Benjamin Seth Youngs when they all nearly died of exposure and hunger. Surely the road conditions had improved in the fifteen years since that episode. Issachar would have likely been in a reflective mood, as the day was his birthday. Issachar was now sixty-six, an old man by the standards of the day. He had closed his most productive middle years there on the western frontier, mingling excitement and danger, struggle and reward, exhilaration and sadness. He remained far from his wife and children, whom he had not seen for over eighteen years and some of whom he would never see again. It is not likely he knew, as he completed that now familiar route between Busro and Union Village, that his life journey had reached its geographical apogee. Since childhood, Issachar's path had taken him to the margins, to places on the edge. New challenges awaited him back in Ohio, to be sure. But as 1824 began, Issachar's frontier days were concluded. Still, the long years working to establish a Shaker presence in Indiana had helped ensure that Shakers everywhere would always associate the name Issachar Bates with the perilous frontier. Issachar may have begun his geographical separation from the Indiana frontier on his birthday in 1824, but his spirit remained linked to that distant region nonetheless.

CHAPTER 9

"Remnant of the tribe of Issachar"

THE BATES KINSHIP NETWORK

IN THE SHAKER EAST

*And now, last of all, but not the least, I must enclose my kind and best love
. . . together with all the kind and good love of all the brethren and sisters
in our family, and of the Elders brethren & sisters at the South House,
and particularly of the Remnant of the tribe of Issachar, all in a lump.*
— Seth Young Wells

Like many other Shaker converts, Issachar Bates entered the
movement in the midst of a large assortment of family members — spouse,
children, siblings, nieces, nephews, and in-laws. Unlike most other converts,
though, he spent the vast proportion of his life as a Shaker far removed from
those biological family members he loved. Among all the old believers in the
Shaker West, Issachar Bates was the only married person and parent forced to
adapt to a life completely removed from his biological family. Singular among
the old believers for his adaptability to the wilderness, his charismatic ability to persuade world's people, his joviality, and his notable gifts of preaching and hymn writing, Issachar Bates continued to cast a shadow back onto
the East, even from his distant position in the West. Meanwhile, the sheer
size and complexity of the Bates kinship network was significant, and many
of his kinfolk in the East exerted influence on their own Shaker communities — another index of Issachar's impact on Shakerism. Several of his children were important and productive members of the New York communities
of Watervliet and New Lebanon, and they leave evidence that they inherited
some of their father's talent for poetry and music, as well as his spiritual
passion.

During his thirty years in the West, the Issachar Bates delighted in news
from his many eastern friends and family members, once remarking of their
letters, "we love the looks of the paper."[1] A gregarious and outgoing man motivated by strong emotions, there is no reason to suppose that Issachar ceased
to love his biological family. His good friend and confidant in Watervliet, New
York, Seth Youngs Wells, enjoyed daily contact with many of Issachar's family,
and it was through Wells that occasional news arrived of the "remnant of the

tribe of Issachar."[2] Because surviving correspondence is only patchy, however, it is difficult to reconstruct exactly how closely Issachar followed the activities of his family back in New York. What little evidence exists points to love, concern, and mutual interest between Issachar and some of his family members. Other kinfolk may have been more obscure to him. Yet close scrutiny of records from the New York communities reveals an interesting picture of the diverse roles played by Bates kin in early nineteenth-century Shakerism.

"Family" provided the key organizing principle of Shaker life. But on the surface, Shaker culture devalued the ties of biological family, urging people to put aside their affections for their "natural relations" in favor of their new "gospel relations." The Church reserved parental titles ("mother" and "father") for an exalted few: Ann Lee and a few of her closest associates of the founding generation of Shakerism, Ann Lee's earliest successors in the East, and the first appointed leads in the West. Within the framework of a spiritual family with "gospel parents," all Shakers were spiritual brothers and sisters. The honorific titles of elder and eldress were accorded to those appointed to positions of responsibility. "Family" was also the concept for temporal organization in Shaker life. Individual collective households were called "families," presided over by teams of four—a first elder and eldress who went by that title, and a second elder and eldress who were designated "elder brother" and "elder sister." Shakers were expected to regard all fellow believers as siblings, to develop familial love and affection for them, and to address them as "sister" and "brother" regardless of natural kinship ties or age. Nonetheless, affections among biological family members probably persisted more commonly than scholars have acknowledged, especially in the early decades of Shakerism. Anyone who examines temporal family membership in most Shaker communities will see people who share surnames. As we have seen, although Shaker communal life called for the reorganization of biological family units into collective temporal family units, many people continued to inhabit households alongside their parents, siblings, cousins, and spouses, making it possible to sustain family bonds at least informally. For Issachar Bates, those bonds were far more difficult to continue, due to his separation in the West.

⁓ *I was married to Lovina Maynard . . . By her I had eleven children. The first was still born, another lived but a few minutes, the other nine are what is called proper children. Namely, Lovina, Artemas, Oliver, Nahum, Polly, Issachar, Sarah, William, and Betsy.*[3]

⮕ *About the beginning of March, 1803, Issachar Bates & family, [8 in number] arrived from Hartford, Washington Co. N.Y. & occupied part of William Carter's west house, in which David Train's family then lived.*[4]

⮕ *So that in March 1803 we moved to Watervliet, all but my two oldest sons with whom I settled.*[5]

Seven children accompanied Issachar and Lovina Bates to Watervliet, New York, in March 1803 to live as Shakers: Lovina (born January 1780), Nahum (b. March 1786), Polly (b. June 1788), Issachar (b. November 1790), Sarah (b. November 1792), William (b. April 1796), and Betsy (b. June 1798). Of these, the eldest daughter, Lovina, is virtually invisible in manuscripts, with scant evidence of her Shaker life and no record of her death.[6] Of Nahum Bates, nothing is known except that he formally confessed his sins in April 1803, when he would have been seventeen.[7] The remaining members of Issachar Bates immediate family—the elder Lovina, Polly, Issachar, Sarah, William, and Betsy—leave ample evidence of Shaker lives that were at least interesting, and in some cases both rich and influential.

⮕ *Give my love to Levina Bates, and tell her, I kindly thank her for taking up her Cross, in Consenting that Issachar might Come to us at first, and in Bearing the cross that he might continue with us.*[8]

Particularly during Issachar Bates's early years in the West, young believers found it remarkable that he willingly accepted his prolonged separation from his wife and children. Indeed, his apparent sacrifice may have helped to explain why Issachar was so persuasive in presenting the requirements of the Shaker gospel to worldly audiences. He was living proof that a mature man with a full and satisfying marriage and many loving children could adapt both to celibacy and to the dissolution of his nuclear family household. Many western converts expressed unfeigned love for Issachar, and as a natural consequence, many wished to reach out to his family members. In a September 1807 letter, Malcolm Worley sent special greetings to Lovina Bates, Issachar's wife, and revealed surprisingly enlightened assumptions about a wife's degree of participation in decisions affecting a married couple. Further he acknowledged that Issachar's presence in the West was an ongoing "cross" for Lovina to bear. Because "the cross" was the term the Shakers used explicitly to refer to the renunciation of sexuality, Malcolm's comments quite pointedly imply that he realized Issachar and Lovina had sacrificed their sex life. The boldness of these remarks might be tempered by the fact that Malcolm himself was a newly remarried widower in 1805 when he converted to Shakerism, one whose wife was pregnant with their first child. By 1807 he and Issachar had spent significant time together, and it is not unlikely that they would have commiserated over the restrictions that Shakerism brought to a marital relationship.

In 1813 Daniel Moseley, an eastern Shaker who had worked in the Shaker West as an "old believer" for nearly five years, wrote a letter to Father David Darrow in Ohio. He included a message for Issachar Bates that he had recently seen and talked to Lovina and the Bates children: "I can tell Brother Isacher that I have lately seen all his family, and heard from them very lately. Levina is a good sister, and the children are young men and women grown, they are all well and I think it would refresh your bowels to see their standing. Elder Brother wrote a letter to B. Isacher about the 23 of Jan. 1813."[9] Issachar was probably gratified to hear that his children were maturing into Shakers of good standing and that Lovina was finding some satisfaction in her life. He had brooded over her happiness and urged her in the note of 1808 to reassure him that she was truly contented.

Lovina and her children had come to the Shaker settlement of Watervliet, New York, in 1803, moving into part of a house also occupied by the family of David Train, also recent converts. The Trains were kin to Issachar Bates (Issachar Bates's older sister Hannah had married David in 1774), and it was the newly married Hannah who may have given a home to the teenaged Issachar and some of her other siblings when their father, William Bates, had remarried in 1777 and moved from the area. Because Lovina was a local girl when she met and married Issachar in 1778, it is certain that she would have known Hannah and David Train, and probably several of the Train children.[10] Whether sharing a house with her in-laws, nieces, and nephews whom she had not seen for seventeen years was a strain for Lovina is unknown. Given Issachar's frequent preaching tours for the Shakers, it may have been a comfort for Lovina to reacquaint with family and share household work with her sister-in-law.

When Issachar had last seen Lovina in December of 1805, she and the children had been on the verge of moving into a house newly built for them at Watervliet. How long they lived in that house is uncertain. But we do know that during the period from 1800 to 1815 the Shaker population of Watervliet was growing, and biological families were being reorganized into spiritual families bound together under covenants to establish spiritual gospel order and economic joint interest. In 1815, two years after Moseley's letter, Lovina Bates signed the newly enacted covenant of the Second Family at Watervliet.[11] She was fifty-five years old. Also called the "West Family," Watervliet's Second

Family was organized around the community's "west house," the house into which the Bates family had originally moved when they arrived in 1803. The household was also referred to as "Seth Wells' family," because Seth Youngs Wells had informal care over it even before the first covenant was signed. It was also Seth Wells' family in a literal sense, as well, since so many members of his own biological family lived there, including his sister Hannah, who was the family's chief eldress, and several of his younger brothers. The Watervliet Second Family was likewise a biological one for Lovina Bates, because in addition to some of her children, she shared the household with two sisters-in-law, two brothers-in-law, and several nieces and nephews. And once she arrived at Watervliet, Lovina Bates remained situated near Seth Wells, who was one of Issachar's confidants as well as the first cousin of Issachar's best friend, Benjamin Seth Youngs. It was Seth Wells who had risen to Issachar's defense in 1804 when a new believer criticized his abrasive preaching style, and it was Wells who wrote many personal letters to Issachar Bates, and who was in a position to convey messages and greetings from Lovina and the family.

Little is known about Lovina Bates's life at Watervliet, New York, but some aspects can be extrapolated. As a member of the Second Family, she would have been a direct witness to the contentious events involving a member of that family named James Chapman. In 1814 Chapman entered Watevliet with his young children, but his wife, Eunice, came to Watervliet to voice her strenuous objections. Her behavior was so disruptive that a group of sisters, including Hannah Train, had to physically restrain her and force her bodily from the house.[12] Lovina may well have been a participant in that scene. Lovina was about the same age as James Chapman, and the two had been paired together by the Second Family elders as "union meeting" partners, a practice in which Shaker brothers and sisters were given structured opportunities for socializing with the opposite sex.[13] Lovina Bates probably harbored an astute perspective on the Chapman family's problems. Like Eunice Chapman, she had initially been horrified when her husband converted to the Shakers. But unlike Eunice, who brought legal action against the Shakers and became one of their most vociferous detractors,[14] Lovina had followed her husband into the Shaker movement willingly and, as a result, was living a comfortable life surrounded by her children and extended family.

The Chapman commotion in the 1810s probably provided some lively punctuation to an otherwise quiet life for Lovina Bates. Likely she worked alongside other women doing domestic tasks. She may have enjoyed music and poetry, because she kept a copy of the Shakers' first printed hymnal, *Millennial Praises*, for her own use. At least a dozen of its 140 hymns were authored by her husband Issachar, something she probably learned through Seth Youngs Wells, who had been actively collecting hymns authored in the West for inclusion in the volume. Lovina's copy of *Millennial Praises* is inscribed with her signature along with the date of April 10, 1813, only a few days after the bound books were picked up by the New Lebanon ministry, demonstrating that she acquired a copy very quickly indeed, perhaps with the assistance of Wells.[15] Lovina Bates was sixty-eight when she died in August 1828, a respectable age for the period. While her death was reported in a letter to the West, how Issachar received the news is unknown. The cause of her death may have been tuberculosis.[16] Her copy of *Millennial Praises* was among her possessions that were passed on to a young sister in the family only days after her funeral.[17]

Also part of the Second Family at Watervliet, New York, were two of Issachar Bates's children, Polly and Issachar Jr. In the 1815 covenant document for the Second Family, Polly's signature is fourth in the column of sisters, and Issachar's is fourth in the column of brothers, in each case, just three names below Hannah Wells and Seth Youngs Wells, eldress and elder.[18] This suggests that both Polly and Issachar Jr. were accorded some prominence within the family, as a pair that were likely to assume some positions of responsibility. At the time of the signing of the covenant in 1815, Polly Bates was twenty-six years old and her brother was twenty-four.

Polly Bates was born in 1788, not long after the family moved to the heavily forested and remote Hartford, New York. When Issachar Bates confessed his sins and embarked on his Shaker life in 1801, Polly had just turned thirteen. The Bates's family's transition into Shaker life paralleled Polly's own transition from childhood into young adulthood. It is hard to know how Polly reacted to the family's move to Watervliet, New York, in 1803 to live alongside the Train family, her aunt, and her cousins, who were virtual strangers to her. Also living at Watervliet were many other large families of new converts from various parts of the region, including the African-American family of Prime Lane.[19] For the adolescent Polly, an abrupt move to such a lively setting, where she could share the company of a crowd of young people more diverse than she had ever known, was probably stimulating and may have compensated for her father's absence. Descriptions of her in surviving Shaker texts suggest she was a sociable young woman able to make friends easily.

By 1815, Polly Bates was a respected sister in Watervliet's Second Family and was being groomed for a leadership position. She must have inherited some of her father's musical and poetical talent. In an April 1815 letter to the Watervliet Second Family, Salome Dennis at the Busro community in Indiana expressed her "kind love and thanks to Polly Bates for her pretty Little token

9.1

"Beautiful Treasure," a song attributed to Polly Bates of Watervliet, New York. From Henry DeWitt, "A collection of songs of various kinds," ASC 882, Edward D. Andrews Shaker Collection. (Courtesy, the Winterthur Library: The Edward Deming Andrews Memorial Shaker Collection.)

of love, we have got tunes fitted to them — They go sweetly," indicating that Polly had sent poems as gifts for the Busro Shakers, including her father Issachar, to sing and enjoy.[20] Several songs attributed to Polly Bates can be found in eastern Shaker music manuscripts (figure 9.1), including one wordless tune of particularly somber beauty (see appendix 3). By 1819, Polly Bates had risen to the position of elder sister in the Watervliet Second Family, which made her the second-highest female authority in that household of perhaps seventy-five adults.[21] She was thus in a position of authority over her mother, her brother, two aging aunts, an uncle, and several cousins, all of whom lived in the Second Family.

Sadly, Polly would not live long. She contracted tuberculosis ("consumption"), and by May of 1823 she was declining fast, as indicated in the letter written by the New Lebanon Ministry to the West Union Ministry that month: "Polly Bates is fast declining with the consumption & cannot continue long in this world — she is much esteemed for her faith & good works. She has so conducted as to find friends here, & we have no doubt of her finding friends in the hereafter."[22] In June 1823, she was officially released from her responsibilities as second eldress.[23] During July, the popular Polly received many visitors, including Issachar Bates's brother Theodore, some sadly remarking that they were there "for the last time."[24] In August 1823, a letter to Union Village from the New Lebanon Ministry informed them that "Polly Bates cannot continue long, if she has not already departed," and asked that they convey that news to West Union, where Issachar was, so that he would realize her death was imminent.[25] Later, when Polly did die, the Watervliet and New Lebanon communities both seemed shaken by her loss, and prompt notification was made to West Union:

> [W]e were called up Stairs to see Sister Polly who appeared to be dying, we kneeled down and pittied her and she revived — we retired and had meeting . . . after meeting we returned to witness the decease of our good Sister Polly Bates, who departed this life about twenty minutes before 3 OC pm. EB (Elder brother) went to inform the Church, who agreed to attend the funeral at 3 OC tomorrow.
>
> This day we attended the funeral and all the Elders and nearly all the young Brethren and Sisters of the Church attended, a very great company and beautiful procession . . . E Brother went to the Chh to carry a letter to send to West Union.[26]

Polly Bates was thirty-five years old when she died on September 14, 1823. Word arrived in the West a few weeks later. At West Union, where Eldress Martha Sanborn had just died from breast cancer, Issachar Bates probably took the news very hard indeed. Evidence suggests that he brooded over Polly's demise for months, and he addressed the deceased Polly in a February 1824 poem called "A Crown" that pays moving tribute to his daughter's "lamb-like spirit." The poem bears the annotation, "A Hymn composed on the suffering of Polly Bates, daughter of Issachar Bates, Ohio 1824" (see appendix 2).

⌇ *The following Hymn was Composed by Big Issachar . . . and is sent in part pay for a pretty little song that was sent to me in the name of* <u>Little</u> *Issachar (a pretty name I wish there was two of them). Big Issachar learned it very quick, and we sing it here, it is Called the Prettyest thing that ever was.*[27]

9.2
Issachar Bates Jr., date unknown. This image appears to be half of a stereograph card. It is inscribed on the back, "Issachar Bates, son of I. Bates, Enfield Conn." The photograph was likely taken during a visit of Issachar Jr. to the Enfield, Connecticut, Shaker community. Item SA 73, Edward D. Andrews Shaker Collection. (Courtesy, the Winterthur Library: The Edward Deming Andrews Memorial Shaker Collection.)

I received the little presents which thou broughtest from the east—for which I thank thee very kindly . . . there were two Anthems. One I have learned, and it is a pretty thing. That of little Issachar's, I have not learned yet.[28]

Issachar Bates Jr. was born in 1790 in Hartford, New York. He was the sixth of his parents' living children, and the couple's fourth son (figure 9.2). Nothing is known about his early childhood. Like his sister Polly, he was an adolescent when his father moved the family to Watervliet. Issachar Jr. may have grown close to Justice Harwood, his first cousin, son of Issachar's sister Dolly, whose family came to Watervliet about the same time. The two were close in age, and in subsequent years, they are often identified in manuscripts as working or taking short trips together. Their names appear together in the 1815 Second Family Covenant, as well as on a later list of Watervliet members. In the covenant, Issachar Jr.'s signature is also directly alongside that of his sister Polly, just under the elders of the family, suggesting he was considered a promising young man suited to future leadership.

Issachar Jr. may also have been mentored by Jesse Wells, a younger brother of Seth Youngs Wells, as a letter written by Seth to Issachar Bates in February 1815 reports that Issachar Jr. and Jesse were working together as carpenters. Later, Watervliet ledgers record that Issachar Jr. was a prolific maker of braided whips, which he produced by the dozen in various lengths.[29] Both carpentry and braiding leather were trades that the young Issachar may have learned as a Shaker. Not yet eleven when his father converted, Issachar Jr. would have been too young to have fully learned a trade in his father's household. There is no evidence that Issachar Sr. was either a carpenter or a whipmaker, in any case. But both were valuable trades: whips were among the small manufactured items that the Shakers marketed in the region, and because the New York communities were growing quickly in the early nineteenth century, carpentry was in great demand. The journal of a contemporary Shaker records that Issachar Jr. sojourned for several weeks at New Lebanon in 1823, helping to build the new meeting house. In fact, he is noted as departing on June 9 and returning on September 30, so he was likely absent from home at the time of his sister Polly's death (though he may have accompanied the large group from New Lebanon noted as attending her funeral). Her passing was likely a bitter thing for the young man. Since he and Polly were close in age and also shared musical talent, they may have had a close relationship.

Because Issachar Bates Jr. did not live in the same community as his father, it was not imperative to find a way to distinguish their names on a day-to-day basis. Many of the younger Issachar's writings — such as songs, poems, and a book of poetry — are signed simply, "Issachar Bates." However, the fact that both father and son wrote songs caused many scribes of music manuscripts to specify one or the other in variousattributions, using abbreviations of "senior" and "junior." The nicknames "Little Issachar" and "Big Issachar" can also be found in just a few letters exchanged by the two with their very closest friends. In addition to the examples found in letters from Busro, Issachar Jr. signs "little Issachar" to a letter written to Isaac Newton Youngs, apparently one of his good friends, whom he had visited in New Lebanon and to whom he was enclosing a song written in four-shape notation.

> Brother Isaac,
> This little song is one that I like, And for this reason I send it to you, believing that after you have learned it, we shall both think alike. But if we fail in this, there is one thing I trust in which we shall agree — That is, never to be covinent breakers. I remember well the covinent that was made between you and I in the Ministry shop the night before I left that place, And it stands good yet on my part, And I have no reason to doubt your integrity. Therefore we must be of one heart & one mind — I have wrote this much to let you know that I have not forgotten you, for I remember the many kindnesses which I received from you & the rest of the brethren & sisters in the Church — And you are all dear to me. Receive these lines with my best love and give it to as many as you feel to. Farewell, "little" Issachar[30]

From this short note, an intriguing picture emerges of Issachar Jr. at about thirty years old, enjoying friendship and shared confidences with Isaac Newton Youngs, who was three years younger. It is impossible to know what covenant the two enacted between them. Isaac's biographer notes that as a young man he struggled both to remain obedient to the Shaker leadership and to manage his sexual desires.[31] The words of Issachar's letter and song suggest that their covenant could have pertained to either issue. In light of the unfeigned devotion shared by "little" Issachar's father, Issachar Bates, and Isaac Youngs' oldest brother, Benjamin Seth Youngs, who were then close companions in the West, the presence of expressed friendship between these two young men is indeed interesting.

Issachar Bates Jr. was evidently seen as a reliable and affable member of the Watervliet community. Documents from the 1810s through the 1830s record his frequent visits to New Lebanon to help with work or to make social calls in company with a few other brothers and sisters, such as one visit in 1819 in a group that included his sister Polly. (Another social visit was carried out in September 1834, with Issachar Jr. part of a group riding to New Lebanon in a new covered wagon.[32]) In 1833 Issachar Jr. was placed in the position of second elder in the South Family at Watervliet, the "gathering order," where he shared responsibility over new believers.[33] In that capacity he was drawn into many discussions with other Watervliet and New Lebanon elders about the handling of difficult new members and recent apostates.[34] In the 1840s Issachar Jr. was made Elder of the South Family.

Among the Watervliet brethren, Issachar Jr. was often entrusted to travel on spiritual errands. There is evidence that he maintained cordial relationships with some of his non-Shaker kin, whom he sometimes visited. His eldest brother, Artemas Bates, who had settled in Jefferson County, New York, was one of the honored few selected to receive a copy of a vaunted Shaker spiritual publication in 1844, Philemon Stewart's *Sacred Role*.[35] Issachar Jr. traveled to Jefferson County to deliver the volume in person.[36] Issachar Jr. continued to serve the Watervliet South Family as elder until his death in 1876 at the advanced age of eighty-six.[37] Of all the Bates siblings, he is the only one of whom identified photographs survive.[38]

My Dear Child & Sister Sally,
An Epistle signed with thine own hand addressing an Old man some
where by the appellation of thy natural father has lately come to me and

was thankfully Received and I wold inform my Dear Sister Sally that the child
that addressed that old man, and the old man thy natural father I hate them
boath. But the father that hath Begotten them in the gospel and the child that
hath received it and kept it ever since and has increased in it and is owned &
loved by the people of God, Boath these I love with my hole heart and this
Child is intitled to the privilege of calling me boath Brother and father in the
gospel. My Dear Sister I accept thy little kind token thankfully and love the
faith that is manifested in it and I am thankful that you have learnt to write
and I desire thee not to forget to manifest thy thanks to Seth for the pains he
has taken with thee and be so kind as to tender my kind thanks to Seth on thy
behalf. The Lord bless thee my Child, my sister, and Build thee up in the gospel.
Farewell . . . from thy father and kind Brother in the gospel, Issachar.[39]

Sarah Bates was born in Hartford, New York, in November 1792. She was
not quite nine years old when Issachar Bates rode to New Lebanon to confess
his sins in 1801, and she was ten when she moved with her family to the Shaker
community at Watervliet. When Issachar visited his family there in December 1805, before returning to the West where he would remain for nearly
twenty-five years before visiting again, Sarah had just turned thirteen. She
was fourteen when she wrote a letter to Issachar in Ohio, to which he replied
at the beginning of September 1807.[40] His reply indicates that he was moved
by her letter, which addressed him as father, and he addresses her in response
as "Sally," apparently his pet name for her from earlier childhood (no other
reference to Sarah Bates as "Sally" is known to exist). It can be inferred from
his letter that Sarah had not yet learned to write when he had last seen her;
her letter to him was evidence of her newly acquired writing skill, taught to
her by Seth Youngs Wells. From the letter's tone and content, Issachar clearly
believed that at fourteen Sarah was old enough to appreciate the gravity of the
spiritual transformation that they each had undergone, but he also acknowledged the awkwardness they both felt at transitioning to a new relationship of
gospel siblinghood in the Shaker spiritual family.

In November 1808, just before Sarah Bates's sixteenth birthday, she was
moved from the dwelling built to house her mother and siblings into Watervliet's "Church family."[41] This seemed to signal her long-term association with
the most devout Shaker families, because at age eighteen she was taken to
New Lebanon to live in the Church Family there.[42] Likely her move was due
to the influence of Seth Youngs Wells, who had been acting as teacher to Sarah.
Seth, who had been a school principal in Albany, New York, before he became
a Shaker,[43] brought experience as both teacher and school administrator and

transferred those interests to his Shaker life, becoming the Shakers' chief early organizer of schools and pedagogy.[44] Not only did he teach Sarah to write, he also mentored and trained her specifically to become one of the school teachers at New Lebanon. Sarah Bates was among the first Shaker teachers at New Lebanon to be licensed by the State of New York. By 1820 she was teaching, as evidenced by remarks from Shaker pupil Rhoda Blake, indicating Sarah was an unusually humane teacher by the standards of the day: "We went to school. Lydia O'Brien and Sarah Bates were the Teachers. They were very kind to me and the treatment was somewhat different, for I had on some occasions seen the schoolmaster bring into the house a bunch of Birch or Beach stick and before the scholars wither them in the embers and for some offence would whip the children like a man would an Ox."[45]

In keeping with Shaker practices of gender separation, Sarah Bates taught primarily female students during her long teaching career at New Lebanon. She worked closely with Isaac Newton Youngs, another protégé of Seth Youngs Wells who taught in the New Lebanon school from the late 1810s until 1846.[46] In all, Sarah taught for more than thirty years as one of the most beloved and respected Shaker teachers in the East. Her effectiveness in the classroom and her pupils' obvious achievements garnered high praise from world's visitors who frequently came to observe the Shaker school.[47] In a peculiarly emphatic 1875 letter to a non-Shaker friend, Sarah reflected on her career:

Dear Hulda, I think you will remember hearing Sister Ann Dodgson, read some little Epistles that I had written to some of my Pupils. I taught the School in this Society more than 30 years, in succession. Had, in all; many Hundred Pupils. And in general; — they were Darling, Intellectual, — and promising children. You are acquainted —With a number of them, here; — and in the families, adjunct. The most part of them; have had Written Recommendations by me.[48]

Sarah Bates became particularly noted for her fine penmanship, an early example of which she had sent her father in Ohio in 1807. The "epistles" written to her pupils were probably the many "rewards of merit" certificates that she penned for her students during her teaching career.[49] But probably the most memorable creative contributions of Sarah Bates are her many "gift drawings," highly complex artworks combining calligraphy, poetry, drawing, and painting, which she produced primarily between 1845 and 1848. Sarah is credited with at least seventeen gift drawings, ranging from large rectangular "sacred roll" compositions more than two feet wide to smaller designs executed on fancifully shaped paper cutouts some six to ten inches across.[50]

9.3 *"From Holy Mother Wisdom to Betsey Bates," attributed to Sarah Bates, April 11, 1847. Item 01-P-152. (Courtesy of the Berkshire Athenaeum.)*

Sarah was one of sixteen identified artists who produced "gift drawings" during a twenty-year period from 1839 to 1859 (figure 9.3), the interlude that coincided with the phase of Shaker religious practice known as the "Era of Manifestations" or the "period of Mother Ann's Work."[51] At this time, the visionary dimensions that had always been present in Shakerism were magnified. Throughout the Shaker world, believers perceived a range of spirits actively moving among them—deceased Shakers, historical figures, heavenly beings—communicating messages and bearing gifts. Each Shaker village had its own "visionists" who conveyed or interpreted messages from spiritual visitors. Many villages also had "instruments," who created artistic renderings of visions and spirit messages using calligraphy, painting, and drawing.[52] Collectively, these artworks are now called gift drawings or "spirit drawings," of which the iconic *The Tree of Life* image, a large sinuously branched fruit-laden tree painted in vibrant greens and reds by Massachusetts Shaker Hannah Cohoon in 1854, is the best-known example.[53] Sarah Bates's smaller gift drawings incorporate poetry and small floral motifs. Her larger ones integrate impressive assortments of meticulously drawn objects—birds, ornate tables and furnishings, musical instruments, architectural structures, flowering trees, and more—together with calligraphy, poetry, and even songs written in a form of Shaker musical notation known as letteral notation. The intricacy and inventiveness of her work has drawn the attention of art scholars, who have examined her ability to integrate prosaic elements of everyday Shaker life—ladders, spinning wheels, floor joists, pails, chairs—together with imaginative and highly embellished objects.[54]

Sarah Bates was actively involved in the extraordinary outpouring of spiritual activity that characterized the period of Mother Ann's work. While she directed considerable energy to the creative production of poetry, music, and elaborate drawings that recorded the outpouring of spiritual gifts from otherworldly visitors to her fellow brothers and sisters at New Lebanon, Sarah was also the recipient of some spiritual messages intended for her personally. One such message delivered for Sarah through one of the New Lebanon "instruments" came from Ann Lee in the form of a charming poem constructed as a warm maternal greeting.

Sarah, Dear child! Come here!
I want to talk with thee!
I never had to call but once,
To bring thee close to me!
How are you Sister? What the <u>Long</u>?
The <u>Latitude</u> you hail?
You <u>once</u> observ'd, "<u>Mother</u> I want,
To have, the <u>good</u> <u>alone</u> <u>prevail</u>!"[55]

By addressing the recipient in an affectionate and conversational tone, such "gift" messages from Ann Lee in the 1840s helped reinforce the spiritual commitment of a rising generation of Shaker adults who had never directly known Ann Lee or any figures from the founding decades of Shakerism.

Sarah Bates also left abundant evidence that she inherited her father's musical talent. Not long after her move to the New Lebanon Church Family at the age of eighteen, she was recognized as one of that family's more talented young singers. In her late twenties, she was selected to be one of five individuals who would learn "singing by note,"[56] which probably meant that she became adept at sight-singing using the four-shape system of named noteheads ("fa-sol-la-mi") that had been popularized in northeastern singing schools of the late eighteenth and early nineteenth century. People able to sing "by note" would have been able to learn, teach, and record music more efficiently. As a former choirmaster and singing teacher for his Baptist church in Hartford, New York, Issachar Bates had certainly known how to sing "by note." His son

Issachar Jr. also knew how, so it is likely that Sarah Bates learned easily. By the 1830s, the singers for the Church Family were divided into two gender-mixed "classes" with about fourteen to sixteen singers in each.[57] Sarah, who had continued as a designated singer, now occupied the position of lead female singer in the first class, and Isaac Newton Youngs was her counterpart, leading the male singers.[58] As one of the Family's best singers, Sarah Bates not only attended regular "singing meetings" but also frequently went to neighboring Shaker families with a few other singers to join in singing meetings or teach a singing school.[59] There is ample evidence that Sarah Bates and Isaac Newton Youngs shared a close friendship for decades, a logical outcome of being thrown together as fellow teachers and fellow musicians, in addition to both being tailors involved in planning and sewing clothing for the Church Family.

Many songs survive that are attributed to Sarah Bates, and they represent a range of Shaker music genres, from hymns to short inspired songs to wordless dance tunes (see appendix 3). Several songbooks compiled by her survive as well. These contain a range of hymns, dance tunes, and inspired songs collected from Shakers in many places, east and west, in addition to abundant compositions of her own.[60] The books also exhibit Sarah's calligraphy skills, along with her facility in using the system of musical notation invented by the Shakers in the 1820s called "letteral" notation, which used lower-case cursive letters in place of noteheads to indicate the notes in a melody. Letteral notation was being fully integrated into Shaker musical culture during the period when Sarah was both a school teacher and a designated singer. Moreover, Isaac Newton Youngs was one of the Shakers' principal refiners of the letteral notation system, so Sarah was ideally situated to become adept at using it herself. She even integrated original letteral notation songs into some of her gift drawings.

Of Issachar Bates's children who became Shakers, Sarah Bates was the most outwardly demonstrative toward her father later in life.[61] Her letter to him from May 1823, addressed to him at Busro, Indiana, is openly affectionate.

> Well Beloved Elder Issachar,
> Thou art a friend known by this appellation with whom I was some acquainted a great many years ago, therefore my pen inclines (moved by the heart) to direct once more with the greatest obligations my never ceasing love and thankfulness to thee, for thy parental care to me. For thou was always a kind parent to me. And I can truly say blameless before my eyes.
> O that I could convey just one little stream from the fountain of gratitude I have ever felt to thee, for thy tender care and instruction to me when I was a child, and unable to help myself; for then thou wouldest

know that thy labor was not all lost. Thou wast the one that first planted the truth of the everlasting gospel in my little vineyard, where I have toiled and laboured ever since. And I think after burning it over and over, and plowing and harrowing it so many years, I have prospects of reaping some good fruit . . . And go on my way rejoicing, making strait paths for my feet to walk in, clothing myself in that manner that I am willing to appear before God when I have done with time . . .

This little book which we send unto thee is one of our school books, wrote and printed in our family. We hope this will be accepted with our unfeigned love.

Farewell————from little Sarah[62]

In the letter she reveals her memories of his "tender care" in her childhood, expresses her gratitude that he brought her to the Shaker faith, and assures him of her unshakable resolve to stay faithful to the Shaker life. The "little book" she sent him as a gift, possibly containing her own calligraphy and some of her students' best work, signals that even at the age of thirty she seeks his approval of her work and contributions to the Shaker community. Her signature of "little Sarah" probably exposes some nostalgia for their earlier parent-child relationship.

As she grew older, Sarah Bates left teaching and spent some time working as the chief office deaconess for the Church Family in the 1850s. She also put her penmanship skills to use, assisting the Ministry by recording copies of correspondence.[63] It is likely that she worked with Isaac Newton Youngs because he served as the office bookkeeper at the same time.[64] Sarah enjoyed excellent health as she aged. She seemed to be a gregarious woman who maintained friendships both inside and outside of the Shaker community, and she continued to correspond with non-Shaker family members. Of all the Bates siblings, Sarah lived to the greatest age. She died in April 1881 at the age of eighty-eight.

    We never learn any thing without a great deal of labour. We can get neither good nor evil if we will not have it, but just what we labor for that we shall have . . . for no one wants to hear the words, "depart from me ye workers of iniquity I know you not." Two years since I came into this room Thursday; & what am I a poor worm of the dust, but I hope I shall be saved at last.[65]

Betsy Bates was born in June 1798, in Schroon, New York, when her family briefly resided there while Issachar Bates preached at Baptist churches in the area. The youngest of the Bates siblings, Betsy was three years old when her father made his Shaker confession, four when when he brought the family to resettle in the Shaker community of Watervliet, New York, and five when he departed for the West. It was the five-year old Betsy who, according to the account later repeated in Ohio, stole tearfully into the woods to detain Issachar when the missionary trio departed in 1805. Of all the Bates children, Betsy probably had the least memory of her father before he converted. Most of her childhood was spent adjusting to Shaker life.

Betsy Bates was only nine in early 1808 when she was moved to Watervliet's Church Family, several months before her older sister Sarah was brought to live there, too. Three years later, at age twelve, she was taken by the New Lebanon Ministry elders to live in the Church Family at New Lebanon, likewise around the same time as Sarah.[66] Little is known about Betsy's schooling, as regular schools were not established at Watervliet or New Lebanon until she was in her late teens. Betsy probably had access to "evening school"—held during the winter of 1808–1809 two evenings per week in the Watervliet Church Family under the direction of Seth Wells, "for the purpose of correcting bad habits in reading & speaking,"[67]—but her writing gives strong evidence that she did not master grammar, spelling, and penmanship with anything close to the proficiency of her sister Sarah. Evidence that Betsy wrote at least one letter to her father exists in the form of an inscription in Issachar Bates's hand in the margin of a piece of devotional prose known by the Shakers as an "anthem." The inscription reads, "A little present from Issachar to his two little sisters at Lebanon Sarah & Betsy with his kind love if they will be little. Thank Betsy kindly for her little letter."[68] It is undated, but would have been written sometime after the middle of 1811, by which time both Sarah and Betsy were at New Lebanon. The same page contains a poem by Issachar inscribed "to his sisters Sarah & Betsy Bates, Dawters by Nature." This material implies the strong possibility of a more extensive correspondence between Issachar and his daughter Betsy that has not survived.

O my soul rejoices, yea my soul rejoices,
To be set free from the bonds of Satan.[69]

During the 1810s and 1820s in the New Lebanon Church Family, Betsy Bates transformed from an adolescent to a grave and pious young woman, inclined to serious thoughts, living among women and men of similar religious devotion.[70] She was a hard worker, taking part in all sorts of manual labor indoors and out, and she was a skilled sewer of women's caps and bonnets. Caps were an essential article of clothing for Shaker women, and Betsy records both the

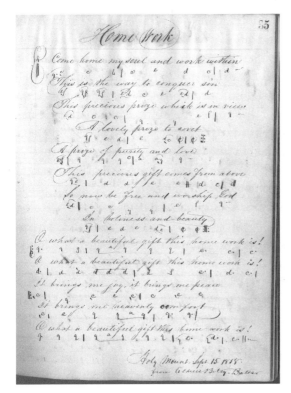

9.4
"Home Work," a song attributed to Eldress Betsy Bates, Holy Mount, Sept. 15, 1858. (From "Hymn & Song Book Written by H. L. Eades, Commencing May 9th 1838," Shaker Manuscripts, IX B 331, Western Reserve Historical Society.)

making of caps and adaptation of cap patterns, suggesting she may have been an innovator in cap design.[71] Like her siblings Sarah, Issachar, and Polly, Betsy produced many songs and tunes (figure 9.4), indicating that many of Issachar Bates's children inherited some of his musical talent. Most of Betsy's songs consist of simple yet profound spiritual expressions set to somber prayerful tunes (see appendix 3).

> (N)othing uncommon to day things rather sober & serious. Joseph is confind yet. I gave him a little tea that was given to me, to increase his appetite, if there was any harm in it I shall never do so again. Every creature has got to learn by what they suffer, I have. When I think I am doing good; but no matter for that, every thing will work right yet.
>
> Sabbath a very holy day; cloudy misty & windy but I hope we shall have some good gift to keep us warm yet for I am sure we need it, for if God don't work Satan will & when Satan works it seams as if evry sail was hoisted to help him. It is so easy to go down stream to destruction, but hard to creep down into the valley of humiliation and repentance. But every soul that is saved had got to come therein, or never reign with Christ[72]

The writing of Betsy Bates indicates she poured her whole self into her spiritual life as a Shaker, ever watchful for weakness, self-critical of the slightest infractions, even in actions that were intended for good. She was utterly determined that her soul would not to "go downstream to destruction." The New Lebanon Ministry clearly found her deportment and character exemplary. After eleven years as second eldress of the New Lebanon Church Family, arguably the most spiritually advanced family of Shakers anywhere, Betsy was promoted to first eldress, sharing with the first elder lead authority in that family.[73] In 1852, she was moved over to the New Lebanon Ministry, placed in the second-tier position of second eldress. In the Ministry, Betsy was partly responsible not just for overseeing the spiritual well-being of a single Shaker family but also for overseeing the spiritual order within the entire Shaker world. In 1856, she was elevated yet again to the highest female office in the Shaker world: First Eldress of the Ministry. In that capacity, as in all levels of the Shaker hierarchy, authority was shared with a male counterpart. But the position of Ministry Eldress held profound meaning in the Shaker world, because the women who occupied that position were inheritors of a spiritual "mantle" that had been passed from the Shaker founder Ann Lee to her successors. Issachar Bates's youngest daughter Betsy became, technically, the successor to Ann Lee, and only the fourth woman to inherit that "mantle" of authority.

O my Elders, O my Elders,
You look like the heavens, you act like the heavens, you are the heavens!
Where would be my heaven, if I was not with you,
I should have no heaven, if I could not see you.[74]

Betsy Bates served as Ministry Eldress for seventeen years, and she was unanimously loved and admired throughout the Shaker world for her patience, kindness, and wisdom, as well as for her deep and profound devotion to Shaker doctrine. Along with the rest of the Ministry, she made visits to all the Shaker communities, east and west. One of her trips to Ohio and Kentucky took place in 1862 at the height of the Civil War, and during that trip she saw firsthand the troubling effects of the war on the Kentucky communities of Pleasant Hill and South Union. But during Betsy's long tenure, the Shaker population was contracting. Shaker villages everywhere faced both economic and spiritual challenges. The charismatic preachers of Shakerism's earlier generation, who had aggressively carried the Shaker gospel into the world, had died out. Membership decline brought with it greater difficulty in running large farm operations. As industrial manufacturing in America increased, Shakers had to develop different marketing strategies. Perhaps because of the changes facing the Shaker world at mid-century, many of the communities began to promote retrospective reflection and writing about the history of the movement. Soon after Betsy Bates assumed the female lead in the Ministry, she and her sister Sarah contributed to this historical turn by compiling a magnificent copy of their father's autobiography in a calfskin-bound volume, together with selections of his poetry. Betsy inscribed it, and during one of her visits to Ohio she presented it as a gift to Naomi Legier, first eldress of the Union Village Ministry. It was an insightful gift. Naomi Legier had been part of the Busro, Indiana, settlement since it was originally gathered by Issachar Bates in 1809 and 1810, and she had lived under Issachar's leadership at Busro for ten years.

> *Died!! Eldress Betsey Bates Died!! ... Elder Daniel Crossman arrived this morning with the sad intelligence of Eldress Betsy Bates decease ... The funeral took place at Mt. Lebanon 2 o'clk p.m. — lasted over 2½ hours — meeting 2 hours long. Every thing was conducted in harmony. Much spoken in praise & in honor of the deceased. She had been a free volunteer from childhood — always true to the cause — her character without spot or blemish. A Mother in Israel! Abounding in charity, love & gospel truth. Ever ready & willing to help all who stood in need of help, &c. It was made known in the meeting that the Mantle of Eldress Betsy would fall on Eldress Ann.*[75]

> "Sung at Eldress Betsy Bates Funeral"
> *The heavens are opened and thou hast come in*
> *To join with the saints who're redeemed from all sin*
> *Prevail thou my chosen, God's judgments are true*
> *But O my Beloved He'll take care of you.*
>   Rec'd from Eld. Isaacher B., Feb. 8th, 1869[76]

Betsy Bates was seventy years old when she died in March 1869. Remarkably, one of the songs sung at her funeral was recorded in a manuscript hymnal as having been brought to her by the spirit of her father Issachar on February 8th, a few weeks before she died. While such spectral visits from spirits bringing songs had been common in the 1840s and early 1850s, they were far more rare in Shaker life by 1869. Apart from the story repeated in Ohio about her tearful childhood farewell to her father and evidence of one letter to Issachar, Betsy left little direct indication of explicit affection for her father. Yet she seems to have been comforted at the end of her life by the notion that her father had appeared to her, singing a song expressing not only his love, but also the reassurance that Betsy would be accepted into heaven. And Betsy's own spectral presence would manifest itself only a few years after her death. *Shaker and Shakeress*, a periodical published by the Shakers in the late nineteenth century, printed a poem — strangely more cheerful than any of Betsy's writings in life — and message from "Eldress Betsy Bates, in the Spirit land."

> Eldress Betsey Bates, in the Spirit Land, sends greetings to the Brethren and Sisters as follows:
>
>> The Angels in heaven and saints upon earth,
>> Are blending together in heavenly mirth,
>> Inviting us all to be of good cheer,
>> And greet ev'ry one with "A Happy New Year!"
>
> Eldress Betsey says: With this receive my affectionate Gospel love; and I should be pleased to have every family share of this Union Greeting.[77]

The "remnant of the tribe of Issachar" included many other people in Watervliet and New Lebanon from the kinship network of Issachar Bates. As already noted, Issachar's two sisters, Dolly Bates Harwood and Hannah Bates Train, entered Shaker life with their large families about the same time as their brother.[78] Theodore Bates, Issachar's younger brother, was also living at Watervliet along with one of his children by 1807. But Issachar's younger brother Caleb initially sought a very different path. Born in 1775, he and William Bates, the youngest sibling, had been raised by their father and stepmother in rural western Massachusetts. After their father's death in 1803, Caleb and William migrated together 250 miles to the northwest to newly settled Jefferson County, New York, where Issachar's eldest son Artemas also eventually settled.[79] There both men married and fathered children. In 1824, Caleb came to Watervliet, seeking information about Shaker life, and in 1825 he returned with his wife, Rebecca, and four children ranging in ages from one to nineteen.[80] One of Caleb's children, Elizaette Bates, was moved to New Lebanon as a teenager, got acquainted with her older cousins Sarah and Betsy, and later held several positions of responsibility as office deaconess.

At the same time that Caleb Bates and his family entered Watervliet, several other children and youth named Bates also arrived, likewise recorded as having come from Jefferson County, New York. These may have also have been Caleb's children, or they may have been the children of William Bates or Artemas Bates, who had also moved to that same region (see appendix 1). One of these youths, Anna Bates, died in 1825 and her death reported to Busro as the "niece of Elder Issachar."[81] Another, nineteen-year-old Paulina Bates, soon made her confession of sins as an adult.[82] During the Era of Manifestations, Paulina functioned as one of the Shakers chief "instruments," individuals who received, interpreted, and recorded messages, exhortations, and prophecies from the spirit world. Her outpouring of spiritual expression during the 1840s was remarkable, and in 1849 her inspired communications were published by the Shakers in pair of volumes titled *The Divine Book of Holy and Eternal Wisdom.*[83]

> *The Broommaking is done chiefly by Theo. B. & is also profitable . . . Seth.*[84]

> *Brother Seth, I want to inform you a little of our fishery here. We have a fish trap on one of our dams, and at this season we catch two or three hundred weight in twenty four hours . . . I think we are about up to Peter for fishing. Issachar.*[85]

> *Now Brother Issachar, before I close . . . Theodore wants to know the name of the great fish which you catch in the Wabash . . . from Seth.*[86]

> *[T]he little note concerning the fish I shall put it into a scrap by itself and send it to Brother Theodore — and then it will be part fish and part flesh . . . farewell from Issachar.*[87]

The chief claim to fame of Theodore Bates, younger brother of Issachar, is the invention of the flat broom.[88] Exactly when he designed and built the innovative broom press is uncertain, but some have estimated about 1804.[89] The exact date of Theodore's entry into the Watervliet community is also unrecorded, but he signed an early Watervliet covenant in 1807,[90] and he may have also shown some promise as a missionary, because he and Benjamin Seth Youngs had been dispatched on a preaching trip to Cooperstown, New York, in 1803.[91] Theodore's circumstances were quite different from those of his older brother. After the Revolutionary War in Templeton, Massachusetts, Theodore had married a woman named Mary Shattuck.[92] She was the daughter of an Elizabeth Shattuck who had been an early follower of Ann Lee and had protected her during the attack by the mob in Petersham, Massachusetts, which Issachar had witnessed.[93] The couple had two daughters before Mary died in 1789.[94] Theodore remarried a woman named Abigail Wheeler, and the couple had three children in the 1790s.[95] However, when Theodore entered the Watervliet community, he came with only one child, his son Theodore Jr.

His wife and his other children all remained outside. By 1819, Theodore Jr. departed and soon married, although he later tried unsuccessfully to return.[96] Theodore himself was the only member of his immediate family to remain a Shaker.

From the many messages relayed between Theodore and Issachar via the letters that Issachar and Seth Wells exchanged, it is evident that the two men shared a congenial relationship. Theodore Bates continued as a stalwart member of the Watervliet West Family, overseeing the growing of broom corn and the manufacture and marketing of flat brooms, one of the most profitable Shaker industries. He also contributed musically to the worship at Watervliet, and several dancing tunes are attributed to him. Theodore died at Watervliet in 1846 at the age of eighty-four.[97]

Sabbath April 1st. William Bates, who has long been hankering after the flesh, & neglecting to improve his gospel privileges, went off this morning in pursuit of his darling object. Thus has he sacrificed his eternal inheritance for a mess of pottage.[98]

At least one of Issachar Bates's children ultimately failed to adjust to Shaker life. His youngest son, William, apostatized in April 1827 after spending most of his life as a Shaker. He did not leave empty-handed. A record of material given to departing apostates shows that he was outfitted with ample clothing and considerable carpentry equipment.[99] It appears that William fell in love with a Shaker sister, Sarah Potter, and several months after his departure, he sent for Sarah: "Absconded. Last night Sarah Potter left this village in a private manner, in company with her mother, who came after her at the request of Wm Bates, who bore the expense of her journey for that purpose.[100] Eventually the two married, and later they returned to visit New Lebanon, possibly to see William's sisters Sarah and Betsy. In September 1839, the New Lebanon Church Family journal records, "Wm Bates and Sarah his wife here today."[101]

Beloved Elder Issachar . . . we make you kindly and heartily welcome to all favors, both spiritual and temporal, which have been bestowed on you and your natural family . . . We are thankful that your faith enabled you to forsake all which you held dear on earth, to go and preach the gospel; therefore what has been done for you and your natural family has been done freely.[102]

Although Shaker doctrine emphasized the dissolution of biological family ties in favor of the spiritual ties of "gospel kindred," extended families were vital to the fabric of Shakerism in its early decades. Scholars of the Shakers have underestimated the extent to which Issachar Bates's contribution to the Shaker movement also incorporated, indirectly, the contributions of his family members. Many of the most productive members of his kinship network were his children Betsy, Sarah, Issachar, and Polly, as well as his brother Theodore. A few, such as Issachar's youngest son, William, lived less-than-auspicious Shaker lives. Yet Issachar's kin accounted for at least thirty-five Shakers at the Watervliet and New Lebanon, New York, communities between 1803 and the middle of the century. Of all the kin in all the branches of the Bates family that entered Shaker life, only Issachar lived in the Shaker West. Bringing his family into the Shaker world, a world constructed upon the metaphor of family, ironically removed Issachar from his own family and made him a virtual stranger to all but a few of his loved ones. But at the same time, Issachar's decision to bring his family to the Shakers enabled many of them to lead remarkable lives.

CHAPTER 10

"The Cockatrice still wants a place in Zion's lovely regions"

TRANSFORMATIONS IN THE SHAKER WEST

The time is now for all to bow, and find their true subjection;
And take good heed unto their lead, for this is their protection.
The lowly mind that's truly join'd unto the true foundation,
Will be secure forevermore, in simple church-relation.
—*From "The Cockatrice Routed," 1833*

Issachar Bates's final decade in the West would be intense and demanding. The events that the Shaker pioneers had set into motion beginning in 1805 were increasingly evolving beyond Issachar's ability to influence, let alone control. Throughout the western communities, dynamics were developing that Issachar found deeply disturbing. Some among the younger generation of Shakers were maturing into a vocal segment that chafed at the guidance of Issachar and his circle. But at the same time, Issachar enjoyed the strong following he had created throughout the region, basking in the love and admiration of many believers of all ages. During his final western assignment as elder at the Watervliet, Ohio, a community on the outskirts of Dayton, he would create a home that he seemed to value more highly than any he had known before. At the same time, he would struggle to bring order to a fractious community. He would reel from the death of David Darrow, lead in Ministry at Union Village, and he would fret over the breakup of West Union, his former home, as the believers there surrendered to years of unrelenting problems. As Issachar settled more deeply into his new role at Watervliet, he would be happily reunited with some of his closest western friends. But the troubling changes in the Shaker West rocked not only Issachar but the whole of the Shaker West.

> Here stands that great City for which we have prayed,
> Her walls they are strong and delightfully laid,
> Each stone is well hewn by a sharp-edged tool,
> And laid in this building according to rule
> [...]

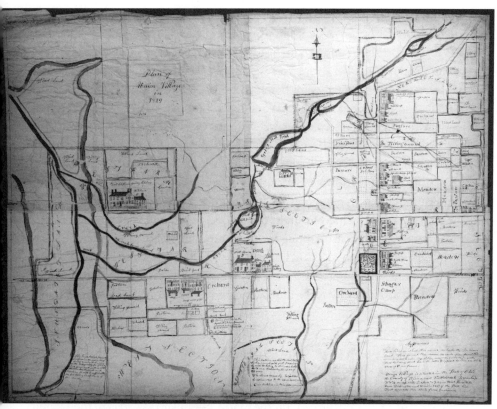

10.1 "Plan of Union Village in 1829." (From Shaker Manuscripts, I A 19, Union Village Land Records, Western Reserve Historical Society.)

No City on earth is so clear and so bright,
Her lamps are still burning by day and by night,
The meek of the earth in her streets may be found,
Here peace like a river shall always abound.[1]

During his decade at Busro, Issachar Bates had not been a stranger to this "Center of Union" for the Shaker West.[2] His arrival at Union Village at the beginning of February 1824 marked his third consecutive midwinter visit, and he had made other visits in 1816, 1819, and 1820. At each arrival, he would have seen changes as the community transformed from the one-time pioneer settlement of Turtle Creek to the largest agglomeration of Shakers west of the Appalachians. Issachar was struck by "the increase of noble buildings," of "industry, cleanliness, and every good work" (figure 10.1).[3]

By now in the 1820s, visitors regularly came from great distances to see

Union Village, with its meticulously tended gardens, orchards, and farm buildings, its six spacious dwellings housing more than five hundred Shakers, and its many workshops and production areas where an array of industries — furniture making, textiles, brickworks, pottery, broom making, seed packaging, cooperage, and more — were being carried out.[4] Near the center of Union Village, on the site of Malcolm Worley's frame house where the Shaker missionaries had been welcomed nearly twenty years before, the spacious brick "North House" now sat beside a large office from which the village conducted its commercial business. Richard McNemar's two-story log cabin still sat a half mile to the east of the center and was now surrounded by the dwellings and outbuildings making up the "East Family."[5] The two-story frame dwelling that Issachar helped to build for the old believers in the spring of 1806 was now a washhouse.[6] Among the most prominent structures was the huge white-painted frame meeting house, completed in 1818 as a replacement for an earlier meeting house that proved to be too small. The new meeting house measured sixty feet by forty-four feet, and its cavernous interior accommodated both Shakers and the many spectators who usually thronged the public services. Opposite the meeting house sat the large Center House dwelling. Neat picket fences enclosed grassy yards around the major buildings, and gravel pathways regulated movement.

Union Village sat at a major crossroads in southwestern Ohio. In fact, it had recently been literally placed "on the map": a popular 1822 atlas of the United States marked "Union" just west of Lebanon, Ohio, along the main east-west route connecting Lebanon with the county seat of Hamilton in the neighboring county.[7] The north-south road running through the center of the village connected Cincinnati and Dayton. From this vantage, the Shakers at Union Village controlled thousands of acres of land. The broken landscape stretching out to the west was still heavily wooded and so swampy as to resist clearing and cultivation. Towering elm and ash trees provided a high canopy for an area sometimes called "crane town," due to the number of cranes that roosted there high above the marshes.[8] What had once been a dense unbroken hardwood forest when Issachar Bates arrived in 1805 had been heavily cleared and replaced with grain fields, pastures, orchards, and gardens; but many areas of woods remained scattered around the premises of Union Village. Issachar the pioneer, who had once written poetry in the rugged mountains of upstate New York extolling the changes that settlers would exert upon a wild landscape, probably found the many changes immensely satisfying.

When I arrived at the Village Father David told me that he did not intend that I should go back again to Busserow, for he had enough for me to do here. This was a pleasing cross to me.[9]

It is not clear why Father David Darrow decided keep Issachar Bates in Ohio in 1824. Perhaps he recalled his initial promise that Issachar's stay at Busro need only be temporary. Darrow could hardly have forgotten Issachar's initial objections, since Issachar himself had recently recorded in a letter, written with Father David's permission, that going to Busro "was the greatest cross" he had ever faced as a Shaker. During Issachar's periodic sojourns at Union Village over the years, he had remained involved in certain spiritual matters, written poetry, consulted with Richard McNemar (who by now went by the pseudonym Eleazar Wright[10]) over doctrine, and undertaken short visits to the Shakers at nearby Watervliet. Issachar was also well aware of key developments in the Shakers' prospects in Ohio by the early 1820s, namely, several potential openings for the Shaker gospel in other parts of the state. Between 1820 and 1824, the Union Village ministry launched overtures in three areas: northeastern Ohio near Lake Erie, west-central Ohio in an area called Darby Plains some seventy miles north of Union Village, and extreme southwestern Ohio, along the White Water River near the Indiana state line.[11] Indeed, Issachar and Richard had spent two weeks preaching at Darby Plains in January 1823.[12] With evangelism work again mounting, the Union Village ministry faced the need of sending able preachers to three different parts of Ohio simultaneously. It is likely that David Darrow wanted to involve Issachar more deeply in these ongoing missionary campaigns, given his experience and effectiveness in working with new converts, and removing Issachar from the Busro ministry served this purpose. Darrow would also have been aware of the occasional tensions between Issachar and Busro elder Archibald Meacham, but removing Issachar undeniably dealt a blow to Busro, which had just suffered the death of Eldress Martha Sanborn. In the space of a few months, Busro's ministry was cut in half. Whatever the reaction of Archibald and others at Busro might have been to Issachar's transfer back to Ohio, no record survives.

At this branch we have had the help of our good Elder Issachar for several weeks, whose everlasting kind love I am requested to forward to you all, with this memorial of his presence, health, and prosperity.[13]

In the weeks following his return to Union Village, Issachar Bates enjoyed reuniting with friends. He relished the company not only of David Darrow but also of Richard McNemar, Malcolm Worley, and Mathew Houston.[14] Because of the late winter season, many of the men were engaged in making sugar at the several sugar camps in the woods around Union Village.[15] Richard, however, was focused on completing the newest edition of *Testimony of Christ's Second Appearing*, the first major published account of Shaker theology, originally written in 1808 by Benjamin Seth Youngs. A second edition had been printed by the eastern Shakers in 1810. Now a third edition was being completed and printed at Union Village, incorporating editorial changes by both Benjamin and Richard.[16] In the first part of 1824, probably in the "elder's shop" — a workshop allocated for the use of the Ministry elders — Richard was overseeing the tedious work of assembling the nearly six hundred printed pages and binding the finished books. Here Issachar worked alongside him. The shared task was probably refreshing, allowing Issachar to revel in the loftier doctrinal aspects of his faith so eloquently expressed by his erudite friend. Lodging there at the elder's shop at the heart of Union Village, working with Richard, and looking out onto a busy road flanked by handsome brick and frame buildings where hundreds of earnest Shakers went about their daily tasks, Issachar seemed to have left the windswept prairies of Busro far behind.[17] The spiritual and temporal climate at Union Village was more stable, the believers less harried. Despite the separation from his particular friends at Busro, such as Salome Dennis, the move was to Issachar's liking, "a pleasing cross." Perhaps the more composed environment of Union Village enabled Issachar to continue grieving for his recent losses; he penned his poetic tribute for his beloved daughter Polly that February, months after learning of her death. As February turned to March, Issachar and Richard may have reminisced about the first March that the Shaker missionaries arrived at Turtle Creek, nineteen years before, as suggested by surviving records, which describe how the entire community shared in an elaborate commemoration of that milestone:

> We had a meeting this evening at 6 oclock in remembrance of E Issachars first coming to this place.[18]

> [T]his day is the anniversary of the arrival of the first messengers of the gospel on this consecrated ground, and some little matters are in circulation in memory of that important event.[19]

March 22, 1824, fell on a Monday, a workday when worship meeting was not normally held. But the date marked the nineteenth anniversary of the Shaker missionaries' arrival at Turtle Creek, and it had been many years since one of the "first messengers" had been present at Union Village on the anniversary. The occasion called for a celebration. All of Union Village turned out, with Issachar Bates and "elder brother" Malcolm Worley, honored as the missionaries' first convert, together at the literal center of festivities.

> Six o'clock P.M the different families met at the brick house and after opening the meeting & singing & laboring awhile, Elder brother Malcham was placed on a chair & taken up by Ashbel & Caleb Pegg, the company then moved with Elder brother in front across the yard & lane into the public yard front of the Elder's shop, where they were intercepted by Elder Issachar, who was brought out of his lodging on a chair by two brethren & so the march continued with singing leaping and shouting into the meeting house. The Elder and Elder brother being placed on their chairs in the centre and surrounded by brethren & sisters, senior and junior, the following verses were sung.[20]

The celebration may have been staged as a surprise for Issachar and Malcolm. To be suddenly hoisted up on chairs and carried outside into the midst of hundreds of boisterous Shakers was hardly normal for a Monday evening. Issachar and Malcolm were borne aloft as standards in a lively parade that crossed the road and processed through the twin doors of the meeting house. They were then feted with a new hymn, probably composed by Richard and practiced in secret by the leading singers.[21] It began with a tribute to the missionaries' journey and arrival in 1805 — "To think that after all their search the diff'rent states around / The 22nd day of March a resting place they found" — before continuing with specific accolades for Issachar and Malcolm:

> The Elder now is on the ground
> Who gave the first pure Gospel sound
> Which hath been spreading all around
> To fill the land with Shakers.
> The Elder brother too is here
> Who first set out his cross to bear
> And did the way of God prepare
> That we might be partakers.[22]

After singing this hymn various exercises ensued, among which were some new gifts exhibited to my sense more glorious than I ever saw before; particularly what is called in the Hebrew tongue Hag, or the circular dance,[23] that which the children of Israel danced after their three days march out of Egypt. To me it felt both awful and glorious, to see such a vast body of well trained believers in a solid body of brethren and sisters alternately move round like the rushing of a mighty wind, while the elder and elder brother sustained the mortification of marking the centre of their circular procession. The exercises continued 'till about 8 o'clock and the meeting was dismissed.[24]

For his part, Richard McNemar was awestruck at the sight of the new dance, two separate wheels of concentric circles of Shakers, each moving as one around the two brothers held high on their chairs at the centers.[25] For Issachar Bates, looking down on the packed dancers wheeling around him, the experience must have been overwhelming. Never before had Issachar been the object of such open and unanimous adulation on the part of so many, literally elevated above the rest. His years of struggle and personal sacrifice — leaving wife and children, confronting wilderness dangers, withstanding ridicule and opposition to introduce the Shaker gospel — had led him to this moment. When Issachar arrived with his companions at Turtle Creek in 1805 and began to testify among the scattered cabins of the cautious Richard and his congregation, little could he have imagined that such a "vast body of well trained believers" would be the eventual outcome. In his letter reporting the March 22nd celebration, Richard McNemar also alluded to the latest — and, as it turned out, last — of the Shakers' expansions in the West.

> When I look toward you wise men of the East, first in opening your treasures to the King of Kings in his second appearing, my views of your "good brethren in the west" are restricted to those whom ye have sent: whom we have always respected as guardians of the purity of the gospel, and unsuspected of any breach of union with their good brethren in the East. If I can be owned among your little children of the West, my highest ambition will be gratified.[26]

Nineteen years to the day after the arrival of Issachar Bates and his companions, the Shaker West was reaching its geographic zenith, with seven settlements, including the recently launched communities at North Union and White Water. But in the same letter, Richard also discussed at length a concern that had begun to plague the Shaker leadership, east and west — namely, doctrinal consistency between the two far-flung halves of the Shaker world. Completing the newest edition of the *Testimony*, together with reflecting back on the missionaries' arrival and the course of their work, had been the catalyst for Richard's contemplation of "whether there be any real difference of opinion between eastern & western believers." Conscious that the entire Shaker

West occupied, in the view of the eastern Ministry, a lower tier in a spiritual hierarchy, Richard emphasized the role of the original three emissaries — and indeed, of all the "old believers" — in representing accurately the essence of Shaker spirituality and doctrine. Because the teachings of the East had been so effectively presented by Issachar and the other chosen emissaries, Richard asserted, it was his conviction that Shaker converts everywhere ought to be "as uniform as the leaves on an appletree." Such reflections on the early missionaries' role — and his own — in creating and integrating the Shaker West, even as he worked with Issachar and reminisced about the events of long ago, were emotionally draining for Richard. His "reflection on this heart-melting theme . . . extracted such a flow from my two little water pots that the paper was in danger of being spoiled." Likely Issachar shared a similar tearful response.

There was probably an attentive assembly in the big meeting house when Issachar Bates preached on March 28, 1824.[27] Though the Sabbath message was usually delivered by Father David Darrow, the mood of reflection warranted an address by the West's most colorful pioneer figure. It was also an opportunity for Issachar to preach to the Union Village families before departing on a journey. On March 30, Issachar set out for northeastern Ohio with Samuel Hooser, an elder from Pleasant Hill, on a compound mission. First, they were to seek out a new settlement called Zoar, two hundred miles away in north-central Ohio's Tuscarawas County, where a group of religious dissenters from Germany had recently formed a communal village. Given Issachar's decade-long acquaintance with the German followers of George Rapp at Harmony, the Union Village Ministry hoped to glean a greater understanding of the Zoarites and whether they shared any spiritual commonalities with the Shakers. Then Issachar and Samuel were to proceed to the new Shaker settlement some nine miles outside of Cleveland, Ohio, a location the Shakers initially called "the Lakes" because of its proximity to Lake Erie but would soon call "North Union."

During their journey on horseback, a spring snowstorm blew into the region, bringing dire consequences for Issachar:

> The third day after we started in the month of March (having a very scarey horse, and showers of snow falling), I took off my hat to shake off the snow, and my horse started, caught the bit in his teeth and ran with me into the woods, and would not quit till he threw me. And as I fell he sent both of his sharp corked heels & hit my leg on the shin bone, just below my knee, and cut a large gash. Samuel caught the horse and I got on him again, and rode 30 miles that day before I examined it, tho' it pained

me very much. Then I went on three days after that, with the wound, till my leg was as large as two legs, and as black as bacon; and I expected it would end my life . . . When I arrived at Zoar, a number of kind young men help me off my horse and carried me into the house. That was about the last I could remember accurately, for I was seized with a violent fever, laid on a bed and lay 47 days, and never was moved in all that time, only by two careful nurses. And whether I had common sense all that time or not I cannot say, and whether I was in this world or not, God knoweth. But I hid myself among the dead to keep out of the way of death, so that I might save my life to return home with.[28]

By riding several days with an open gash in his leg cut by his horse's hooves, Issachar Bates developed an infection that nearly cost him his life. Fortunately the people at Zoar received him with compassion and gave him what medical attention they could. In fact, it was probably providential that he landed at Zoar with his injury instead of the new Shaker settlement that had been the brethren's ultimate destination. Joseph Bimeler, the leader and founder of the village of Zoar "separatists," also acted as that community's physician. His keen interests in medicine and in human physiology are reflected in his surviving writings.[29] Conscious of the assistance they had received from other intentional communities since arriving in Ohio in 1817, the Zoarites were hardly likely to treat the Shakers with anything other than hospitality.[30] For over six weeks Issachar lay at Zoar consumed with fever, hovering between life and death. The swelling throughout the length of the affected limb was so severe that the skin of his foot burst. His survival at age sixty-six confirms that his constitution was exceptionally strong. But the ordeal took its toll. The high fever that ravaged Issachar's body cost him all of his hair and nails and left him emaciated.[31]

Last evening Samuel Hooser arrived here from Zoar with tidings of Elder Issachar being near death's door from the kick of his horse.[32]

As soon as the alarming news of Issachar Bates's accident reached Union Village, the ministry acted. Two brethren with medical training, Calvin Morrell and Charles Hampton, rushed to Zoar,[33] but by the time they arrived, they found Issachar past the crisis point. Indeed, although he was still bedridden, he had rallied enough to try and preach to his caretakers. Perhaps Issachar realized that he was being cared for by the community's leader, himself a fellow religious visionary, which would have stimulated him to engage in doctrinal discussions: "Notwithstanding my distress, I was most of the time in great labor. I lost no time. I was striving to gather up a people into a joint interest, and tho' they seemed anxious to effect it yet I could not get them to touch it in its order."[34] Articles of communal living had been formally enacted at Zoar just that spring,[35] but the language barrier between Issachar and the Zoarites probably impeded their exchange of spiritual ideas. Though Issachar received the ministrations of Bimeler and his followers gratefully, he regarded Zoar as a spiritually "dead" place. When the Shaker brethren arrived, he was glad to depart, writing later: "Home! Home! was what I was after."

Though the Shaker brethren urged the Zoarites to accept payment for the care given Issachar, they refused. The journey home was made by way of a carriage owned by Union Village, driven up by Mathew Houston expressly to give Issachar a more comfortable ride. Still unable to sit or stand upright, he traveled on a bed of straw. Back at Union Village at the end of May, there was "Great rejoicing to see E Issachar home alive."[36] In a particularly appropriate tribute, the nephew and namesake of Richard McNemar (a young man in his twenties) celebrated Issachar's return with a poem that began: "I'm thankful Elder Issachar he has returned again / His cross he Bore and went to Zoar in sorrow grief and pain."[37]

~ *[J]ust three months from the time I lay down at Zoar; which was the fourth day of April, to the 4th of July, I was able to kneel for the first time.*[38]

Issachar Bates rejoiced in a full recovery from his leg injury. Kneeling was an important part of Shaker life; Shakers knelt in prayer several times a day, both privately and collectively. Because of his active role in leading the "labor" of the dance, Issachar especially valued his agility. July 4, 1824, a public holiday, fell on a Sunday, and the public meeting at Union Village was even more crowded than usual with local visitors (who "behaved well" according to accounts), with at least 1,500 people crowded around the meeting house.[39] Relishing his restored health, Issachar was probably also stimulated by the dynamic atmosphere of Union Village. Though Shakers did not explicitly celebrate Independence Day, the veteran Issachar likely indulged in some private reflection on his own small role in the fight for American independence. After all, his hymn paying tribute to George Washington and the cause of American freedom, "Rights of Conscience," had been printed in *Millennial Praises* years before. But regardless of whether he made open expression of his private patriotism on that day, he could openly celebrate his recovery.

With Issachar again ambulatory, David Darrow wasted no time in sending him back out on the road. Later that summer Issachar accompanied Mathew Houston to visit the new community at White Water, some thirty-five miles to the west. At the beginning of September, he set out once more for northern Ohio, traveling by carriage with three other Shakers and stopping en route for preaching engagements. This time he reached North Union and spent more than two weeks working with the new converts there. He returned to Union Village in mid-October, where surprising news from David Darrow awaited him.

> ⮑ *Father opened the matter what he wanted of me. Next I was to go and take charge of the people at Watervliet. I was almost speechless for I was opposed to it in my heart for these reasons. I had never felt myself capable of taking the first care of any people and had said I never would do it. And I knew that a number of them were very active in running over their leaders and this I dreaded, but dare not refuse, but said I was not willing. But Father was very merciful and told me he would not lay too heavy a burden on me in my old age, but said he, go and stay there three weeks and then if you do not feel satisfied you may return in union.[40]*

Issachar's reaction to Father David's directive that he "take charge" of the small Shaker community at Watervliet, Ohio, was similar in some ways to his initial response to the Busro assignment almost fifteen years earlier. And Father David's rejoinder was similar, namely, that Issachar need only stay for a short time if he truly objected. But in one important respect, this instance was different. Father David intended that Issachar be "first in care" at Watervliet.

Since the beginning of the Shaker West, it had been customary to place old believers in the foremost leadership positions wherever possible. Issachar had been second elder at Busro, serving under Archibald Meacham. Now, as in 1811 when preparations for the Busro Ministry were being laid, Issachar downplayed his leadership potential, resisting not only the top position but any position whatsoever. Although the charismatic Issachar excelled at inspiring people to action through his captivating speech and engaging hymns, he seemed to doubt his own leadership abilities and even to question whether he deserved the moniker "old believer."

> Inasmuch as I am numbered among . . . those who were sent to this Western land, to declare that salvation which we received — for which cause I am called an Old believer <u>here</u> — tho the last and least of all, as pertaining to age and privilege in the gospel — and among all my big feelings, and

high sense, I never yet felt myself worthy to be equaled with those who are called Old believers.[41]

Even as late as the 1820s, Issachar was acutely conscious of having himself been "young" in the gospel when he was first sent to the West in 1805, having only confessed his sins a few scant years before. Yet to the "young believers" in the West, Issachar was not only counted, somewhat ironically, among the "old believers," he was the object of the effusive admiration — even approaching hero worship. Over the next decade, the gratification Issachar drew from this admiration would become troublingly evident. For now, while he might privately enjoy his popularity, he claimed to be unequal to the tasks of leadership reserved for old believers. In truth, perhaps he chafed at the responsibility that came with accepting the title. Issachar treasured his mobility and opposed routine. He resisted accountability, never even keeping a journal for any part of his long life, despite the fact that the Shakers encouraged journal-keeping. Given this array of characteristics, his concerns for his own leadership suitability were well justified. Notwithstanding his reluctance, Issachar accepted this new directive. When he arrived at Watervliet, he was greeted as "Elder" and as "as an incipient nucleus to a future ministry." In accordance to the practice in the Shaker West of attic rooms being used as quarters for elders and eldresses, Issachar, "was placed up garret in the ministerial order."[42]

> We were gladly received. And here I went at the work of regulating affairs for they were in confusion opposing their Elders, opposing their Deacons, and opposing one another. It was bite bit the biter all round and in debt to the world besides. At last they got to confession and settling with one another as fast as they could.[43]

Likely Issachar Bates was dismayed at being charged with the task of calming the "confusion" at Watervliet in 1824, a community in whose genesis he had in fact been instrumental many years before. He had first traveled to the pioneer settlement of Beaver Creek in May 1805 to preach alongside Benjamin Seth Youngs. He and Benjamin, together with Richard McNemar and others, returned in the spring of 1806, when many of the initial conversions occurred.[44] Over the next several years, visits between the two sites were almost constant. Several converts from Beaver Creek came to live at Turtle Creek, and vice-versa. A large two-story log meeting house was constructed for Shaker worship in 1811 and the settlement renamed Watervliet in honor of the New York settlement near Albany, the home of so many prominent early Shakers, including Ann Lee.[45] But the people of the West's Watervliet were a disjointed group. Although a large brick dwelling had been finished in 1820 and numerous other buildings erected, there were many deviations from "gospel order." A journal kept by one Watervliet Shaker indicates evident discord among the various families in the early 1820s,[46] and soon after Issachar arrived, several babies were born, including one to a couple that had signed the Shaker covenant more than ten years before. But the community seemed potentially prosperous in other respects; a group of new converts had just arrived a few months before, and a second dwelling was under construction to accommodate them.[47] Issachar was well acquainted with the community and its challenges. In addition to the time he had spent there in its foundation years, he had made several visits during his periodic sojourns to Ohio from Busro.[48] Issachar's first priority when he arrived that October was thus to repair the spiritual dimension of the community, and he set about doing this by re-introducing the fundamental Shaker practice of confession of sin. Near the end of November, Issachar made a trip back to Union Village, suggesting David Darrow must have adhered to his promise of offering Issachar an "out" after a few weeks,[49] but he soon returned to Watervliet, indicating his ultimate acquiescence to Father David's wishes.

> In a few months they paid off their debts and they finished off the north brick house and moved into it and moved a family into it between Christmas and New Year. And the first day of January 1825 we all came together and agreed without a dissenting voice to build a meeting house and we went to work at it like men. And the 26th day of May the same year it was raised with the help of the young men from Union Village. The house is a frame house 50 by 40 feet and in the month of June we held meeting in it and had a joyful dance.[50]

In beginning a new year at Watervliet, Issachar probably showed good judgment in giving the fractious assemblage of Shakers there a common goal. Constructing a meeting house kept their focus on the spiritual beliefs they held in common, rather than the various issues that divided them. Ironically, when Issachar had left Busro one year earlier, work had just begun there on a frame meeting house to replace a log structure. Issachar was no doubt aware that this new building — whose size was identical to the structure proposed at Watervliet — had been completed in December, a fact he might have used as a catalyst for the Watervliet believers, urging them to work together to bring their village in line with the architectural standards of the other communities. The work proceeded quickly during the winter and spring of 1825.

In April, a message from Issachar was enclosed in a letter going from Pleasant Hill to New Lebanon, showing that he found humor in the fact that in twenty years he had gone from one "Watervliet" to another.

> It is now about twenty years Since I left Watervliet, and I have traversed this Western World since that time in almost every direction and behold I am at Watervliet after all the fuss. But if I can do any good here, that is all I care about . . . I should be thankful if the kind Ministry would remember me when they write to the East, for I have no chance in these times to let them know where I am. For I am here in this place, running in a gang by my Self.[51]

Issachar's tone suggests he felt a bit displaced at Watervliet. During most of his stationary interludes in the Shaker West, he had been accustomed to being with other old believers, or at least with longtime friends. As a solitary "gang by my Self," he was trying to shepherd Watervliet through a sensitive transitional period. But the increasingly optimistic mood at Watervliet was muted by troubling news from Union Village. Father David, seventy-five years old and in declining health for several months, had died on June 27, 1825. Issachar went immediately to Union Village: "And good Elder Issachar was early notified and arrived about six in the evening and took his full share in the duties of the scene. His presence and aid have been a special strength and comfort to the Ministry and to us all."[52]

As senior among all the old believers, in terms of age, Issachar naturally assumed a leading role in the funeral service and burial, which were attended by more than 500. A Union Village letter written on July 4 reporting on Darrow's funeral recorded that Issachar "rendered quite important assistance thro' the Procession of the day."[53] But the same letter suggests that Issachar had moved into the Union Village Ministry, and it places Issachar's movements since he left Indiana in quite a different perspective: "Those of us in the meeting house with Elder Issachar are all in usual good health . . . P.S. Elder Issachar has been here a considerable length of time, & it is agreed upon & concluded for him not to return back to West Union any more to abide; but to take up his residence in those parts and devote his time and attention to the people in those regions for the future."[54]

By the 1820s, certain housing practices had developed in the Shaker West. As early as 1816, family elders and eldresses at Union Village inhabited rooms in the topmost story or "garret" of each family's dwelling.[55] Ministry elders and eldresses inhabited rooms in the upper story of the meeting house.[56] Many manuscripts simply refer to an individual moving "up garret" or "to the meeting house" as euphemisms for shouldering leadership positions. For these reasons, a reference to Issachar, whose 1824 lodging at Union Village had been in the "elders' shop," residing in the meeting house in July 1825 after David Darrow's death, is significant. The letter containing this reference is clearly signed "the Ministry."

Another interesting aspect of the letter is its reference to an agreement that Issachar not be sent back to West Union (Busro). Issachar's own writing shows that, at least from his perspective, this decision had been made more than a year before, by Darrow, indicating further subtle evidence of a close relationship between Issachar and Father David and implying that the two were accustomed to meetings and discussions to which others were not privy. In total, the letter offers subtle yet potent evidence of two things: first, Issachar's close relationship with Darrow and, second, the probability that in the days immediately following Darrow's death, Issachar was regarded as part of the Ministry at Union Village, perhaps even as Darrow's rightful successor. Perhaps another token of their close relationship was that Issachar laid claim to one symbolic piece of Darrow, namely, a particular large chair that Darrow had used. Writing a few years later of his room at Watervliet, Issachar notes that his furnishings include "Father David's great chair."[57]

Over the next several years, the chief leaders in the Shaker West scrutinized this very question of Father David's rightful successor. Darrow had named no male successor, nor had the eastern Ministry at New Lebanon voiced its wishes. Because names of David Darrow and Ruth Farrington, his female counterpart, were written in the Union Village covenant as the individuals who held lawful authority in the community, many worried that Darrow's death without the naming of a successor rendered the covenant void.

> At the decease of Father David there was some anxiety relating to the security & stability of the foundation and various senses began to come in contact. David Darrow & Ruth Farrington were mentioned in both the first & 2d covenant as the ministry to whom teaching obedience was to be rendered & no provision made for any succession in office at their decease . . . the fact is that nothing was done before Father's decease to settle or regulate the order of things in future.[58]

Richard McNemar, who by 1825 had already represented the Shakers in court and had mastered the intricacies of the western Shaker villages as legally constituted entities, began to study the matter closely and concluded that "in a law sense Father David died intestate" and that the remaining Ministry elders proceeded "without consulting or conferring with any other authority."

Although the letter written immediately after David Darrow's death in late June 1825 implies that Issachar had been elevated to the Union Village Ministry, events that unfolded during July 1825 point to something very different. Solomon King, who had served as second elder in the Union Village Ministry, accompanied Issachar Bates back to Watervliet, and the two worked together to adjudicate the conflicts that remained there. It was decided that Issachar would remain at Watervliet as the "lead," or first elder, and the people declared their support for him.

> I tarried there till the 4th of July and then returned to my appointed home and the Ministry came home with me. In this visit of the Ministry there were much labours made with the people to get them to settle their former broils with their Elders and one another which was effected in a good degree. Then Elder Solomon had them all assembled in the meeting house and spake to them in a wise and pleasant manner. He asked them if they felt satisfied with me. They all answered that they did. He asked them if they were all willing to take me for their lead and council and be subject there unto. They all answered Yea.[59]

Solomon King succeeded Darrow as lead at Union Village, although the parental title of "father" was never again used in the Union Village Ministry.[60]

> *This people while humble and obedient were blest and prospered in all things equal to any in the land. They bought 100 acres of land, for which they paid 2100 dollars without difficulty. They built a two story house on it for the young order 40 by 30 feet. Built a first rate saw mill with two saws and excellent grist mill with two runs of stone all finished off in the best manner besides their Meeting House, and many other improvements.[61]*

Over the next year or so Issachar Bates seemed to be a "hands-on" leader at Watervliet. In many Shaker communities, the principal leaders set themselves somewhat apart from daily work activities, even to the extent of eating alone in separate dining areas. This separation arguably allowed ministry and elders to maintain their spiritual focus. But Issachar visited the individual Watervliet families constantly, attending their weeknight worship meetings and social meetings, and often taking meals with them. A journal kept at Watervliet for 1825 and 1826 abounds with phonetically rendered entries such as "Elderisiker comes here today and eats supper," "Elder Isiker comes to see us and we git matters settled," and "Elder Isiker speaks in meeting . . . things get lively."[62] He counseled the believers on reconciliation of their disagreements, sought their suggestions on more building projects, showed concern for the sick, and organized a work schedule for the sugar-making season. In May 1826 Issachar instituted a foot-washing ceremony at Watervliet, something that new converts had once performed to honor Issachar and the other old believers. All the while, Issachar made frequent visits to Union Village — at least nine individual trips over a one-year period from the summer of 1825 to the summer of 1826, with stays of a few days to a few weeks, suggesting that he wished to be on hand to confer regularly with Solomon King and others there.

In the summer of 1826, Issachar Bates was reunited with his former Busro comrades after a separation of more than two years. Archibald Meacham, together with Salome Dennis and others, arrived at Union Village early in June. They had come so Archibald could rendezvous with Union Village brother Andrew Houston, a promising young elder and the son of Mathew Houston,[63] so that the two could make a trip to New Lebanon. Chronic problems at Busro were causing the New Lebanon Ministry to consider disbanding the community altogether. Busro's tribulations were many: sickness that continued to vex believers, the loss by disease of many stalwart early Busro believers leaving behind obstreperous offspring who were less committed to being Shakers, the impact on the believers of Indiana's laws stipulating militia service.[64] Archibald was summoned east for deliberations over Busro's fate. In his absence, Issachar was to make a visit there.

> Now on the 8th day of June 1826, Elder Archibald, and company from Bussrow arrived at Union Village, and Elder Archibald and Brother Andrew Houston went on a visit to the East; and I was requested by Elder Solomon to go and make a visit to Bussrow. Accordingly on the 29th day of July I started in Elder Archibald's carriage with Br. Joshua Worley and Eldress Salome Dennis & Sister Eunice Bedle. We arrived at Bussrow the 4th day of August evening. Our labors were to reconcile them to be of one mind, in case the removal should take place.[65]

Issachar traveled back to Busro together with Joshua Worley, the twenty-six-year-old son of Malcolm Worley and a rising young elder in Ohio, and with Salome Dennis and Eunice Bedle, with whom Issachar had a long history.[66] He had been present at the two women's conversions more than twenty years before at Turtle Creek. They had been among the first young believers selected to take up residence in the first dwelling built for the old believers in 1806. Salome had been at Busro with Issachar since nearly the beginning of the community, and after the death of Martha Sanford in October 1823, she had moved into the position of first eldress and Eunice Bedle had

arrived from Ohio to take the second eldress position. The eldresses probably enjoyed showing Issachar the changes at Busro. No doubt Issachar was
delighted at the opportunity to lead singing and dancing in the new meeting
house whose construction had barely begun when he last saw the site in early
1824. Yet the visit was not without complications:

> They were all glad to see us but they were divided. There was the move
> proposed and some were for it and some against it. Brother Joshua and
> I both labored with them heard their complaints. My sickness was heavy
> upon me, but all the time I was able, I was among them. They received my
> words kindly, confessed their confidence in me, and their love towards
> me. But I had left them and they never believed that it was right and a
> number of such like complaints . . . Their faith in general appeared strong
> amidst all their afflictions.[67]

Being back at Busro was physically and emotionally taxing for Issachar,
who was now approaching seventy. Partly because of the late summer season
and partly due to the exertion of the trip, he suffered a severe relapse of his
malaria.[68] He was deeply troubled to realize that many of the Busro Shakers
still resented him for leaving them unexpectedly more than two years before.
The community was well aware of the ongoing deliberations over Busro's fate,
and anxieties for the future placed the whole population on edge. A group
of recent converts from Adams County, Ohio, had lately been moved out to
Busro in an effort to bring an infusion of fresh energy and commitment. But
many of those new arrivals contracted malaria and grew discouraged. Issachar
was sick and his spirits were muted when he left Busro in mid-September to
return to Ohio. His regrets over Busro had been reawakened, and he probably
realized he would never see the community again. He could not know that
Busro's fate would continue to plague him and the rest of the Shaker West.

> ⁓ I was very unwell, yet I started on horseback with Br. Joshua, leaving the
> Sisters there. And in five days arrived at Pleasant Hill 190 miles . . . But here we
> found a number of those wild creatures who had begun to weave their spiders
> web and hatch their cockatrice eggs. And I expected then they would soon
> back out in a viper, which came to pass in the year [18]27.When the Busserow
> Society broke up here was a number who took advantage of this move to
> strengthen their unbelief that the gospel is not what it is testified to be. That
> all other Societies are liable to break up as well as bind![69]

From Busro, Issachar and Joshua Worley journeyed on horseback to Pleasant Hill for a visit, instead of returning directly Ohio. Conditions among the

Kentucky Shakers worried Issachar deeply. Word had spread that Busro, a large and reasonably stable society that had steadily grown and prospered despite difficulties since retaking its evacuated site in 1814, would soon be ordered to disband. Since the hundreds of members of West Union were signatories to a legally binding covenant enacted in 1815, no one knew what the ramifications of a breakup would be for the people and for the economic joint interest they had worked so hard to build up. At Pleasant Hill, Issachar and Joshua found some young adults who were particularly strident in voicing their opposition to developments in the Shaker West. Richard McNemar, who soon was sent to Pleasant Hill to probe the role of its young adults in what was turning into a mounting rebellion, pointedly attributed the brewing trouble to the Busro breakup:

> The church was in peace and usual prosperity in 1826 when the mixing of spirits began through the door that was opened toward W Union. From the adversities of that society a spirit of jealousy had got up against the Ministry as the cause in some it rose into rebellion & spread like fire till it spread in a general schism. This jealousy & lack of confidence had its ministers & agents . . . who in consequence of the dissolution of the order at West Union felt themselves free & independent to say & do as they pleased.[70]

When Issachar Bates returned to Ohio later in 1826, he was relieved to be away from the rancor he had found in Indiana and Kentucky. But the impending breakup of Busro hung like a dark cloud. Archibald Meacham returned in October with the confirmation that the community's land and assets were to be sold and the people evacuated early in 1827. The Busro believers would spread out over the other communities in the Shaker West, most going to communities where they felt the strongest link by virtue of kinship or acquaintance. Issachar went to Union Village in April 1827 to be there when some of the Busro people arrived, including the Busro Ministry. Archibald soon was moved to take charge of the new community of White Water. But the two Busro eldresses, Salome Dennis and Eunice Bedle, accompanied Issachar back to Watervliet. Once there the, "[t]he order of Eldership was radically changed. Elder Brother Robert (Baxter) dropped his title and went into the Garret to live with Elder Issachar & became Brother Robert. Eldress Salome Dennis & Sister Eunice Bedell went into the opposite garret room. Thus constituting an Eldership for the family and a Ministry for the whole society. This order of things continued till April 1832."[71]

Such had been the disarray at Watervliet that the normal practice of paired elders and eldresses providing leadership for each family had been suspended, at least in part, since before Issachar's arrival in 1824. Although some of the families had been served by elders and eldresses who were longstanding residents of the community since its earliest days, Issachar had stood more or less alone as the lead of the community overall. Such irregularity was sharply at odds with Shaker wisdom, as articulated by the New Lebanon Ministry in a letter to Ohio that spring, making urgent recommendations for the Ohio communities: "It is true brethren may go & preach the gospel to the world of mankind, & they may help young believers on their way for a time. But their ministration will be of short duration, & the travel of the young believers will come to an end, unless the female has her corresponding place & her just right in the government. One pillar, let it be never so big is insufficient to hold up the building."[72] Insightfully, the Ministry in the East recognized that being gifted as a preacher or as a problem-solver in a struggling Shaker family did not necessarily translate to being a good elder. And it reasserted the vital importance of the female lead, the female half of Shaker governance. But likely the New Lebanon Ministry did not realize that Issachar's solution for restoring the female role to the leadership at Watervliet would be so disruptive. Salome Dennis had been criticized at Busro for being divisive in exercising her authority over the women there: "The sisters also become much dissatisfied with Eldress Salome, which was not without grounds . . . she was accused with harshness and severity towards the Sisters, at least her disposition was not very smooth. She was also accused with partiality, &c."[73]

In addition to Salome and Eunice, who were moved into the "garret" as eldress and elder sister, several other Busro people came to Watervliet expressly because they retained a loyalty to Issachar Bates. Naturally, some Watervliet Shakers were ruffled. The perception that Issachar Bates was installing his special friends at Watervliet, placing some of them in positions of authority, did not bode well. To make matters worse, Watervliet seemed to garner the special attention of the Union Village Ministry in early 1828 on the problem of alcohol consumption. Writing on behalf of the Watervliet elders, Issachar repudiated "DOCTOR BRANDY," declaring that medicinal use of ardent spirits "gives power to all that are naturally given to appetite, to put the knife to their throat." At that time, the community pledged to curtail "the needless wicked use of ardent spirits," affirming "with uplifted hands and a loud Amen."[74] But the drinking was only one symptom of a larger set of problems.

Dynamics in the Shaker West were building to a near crisis. Disaffected young adults from Busro remained bitter over the dissolution of that society and the loss of the property that they had invested in Busro's joint interest.

They carried their grievances with them to their new homes in Ohio and Kentucky. Two particular malcontents who came to Watervliet and Union Village were credited with sowing seeds of dissension:

> We need only name an Andrew Martin & Danl Rankin who alone were sufficient to spread darkness over the whole church to defame every character in it, the ministry not excepted. Martin could lecture to the young people largely on his experience that he had passed through all the degrees of Shakerism & found it to be all rotten . . . Rankin had gained enough from his experience in the office to excite jealously enough towards that department & his stock of infidelity was sufficient to subvert the faith of all who lay under the least trials or would listen to his abominable stuff.[75]

Issachar Bates was deeply pained to see young adults whom he had helped gather to Shakerism and had mentored over long years now working to tear down the Church in the West. Several of these young men, including Daniel Rankin, he had brought to Watervliet, not realizing by doing so he was bringing vipers into the nest. A series of defections from Union Village, Watervliet, and Pleasant Hill began in 1828 and continued over the next few years, mostly affecting adults under forty, which was exactly the population that the societies could least afford to lose. Many of the malcontents were the children of the early western converts, and they represented the future of Shakerism in the region. Issachar wrote, "Who but . . . a suffering follower of Christ can judge of the trials and see suffering that must be endured by those who have the care, the concern, and over sight of such beings?"[76] Many of the "younger set" resented a hierarchical authority structure that marginalized their voices, yet the older generation clung to the necessity of retaining firm control, believing that "[m]uch, yea very much depends on the few survivors of the old stock & their examples in managing Church affairs. Many heats have been taken on the metal, & it has been hammered & shaped this way & that, by different ministers of the Patriarchal Order, but the last thing is to give it the kind temper, & this depends much on the last surviving few.[77] And Issachar was among that "surviving few." He had reached "three score years & ten," considered then to be the average limit of the human lifespan.

Many of the believers under Issachar's care at Watervliet seemed, if not satisfied with him as a leader, at least genuinely fond of him as a patriarchal figure. In 1828 he convened a birthday celebration for himself:

> When I was seventy years of age, I felt as tho' God had been very merciful and kind to me to honor me with such a good old age (seeing I had so

narrowly escaped with my life so many hundreds of times and a number of times been at death's door); I felt so thankful that I concluded I would notice that birthday, for the first time that I ever noticed one, & perhaps it would be the last. So I called all the society together that evening, old and young, and made a feast, and we had a joyful meeting . . . Now I verily thought at that time that I had but a few more days to spend in this world, altho' I had middling good health, and could do a good day's work in my garden. Could ride to Union Village any time in four hours, a distance of twenty two miles. I could not find that I had failed much, yet I thought I had lived long enough. But the people would often tell me that I had got to live twenty years yet, for I could dance and play in meeting about as spry as any of them.[78]

It was in the late 1820s that western leaders began making more trips to the East for advice and discussions. Benjamin Seth Youngs and the South Union Ministry traveled east in 1827, carrying an upbeat letter from Issachar, in which he uses the metaphor of a shotgun to express his desire that his good wishes be dispersed widely among his friends: "[I]t will please the old hunter mighty well; not that I expect to kill any of you, but that ye may know by the noise of Issachar's Gun that he is yet alive and in good health, able to do a good days work every day."[79] Richard McNemar made a trip in 1829, partly to carry out the somber task of escorting Lucy Smith back to New Lebanon. She had been the female lead at Pleasant Hill for twenty years, but defections and a series of lawsuits relating to the recent revolt had stressed her greatly and left her physically weakened. In 1830, Issachar had his own opportunity to return east, and he joyfully embarked with Solomon King on his first trip back to New York since 1805: "Now on the first day of June, I started with Elder Solomon on a visit to the East, to visit our ancient gospel friends in the land of our nativity . . . And in a few days arrived at WaterVliet the place of my former residence. This began to feel like a new World. We visited and feasted on love and good will."[80]

By 1830, canals and steamships had made travel to New Lebanon far more efficient (figure 10.2). Along the way, Issachar and Solomon visited the Shaker villages of North Union and Sodus Bay, the latter settlement one Issachar would have been excited to see for the first time. A promising location situated dramatically on the shore of Lake Ontario, Sodus Bay had been established just a few years before, and many of its inhabitants had family connections to Shakers in Ohio. Conveniently located halfway between the New York communities and North Union, Ohio, Sodus regularly hosted traveling Shakers.[81]

10.2 Canals of Ohio, 1825–1913, *published by the Ohio Historical Society,*
Columbus, Ohio, 1969. (Courtesy of the Ohio Historical Society.)

Arriving at Watervliet, New York, Issachar was reunited with his son and namesake, Issachar Jr., along with his brother Theodore and many other relatives and old friends. After a few days there, the travelers moved on to New Lebanon, where Issachar found his daughters Sarah and Betsy and, given the letters and gifts that had passed among them over the years, a joyful reunion indeed. Betsy, now a second eldress in the Church Family,[82] accompanied her father along on a visit to the young women and girls of the North Family or "gathering order," where Issachar had a chance to speak to young Shakers for whom the West was like another planet. He preached to captivated audiences and attended many singing meetings, during which he was surely gratified to witness his daughter Sarah among New Lebanon's leading singers. In their turn, the New Lebanon Shakers were intrigued at this elderly yet animated figure, whose frontier exploits were the basis of tales: "Elder Issachar is 73, a very bright, active, intelligent elderly man. Simple, childlike, affectionate & wise . . . Issachar traveled & preached much, met with many curious adventures — was Elder at Busro while that Society remained there . . . A large concourse of Spectators attended our meeting & Elder Issachar addressed them. Manifested much energy & spoke very loud."[83]

The visit extended eastward still further. Issachar and Solomon were escorted by New Lebanon Ministry elder Rufus Bishop on a tour that included two different stays in large and prosperous Hancock, Massachusetts, and visits to Enfield, Connecticut, and the small but vibrant Tyringham, Massachusetts.[84] At Enfield, Issachar became acquainted with fellow musician Russel Haskell, whose passion for collecting and recording hymns led him to document numerous western songs that Issachar shared during the visit. While Issachar was visiting these three villages for the first time, it is safe to say that he relished returning to the region of his birth and youth, where he could mingle with people who shared the New England accent and mannerisms he still retained. Feted wherever he went and reveling in the constant conviviality, the West and its troubles must have seemed very distant. Yet all too soon, the travelers' route turned westward again. Issachar and Solomon tarried at Watervliet, New York, for their journey's final week. There, Issachar visited the cemetery, where the graves of his wife, Lovina, daughter Polly, and niece Anna were all clustered in the northwest corner.[85] And then it was time to embark westward on the Erie Canal. Issachar enjoyed the mostly water journey to Ohio, calculating their progress at an average rate of one hundred miles for every twenty-four hours. He took great delight in one particular leg of the trip, the crossing from Buffalo to Cleveland on Lake Erie where "the Lake was very rough which caused a wonderful discharge of provision through the teeth of many, and heavy praying as well as vomiting."[86] Still a hardy traveler, Issachar seemed immune to seasickness, but Solomon was still ill when they arrived back at Watervliet, Ohio, more than a week later.[87]

Issachar's trip to the East had been a joyous distraction. But back in the West, he found that the disorder had only worsened: "But to my grief and sorrow of my soul I found an increase of apostasy . . . they had heard that there was a new covenant that would be brought forward, and they had an idea that it was because the old one was weak and now was their time to crawl out of any covenant. For they had fallen into the same plan with those reprobates at Pleasant Hill to break the covenant and divide the inheritance."[88]

A Shaker at Union Village wrote, "Mad dogs are raging thro' the country," by which he meant the many apostates that continued to plague the Shakers, coming to the dwellings to talk to friends and relatives. Elders tried to limit their influence by urging faithful Shakers to send any apostate to the village office to be "attended in good order."[89] Because a common theme in the grievances was concern over the stability of each community's covenant, the Ministry increasingly pushed, first, for an open reassessment of each believer's commitment and, second, for a revision of covenants at Union Village and Watervliet to reflect the "post-Darrow" reality. "We believe it is high time that we should come to the light & declare openly to each other what we believe," Richard McNemar wrote.[90] However, that process provoked even more apostasies. Issachar Bates wrote bitterly of this interlude:

[I]n 1831 after dishonoring themselves and their profession the covenant was brought forward and read and any one that felt free to sign it might and none else . . . so the matter went on till 1832 and they found that a sacred covenant with God and each other was not so easy to break as they had calculated on. And they themselves began to break and to scatter to the four winds on their ways to destruction and there I must leave them. Amen. They were naturally likely young men and women that went off and they were natural and after that which is natural. And they have got it and they are welcome to the whole of it for me . . . And on that ground I leave them.[91]

Richard McNemar spent Christmas 1831 at Watervliet, Ohio, with Issachar. The two jointly composed a Christmas hymn, which took the form of a dialogue between the brothers and sisters. Issachar's wit, Richard's theological acumen, and the poetical skills of both combined to produce a hymn that still stands as the best explication of the Shaker perspective on the Christmas story—along with a vigorous endorsement of female equality.[92] Spectators to the Shaker meeting on December 24 may have been surprised to hear the Shaker sisters sing, "For it is the woman's day!" Richard preached a Christmas message, and later the Shakers held a celebratory evening meeting in a newly completed meeting room over the kitchen wing in Watervliet's center dwelling, with "a great deal of lively exercise."[93] But the Christmas tradition also included the practice of individual confession before an elder, and one Watervliet brother, John Martin, refused to comply. Issachar and Richard confronted him, but in vain. A few days after Christmas, Martin became the latest apostate.[94] Issachar later expressed his frustration: "How many in this day of God Almighty I have seen, who have received the everlasting gospel . . . believed it and received it with joy, turn away from it like a dog to his vomit again; for no other cause than this. Because they had not a good and honest heart . . . I have labored with such people often, and it is like throwing water against a goose's breast: it cannot enter."[95]

With the opening of 1832, Issachar Bates had been a Shaker for a full thirty years. He was nearly seventy-four years old, an advanced age for the period. His recovery from one dire accident and his ability to still withstand long and difficult journeys were proof of his continued physical vigor. A jolly interlude in the land of his youth where he was a celebrated and storied figure, while invigorating, had done little to relieve the anxiety of leadership. Instinctively Issachar had shied away from leadership positions, likely because he knew his own limitations, and as an old man, he was perhaps less interested in leading and more interested in creating a comfortable home at Watervliet surrounded by beloved friends. Facing a cauldron of dire developments in the Shaker West that were far beyond his ability to control, Issachar would flounder.

CHAPTER 11

"Tribulation Worketh Patience"

A BITTER CLOSE IN THE WEST

Perhaps you may have the brains beat out of your soul some day,
and then you will know what heart-rending sorrow is and not till then.
— Issachar Bates

As 1832 opened, Issachar Bates found his position at Watervliet under scrutiny. He was to be removed from office and the eldership transferred to Richard McNemar, who had come to Watervliet ostensibly to sort out details of a much-needed new covenant. On the surface, Issachar was happy to be relieved of responsibilities. But he chafed at being sidelined in the community's day-to-day operations, seeming to have no useful purpose. Perhaps because Richard brought with him to Watervliet his aspirations to establish a printing press there, his presence seemed to encourage Issachar to indulge his literary interests and undertake more writing. At Richard's urging, he wrote his autobiography, and with Richard and others he collaborated on a hymn book, an ambitious volume that would be only the second hymn book ever printed by the Shakers. Issachar also became embroiled in a controversy over military pensions that brought strong criticism from the New Lebanon Ministry. Freed from responsibilities of eldership, he traveled to visit other communities, but his health suffered. Frustration seemed to cause Issachar to lose some of his emotional moorings. He grew cantankerous and suspicious, trying the patience of his closest friends. By 1834 it was clear that Issachar's continued presence in Ohio was more hindrance than help, even though he retained the love and admiration of most. A summons to return permanently to New Lebanon in the spring of 1835 could not have been a surprise.

My past imperfections I'll not justify,
But when sharply reprov'd my old nature may fry: —
From "A Good Determination," by Issachar Bates

The property and structures of Watervliet had prospered under Issachar's leadership by the early 1830s (figure 11.1). Outwardly, at least, order seemed to prevail. But Issachar and Richard McNemar had together begun to probe

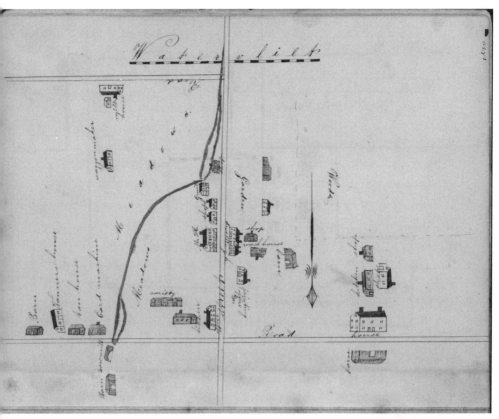

11.1 *"Watervliet" from* Sketches of the various Societies of Believers in the states of Ohio & Kentucky . . . Copied from Isaac N. Youngs Journal, July 1835 by George Kendall. *(Library of Congress Shaker Collection.)*

the community's internal discord during Richard's Christmas visit. Richard returned in February 1832, a gloomy time for the Ohio Shakers. Unusually warm and rainy weather that month had produced the "greatest flood ever known in the country," damaging property at Union Village and making the area's roads nearly impassable.[1] Mud notwithstanding, Richard struggled the twenty-five miles from Union Village to Watervliet to continue the process of reviewing that society's records and assessing how the Watervliet covenant should be updated so as to reflect the current state of the society.

Friday February 10th 1832 set out for Watervliet about 10 oclock — The road very muddy — arrived about sunset and was kindly received . . . Lodge tonight in the garret as usual, find it an incumberance to the order, and conclude to propose some other arrangement for my accommodation during my stay.

*Saturday morning clear & pleasant — talk over matters & things, with
the company & with James Ball from which it appears that my present &
immediate concern is about the affairs of the office particularly the office books
of account and record. Propose to Elder Issachar to put up at the office which
meets his entire approbation. After breakfast all being agreed Elder Issachar
conducts me to the office where I am soon located in a commodious room. The
books produced & I commenced examining them . . . It was but a few minutes
after I got to the office till the thunder began to roar & the lightning to flash &
the rain to pour down in such torrents as produced the greatest flood that has
lately been seen — Among all the office books I found no book of records, &
could not learn that any had been kept in the society except by Nathaniel.*[2]

It was not Richard's first trip to Watervliet for this purpose. The previous
April of 1831, he and Mathew Houston had together gone to Watervliet where
they "took their stations in the garret as helps to the ministry in regulating
and arranging the affairs of the church & society." Considering the transitions
that had been under way in the Shaker West since the death of David Darrow
and the dissolution of Busro, renegotiation of the covenants that governed
the Shakers' joint interest was clearly warranted. Richard, with his excellent
grasp of the legalities of Shaker life, was the best person to undertake a review
of Watervliet's records and to author a new covenant. But things did not begin
auspiciously. Even his usual practice of lodging "in the garret" with the elders
proved divisive, though for whom Richard does not clarify.

Not long before, in the spring of 1831, Richard and Issachar had presided
over a series of meetings with the believers at Watervliet to re-evaluate the
covenants throughout the Shaker West and to solicite people's views on how a
revised covenant might best be tailored to Watervliet while remaining consistent with the covenants of the other communities. Ultimately, a revised covenant was prepared and read to the people. But instead of signing it, they put it
aside for further consideration, a frustrating stalemate for Richard, who later
remarked of that effort, "We made a draft and offered it but the state of matters & minds vetoed the transaction, so we backed out & left matters as they
were."[3] The bone of contention lay mainly in people's understanding of the
term "joint interest," and whether individual signatories to the covenant had
forever surrendered their right to have input into the dissolution of property
that had once been theirs. Richard later reflected, "Thus matters apparently
grew worse & worse till the next February when I was sent up to examine the
books and papers and things, and make out a regular record of society matters
from the beginning to the then present date."[4] Now as 1832 began, Richard,

who had been acting as legal counsel in the Shaker West for several years, set about assembling all the relevant records.

That stormy February, Richard's task did not get off to a good start. Issachar Bates was entirely willing that Richard review all available information and helped him to get settled at the office where he could be closest to the materials he needed. But Richard found to his dismay that scarcely any records existed, apart from a journal that had been kept for a few years by Nathaniel Taylor, a deacon at Watervliet. The raging thunderstorm outside seemed an appropriate reminder of the rocky times that had gripped the Watervliet community virtually since Issachar's own arrival several years before, as well as a portent of the troubles that would continue. Richard was forced to appeal to the entire community for help in piecing together the course of past events such as land transactions, changes in membership, and details of how the various families were organized. To his surprise, no previous covenant could be produced. Richard discovered "that even that was not to be had, it having been taken to U.V. for safe keeping." Indeed, the disarray at Watervliet was even worse than Richard had feared. As the highest-ranking elder, Issachar bore at least some blame. The responsibilities of a Shaker family elder admittedly did not include explicit oversight of temporal matters, which tasks were left to the office trustee. However, Issachar had pointedly put aside many aspects of normal Shaker order during his nearly eight years at Watervliet, working in a remarkably hands-on fashion and taking direct interest in temporal and spiritual matters alike. For Issachar to assert now that he had always been completely oblivious to the regulation of temporal matters at Watervliet was disingenuous. Richard seemed aware that Issachar was hoping to avoid accountability for the many thorny difficulties that had developed during his tenure. While sympathetic to the legitimate assertion that Watervliet lacked members to whom responsibility could be delegated, Richard also recognized that the Watervliet people were vexed by a perceived lack of strong leadership among the community elders.

> Elder Issachar most feelingly declared that he had no other word of God
> for the people than what he delivered & on the other hand it appeared
> that his helps felt unable to stand under the weight of burden of the oppo-
> sition that was generally felt to his ministrations. On the delicate subject I
> could not but sympathize with both sides believing all were conscientious
> and sincere. On the one part it is a fact that the society is much lacking
> for talented members to establish chh. Order in a manner that would suit
> Elder I's faith & feelings . . . On the other hand the people are as sensible

of lacks in the order of government for which they are not responsible & which it is out of their power to remedy.[5]

Richard's primary purpose in coming to Watervliet that February had been to return to the question of the revised covenant, review records in light of the concerns that the Watervliet believers had previously expressed, and draft a new covenant that the society would be willing to sign. But the airing of people's concerns about the covenant quickly morphed into concerns about the Watervliet leadership in general. Richard found himself in the middle of a conflict between Issachar and some vocal members of the society. Issachar recognized that the Watervliet society was seriously deficient in "church order," but blamed that on the absence of believers with suitable talents. He lost no opportunity to expound on the believers' faults in preaching. But the people at Watervliet recognized faults in Issachar and the other appointed leaders for not doing their best to regulate the day-to-day operation of the society, and they were tired of bearing the brunt of criticism. Things soon grew even worse. At the end of the month of February, a recent apostate from Watervliet confronted Issachar:

> William Martin came to the village replete with malignity. Elder Issachar inadvertently stepped into the clothes shop & found him there, altercation ensued which on Martin's part burst into a flame, most profanely & abusively urging the good Elder to say to his face what he had preached about him post tergo ["from behind"]. "Well," said Elder Issachar, "I have said you were a mean man," for which he instantly rec'd a blow on the mouth & but for the intercession of Isaac who held the reprobate the assault & battery would have been pursued until it would have been terminated in the murder of an innocent & respectable man in the 74th year of his age.[6]

Isaac Martin, brother to the man who assaulted Issachar and Issachar's one-time trusted assistant, left Watervliet a few weeks later. Clearly, the plague of apostasies was not over yet. News of the assault on Issachar reached Union Village, and Solomon King took the precaution of telling members not to speak with "reprobates" and to lock their doors and secure their property.

Possibly to distract Issachar while the review of Watervliet's many problems was underway, Richard proposed that Issachar write his autobiography. Richard probably had several motives. In addition to giving his friend a pleasanter project to occupy his energies, Richard hoped that Issachar would produce a manuscript to complement one of Richard's own recent occupations: publishing. For over twenty-five years, Richard had nursed the ambition to operate a printing press.[7] Since 1807, he had overseen the publication by outside printers of his own first major literary work, *The Kentucky Revival*, the Shakers' earliest large-scale theological treatise, *The Testimony of Christ's Second Appearing*, and numerous smaller tracts. But using outside printers was cumbersome, necessitating constant trips to printers' offices to attend to details. Observing the power of apostates' published accounts to spread anti-Shaker slander, Richard had long urged Shaker leaders to be more proactive in publishing their own doctrines. Further, given the desire of Shakers to maintain separation from the world, the astute Richard reasoned that the Shakers might benefit from operating a printing press on their own premises. He had been instrumental in setting up a printing press temporarily at Union Village in 1823 for the revised edition of *The Testimony of Christ's Second Appearing* (which Issachar had helped him to complete in early 1824), but that equipment had been sold after the job was completed. During Richard's trip to the East in 1829, he had gained the eastern leaders' confidence for setting up a printing press in Ohio to publish a variety of works. By early 1832, he had assembled the necessary equipment, and he brought it with him to Watervliet. His intent was to launch a printing enterprise that would give the Shakers an outlet for a range of printed literature, from legal documents to theological treatises to historical accounts of the opening generation of the western Shaker enterprise. Richard had begun collecting material for potential publication the previous year, an activity that flowed naturally from his assignment to travel the Shaker West and review covenant documents. Having observed that "the first or aged class of Believers who had borne the burden & heat of the day, were gradually passing off the stage of action,"[8] it was natural for him to urge people like Issachar Bates to set down his recollections. Not only would they benefit later generations of Shakers, but they could also be an asset in the present fractious atmosphere by reminding people of the ideals, motives, and sacrifices of earlier Shakers.

> ⬯ [N]ow presented here for the press, is a manuscript . . . The title of it is *The Life & Experience of Issachar Bates*, written by himself. To my own part I consider it a well written affair, & worthy of all acceptation. Perhaps I feel some partiality towards it, as I was among others who requested him to write it.[9]

Others besides Richard McNemar sought to persuade Issachar Bates to record his life story, an unusual undertaking for Issachar. Throughout his life he had seemed to resist making narrative records of his activities available to the Shaker society at large.[10] He had kept no journal. His letter-writing was spotty, though the letters that survive are remarkable both for their detail and for their well-crafted prose. His primary mode of recording his thoughts and actions had long been poetry, though here again he was known as an avid storyteller whose mind was a virtual "museum," comprising "humorous incidents of his life and past events, unknown to anyone else."[11] So producing a prose account was a departure, but his closest friends persuaded him it would be a valuable exercise. He wrote over 120 pages in only a few weeks' time.

> I have as it were ransacked my whole life according to the best of my remembrance, from the year 1758 to the 26th day of March 1832. And it has been my sincere endeavor not to state anything, but what was fact, and to avoid exaggeration as much as possible . . . for I never should have undertaken this heavy task in this my advanced age, had I not been strongly solicited by some of my best friends, who urged it as my duty, to leave a record of these things behind me for the satisfaction of those who come after me.[12]

The draft that Issachar brought to a preliminary conclusion on March 26, 1832, was remarkable in its scope and winning style. For some, its completion seemed to represent a logical transition point in Issachar's duties. It was abundantly clear that Issachar had been struggling as chief elder at Watervliet for quite some time. On April 1, 1832, with the Union Village Ministry present, Issachar was formally removed from his office and replaced by Richard McNemar. The "Church Record" for Watervliet, a type of document standard in all Shaker villages for the recording of major events (but one that only commenced at Watervliet once Richard assumed eldership), noted for April 1: "Elder Eleazar Wright succeeded Elder Issachar as lead of the society and family, the latter being this day released from his burthen." Speaking of himself using the initials of his pseudonym, Eleazar Wright, and ruefully alluding to the disorder that had dominated Watervliet, Richard wrote that on that day, "the Ministry being here, Elder Issachar was released from his charge and E.W. put into his place (whatever it might be) among an unorganized people." No one objected to the change.

Issachar himself may initially have been relieved to be removed from the burden of eldership. However, he continued to reside at Watervliet, creating dynamics that were awkward at best and outright disruptive at worst. His special friends remained both deferential to him and attentive to his personal needs, even though he had no formal standing as elder. Eldresses Salome

Dennis and Eunice Bedle lavished him with personal attention, tending his room, caring for his clothing, and preparing his food. His role as "public minister" continued much as before. In the public meetings held each Sabbath, Issachar delivered sermons and led singing as usual:

> Altho he was released from the burden and first care of this society yet he continued his ministration both to the world and believers whenever he felt able or an occasion required it or an opportunity presented. He generally spake in public meeting about every other Sabbath while public meeting lasted. There were four brethren in this society that spoke in public meeting in these times. Namely, Elder Issachar, Elder Eleazar, Henry Miller, and William Phillips . . . Elder Issachar and Henry Miller would speak one day and then Elder Eleazar and William Phillips the next . . . This regulation continued with but little interruption until May the 21, 1833.[13]

Richard McNemar's role at Watervliet was murky. Although he was technically the lead, the fact that no revision of the Watervliet covenant had yet been agreed to kept conditions in limbo and made Richard's task difficult. He later characterized much of the remainder of 1832 as a time of "retirement and cool reflection."[14] Richard used the interlude as an opportunity to launch his new printing press in earnest. In May he printed a circular dedicating the new press. Sometime during the summer or fall, he launched an ambitious project — the compilation of a hymn book. The finished volume was printed the following year and titled *Selection of Hymns and Poems for the Use of Believers*. A robust work, it comprised about two hundred hymns.[15] It was probably logical for Richard to include Issachar in the project. The interest the two men held most strongly in common was their passion for music and poetry. Both were accomplished singers and poets — indeed, two of the most prolific and skilled poets in the Shaker world. Compiling the hymnal involved sorting through hundreds of hymns and poems generated during their lives as Shakers as well as works from other Shakers, both east and west. Working together in the small frame "print shop" at Watervliet (figure 11.2), they included hymns on a variety of themes: doctrinal, historical, spiritual, hymns for Christmas and New Year holidays, hymns for funerals.

The experiences of both Issachar and Richard left them well-suited to the task of producing the hymnal. Both had nurtured and promoted music in Shaker worship for nearly thirty years. They had helped compile the Shakers' first hymn book, *Millennial Praises*, more than twenty years earlier. Since then, the mobility of both men throughout the Shaker world allowed them to lead

11.2 *Richard McNemar's print shop today. No longer on its original site, the print shop has been moved to Carillon Historical Park in Dayton, Ohio. (Photo courtesy of Dayton History, with thanks to Steve Lucht, lead interpreter, Carillon Park.)*

worship and take particular notice of music wherever they went, encouraging the efforts of other songwriters. Both were acquainted with leading Shaker hymn writers throughout the country. Issachar's two particular friends, Salome Dennis and Eunice Bedle, were also drawn into the effort, and the group worked together as an editorial team, sorting, soliciting, and organizing material for the hymnal.

Richard's motives were complicated. In the volume's preface, he expressed his purpose to "promote general union among Believers and perpetuate the various impressions attending those gifts in their first operations: For in singing a lively hymn, or perusing a striking piece of poetry, it is not uncommon to imbibe a degree of the spirit that dictated it."[16] Yet Richard's recent struggles at Watervliet had highlighted the difficulties that could result through inattention to record-keeping, and he was conscious that the first generation of Shakers in the West — Issachar and himself included — were aging and would soon pass from the scene. Richard was a believer in the power of music and verse to inspire, soothe, and unite. Looking around him, he saw a troubled Shaker West desperately in need of union and inspiration. Richard's use of the pseudonym "Philos Harmoniae," or "lover of harmony," signals his wish that the hymnal would be an antidote for a fractious community. And he hoped the work might be a productive focus for Issachar, who seemed to be losing a clear sense of his function in the community. Together, culling through the rich poetry and music produced by Shakers during a full generation, much of it their own work, Richard and Issachar could enjoy "a joyous and wistful exercise"[17] and complete a volume that would encapsulate the many dimensions of the western Shaker experience of which they themselves had been such a vital part.

For all his work on Richard's hymnal as a tool to achieve harmony, Issachar Bates himself stood in great need of soothing after his removal from leadership in 1832. A rift had developed between Issachar and Solomon King, first elder of the Union Village Ministry, possibly because Issachar projected onto Solomon the resentment he felt over the inauspicious end of his leadership stint at Watervliet. In July Issachar refused to attend a Saturday-evening meeting at which a letter from Solomon was being read. The message he sent via Eunice Bedle clearly indicated he was brooding over a directive from Solomon: "[H]e don't like that road & intends to have no more to do with our order." Richard went to Issachar before Sabbath meeting the next morning and persuaded him to stop sulking, writing later: "Is(sachar) visited by Eleazar & becomes more reconciled, requests to take his place behind Robert in the march."[18] But as the year continued, Issachar's dissatisfaction with his new status continued to generate friction. Issachar's friends, too, remained uncomfortable under Richard's leadership. In November, Richard wrote of being "[t]racked on every side" by Issachar's special allies, who tried to be Issachar's eyes and ears.[19] By December, when two senior Shakers from Union Village, Melinda Watts and Ashbel Kitchell, arrived with the directive to assume eldership positions at Watervliet, Richard was aggravated by Issachar's irrational interventions.

> Heavy labors with E.I. (Elder Issachar). His trials are heavy at the Eldership for acting in any matter without his knowledge and judging of every thing that transpires. Three hours spent to satisfy him that we had done nothing yet secretly, that Melinda Ashbel &c were sent here as much without our knowledge as his . . . It is all a farce about his surrendering his gift & authority to Eleazar. There is nothing of it. His long labors among this people gives him a claim that he never means to relinquish.[20]

Part of Issachar's behavior may have stemmed from pent-up frustrations over the abrupt new course that his life had taken. Accustomed to both mobility and influence, increasingly he now had neither. Since returning from his journey east in 1830, he had been practically static at Watervliet for more than two years, save a handful of short trips to Union Village. And all the while, Issachar was witnessing the Shaker world he had helped to build in the West fraying around the edges. People he had nurtured and mentored were apostatizing; some had even turned on him with violence. His friend Richard, whose confession Issachar had heard back in 1805, had now supplanted him as elder. Although Issachar had found some momentary respite in the literary pursuits of writing his autobiography and helping to organize Richard's new hymnal, it was plain that he needed to carve out for himself a very different role. As yet, he did not know what that might be.

One pursuit that Issachar Bates apparently reveled in during this period was gardening. Manuscripts contain multiple tantalizing hints that Issachar had long harbored interests in gardening and tree husbandry. As early as 1810, he had taken a special interest in planting and tending nut trees at Turtle Creek, and at Busro he had laid out extensive fruit and nut orchards. By the 1830s, garden seeds were a major industry of Shakers everywhere, including the western communities. Richard McNemar's writing indicates that it was Issachar who was in charge of harvesting, sorting, and packaging garden seeds at the end of 1832.[21] From that time until Issachar's final departure from the West in 1835, there are several references to Issachar tending a large and productive garden at Watervliet, including remarks by Richard reflecting sensitivity to just how important an outlet gardening had become for Issachar.[22] Gardening would have entailed tending vegetables, herbs, and medicinal plants, as well as preserving seeds for sale. For the sociable Issachar, gardening would have given him ample opportunity to interact with women and men all over the community, from the cooks and nurses to the trustees and deacons who oversaw the preparation and sale of garden products.

Sometime in the summer of 1832, the Shakers at Watervliet learned that the U.S. Congress had passed a new service-pension law, which both regulated and liberalized pension claims for surviving veterans of the Revolutionary War.[23] The information probably came to them through local newspapers. For the Ohio Shakers, practical yet pacifist, this presented a dilemma. Shaker men who had participated in the Revolutionary War in their pre-Shaker lives now rejected violence, and all Shaker men refused to bear arms. But should Shaker veterans also reject lawful pensions for past service? Was the act of claiming a pension for military service tantamount to approving that past service? Richard McNemar and other Shaker leaders in Ohio considered that question in September 1832, soon after they learned of the recent law: "Today a counsel was called to deliberate on the subject of Church members accepting & receiving pensions for military services in the revolutionary war. After due consideration it was agreed that there was no impropriety or inconsistency in any of our brethren accepting of the provisions & benefits of the act of June 7, 1832."[24]

They decided that there should be no "impropriety" attached to any pension claim on the part of any Shaker veteran:

> Nor for the Church to admit as a part of the consecrated interest those pensions appropriated by the government for their support & benefit. Inasmuch as the Ch[urc]h contributes their equal part for the support of the government & our aged brethren are least maintaining themselves or fulfilling the common obligations of Ch[urc]h members in supporting the interest by their actual services, it is highly proper that they should be released from those obligations & enjoy the benefits of those provisions rightfully merited from government in their younger days . . . It was further agreed that the following brethren to wit Francis Bedle, Joseph Stout, John Houston, Abner Bonnel, Reuben Morris, Benjamin Howard, Abijah Pelham & Benjamin Cox be encouraged to prepare & forward their respective applications according to law — & that Eleazar wait upon each of them & take the minutes of their several terms of service.[25]

The Ohio Shakers' rationale was logical enough. Because the Shaker communities paid taxes, all individual members supported the government lawfully. As members aged, their ability to contribute to the material welfare of the community diminished. Consequently, it seemed reasonable for them to draw a pension to which they were entitled for past service to the government, lest they otherwise be a drain on the community's resources. Moreover, Richard's statement on pension matters, written while the renegotiation of covenants in Ohio was still going on, seemed to say that pensions claimed by Shaker veterans belonged to those individuals alone and were not to be regarded as part of the "consecrated interest" of the community. Richard confirmed his approval of the pensions by identifying several elderly Shaker men who were eligible to apply for pensions, and at a meeting held on September 13 he offered his own services as scribe to record each man's testimony of his service as part of the application process.

For one obvious reason, Issachar Bates's name was not among the eligible veterans identified by Richard McNemar during that meeting. In fact, Issachar had already applied for his pension at the Montgomery County courthouse in Dayton, Ohio, on September 11.[26] Rather than waiting for the Union Village Ministry and Watervliet elders to assess the Shakers' position on pensions, Issachar had gone to the courthouse on his own initiative. The fact that Richard convened a meeting just two days after Issachar had applied for his pension suggests that Issachar's action brought the matter to a head, forcing the elders to formulate a formal policy on pensions.

The primary feature of the pension application was a statement of military service. In Issachar's case, this statement comprised a substantial narrative of about one thousand words. Its coherence, complexity, and organization suggest that he had previously prepared it, then copied it by hand into the application. Probably the fact that he had just written his autobiography a few months before made the task of recounting his wartime service somewhat easier. But Issachar did not simply repeat that portion of his autobiography that deals with his soldiering life. Rather, he constructed a separate account that detailed places, engagements, and officers, and described actions and duties. Also, the application process required him to bring two character witnesses. For that, Issachar was accompanied by Henry Miller and James Ball, two senior Watervliet brethren. James Ball had joined the Watervliet community some fifteen years before and had numerous relatives both at Watervliet and Union Village. Henry Miller had been part of the Busro community until its breakup, after which he chose to come to Watervliet, possibly out of loyalty to Issachar, a desire to remain with the other Busro Shakers, such as Salome Dennis, who were resettling at Watervliet, or both. Since his arrival, Miller had partnered with Issachar in preaching at Sabbath services. In an interesting departure from Shaker practice, Miller identified himself as a "clergyman" on Issachar's pension application, despite the fact that Shaker preachers rejected the titles and trappings associated with clergy. Issachar seems also to have garnered the assistance of one of Dayton's foremost attorneys, Robert A. Thruston, described as "the most brilliant and fluent speaker of his day at the Dayton Bar."[27] Thruston's signature is also on the application, and he is named as the individual to whom the official pension certificate was to be issued.

> ⌒ *In the evening we have a conference relating to signing the Chh covenant and council the causes why it was not signed when first proposed and in relation to the eldership being any means of frustrating the business by unwise speeches. All conviction on that ground was spurned with this expression "I am not sorry for any thing I said nor never shall I be." — So the matter stands forever unsettled. Bro. Robert has gone thro with H. & T & they stand as they did perfectly aloof from Eleazar . . . & he thinks that there are ten opposed to signing the covenant.*[28]

As 1832 closed, Watervliet's covenant still remained unresolved. Lines seemed to be drawn within the community, with some of Issachar's allies still obstructing the new leadership of Richard McNemar. At Union Village, a hymn by Richard's son James marked the end of 1832 with the wry observation, "Come let us all be of good cheer / We've lived to see another year / We have been safely carried thro' / The tedious year of thirty-two." Richard and Issachar featured this text in their new hymnal, an acknowledgement that the western Shakers were enduring rough times.

As 1833 began, Issachar began to insert himself more regularly into the ministerial dealings of the community, a sign that he rejected his role on the sidelines:

> A conference was held relating to the settlement of West Union matters. Members present were Elder Issachar Bates, Elder Samuel Turner, Br. Joshua Worley, Henry Miller, Ashbel Kitchel, and Eleazar Wright . . . Elder Issachar proposed to cancel certain trials that had been opened to him by Henry Miller against Eleazar Wright as superintendent of the West Union affairs.[29]

Nearly six years after the breakup of Busro, many matters relating to the sale and disposition of the land, buildings, and other property remained unresolved. Richard McNemar (under his pseudonym of Eleazar Wright) had been sent to Busro in the fall of 1826 to begin the process of overseeing its evacuation and the sale of the property. The fact that discussions were still taking place in early 1833 over "the settlement of West Union matters" hints at one source of grievances held by some at Watervliet toward Richard McNemar. It appears that Issachar was attempting to shield Richard from aggressive actions on the part of former Busro members. Issachar presided over another meeting just a few days later at which a "general council of aged brethren" advanced recommendations to the Union Village Ministry about desired changes in the family eldership of Watervliet, although they recommended leaving Watervliet's first elders (Richard McNemar and Salome Dennis) intact. Such brief glimpses of business transacted at Watervliet help to illuminate the complicated relationship between Issachar and Richard. Although they were cast into an antagonistic situation, and although they experienced one another's negative emotions and may have been perturbed by one another's actions, their friendship had not yet wavered.

Among Issachar's closest friends, the one with whom he had had relatively little direct contact since taking up residence at Watervliet, Ohio, was Benjamin Seth Youngs. The idea for Issachar to plan an extended visit with

Benjamin may have been his own. Or it may have been Richard's solution to Issachar's awkward entanglement in Watervliet's affairs. Whatever the case, Issachar set the wheels in motion:

> [I]n the year 1833, I wrote to Elder Benjamin and informed him that if he would come and make us a visit that spring, I would go home with him. Accordingly he came, and made us a lovely visit.[30]

> May the 21, 1833 . . . Elder Benjamin paid him a visit from South Union. He came alone by himself and tarried with us five days. And Sabbath the 26th Elder Benjamin spoke in public meeting on the subject of Christ's second appearing in the female . . . There was quite a respectable audience, and many people from Dayton. And in winding up his sermon he left his blessing on the people of Dayton for their kindness and friendship they showed to believers from the time they first came into this country to the present day. And on Monday the 27th of May Elder Issachar started on his last visit and journey to Kentucky with his old friend and fellow traveler Elder Benjamin S. Youngs, who he came into this country with.[31]

Issachar Bates was clearly delighted to see his old friend Benjamin Seth Youngs. Benjamin remained the first elder in the Ministry of South Union, Kentucky, a position he had filled since 1812. He rarely came to Ohio, and he had last seen Issachar when he visited Union Village on his way home from a visit to the East in 1827. It was widely understood that this would be Issachar's final visit to Kentucky. Although he had not been explicitly summoned back to the East, letters between the Union Village and New Lebanon ministries had hinted at the advisability of his return. Of the old believers who had been sent west, several had died, and others had returned east immediately after vacating the offices they held. In one case, Archibald Meacham had been given the opportunity to return to New Lebanon upon the breakup of Busro, but he chose to remain in Ohio and assume the position of first elder at the fledgling White Water community.[32] There was simply no precedent for an old believer to remain in the West in limbo, as it were, with no specific office or assignment. Issachar must have realized that the arrival of a formal summons back to the East was only a matter of time. But he could engineer circumstances to delay it as long as possible. Travel between eastern and western communities remained a major undertaking, requiring orchestration of months or even years. No one would expect an elderly man in his seventies to travel during an inclement season of the year. So Issachar knew, when he departed in May 1833 with Benjamin for a visit of several months in Kentucky, that he remained safely ensconced in the West until at least the following year, and perhaps longer.

> 🖙 *Arrived safely at South Union, where we were welcomed with joy, without mistake. Here I stayed taking comfort, for there was nothing here to make me uncomfortable. Here I could preach, pray, sing, and dance with freedom, for I was among my old acquaintances. I took more satisfaction here than I can describe, for it felt good all round about.*[33]

The journey from Union Village in southwestern Ohio to South Union in southwestern Kentucky was accomplished via a steamboat down the Ohio River to Louisville, followed by a hired carriage the rest of the way. There were concerns over cholera that spring and summer, and cities on the Ohio River were particularly vulnerable,[34] but the two elders made it to South Union without incident.

Issachar Bates was a popular and beloved figure at South Union. Because the first missionaries to carry the Shaker gospel to the Gasper River settlement in September 1807 had been Issachar and Richard McNemar, Issachar's history with South Union's oldest members went back even farther than that of Benjamin Seth Youngs. Over the years, he had made many extended visits to South Union and had seen it grow and change. At South Union, Issachar delighted in visiting his many friends among the various families. Among his close friends were members of the Eades family: Sally Eades, who had confessed her sins to Issachar in the autumn of 1807, was now one of the principal poets and hymn writers at South Union; her son, Harvey Eades, who had been six months old when his parents converted, had also developed a gift for music and poetry. Songs from both mother and son had been included in Issachar and Richard's *Selections* volume, and Issachar undoubtedly spent time with Sally, Harvey, and other South Union musicians, singing old songs together and sharing new ones. Issachar also had an opportunity to enjoy a reunion with many former Busro Shakers who had resettled at South Union, such as Samuel McClelland, Busro's physician and an able hymn writer.

Altogether, Issachar stayed more than a month at South Union, and he wrote one of his most unusual songs while there. Called "Ode to Contentment," it would be widely reproduced in more than a dozen music manuscripts, beginning with a South Union manuscript where it is recorded as "Given on June 20, 1833."[35] The song's most unique feature is its use of three-part harmony. Shaker music of the early nineteenth century was overwhelmingly monophonic. The practice of "carrying parts" was associated with worldly singing, something the Shakers generally avoided. But in one corner of the Shaker world, South Union, songs in two- and three-part harmony *were* being written and sung in the 1830s.[36] The three parts of "Ode to Contentment" are independent interlocking melodic lines, after the manner of New England singing-school repertoire of the late eighteenth century. The main melody, as well as the rhyming pattern of the first verse, closely match the melody and rhyming pattern of an early singing-school exercise that the one-time choirmaster Issachar almost certainly would have known, especially in view of his proven ability to retain vast numbers of songs. In rich poetry that evokes the poetic "odes" of the late eighteenth century, the words express a longing to find contentment by rejecting pride, lust, covetousness, hypocrisy, laziness, and a range of other vices. Given Issachar's recent struggle to hold onto his own contentment, the text seems to be an expression of his own emotional state. By using the three-part melody Issachar was harking back— consciously or not—to a much earlier time of his life that was perhaps less complicated and more filled with contentment.[37]

At the culmination of Issachar Bates's visit, on July 20, 1833, the South Union singers paid tribute to Issachar with a farewell hymn composed by Sally Eades:[38]

> Farewell, farewell, what shall we say, Kind Father to us in the West,
> You've finished here your little stay, For which we have been greatly blest.
> Farewell, farewell, you've been a Parent in the West,
> Farewell, farewell, and may you ever more be blest.
>
> You sacrific'd all things below, To suffer with us in the West
> First gave thyself the fatal blow, Which fitted thee to help the rest.
> Farewell, etc.
>
> Your bright example we adore, We love to even speak your name
> May Heaven bless you ever more, We thank the Lord that here you came.
> Farewell, etc.
>
> But so it is—and we do know, That Mother's Children for you call
> Do take our love where ere you go, And give to Mother's Children all.
> Farewell, etc.

By the 1830s, special songs that both greeted and bade farewell to visitors were standard fare across the Shaker world. But this particular farewell song contains more than laudatory platitudes. Rather, it reveals several noteworthy aspects of the relationship between the community that generated it and the person being honored, Issachar Bates. First, the song immediately addresses Issachar as "Father." Parental titles were so highly valued in Shaker culture that they were bestowed only on a select few. In the West, only a single person — David Darrow — had been accorded that title, and after his death, the Union Village leaders declared that the "titles of Father and Mother have become obsolete."[39] Yet here was a song celebrating Issachar Bates as "Father" and "Parent in the West." Clearly, formal directives were one thing and emotional impulses were quite another. Many at South Union and elsewhere genuinely regarded Issachar as a father figure. The song also reflects an awareness of all that Issachar had sacrificed to remain in the West. Instead of remaining in the East with his own wife, children, and extended family, he had accepted "the fatal blow." By forsaking his own family, he embodied powerful evidence to Shaker converts that the demands of celibacy and communal living outside of family units could be met. The song also alludes to the uniqueness of Issachar's name and to the affection it evoked in those who spoke it. Finally, the song portends Issachar's departure to the East, which the South Union Shakers probably knew beckoned not far in the future.

> *After I had tarried here thirty-six days, I was taken in a carriage . . . to Pleasant Hill, 130 miles. We arrived in five days, and were joyfully received. Here we had a hearty visiting . . . and we had joyful times. Here I staid and took comfort, in visiting, preaching, dancing, and singing; till the latter part of the time I was quite unwell. But all the kindness was shown me by the nurses from every quarter that was possible. But I was afraid I should have to be bury'd in Kentucky. For here I had to stay longer than I meant to, waiting for Elder Benjamin to come; for the people at Pleasant Hill were determined to see us both together, once more in this world. And he and I had agreed to have it so. And about the latter part of August, Elder Benjamin came on by stage, and we went at our business. We visited every family. Benjamin and Issachar together, once more like former times, which was a great satisfaction.*[40]

Issachar had last been at Pleasant Hill in the autumn of 1826, shortly before the breakup of Busro. That visit had been clouded by the recent death of Pleasant Hill elder John Dunlavy, as well as by the fallout from Busro's demise that had already begun spreading to other sites. This visit was much more upbeat. The worst of the apostasies and other trials seemed to have passed. Issachar could enjoy himself among believers who had known him from his earliest days as the Shakers' leading frontier preacher. Because Issachar and Benjamin had once been so inextricably linked, the Pleasant Hill Shakers reveled in seeing them together once more. Issachar was seventy-five and Benjamin nearly sixty, two aging friends who had endured much to help create the Shaker West. Yet while Issachar displayed his customary energy and zeal—preaching, singing, and dancing—the taxing journey in the summer heat took its toll. He became ill while at Pleasant Hill and worried that he might die before reaching Watervliet again:

> We went on our journey and arrived at Union Village, 140 miles, where we were welcomed. Here we tarried a number of days, and I had to do my best to keep up and visit with my little lovely company that came with me, for I was sick enough to be abed. But after a few days we went on to Watervliet, where we were joyfully received; and I was glad I had got once more so near to my grave; where I expected shortly to be laid: (the place which I had appointed myself).[41]

> Last Monday 2 weeks ago Elder Issachar arrived from his long visit to Kentucky accompanied by two brethren & two sisters from Pleasant Hill. The particulars of his journey & the state of matters there you will receive in a long letter which he is now preparing[42] . . . I need only say that his constitution is much impaired, his health poor & his life is deemed pretty precarious. Yet he is not bedfast, moves about with uncommon vivacity & his zeal for God & the gospel is not in the least abated.[43]

Issachar's friends were happy to see him return safely to Ohio after an absence of more than four months. Although clearly ailing, Issachar carried on with his usual vigor as autumn continued. Inwardly, he was relieved to be back at Watervliet, where he expected to die soon. In his absence Richard Mc-Nemar had remained focused on completing revisions to the still unresolved Watervliet covenant and had corresponded with easterner Seth Youngs Wells on the subject. Seeing Issachar so ill alarmed Richard, and he wrote to Wells soliciting final suggestions on the covenant draft, indicating some urgency lest Issachar die before its completion: "I shall . . . be glad to have yours as soon as possible for several reasons particularly on Elder Issachar's account: as he may not be long in this world, it would be very desirable to have his signature to this long-to-be-remembered test of union."[44]

Upon returning, Issachar spent considerable time recuperating from his illness. He found a pleasant surprise: his friends had spruced up his room, which was in the kitchen wing of the principal dwelling at Watervliet. Because of the heat generated by cooking, rooms over the kitchen would be warmer. Also, having his room on the upper floor of the kitchen wing placed him adjacent to the spacious community meeting room, used for evening socials and singing meetings as well as for Sabbath meeting during inclement weather. With much of the extroverted Issachar's activity centered upon singing and preaching, no location could have been better.

Issachar describes his room in a letter written to South Union not long after he returned from Kentucky. Generally, Shakers rejected purely decorative items, but Issachar refers to having "pretty things," probably mementos from his friends, suggesting that while his room corresponded in the main to other elders' rooms, there were a few exceptions. One of these mementos was a bundle of peacock feathers, probably hanging from the ubiquitous peg-rail that encircled all Shaker rooms. South Union was known for having resident peacocks, and Eldress Molly Goodrich had evidently presented Issachar with the gift of a peacock tail. Issachar also had plenty of books to read. Whether he refers in his letter to books produced by Shakers is unknown, but since 1824, the Union Village Ministry had made several efforts to eliminate the reading of "worldly" books, going so far as to stage a book burning.[45] Yet Issachar's age and status likely permitted him more latitude in reading matter. A further unusual feature of Issachar's room was the presence of a supply of money, which he indicates he could freely use to purchase articles such as pipe tobacco.

> While I was in Kentucky, my good friends fixed off my room in the best manner. — Put a second coat of plaster on the wall, spread the floor over with new carpets, and furnished it with all necessary furniture. Now I mean to be very particular and simple in describing my present accommodations; & perhaps I shall be excused if I am a little silly in my old age.
>
> Well this is a handsome room with two twenty light windows, with nice window blinds, a good little stove and fire place — a good husk bed with the best of bedding — a bureau with four drawers in it — a table — a wood box — a looking glass — a comb case — the little spotted trunk you know,[46] Father David's great chair, and three others besides. Spit box, fire shovel & tongs — blow-pipe and matches — brooms and brushes — pipes & tobacco, and money to buy more with. Candle, candlestick and snuffers — pitcher and wash bowl, chip-basket and bed-mug — razor — lather box and soap, and a number more useful and pretty things. A nice little clock, that keeps very good time, and Eldress Molly's pretty little Peacock's tail hanging up in sight, and as many books as I wish to read — and pen & ink, and you know that I have a plenty of writing paper of the best kind — and what doth hinder me from writing as much as I am able . . . So

I will venture to say that there is not a Bachelor or knight on the earth that is better provided for to live than I am.[47]

The cost of many of these items, along with the expenses of his long visit to Kentucky, had probably been partly defrayed by the money that he had begun to receive from his Revolutionary War pension. His pension record indicates an amount of $238.75 issued in April 1833, and Richard's written recommendation from the previous fall indicated that pension money was to be controlled by individual recipients instead of being placed in the general coffers.

Issachar apparently mentioned his pension to eastern Shakers with whom he corresponded, and in November 1833, the Union Village Ministry received a letter from New Lebanon expressing surprise and dismay that Issachar was accepting "blood" money:

> Having wrote to you so late on the 18th of last month we did not expect to write again so soon. But having seen a letter which Eldress Elizabeth received from Elder Issachar we feel it our duty to write at this time. The aforesaid letter was in general very edifying, but there was one portion of information therein which cased serious reflections.
>
> The Subject alluded to is where he informed her that he has been taking his pension for his Revolutionary services! Can this be a fact? Can it be possible that so good a man as Elder Issachar, who has suffered so much for the cause of peace and salvation, could after all take a reward or pension for having heretofore aided in a work of death and destruction? a work which the true followers of Christ have ever borne a pointed testimony against; and which Elder Issachar would be one of the last men on earth to perform.
>
> Doubtless he considers that his revolutionary services were performed under nature's darkness, when he thought he was doing his duty and that he can now put the pension money to a better use than the world would if they were to keep it . . .
>
> It has never been the practice of believers to accept of pensions, bounties, nor pay for military services. Our Parents and Elders in the gospel have, from the first of our faith, considered such money as the price of blood . . .
>
> We have a great deal of love for Elder Issachar and respect him much for the good which he has done, and feel very unwilling that he should do anything to dishonor himself or the testimony in the decline of life, as did most of the good kings of Judah and Israel.[48]

Issachar could not have been pleased at such a harsh reprimand. After all, the Ohio leadership had openly encouraged the collecting of pensions, and Richard McNemar had personally assisted most of the Shaker veterans in preparing their applications. Likely he felt unfairly singled out. He would have been even more vexed to learn that Richard included in a letter to Rufus Bishop of the New Lebanon Ministry a remark mocking him as "my reputed predecessor, who at this time is known to be quite a monied man."[49] But the New Lebanon Ministry had not realized the different approach taken to pensions in Ohio. After further review of the matter, a second letter from New Lebanon struck a considerably softer note and must have comforted Issachar:

[W]e feel full union in letting the matter concerning Pensioners rest perfectly still, both in the East and West; and, as you wisely observed, "let it die a natural death;" which it will before long, provided you and we are careful to keep the matter within due bounds. There are but very few here who know that you and we have pursued different courses, in this particular, say a few of the Elders, and the fewer the better . . . Give our best love to Elder Issachar, and tell him to cease from his tribulation, "for as the Lord liveth, he who hath wrought so great salvation shall not die," nor lose his union for what he has honestly and innocently done in accepting his pension.[50]

This pointed apology to Issachar was probably timely. His health remained precarious, and fretting over the pension issue had been a further drain on his energy. That winter the community believed that Issachar's end was near, and his closest friends assembled to hear his last wishes.

Elder Eleazar, Robert Baxter, and Moses Eastwood, Eldress Saloma, Eunice Bedle & Patience Naylor, were called into the room where he then lived, in the west end of the kitchen, second floor, southwest room . . . He said he had helped lay out the graveyards of all the societies of believers in the western country and now his desire was when he died to be buried in the graveyard here at Watervliet, in Ohio, and that he would like to be buried on the right hand side of the ally leading into the grave yard from the north side of the yard, where there had been a large oak stump dug up some years previous, by his own hands. His will was, that all his property and money including his pension money, the two carriage horses, one cow, and bull, together with his right & claim to the same, should be given to the Elders, for the benefit of the Society.[51]

In fact, Issachar's time had not yet come, but as 1834 continued, he struggled physically and emotionally. Being confined by sickness left him bored and cantankerous. He annoyed the entire household with a series of vocal complaints over unnecessary noise in the dwelling house during the course of an average day. Describing this "wooden thunder," Issachar's meticulous calculation of the number of doors slammed and armfuls of wood flung noisily into stoves must have exasperated even his most loyal friends. After presenting his grievances in meeting, he recorded them in a detailed essay:

> I hate to see or hear a heavy footed brother or sister thumping across the floor, co-lump, co-lump, co-lump . . . Now perhaps you may be offended at me for being so plain and blunt on these matters. But I suppose you know that I don't care for that. And perhaps some may think, "it means me." Well if it does you will please me very much if you will quit it; and if it does not mean you, then you are safe enough.[52]

Nonetheless, Issachar remained endearing. He especially delighted in the company of the community's children and youth. One unidentified Ohio Shaker sister recalls Issachar's appearance and demeanor around this time, when, as a girl of eleven, she would accompany the eldresses to his "retiring room" to "help spread the bedclothes on his bed."

> This privilege I could have, if I walked so quietly that he would not hear my footsteps coming up the stairs, for he disliked heavy walking or any loud noise in the house. I was fair charmed with him the first time I saw him . . . He looked so plump, so clean, so good, so kind, so pretty, his eyes so blue, and had such a lovely twinkle in them, reminding a child of "Twinkle twinkle little star, How I wonder what you are." His head leaning towards the right shoulder, with a slight inclination downwards and keeping up a perpetual little noddle, all so cunning . . . his noble head obeyed its own inclinations, as the Aspen leave obeys its own perpetual motion.[53]

As spring approached, Issachar sought a medical procedure known as the "Thompsonian order," which was then in vogue. It involved steam baths to induce perspiration, accompanied by herbal emetics.[54] Perhaps this was effective or perhaps the change of seasons provided a natural tonic. By summer, Issachar was on the mend physically, but he remained emotionally feeble: "I then got into my garden and nurseries: and this was the best nurse I found. So I kept about my work all summer, tho not without pain, sorrow, and affliction; for it felt to me I had no more business in this world. And I did not see any use in my living."

That same summer, "Br. Rufus Bishop, and Br. Isaac Youngs, made a visit from the East."[55] Isaac Newton Youngs was the younger brother of Benjamin Seth Youngs. He was an intelligent and accomplished forty-one-year-old when he and Elder Rufus Bishop toured the western societies in the summer of 1834, and already known to many western Shakers by direct acquaintance or by reputation. As a chief singer and hymn writer at New Lebanon, he was familiar to both Issachar Bates and Richard McNemar, who greeted him excitedly when he arrived at Watervliet. Isaac highlighted their inspection of Issachar's garden in his journal, noting that it was quite nice and that a German immigrant living nearby had exclaimed, "dat dis is de baradise garden!"[56]

But for Issachar, the visit ended on a sour note. He had written a hymn to honor the departure of Rufus and Isaac, but Solomon King attempted to hasten the travelers on their way, deflecting attention from the hymn. Issachar vented his anger to Richard:

> Today Elder Issachar came into the shop apparently in the utmost distress refused to be amused or comforted said he had settled it in his mind not to go to the village. That Elder Solomon . . . hated him & meant to take every advantage to afflict him. Mentioned what took place in the hall the morning Elder R[ufus] & I[saac] were taking their leave, in rejecting his hymn publickly in a scornful manner treated him every how like the meanest underling, that such has been his conduct toward him for years.[57]

And Issachar's animus toward Solomon King only intensified. When the eastern visitors prepared to leave Union Village in September and invited Issachar and Richard down for the occasion, Issachar was nearly beside himself, exhibiting paranoia and playing the martyr.

> Today Elder Is came to the shop & stated his feelings in relation to his going to the village to meet the Eastern visitants. That he had no feelings to go. That the invitation which he had rec'd by letter from E.S[olomon] was not, in his opinion, an expression of real feeling — but he had been excited to it by E[lder] R[ufus] & I[saac] N[ewton]. That he expected E.S[olomon] had given his character to the visitants in the darkest colors, & it would go to the east that he was a poor old creature that never had any spiritual gift, — and never was qualified to lead a society &c &c. That should he go down . . . he wished me to accompany him, & that he would stay with me at the office & make as little trouble as possible and pay for his boarding.[58]

At the same time that Issachar and Richard were diverted by the visit of the eastern brethren, they continued a series of deep conferences over the finalizing of the Watervliet covenant. Richard wished to incorporate a histori-cal preamble that recounted the changes in eldership at Watervliet since the community's inception. For obvious reasons, he had no intention of using the covenant document to exhibit the disarray that the community had been in for several years. Through scrupulous consultation with his "aged friend," Richard attempted to perceive the community's troubled past from Issachar's point of view:

> He said I did not understand him, that he did not mean that he was a regular or actual Elder, but that all would have to acknowledge him in that relation. I very cordially admitted that he was & would forever be ac-knowledged & respected in his proper order & relation to us all & doubt-less rewarded for all the good he had done. As to his special relation to this society he was respected as a father, but first and last our mutual gift and calling had been as helps to the ministry. [T)]his he had repeated[ly] stated as a special communication from F[ather] D[avid] in his own words; that he F.D. had often said, you & Eleazar are my ministers.[59]

Two things were now clear — that Issachar now required constant reassur-ance of his value to the society and that among his chief motives was self-preservation. In his retrospective assessment, his role at Watervliet was to have been chiefly spiritual and advisory. The onset of the disarray had been the arrival of the Busro eldresses (Salome Dennis and Eunice Bedle). With their arrival, other elders had been displaced and "the consequence of this sin-gular change was total confusion." Individuals who had held temporal respon-sibilities "became powerless" and "the whole burden of everything spiritual & temporal fell on . . . Elder Issachar." Issachar recalled "[t]hat in this situation he became exhausted not so much in body as in mind & most cordially & thankfully accepted of Eleazar as a help to lighten his load, but by no means to release from his original gift of care & bury him before he was actually dead." The fact that leaders and rank-and-file believers alike at both Watervliet and Union Village continued to regard him as released from his original responsi-bilities of spiritual oversight continued to vex Issachar sorely.[60]

In the midst of such frustrations, Issachar embraced yet another activity: basketry. Whether he had ever made baskets before is a mystery as his first mention of the task is in his account of his last winter in Ohio. Determined to remain productive, he doggedly produced willow baskets with the elderly Francis Bedle and Joseph Stout, two other Revolutionary War veterans:

> Now after I had got all my garden stuff secured, and the garden manured, on the 11th of November, I started for Union Village; and there I went to

making baskets with the brethren, Francis Bedle & Joseph Stout. And there staid till the first of January 1835. Then returned to Watervliet, and made willow baskets, till the 27th of the same month. Then back to the Village and made baskets till the 9th of March . . . And about this time I received a letter from the Ministry at New Lebanon with an invitation in it for me to come home (as it was called). Then I thought of my grave! But no way to get into it without help, and no one to help me. But O Lord God, why was I born to sup sorrow forever! But there was no discharge in this war, I must go.[61]

Issachar's summons from New Lebanon arrived in March:

You have spent your life & strength both of soul & body for the good of others . . . Then if you depart in justification & union you will . . . become a bright zealous young man again! And if your ministrations or eldership should be eclipsed after serving threescore & seventeen years in your clay tenement, no doubt you will find space & work sufficient in the spiritual world if you go there reconciled & well prepared. Hence you have nothing to fear on that score. And as to the dishonor of your resigning & returning home, there can be none; for who else has continued in the ministry or eldership to such an advanced age in any Society of believers since the first opening of the gospel of Christ's second appearing. Again if you believe that you can yet do good there for a time, or even think the believers there cannot do without you, it is nevertheless certain that they will have to do wholly without you very shortly for your age is such that you do & will fail whether you are sensitive of it yourself or not. Therefore . . . you will end your gift & your days more honorably if you return to this country.[62]

Richard McNemar and others soon heard the news. The "sisters," Salome Dennis and Eunice Bedle, initially thought Issachar felt relieved that at least he need no longer fret over when and if his "invitation" might arrive. But then Richard heard that Issachar was "bathing his cheeks with tears," which he reported in a letter to Solomon King, who harbored concerns over how Issachar was receiving the news.

[A]fter venting his feelings alone we were called together and the letter was read, and after repeating his objections against returning. That all those who had returned had a home to return to but he had none . . . The idea of his requesting to be released he pronounces a positive falsity & would affirm before any court in heaven earth or hell that he never made any such request nor never thought of such a thing. This at present

seems the weightiest matter that he holds against any of us and if not settled will undoubtedly go to the east as a key to the whole story & may do
mischief.[63]

Richard also detected that Issachar continued to be distressed over his
pension money. Although the matter of western Shaker veterans drawing
their pension had appeared to be resolved more than a year before, some recent event had re-ignited the issue. Possibly some believers were concerned
about the manner in which Issachar used the money. Richard wrote to Elder
Solomon:

> His feelings appeared to be much excited on the subject of binding him
> about his pension money that it was repugnant to all laws human or di-
> vine to debar him from giving & disposing of it as he chose, of course that
> he was justified in giving M.Smith 10 dollars the day before. These two
> things I mention not to augment the difficulties between you but to excite
> your attention if possible to have them settled should you think it of im-
> portance for him to bear a good report to the east.[64]

Between receiving his summons back to New Lebanon in late March and
his actual departure in mid May 1835, Issachar wore his heart on his sleeve. He
bitterly mourned his impending exodus and let everyone know it:

> So I wandered up and down bewailing my fate, but all to no purpose; I
> must go and leave my people, that felt dearer to me than my natural life.
> For if I could have died and been buried on the ground that I had pur-
> chased with my life, I could have laid my old head down in peace. But
> perhaps the reader would say I am exposing myself, that it shows an un-
> reconciled mind. Well what of all that, I am writing my experience and I
> mean to be honest about it. Perhaps you may have the brains beat out of
> your soul, some day, and then you will know what heart rending sorrow
> is and not till then.[65]

Many believers at Watervliet were equally shattered by Issachar's departure.
Jane Patterson, who had been one of the first Watervliet converts to confess
her sins to Issachar as early as 1807 wrote him a letter in his final days, expressing her sense of impending loss and her appreciation: "I ask myself is this
the last sight? Shall I see you no more? . . . I have looked back to the first day
that I ever saw you . . . how firm and unshaken you have stood through it all,
to establish the Gospel in this land."[66] Others at Watervliet blamed Richard
McNemar for orchestrating Issachar's removal, even though Issachar person-

ally saw Solomon King "as the prime instigator of all his troubles."[67] Robert Baxter, an elder at Watervliet who had stood "aloof" from Richard for some time, refused to speak to him after Issachar's summons arrived and sent a message through one of the eldresses that he would be leaving the village as soon as he could make arrangements.[68] In fact, Baxter left on April 16, the same day that Issachar traveled to Union Village to make his final good-byes there.[69]

So great was Issachar's consternation over leaving Ohio that he manipulated his departure down to the very day. Elaborate arrangements had been made for him to travel with his best friend, Benjamin Seth Youngs, and two Kentucky eldresses, Hopewell Curtis and Mercy Pickett, who were also returning east to live. Young Harvey Eades was also to accompany them for a visit. Issachar was to travel by carriage to Cincinnati, escorted by Richard McNemar, where he would meet the Kentucky party and they would proceed on together. Their route would take them up the Ohio River to the mouth of the Ohio-to-Erie Canal at Portsmouth, and they would proceed up the canal to its terminus at Lake Erie before continuing by steamship to the Erie Canal and on to eastern New York. But whether to avoid being escorted by Richard for his final departure or to snatch a final few days at Watervliet, Issachar abruptly announced at Union Village only days before he was to leave for Cincinnati that he would not go as planned. Rather, he would return to Watervliet and in a few days time he would travel by wagon east to Circleville, Ohio, which lay on the canal. There he would rendezvous with his Kentucky friends. Issachar's lack of cooperation threw the elders into confusion. Richard had to continue on to Cincinnati alone to meet the Kentucky party and inform them of the new itinerary.

On April 30, 1835, Issachar and Richard parted for the last time at the center of Union Village, close to the very spot where they had first met thirty years before, nearly to the day. It was a distressing moment. Although they had maintained their warm friendship despite the challenges of these latter years, the final months had taken their toll. Issachar's anxieties over leaving caused a near emotional collapse. At the end, he declared that he was being driven off, and his final words to Richard were unkind.

On May 14th, Issachar left Watervliet for the last time, escorted by his beloved friends Salome Dennis, Eunice Bedle, and others. Since receiving his summons from the East, he had seized every opportunity to record his sorrow in poetry and songs. He produced poems at every opportune juncture, including the evening meeting with the Watervliet family on the night before he left. Still more music followed on the day of his departure. As the group rode east from Watervliet, Issachar sang a tune from his days as a fifer, declaring it his parting "retreat."[70]

> I told sister Eunice Bedle that this is my retreat. I have played it on the fife; many a time; but I never had such a retreat as this before. And if she would learn the tune I would send her some words to it, if I should live to get thro. So she learned it, and I sent her the words.[71]

Appropriately, Issachar Bates exited the Shaker West with music on his lips.

Unlike the other old believers in the West, Issachar Bates had been so new to Shaker life when he came to the West that he had not yet established a settled home in any of the eastern communities. A thirty-year absence had created a gulf between him and his biological kin who were Shakers. His wife, Lovina, and daughter Polly were dead, and his other Shaker children were grown and scattered between New Lebanon and Watervliet. His closest friends were all in the West. In declaring that the other old believers "had a home to return to but he had none," Issachar was not simply being melodramatic. He was stating a fact. After thirty years, his roots were now deep in the West. Like the old oak tree at Watervliet, whose stump Issachar had personally wrestled from the ground at the very spot in the graveyard where he later declared his wish to be buried, Issachar was himself uprooted. But his desire to be obedient to the Shaker leadership compelled him to leave his home in Ohio and embark on his last journey.

CHAPTER 12

"So I'll relinquish all demands"

JOURNEY'S END AT NEW LEBANON

So I'll relinquish all demands For any good I've ever done;
I'll throw my soul into thy hands, And trust thy mercy, that alone.
— *"Nightly Prayer," Issachar Bates*

Issachar Bates took up residence at the New Lebanon, New York, Shaker community in June 1835. It was relatively unfamiliar, but not entirely unknown, territory for him. For more than a generation, New Lebanon had been the center of the Shaker world, the largest concentration of Shakers anywhere. Issachar had confessed his sins there in 1801. More recently, he had traveled there in 1830 along with Solomon King, where they were honored as two venerable representatives of the distant West. Now he arrived to stay, a storied figure from Shakerism's western flank, known to most easterners only by reputation or from his many poems and hymns.

Issachar Bates's desperate and unsatisfied desire to remain in Ohio, coupled with the stress over the West's many difficulties and recent quarrels with his closest Ohio comrades, had left him a shattered man. Upon arriving at New Lebanon, the seventy-seven-year-old Issachar was probably as depressed and anguished as he had been in his life. But he was not finished yet. Drawing on his gregarious nature and his many personal resources and talents, he displayed remarkable resilience during his final interlude at New Lebanon. Issachar found comfort in his favorite activities — singing, preaching, poetry, gardening. He corresponded with western friends and tried to rectify the troubles he had left behind in Ohio, at the same time embracing his new situation. Issachar finally completed his life's journey having cultivated a place in yet another Shaker family, where he was loved, honored, and long remembered.

    We went on to Cleveland. There we staid more than two days, and the Elders from North Union visited us one day. And on Saturday we went on board the steam boat, William Penn, and arrived at Buffalo in thirty hours; then stepped into a Canal boat and went on to Schenectady. Then hired a carriage and went to Watervliet, where we were kindly received and well treated. Here we staid and visited more than a week. We visited every family, and I took all the comfort I had any room to receive; for there was comfort enough to have comforted a regiment of men . . . But what effect could all this have on a Job, when he was curdled like cheese, & his gall poured out upon the ground. Now will you think that I am exposing myself again. Well let it be so, I am writing my experience.[1]

Issachar fretted for much of the eastward journey. When the group reached Cleveland, they were expected to ride over to North Union, some twenty miles from the canal. But pleading illness, the elders and eldresses remained at a hotel while young Harvey Eades ventured to North Union by himself. Possibly Issachar was in such a funk that he felt unable to conduct himself cheerfully during a visit there. Dismayed to learn that the main group was not coming, the North Union elders went to visit them briefly at their lodging.[2]

When the group embarked on Lake Erie, Issachar rallied somewhat, walking about the boat with Benjamin and busying himself seeing to the security of the group's luggage.[3] Having enjoyed his 1830 voyage on Lake Erie, it is likely Issachar was exhilarated to be on the Great Lakes once again.

> Issachar Bates Senr, of Watervliet Ohio, having come by steam-boats & canals & land carriage from South Union in 22 days, from Louisville in 21 days, and from Cincinnati in 19 days. Issachar, Mercy, and Hopewell expect to reside at N. Lebanon.[4]

The group stayed at Watervliet for more than a week, where they were cordially welcomed. The visit would have included Sabbath worship, as well as weeknight meetings for singing and socializing. Issachar's note that he made the rounds to each family confirms that was reunited with his kin at Watervliet—his brothers Theodore and Caleb, sisters Dolly and Olive, son Issachar, and a multitude of nieces, nephews, and in-laws. He probably also spent time with Seth Youngs Wells, with whom he had corresponded throughout his thirty years in the West and probably his closest friend among the eastern Shakers. Likely the stay at Watervliet allowed Issachar to decompress from the anxieties that had attended his departure from Ohio. On June 9, Watervliet brethren used two wagons to transport the group and their luggage on the final leg of the journey to New Lebanon.[5]

> The brethren that were expected from the west arrived at the office at 6 oclock this evening . . . 2 sisters & Issachar Bates from Watervliet, Ohio, these 3 last have come to stay here and make it their home.[6]

As soon as he arrived, Issachar met with the New Lebanon Ministry, to whom he aired his various grievances: "The next day I had the privilege to pour out my feelings to the Ministry. And altho' I had not a doubt of their being full of mercy, charity, and pity, yet nothing there for me. But I might have the privilege to go and make my home at the Second Order in the Church. I waived the matter for that time."[7] Issachar probably did not "pour out" his objections to returning to the East, per se. Disobedience to the "lead," namely, to the elders standing in authority, was among the most serious infractions of Shaker life. The Ministry already knew that Issachar had returned against his will. But subordinating one's own will was the essence of Shaker life. Even Richard McNemar had observed that after Issachar's initial venting, "he said he would comply: and has expressed no other feeling since."[8] More likely, Issachar would have voiced his anxieties over Solomon King's management of affairs in Ohio, his impression that Solomon had led some to believe that Issachar wished to be removed from office and sent east, and the recent objections over Issachar's handling of his pension money.[9] The audience left Issachar unconvinced that the Ministry fully appreciated his perspective, but he decided not to press matters further. He did hand over a sealed letter that he had brought with him from Ohio (whose contents are lost), addressed to the Ministry from Richard McNemar. The New Lebanon Ministry's reply to Richard offers an indication of its reception:

> This short communication is to let you know that your letter of May 10th by Brother Issachar was duly received, and its object well understood by us at least we think so; and we consider it a pretty curious wrought piece for the purpose of removing his trials in relation to you, provided he should not travel out of them on his long journey. And we felt more than willing to do all in our power to make him comfortable both in body and mind, in his superanimated state. So we gave your letter a public hearing and it seemed to pacify his feelings very much; and he has since appeared about as comfortable in body and mind as we could expect, considering all circumstances.[10]

It is safe to assume that Richard had composed a letter offering his perspective on the eldership succession at Watervliet, from Issachar to himself. In it he was probably careful to highlight Issachar's honored place as the community's spiritual founder and acknowledge that many Watervliet residents would always look to him as a spiritual authority regardless of his formal title. The Ministry recognized the letter for what it was, namely, an effort to assuage a very distressed Issachar. The respite of the long journey may have partly diminished Issachar's anguish, but to the Ministry he still appeared "superanimated." Whatever the contents of Richard's letter, it allowed Issachar to recover some dignity. Still, the Ministry realized that Issachar had been sorely tried. The Ministry was also well aware that the problems in the West extended far beyond those that were of Issachar's making. New Lebanon was indeed scrutinizing the leadership of Solomon King and of all those whom he appointed, including Richard. Solomon and Richard had known that, which explains their concern that the manner in which Issachar might present his grievances once he reached the East "may do mischief."

Issachar Bates began the difficult adjustment to his new situation. He was sent to live in the Second Order of the New Lebanon Church Family:

> [T]he next day I told the Office Sisters that I must gather up my things and go to the Second Order and try to make a home there; but I had nothing to make it with but a pen knife. But . . . they welcomed me and showed nothing but kindness and love, all over the house: and they were justified according to the testimony of Christ; for I was really a stranger, and they took me in. But as far from being a member as Ohio is from New Lebanon. But they were laboring all over the society to make me comfortable: old and young, Ministry & people. had not a doubt of that, but what effect would all this have upon a Rachel, seeing the children were not. Now every where I went, and every believer I met, was full of loving kindness, and tender compassion for me . . . But they almost provoked me to anger with this repeated saying, be comfortable, be comfortable; when they might as well have told a toad to be comfortable under a harrow, for I could not reach it! It was my hour of temptation.[11]

In the 1830s, the Church Family at New Lebanon was considered the most stalwart and committed collection of Shakers in the community, and indeed, some of the most devout Shakers anywhere. At that time, its division into a First Order and a Second Order was probably more a reflection of the large population numbers in the New Lebanon Church Family than of an effort to assign a spiritual ranking of one above the other.[12] The adult population of the Second Order numbered just over sixty, equally divided between males and females.[13] The Second Order inhabited a group of buildings including a large three-story house and several workshops located about two hundred yards south of New Lebanon's meeting house along the main road through the village,[14] a short walk from the neighboring First Order. The size and complexity of New Lebanon, an abrupt contrast to the more compact scale of Watervliet, Ohio, probably overwhelmed Issachar. And the outpouring of kind welcome from the Church Family Shakers grated on his nerves, though he knew they meant well: "Elder Brother Samuel Johnson and Elder Sister Lucy Darrow are first in care, & with them Amos Stewart & Sally Lewis. And to add a little to my comfort there are some of my old friends here, such as Daniel & Constant Moseley, Hiram Rude, Lydia Obrien, and Hannah Train jun . . . a very kind agreeable family."[15]

The presence in the Second Order of a few old friends and acquaintances was considerably reassuring to Issachar. Lucy Darrow, first eldress, was the daughter of Father David Darrow of Union Village, to whom Issachar had been devoted. Daniel Moseley and Constant Moseley (who likely were brothers) had each spent several years among the old believers in the West.[16] Daniel had been part of the group dispatched to Ohio in the summer of 1805 at the request of the original three missionaries, and he had remained there for seven years. Constant had come west in 1806 and stayed for five years, assisting mainly with the foundation of the Pleasant Hill, Kentucky, community. Issachar would have well recalled working alongside both men. Hiram Rude was a much younger man in his thirties, who had come into Shaker life as a child in Ohio. Hiram had lived at Union Village until 1820 when he turned eighteen, at which time he had been taken to New Lebanon to escape the erratic interference of his estranged non-Shaker mother.[17] Rounding out the group of his named friends, Hannah Train "jun" or "junior" was Issachar's niece, the daughter of his older sister Hannah Train.[18] Nonetheless, he remained troubled and homesick.

Issachar Bates took up residence at New Lebanon in early summer, always a busy time. On Thursday June 11, the very day that he moved from the office down to the Second Order residence, a major operation was taking place at the center of the village: the newly purchased "great bell" had arrived and was being hoisted into place in a belfry affixed atop the "Great House," the immense three-story residential dwelling that sat just south of the meeting house and housed the First Order.[19] Watching this spectacle would have been an unusual distraction for the whole village, Issachar included. A few days later, Giles Avery, a brother in the Second Order, realized that in the excitement over the new bell he had neglected to note Issachar's arrival: "Forgotten last Thursday brother Issachar Bates came to this family to make it a home. He is joyfully accepted."[20] The very night of Issachar's arrival, the Second Order convened an hour-long singing meeting, with dancing and marching.[21] In the days after, Giles Avery noted uncommon heat: "Weather is extremely warm so that it fairly seems to suffocate a person." This was followed the next day by one of the worst thunderstorms ever witnessed at New Lebanon.[22] For

12.1 *Second Order, Mount Lebanon. This stereographic image was probably produced about 1870. It shows the extensive gardens, which would have been present between 1835 and 1837 when Issachar Bates lived there. (Courtesy of Hamilton College Special Collections.)*

Issachar Bates, the weather probably felt reminiscent of the cycle of sultry heat and violent storms he had grown accustomed to in Ohio and Indiana.

> *I soon got to work in the garden where I could vent some of my feelings on the weeds. First in Br. Gideon's Botanical garden at the Second Order; then in the ledge garden. Got acquainted with B. Eliab and Garret, picked roses for the nurses, picked over herbs in the dry house with the sisters, got some acquainted with them, and could feel a little freedom.*[23]

Working outdoors in the gardens at New Lebanon was the powerful tonic that Issachar needed (figure 12.1), and he was partnered with a pleasant bunch of Second Order brethren. Issachar was already acquainted with Eliab Harlow, who had visited the West in 1810 together with William Deming, and Issachar had spent time showing them the pecan trees he had planted at Turtle Creek. Possibly he and Harlow had discovered back then that they shared an interest in trees and plants. The "Botanical garden" was nearly an acre in size and lay on the west side of the main road through the village, directly opposite the Second Order dwelling and the neighboring "Sick House."[24] By "ledge garden," Issachar probably meant a small garden that sat somewhere in the Second Order area directly along the road on the east side. New Lebanon was laid out on a north-south axis along a road that had been cut into the side of the mountain that lay to the east of the village. Thus, areas on the east side of the main road lay generally uphill of areas on the west side, and in places the uphill areas had probably been stabilized with retaining walls, creating "ledges" and offering locations for smaller garden plots, such as "kitchen gardens" that would provide cooks with ready access to herbs. With abundant rainfall and heat to begin the summer season, Issachar likely had his work cut out for him in weeding. Later in July a second severe storm brought two and a half inches of rain in fifteen minutes that "gullied roads [and] brought much rubbish down from the hills."[25] Issachar's ledge garden and the larger botanical garden were doubtlessly impacted. Well accustomed to hardship and setbacks, Issachar probably took it in stride and went about the repairs to the gardens with good humor.

A letter composed by Issachar during his first summer at New Lebanon to his beloved friends at Watervliet, Ohio, illuminates not only his emotional state and his manner of adjusting to his new home, but also details of spiritual and social life in the New Lebanon Church Family:

I have not forgotten you . . . I am trying to make another home in my old age, and I hope I shall succeed—Altho it was more than tenfold harder than natural death to be separated from my friends in the West, yet I find there is great room for me to gain something further, and in some particulars more to my satisfaction, especially in the worship of God. For it has been a great grief to me for some years past to see that life-giving worship of God so neglected in the state of Ohio . . . I moved to this family on Thursday, the 11th of June. That night at half-past seven the bell rang for retiring. At eight the family assembled. They sung fifteen songs & hymns in that meeting, and labored and marched ten of them, which took one hour. On Friday was union meeting one hour. Saturday night half an hour retiring, and at eight assembled. There was considerable power and bodily exercise: eighteen songs & hymns sung and twelve of them labored & marched, the meeting continued nearly two hours. — On Sabbath day it seemed as tho' the greater part of the day was taken up in meeting at home or at the meeting house . . .

There is but very little preaching in meeting, but many warm exhortations from every quarter, old and young, male and female. All is freedom—no bondage.

Now judge ye how it must feel to a poor old half-blooded saint to come into such an order as this, after running a race of more than thirty years, preaching & ministering order, and being faithful to attend to every order according to my understanding.

Now I have got to make as real a beginning as when I first confessed my sins, and learn it all over again . . .

Now I suppose you would like to know how my hands are employed, as well as my mind. Well I will inform you. I have entered into copartnership with Br. Gideon Kibbee in a botanical Garden, and we agree very well so far. But I confess that when I get at work in the garden, my mind and will keep running back and thinking of S-and-E and J-and-C and V-and-P & forty more . . . I told you that I intended to get as near you as I could reach with this paper; and the more I can inform you of little childish things, the nearer I think, I shall get to you. So you will bear with me a little in my folly. Now you know that I am old, and another has to guide me. I will tell you about it. Brother Daniel Mosley is my file leader in meeting and at the table. He sends his best love. I live in the room with him and others. I sleep in the room where Br. Jethro Turner sleeps — he sends his love. Sister Lydia Obrien takes care of my clothes. She sends her love. And finally they are all as kind as they possibly can be.[26]

Shortly before Issachar Bates arrived at New Lebanon that June, the First and Second Orders of the Church Family had donned summer attire for Sabbath meeting — striped linen trousers for men and white linen dresses for women.[27] Issachar would not feel left out; soon a pair of striped trousers had been sewn for him by the tailors.[28] The First and Second Orders met together for Sabbath meeting in the village's enormous meeting house, with its vaulted ceiling and two-story windows. For Issachar, this would have meant seeing his daughters in meeting, perhaps spotting them across the vast space somewhere in the ranks of the white-clad sisters. Issachar was struck at how different the manner of worship was from Ohio's. He would have reveled in the singing and dancing, and he would have known many of the hymns. Indeed, possibly some of the hymns were his own compositions. Always a quick study in anything musical, he would have rapidly learned the less familiar songs. He seemed surprised, however, to find so little preaching in Sabbath meeting. After three decades of organizing Sabbath meetings in the West, featuring sermons up to an hour long, delivered by appointed elders, this manner of meeting with short "exhortations" uttered freely by sisters and brothers alike seemed entirely novel to him. Issachar felt he was beginning his Shaker life anew. Though he grieved for his Shaker family in Ohio, he resolved to realize some spiritual gain out of this latest challenge. But in spite of the upbeat façade that Issachar presented to his friends, he was feeling the effects of old age. In concluding his letter to Ohio, he remarked on the pain of his arthritic knuckles, and he asked his Ohio friends to send him his spectacles, which he had accidentally left behind.

12.2 *A circle dance like that depicted in this print was performed frequently in western and eastern Shaker worship and was familiar to Issachar Bates. Here it is depicted in the New Lebanon meeting house, where he worshiped from 1835 to 1837. ("The Shakers of New Lebanon - Religious Exercises in the Meeting-House," Mount Lebanon, NY, by Joseph Becker [1841–1910], published in Frank Leslie's Illustrated Newspaper, 1873. Wood engraving, ink on paper. I am grateful to Jerry Grant, Shaker Museum|Mount Lebanon, New Lebanon, New York, for assisting my access to this image.)*

Even as Issachar was impressed and exhilarated at the spiritual substance of meetings at New Lebanon, where one of the favorite worship dances was the same circular dance performed at Union Village specifically to honor Issachar more than ten years before (figure 12.2), he probably did not realize that for some New Lebanon Shakers, his own presence and contributions were a welcome infusion of energy. Not long after his arrival, he was called upon to speak in meeting and relate greetings from the West, an occasion that, one listener wrote, "really seems to impart new life & animation."[29] Before Benjamin Seth Youngs returned west later that summer, he and Issachar "spake considerable relative to their first start to preach the gospel in the far west, spake of their success in their undertaking and a great deal that was truly edifying to those who were in a great measure ignorant of it."[30] The Church Family Shakers were taken aback at the charisma and dynamism still exuding from this aging pair — the elderly and once robust Issachar and his tiny slip of a friend Benjamin, who had together braved the uncharted wilderness.

We have a very cheerful meeting for brother Issachar made a very nice display of gestures added to the remodeling of the tune called the Stubborn oak & we think the handle to it is very smooth. We try to learn to motion it after seeing him sing dance & motion it all alone to show us how & in the course of the meeting the family get the order of it nicely and perform it all together.[31]

We have meeting at home among our selves and it is so dull that one would scarcely know whether we were trying to serve God or something else: however we get Brother Issachar Bates to sing the stubborn oak with his handle to it & after dancing it tolerable lively we begin to wake up some.[32]

As Issachar settled further into his new situation, his new family at the Second Order began to truly appreciate his singular gifts of infectious singing and dancing. "The Stubborn Oak" was a short spiritual song that had been sung in the East for at least a dozen years.[33] Whether Issachar already knew it is unknown, but he set about improving it by innovating a new set of dance motions that he taught to the entire assembly. In nearly thirty-five years as a Shaker preacher, Issachar had taught songs and dances in myriad settings: from puncheon-floored open air "stands" in forest clearings to log meeting houses to the frame and brick meeting houses of Ohio and Kentucky. Now in his old age he continued to captivate believers with his singing and dancing in the largest meeting house of the Shaker world. The Second Order could rely on Issachar to stimulate their zeal even in the occasional dull meeting.

Now the beloved Ministry, in short time showed their mercy and kind charity to me, as well as to others, for they sent Elder David Meacham, Eldress Betsy Hastings, Luther Copley, and Joanna Kitchel to help them beloved children in the west. This took off a pound or two of burden for me. After awhile Elder Solomon, Eldress Rachel, and Eliza Sharp came on ... and this took off a few more pounds, for this was in my favor. For Eldress Rachel came into the family where I lived, and I had my old Mother again ... After a few weeks the good Ministry sent Daniel Hockings and Stephen Wells, deacons, to help these beloveds in their temporal affairs. This took off a little more burden; and after Elder David returned home with Elder Mathew Houston I was glad; and when he related how matters were regulated there I was gladder yet, for I was perfectly well satisfied with all that was done; and this took off full half of my burden ... Now about this time I found some more good news. The good Ministry had been to Watervliet and had appointed Elder Freegift Wells to go with Elder Mathew to the West, and I hope to stay there. This was quite agreeable news to me; and I understand very pleasing news to them in the west; so that my burden still grows lighter and lighter.[34]

Issachar Bates had carried the problems of Watervliet and Union Village with him to New Lebanon, and he continued to fret and worry over situations far away. Issachar was more than pleased when in the late summer of 1835 a team of four, including an elder and eldress and another pair of devout Church Family Shakers, were dispatched to Ohio to inspect the troubled leadership situation. They were charged with the authority to intervene and make changes. Once in Ohio, they began intensive consultations with the elders at both Union Village and Watervliet.[35] Elder Solomon King was invited to step down from his office and return to New Lebanon, along with his partner in eldership, Eldress Ruth Johnson (who went by "Eldress Rachel").[36] Issachar's remark that Elder Solomon's return "was in my favor," offers further evidence of the conflict that had existed between the two of them when Issachar had left Ohio. Apparently, Issachar regarded the Ministry's demotion of Elder Solomon as vindication of the grievances he had been nursing. Ruth Johnson returned to New Lebanon at the same time. As Solomon King had been in Ohio since 1805, and Ruth Johnson since 1807, it is possible that the New Lebanon Ministry recognized the value in a complete turnover in eldership. Probably better for Issachar, lest he still harbor hard feelings, Solomon went into the First Order to live. But to Issachar's satisfaction, Ruth Johnson, whom he had regarded as a spiritual "Mother," came into the Second Order. Issachar was happy to have Ruth, a close friend, spiritual mentor, and fellow "old believer" who had shared so many western hardships, joining him in the same household.

All during the fall of 1835, Issachar followed closely the news of the New Lebanon Ministry's work to assist in regulating and stabilizing the troubled affairs in the West, particularly at Union Village and Watervliet. The whole New Lebanon community had been alarmed to hear in early September that Nathan Sharp, who had held the important office of trustee at Busro and had since been based at Union Village where he continued to carry out vital transactions relating to sale and disposition of the Busro property, had absconded and stolen several thousand dollars. This news must have been emotionally shattering to Issachar, who had worked closely with Sharp for many years. But it also caused a further financial tailspin in Ohio, bringing Issachar more worry, and he was relieved when two stalwart New Lebanon deacons were sent to help Union Village recover from the loss. Because Issachar had been part of the Busro Ministry, his attention to the ongoing resolution of issues relating to Busro was more than just residual concern for his old home. Rather, Issachar had been required to give up his power of attorney before leaving the West, in case the ongoing efforts to resolve Busro's dissolution required signatures or testimony from those who once held office in the Indiana community.

In late 1835 western Shaker Mathew Houston journeyed back to New Lebanon along with Elder David Meacham, to report the progress and changes at Union Village. Issachar was happy to see yet another familiar face, even for a short time. During a stay of a few months, Mathew probably filled Issachar in on how the changes were impacting his closest friends. Richard McNemar had been relieved of his office at Watervliet and was in the process of relocating to Union Village.[37] Salome Dennis had likewise been removed as eldress at Watervliet and had been reassigned to a deaconess position at Union Village. Eunice Bedle remained at Watervliet and was now elevated to eldress. Soon Issachar's western friends would welcome an eastern Shaker to their midst. Freegift Wells, the younger brother of Seth Youngs Wells and a lifelong devoted Shaker from the Watervliet, New York, community, was to be dispatched to Union Village to assume the lead. Issachar derived considerable satisfaction from this news and believed that Freegift Wells potentially offered an antidote to Ohio's ills.

> A friendly caution —
>
> Sister Salome } You have publickly & privately & repeatedly said that you always respected me as a father. It is therefore presumed that a word of counsel from me will not be offensive. Then I say — Hearken O Daughter, and consider, & incline thine ear, Forget also thine own people & thy father's house, so shall the king greatly desire thy beauty for he is thy Lord & worship thou him. Forget, I say as fast as you can. But it would be nothing to your honor to traduce or demean your father or grandfather or any of your own people or the people that you have owned as your kindred in the gospel. This is what your father never did.[38]

A personal note from Issachar Bates to Salome Dennis written about this time is couched in metaphor and biblical language, but the meaning is clear. Her esteem for him as a father figure had been publicly owned. Because of that he was giving her strong fatherly advice to accept both his fate and her own, namely, her inevitable move from Watervliet ("thy father's house"). His words suggest he believed Salome (whose abrasive personality is noted in some sources) had dishonored herself by openly lashing out against specific leaders, including Issachar himself.[39] Such notes hinting at the intimate and complex nature of interpersonal Shaker relationships are rare and valuable.

12.3

This enormous willow basket, holding approximately five bushels, matches the size of those made by Issachar Bates, who wrote of making dozens of such baskets between 1835 and 1837. No record of its age or origin exists, but this item was owned and used at New Lebanon, and given its probable age, size, and materials, it could have been made by Issachar. No other New Lebanon Shaker is recorded as constructing such baskets. (With thanks to Jerry Grant, Shaker Museum|Mount Lebanon, New Lebanon, New York.)

Far removed physically, if not emotionally, from the continuing turmoil in Ohio, Issachar settled into a comfortable new routine. He enjoyed new friendships and renewed old ones. In his garden work and attention to herb preparation, he contributed to the economic welfare of the Church Family:

> After I had kept the weeds conquered all summer & frost stepped in to help me, then I went to work with Br. Eliab in the brick shop, pressing herbs and putting up roots and herbs, and here was a comfortable soul to work with, and when he and Garret were both there, or either of them, it was impossible for me to feel uncomfortable; for I had hardly time to think of any thing but their comfortable spirit and agreeable conversation . . . Now after we had done pressing and putting up roots and herbs, I went to work making willow baskets: I made 28 baskets generally holding from one to five bushels and when I had got thro' with that I had liberty from the Ministry to make a visit to Watervliet.[40]

As a wintertime occupation, he worked at basketry just as he had done in Ohio, producing large willow hampers. His first baskets, made during his first winter at New Lebanon despite the arthritis that must have reduced his grip and his hand strength, were enormous — holding up to five bushels (figure 12.3).

Although Issachar Bates has received previous attention from Shaker scholars for his music, poetry, and preaching, he has never been particularly associated with any of the Shakers' many handicrafts or industries. For that reason, what he says about his wintertime occupation of basketry deserves notice. Black ash has been identified as virtually the only material used by the Shakers in their basketry, but research has mainly concentrated upon baskets produced in the eastern communities for commercial sales after the 1830s.[41] In examining surviving Shaker baskets, it has been notoriously difficult to differentiate among baskets made in Shaker communities, baskets purchased by the Shakers in their surrounding neighborhoods, and those brought into Shaker communities among the private possessions of converts. Issachar's remarks — identifying the making of utilitarian baskets, their sizes, and the materials used — offer a rare and valuable glimpse into Shaker utilitarian basketry of the mid-1830s.

Issachar had declared that he spent his last winter in Ohio making willow baskets, sometimes working with two other elderly men. A year later at New Lebanon, he was again at work making willow baskets or hampers. Woven hampers would have had a range of uses, including carrying and storing garden products and carrying laundry. Hampers on the larger end of the size range Issachar mentions probably were used to carry and store higher-volume materials of lighter weight, such as wool fleece for carding and spinning (a five-bushel hamper of apples or of wet laundry would be impossible to lift!). In all descriptions of his baskets, Issachar identifies willow as his material even though scholarship on eastern Shaker baskets indicates overwhelmingly that splintered or shaved wood was the dominant material. Thus, it is possible that Issachar Bates had learned the technique of willow basketry in the West and introduced it to New Lebanon when he returned in 1835. Many species of shrub willow are native to North America and Europe alike, including low-lying meadows and riverbanks of both the Midwest and Northeast.[42] In addition to providing material for baskets, shrub willow could be trained for hedges. But significantly, there is no record of the New Lebanon Shakers using shrub willow for baskets or hedges until after Issachar Bates arrived. In the spring of 1836, after Issachar had joined the ranks of the garden caretakers, willow slips were for the first time cultivated in the garden, expressly due to Issachar's initiative. Another Second Order Shaker, Barnabas Hinckley, who helped with garden work in the spring of 1836, writes of "ploughing the ground for peppermint & for I Bates willow slips. I Bates & Eliab Harlow set out the slips."[43] They could have been planting the willow for a hedge. They could also have been trying to actively cultivate the willow to establish a supply of Issachar's preferred basket-making material close at hand, eliminating the need to trek into nearby meadows and thickets to find it.[44] The following winter was even more productive for Issachar, who wrote in February 1837 of producing more than three dozen willow baskets.[45]

When Issachar Bates had been part of New Lebanon's Second Order for about a year, the family welcomed yet another Ohio transplant to its ranks: sixteen-year-old Hannah Agnew, a popular young sister from the White Water community.[46] Hannah arrived homesick and overwhelmed, separated from her biological father, White Water elder Joseph Agnew, for the first time in her life. She probably welcomed the companionship of the grandfatherly Issachar Bates, who was known for his warmth and affection and whom she probably recalled from his visits to White Water. Hannah's later writing suggests that Issachar mentored her, particularly in her fondness for writing poetry.[47]

Soon after Hannah's arrival, the entire Second Order gathered for an unusual meeting, where according to a previous arrangement, the Second Order believed that some of the Shakers from distant White Water traveled in spirit to check on the welfare of young Hannah Agnew: "This evening we are blessed with a visit with the invisible souls at Whitewater which had agreed to meet with us this evening to see if Hannah Ann is comfortable."[48] The date was July 4, and the meeting was a novel way to mark Independence Day. In addition to recalling his war experiences as he probably always did on July 4, Issachar may have also empathized with young Hannah's homesickness and wondered if he could make his own spiritual visit to his beloved Watervliet, Ohio.

> ⌒ *Sat. August 13 — Extraordinary northern lights continued all last night — continues very cool for August. Artemas Bates came here to see his father whom he had not seen for about thirty-three years.*[49]

At least two New Lebanon journals record the visit in August 1836 of Artemas Bates, Issachar's eldest son, about whom relatively little is known. Born in 1782, he was nearly twenty years old when his father confessed his sins and urged the rest of the family to become Shakers. Issachar's autobiography refers vaguely to "my two oldest sons with whom I settled" in 1801, suggesting that some of the family property was given to Artemas, who elected not to follow his father into Shaker life. Possibly Artemas was already married. By 1820 Artemas had migrated across upstate New York to Jefferson County, near the eastern end of Lake Ontario.[50] This was the same area where Issachar's two youngest brothers, Caleb and William, had moved in 1803 after the death of their father. It seems likely that Artemas was induced to follow his uncles to that area after his own parents and most of his siblings had gone to live among the Shakers. In any case, Artemas's journey to see his father from his home in northwestern New York would have been arduous, not a casual undertaking. The distance was well over two hundred miles, and the time and expense for a middle-aged working man to make such a trip would have been daunting in 1836. The fact that Artemas even knew that Issachar was back at New Lebanon suggests that there was some correspondence among the Bates family members. Caleb Bates's family, who had come from Jefferson County when they entered the Watervliet community in 1824 and 1825, may have continued to correspond with Artemas. Or the Bates sisters at New Lebanon, Sarah and Betsy, may have taken it upon themselves to write their eldest brother to inform him that his aged father was back in New York. Whatever the communication venue, Artemas arrived for a visit. How Issachar may have felt reuniting with his eldest son whom he had not seen for thirty-three years is impossible to imagine. No further record of their visit is known. But another journal records that Artemas's time at New Lebanon also included visits with Betsy and Sarah.[51] The occasion must have been cordial, leaving Artemas wishing for future visits with his father, because the group made preliminary plans for Artemas to visit again the following summer.[52] Given Issachar's lifelong fascination with "signs and wonders," it is likely that he noticed that the occasion of Artemas's arrival coincided with a remarkable display of northern lights.

Although Issachar was seventy-eight in 1836, his health seemed to have improved markedly since his move to New Lebanon. He certainly maintained a high level of physical activity between his daily outdoor garden work and the vigorous worship dancing several times per week. That, combined with reduced stress from the absence of vexations from the Ohio communities, improved his quality of life, even though his homesickness for Ohio never entirely subsided. He also traveled less once he arrived in New Lebanon. Besides a visit of several weeks to Watervliet, New York, in February of 1836, he primarily stayed with the Second Order. However, he refused to be confined, and in fine weather he enjoyed going on long rambles up onto the mountains surrounding the village.[53] "Motion" remained at the core of Issachar's being, even though much of his motion now comprised the exuberant action of meeting-house worship. One of the songs he composed after moving back to New Lebanon reflects his propensity to always remain in spiritual and physical motion, whether in the labor of the dance or the activity of daily life, while it also points ahead excitedly to the end of the life journey.

Wake up my soul and move in earnest, You was form'd for endless day, Soon from flesh you'll be unharness'd, Soon you'll burst this clog of clay.

Wide awake, Wide awake,
Wide awake and view your kindred, Safe in yonder mansions where
Keep the step, Keep the step,
Keep the step and don't be hinder'd, Straight ahead you'll soon be there.[54]

On an autumn day in 1836, Issachar was part of a large group released from their normal duties and treated to a day-long outing on the mountain-top looming over nine hundred feet above the village. It was September 22, a Thursday. Annie Williams, a middle-aged sister from the Second Family,[55] was invited along and recorded the occasion:

> Two brethren & a number of sisters from the second order, took a walk up to Mount Zion; Their names were as follows Issachar Bates, Hiram Rude, Permilla Dickerson, Rhoda & Hannah Blake, Rhoby Bennet, Rachel & Joanna Vining, Leah Taylor, Sarah Ann Lewis, Eliza Avery, Mary Stewart, Jane Ray, August & Terrissa Lenure. They invited Elder Sister Rebecca Anne Davis & myself to go with them. We had a very pleasant walk, and took dinner on top of the mountain. John Remington came to us just in time to take dinner; The young sisters sang many a pretty song & so did Br. Issachar. We returned by way of the Pinnacle and had a circular dance, and a full view of the church & village, and with the help of our spy glasses we brought objects very nigh. We returned by way of the south House, called in and rested a little & returned home.[56]

A hike of several miles up the forested slopes of a mountain for a day's outing with a group of young people was probably not the normal activity expected of near-octogenarian Shakers. But Issachar Bates was unique. The large party consisted of mostly women and girls, most in their twenties and thirties and some as young as twelve.[57] Three among the group were in their early fifties, but Issachar was far and away the eldest present. As the lively band made its way up the mountain, perhaps Issachar regaled them with stories of his many adventures in the mountains of Kentucky and the wilderness of Indiana. Most of the sisters with Issachar that day had not even been born when he had set out to carry the Shaker gospel across the Appalachian Mountains. Or maybe Issachar reached even further back into his memory to recount episodes of his pre-Shaker life in the deep woods of the Adirondacks. On a bright September day, surrounded by the laughing voices of his young women companions, those times must have seemed very distant indeed. At the top of the mountain, the girls sang songs. Of course Issachar could not resist joining in, and he probably taught them songs from his years in the West. High on the mountaintop overlooking New Lebanon, the group amused themselves with spyglasses they had carried along to better view the distant buildings. Observing the village from the pinnacle above, they would have been facing west. Perhaps Issachar trained the spy glass toward the horizon and imagined he could close the distance that separated him from the places he loved so well. He had led outdoor worship on countless occasions and rarely without drama: camp-meeting revivals, makeshift platform "stands" in forest clearings surrounded by the taunts of persecuting neighbors, the frozen hilltop in Indiana Territory in 1809 when he and his companions so nearly died of exposure. On the wind-swept summit with the stately buildings of New Lebanon visible below and autumn colors painting the surrounding hillsides, Issachar surely found considerable joy in the exhilarating open-air dance, together with a happy group of young and zealous Shaker sisters.

As 1836 concluded, Issachar enjoyed even more attention from long-lost family members. His son Artemas had evidently returned home to encourage his daughter, Issachar's granddaughter, to visit. She was a young married woman and arrived for a visit with her husband late in the fall. But Issachar's spiritual family in the Shaker West remained in his thoughts nonetheless. That winter of 1836–37, soon after his seventy-ninth birthday in January, he composed his final letter to his friends at Watervliet, Ohio. They had written him with news of the community's latest happenings, including such rich details as a run-down of the room assignments. Apparently, the letter also detailed an important new development at Watervliet, namely, the complete renunciation of the use of opium and medicinal alcohol, something that Issachar addressed at length in his reply.

> Your verry acceptable letter of Febr 1st came safe into my hand the 16th and you may be sure I was glad that you had not altogether forgotten that I once lived at Watervliet . . . I concluded to take courage and try my old hand once more seeing I have got my old eyes again which I left behind among the rest of my troubles, and with them I can see yet and with no others . . . It was a satisfaction to me to hear their names and rooms they live in. I could see every one of them as I read their names; just how they looked and how they acted but could not speak so as they could hear me . . .
>
> . . . In particular I am thankful that you have a divorce from opium and ardent spirits for I have found out that habit is an unreasonable physician. For about ten years after I confessed my sins I would not taste a thing that had spirits in it. But by sickness and being urged by those whom I thought

knew better than I did, I began to take a little medicinal bitters once in a while, till at length it began to grow into a habit. And as it was common custom among those whom I esteemed better than myself I felt justified. After a while it began to be whispered about that they did not make use of spirits at the East and some began to take up their cross. But at that time I had a very sick winter and there were various kinds of medicines prepared for me to take . . . I felt as tho I could not get along without them nor hardly with them. I mention these matters to you to let you know in good conscience that I never made use of any kind of spirits since I confessed my sins for any purpose than meaning it for my health. And I never have drank a teaspoonful of raw spirits since the day that I confessed my sins, and I am sorry that I ever had any thing to do with the stuff. For I never have meddled with it since I have been here and I am better off without it . . .

I will love you all together and bless you all together forever. Amen. Amen.[58]

In concluding this letter, Issachar informed his friends of his continuation of work in the garden and herb shop, punctuated by sadness over the recent death of his new friend and working companion, Garret Lawrence. He also stated that his production of willow baskets was booming. But the most noteworthy feature of this letter lies in Issachar's frank remarks about his own relationship with alcohol. Issachar had introduced his own propensity toward alcoholism with a few comments in his autobiography addressing his soldiering life during the American Revolution, when he began to "partake of the substance" and to embark on a "school of vice in which I was not slow to learn." Apart from casual comments in a few letters about the enjoyment of fermented cider, nowhere else does Issachar so openly express his views about alcohol. The letter represents a virtual confession of his longstanding temptation for alcohol. Issachar admits that he used sickness as an unwarranted justification for drinking hard spirits, although he suggests that others shared blame for luring him into it. The letter alludes to the contrasting views on alcohol held in the East. Issachar finishes by declaring that he has now put aside the consumption of spirits once and for all. In light of the "confessional" aspect of this letter, Issachar's dark period from the autumn of 1834 through the spring of 1835 perhaps makes more sense. It was during this time that Issachar struggled with both health problems and apparent emotional instability — overreacting to others' actions, exhibiting paranoia. If during this period Issachar was regularly consuming raw spirits, albeit with medicinal intent, possibly along with opium preparations, his erratic behavior comes into better focus.

> ⌒ I wish you to give my love to Br. Issachar, tell him that if I ever treated
> him with cold indifference or impertinence I have been well paid for it since
> this time last year & I do not expect to die in debt to any of my predecessors.
> You may tell him . . . that about a week ago he paid me a friendly visit in
> a night vision and after an agreeable interview he took his leave saying,
> "farewell my son," to which I responded, "Farewell Father," after which I
> awoke with comfortable feelings which are particularly manifested in the
> pains I have taken in sending him Elder Br. Eli's vision . . . Farewell from
> Eleazar[59]

In more than eighteen months at New Lebanon, Issachar Bates had followed events in Ohio from a distance, had welcomed other Ohio friends to New Lebanon as visitors or fellow residents, had received news from many of his friends, and had composed warm chatty letters in reply. But there was one person with whom Issachar had had no further communication, since parting from him in April 1835. That person was Richard McNemar. Issachar had written no letter to Richard, and he had received no communication from him. In November 1836 Issachar was called into the Ministry shop to hear a letter from Richard read aloud. The letter contained a short message for Issachar. Remarkably, the proud Richard not only apologized for their past misunderstandings, he also exposed the warm paternal emotions he still held for Issachar. Richard's letter to New Lebanon also recounted the final departure that fall of Benjamin Seth Youngs, the last of the three original Shaker missionaries to leave the West.[60] On that occasion, "Elder Br. Eli," probably Union Village Second Family elder Eli Houston, had a vision apparently involving the relationship of the Shaker West to the Shaker East at that momentous juncture, namely, the formal departure of the last of the original missionaries. Believing that "there should be a clear correspondence between the Alpha & Omega of the work in this country," Richard apparently used his printing press to record "Eli's vision," a copy of which he addressed to Issachar, with the words "as a Memorial of our former freedom."[61]

Seeing Richard's message, Issachar was probably awash in memories of times spent together both thirty years before and much more recently, worshipping, preaching, singing, dancing, journeying, working side-by-side in myriad tasks. He resolved to end his silence toward Richard. On December 27, 1836, he composed a letter, addressing it to "Brother Eleazar" in deference to Richard's expressed preference for his pseudonym Eleazar Wright, which deserves to be reproduced in full.

Ever Esteemed Brother Eleazar. —

The time has felt long to me, to be shut out from any kind of communication with one, with whom I have spent thirty years with so much freedom, and friendship — one year and six months has passed away in lonely silence without one breath from Eleazar, either by word, by spirit, or by letter. — and not even a dream by night, — but a multitude of trying thoughts by day. Till some time in November past, — The ministry returned from Watervliet, and brought me a letter from the first order of Elders in behalf of the Church at U. Village. (for which I was thankful) and with it they brought that little printed sheet, you sent me with a few lines written, which felt healing to a sore spot — in particular the following words [as a Memorial of our former freedom]. The next day Brother Rufus invited me in to the Ministry's shop and read a letter that you sent him, and in it you stated that you had found E. Brother Ely's vision, and had sent it onto me — then he read your dream, and I said Amen. In a few days I received the rest of the packet of letters, brought by E. Benjamin, the vision among the rest, with your remarks on it. — (and now in this spot, I return my kind thanks to you, and desire that you would convey my best love, and kindest thanks to him E Brother Ely for this favor, for the vision is much esteemed here by all who have seen it) —

Now after all these good things, it brought you so near that I began to dream. But my dreams were all too short to fill my mind. — First I dreamed that I was at work in the Brick shop pressing herbs with Br Eliab (where I have been at work all the fall). I thought I sat filling a Box for pressing, and you came in at the door behind me and said thus — well you keep at work yet. — I answered yea, and I always intend to work. With that I looked round and behold it was Eleazar, but you had just turned your back to go out of the room, but I expected your return soon. But I awoke and that was the last of it, and I was sorry. — The next dream I had was a few nights past.

I dreamed that some of the Brethren told me that Eleazar had moved to New Lebanon to live, that he had been here two or three days, but could not tell me where he was. — I thought I went out back of the buildings and I heard some body at work in a small Barn. I went into it and there was Eleazar sure enough. And after we had gladly saluted each other, I asked you what you was doing there you said you was thrashing Rye. I observed that as you was placing the sheaves for thrashing some would lay on the floor, and some you would throw out door into the barn yard. — I asked you what you did that for — You said that was your orders, to throw all the blasted sheaves into the barn yard for there was not one grain of Rye in them. But I had no feeling to take up time talking about the Rye, for I was in haste to bring forward a matter that I wanted just such an opportunity as this to open it. — And just as I was about to open it I awoke and behold it was a dream. — And I was so disappointed that I was determined that I would go to dreaming wide awake, that I would write to you. — It is in relation to the last words that I ever spake to you, or ever expect to speak to you in this world face to face. —

The words were these — Farewell, and when thou art converted strengthen thy Brethren. I cannot suppose that you ever thought that I meant to be converted to the faith. Nay I never scrupled your faith from the beginning, any more than Jesus Christ scrupled Peters faith, but he saw wherein he was lacking and had to be converted into it. And notwithstanding your eminent gifts and talents I could feel a lack in you of one of the most blessed gifts that is in heaven, or on earth — which is Mercy — No doubt you have seen more lacks in me than one, but I know that I do love Mercy, and I do love to be merciful. I was taught it when I was first sent out to labour with souls if I felt never so sharp against the flesh to be sure and hold the soul in Mercy, and I never forgot it. Blessed are the Merciful, for they shall obtain Mercy — I do not despise judgment, I love it in its place, but Mercy rejoices against judgment and I am thankful for it. — I suppose that it was generally judged that my being removed out of office was the cause of my trials and sufferings. — But that is a false judgment, I know better than that, and always shall know better. — It was because I had to take up with jealousy instead of Mercy from those who stood before me. — But enough of this for I did not mean to stir up these old things, they feel too dreadful to me, but rather to stir up a reconciliation, for it would be a wonder if I should come out Blameless in the end myself.

So Brother Eleazar I love to feel Merciful to you — and if you feel Merciful to me I shall be thankful and you may let me know when it is convenient.

And now I shall close these few crooked lines by saluting you with the same love that I had for you from the beginning, giving you liberty to make as free with my love to every good soul as you feel to, But in particular to your good old room mate Brother Matthew.

Fare Well———Issachar[62]

This was Issachar's final letter to Richard McNemar, and one of the last letters he wrote in his life. Rarely does a piece of Shaker correspondence display such emotional complexity as this. The letter thoroughly exhibits his regrets, as expressed first in his series of dreams and then in his heartfelt apology. Ever since parting from Richard in April 1835 at Union Village, Issachar had nursed misgivings over the last words he spoke to Richard, words that were an exact extraction from a verse in the Gospel of Luke (Luke 22:32): "But I have prayed for thee, that thy faith fail not: and when thou art converted, strengthen thy brethren." The context of the verse is Jesus chiding Peter for his lack of faith and essentially telling Peter to put his own house in order so that he may be of better service to the other disciples. Issachar's utterance of those words to Richard was a clear statement that he then believed Richard to be spiritually adrift. But Issachar repented giving the impression that he had doubted Richard's underlying faith. As simply and directly as he could, Issachar confessed to Richard what had most unsettled him—that Richard had appeared to put judgment ahead of mercy. He expanded his confession to encompass the whole source of his vexation during that troubled time. Issachar's worry had not arisen from being removed from office, but from feeling jealousy and judgment instead of mercy and compassion from "those who stood before," by whom he meant those in authority over him, namely, Richard and Solomon King. The passage of time and the benefit of distance had soothed Issachar and allowed him to sort out his feelings and admit his own shortcomings. Moreover, he composed this letter two days after Christmas. For Shakers, one solemn aspect of the Christmas celebration was renewing one's confession to one's elders and brethren alike, expressing remorse for any wrongdoing. Seen in that context, the timing of Issachar's confession to Richard takes on extra significance. In this letter of confession to Richard he sought to restore their friendship and end their correspondence with the same loving spirit that attended their first meeting and sharing of the Shaker gospel in 1805.

Richard McNemar must have been emotionally affected by the letter. Letters took two to three weeks to travel between New Lebanon and Union Village, and the fact that Issachar had received a reply sometime before February 14, 1837, means that Richard composed and posted a letter to Issachar immediately. Unfortunately, that letter has not been located and may not have survived. But Richard must have accepted Issachar's apology and offered comforting words of his own, because Issachar's satisfaction with the reply was recorded in a note to Richard written by Seth Youngs Wells and posted on February 17.

Your letter to Br. Issachar has been received. On Tuesday the 14th he brought it to me to answer your request in the P.S. As I had not the laws of Massachusetts by me, we concluded to have him go over to Hancock & get them. Accordingly, he went over there yesterday and got the Revised Statutes of that state which were published last year & from which I have transcribed the most important passages, which if they could be in substance, incorporated into the laws of Ohio, would be of essential service to the Believers in that state . . .

Br. Issachar was much pleased with his letter, and gladly went over to Hancock after the law-book, and expresses his thankfulness for the privilege of doing so small a favor for his western friends. He also sends his everlasting love and kindest thanks to Brother Eleazar for his most acceptable letter, and desires him to make free with his increasing love to all his western friends.[63]

It appears that, in addition to mending fences with his letter, Richard asked Issachar to perform a small task. Pursuant to his work on perfecting the new Ohio Shaker covenants, Richard was trying to compose a portion addressing the Ohio laws of religious freedom. For comparison, he wished to see the portion of the Massachusetts constitution on religious freedom. Issachar brought the matter to Seth. They decided that Issachar should be dispatched to ride over to the neighboring Shaker village of Hancock, Massachusetts, which lay about ten miles away, just across the state line. There he could borrow the necessary volumes so the relevant passages could be transcribed and sent to Richard. Issachar's utter delight in being able to perform a small favor for Richard was touching. Although only a few hours' ride by horse, Hancock lay on the other side of a high ridge in the Berkshire Mountains. In 1837, a ten-mile ride alone over a high Berkshire pass in mid-February would have been well beyond the capacity of most seventy-nine-year-old men. But not for Issachar Bates. His friend Richard required his help, and nothing could stop him from rising to the occasion.

But the midwinter ride to Hancock would be among the final tasks that Issachar Bates would perform for Richard McNemar or for anyone else. His life journey was drawing to an end. That winter there had been many people seriously ill in the Second Order and a number of deaths. Issachar was still reeling from the death of the relatively young Garret Lawrence in late January, and on March 7 Issachar attended the funeral of yet another Second Order friend.

After returning from the funeral, he (Issachar) attended the evening union, was remarkably bright & cheerful, sung & conversed with much freedom, said he had enjoyed better health the year past than for 15 years before. One of the sisters told him she hoped he would not take this fever (then prevailing in the Chh. of which 11 in that family were then, or had been down). He replied, "If I do take it, I hope it will be my last sickness, for I shall want to go right on." He was taken the same night. In his sickness his earnest feeling was to die. He said he had done all the good he could do in this world, and he chose to die. He had some time previous composed a hymn (the last he ever composed), which he called his Nightly Prayer, and had several times sung in union meeting. This he requested might be sung at his funeral, that the Brethren & Sisters might know his feelings.[64]

Issachar's last illness lasted only ten days, and he was fully prepared to die. His bright and happy demeanor at the end was probably a reflection of the reconciliation he had just managed to achieve relative to his good friends in the West and to his troubled latter years. At the time that he and others in the Second Order were battling an infectious respiratory illness and fever, he was comforted by the presence of his good friend and "mother" from Ohio, Eldress Ruth Johnson, who stayed at his bedside and served as his nurse. His suffering grew considerably worse, and Shakers from the all over the Church Family grew concerned. Brother Giles Avery reported that "Issachar's dissolution seems to be near. The first order are still quite liberal to watch & 2 come for that purpose every night."[65] Giles Avery does not identify those from the First Order of the Church Family who came to stand vigil by his bedside each night, but it might have included his daughters Sarah and Betsy. Eldress Ruth Johnson later reported that during Issachar's last few hours of life, "three bright lights were seen hovering over him, about three hours before his death from which time he was more calm and easy than before until he died."[66]

On the afternoon of March 17, 1837, New Lebanon Ministry elder Rufus Bishop sat writing a letter to the Ministry at Harvard, Massachusetts. As usual, he reported on the health of the various families, before going on to other matters and finally concluding the letter.

At the Second Order they have a number of severe cases, and some of them are yet confined to their rooms & not out of danger, particularly Benjamin Lyon, Gideon Kibbee, and Issachar Bates; and it is yet uncertain how it will turn out with some of them, particularly Gideon & Issachar. It was once or twice thought that the latter was struck with death, but afterwards there seemed to be some hopes that all of them would recover in due time . . .

N.B . . . While filling the blanks in this page, word came that aged Issachar Bates departed this life about 10 minutes past 3 Oclock this afternoon, in the 80th year of his age since January 29th.[67]

Issachar Bates's funeral was held the following day, March 18, in the cavernous New Lebanon meeting house. As Issachar had requested, his final hymn,
"Nightly Prayer," was both read and sung, along with several other hymns.

Funeral was attended 18th inst. 2 o'clock afternoon.

At the commencement Elder Br. Samuel Johnson said . . . it would be
well to give some information concerning Brother Issachar's first setting
out in the gospel.

By Mother's gift he was sent to the West in the cold dreary season of
the year to preach the gospel to the world. He passed thro' heat and cold,
persecution and sufferings, more than any one present ever had . . . Br.
Daniel Boler then said he could witness to the truth of what had been
spoken concerning the deceased. For he had truly forsaken all that was
pleasing, near & dear to a natural man. Father, Mother, Wife & children
house and land . . . That his soul seemed to breathe forth courage, courage! And that he had, ever since he knew him, been truly a living soul . . .
That Elijah left his mantle for Elisha, and Issachar had left his for us, and
we could divide the River Jordan as well as ever Issachar did, by bearing
the same cross that he had borne, &c.

After singing many beautiful songs appropriate to the occasion . . .
Elder Brother said we might attend to the burial of the corpse.[68]

Br. Issachar, notwithstanding his eccentricity & natural bluntness, was
evidently a very zealous Believer, always alive & active in the faith of the
gospel & in the worship of God, and was a real cross-bearer. It was testified by the Elders, at his funeral, that they believed he had done his work
faithfully, according to the best of his understanding — that in the early
part of his faith he had readily & literally given up all for Christ's sake &
the gospel's, and set out in faith and obedience to explore the western wilderness, without knowing whither he was going, what trials & conflicts
awaited him or what success he should meet with; but still he pressed forward with his companions, determined to fulfill his mission & preach the
everlasting gospel to a lost world.[69]

Issachar Bates was interred in the Church Family burying ground located
just west of the gardens where he had recently labored.[70] The procession carried his coffin down the main road of the village from the meeting house,

through the Second Order, past his "ledge garden," and turned west down the intersecting road alongside the botanical garden to the prepared grave.

One of Issachar's final songs written after his return to New Lebanon is also one that has received modern attention outside of the Shaker world.[71] Though short, it pulses with the exuberant spirit of a man who, once he came to Shaker life, never stopped moving. Like David, the ancient Hebrew poet who danced secretly before the altar of god while Saul's daughter "Michal" jeered him, Issachar took "nimble steps" his whole life. He defied the naysayers and heralded the Shaker message as he continued his journey.

Come life, Shaker life, Come life eternal,
Shake shake out of me all that is carnal.
I'll take nimble steps, I'll be a David,
I'll show Michal twice how he behaved.

"Elder Issachar seems to be continually at hand"

This now ends the life and labors of Elder Issachar Bates . . . For he was a man raised up by the hand of God to do the work he has done . . . a man well calculated to be the pioneer of the gospel.
— Moses Eastwood, Watervliet, Ohio

The process of summing up the meaning of Issachar Bates's complex contributions began soon after his funeral. Isaac Newton Youngs, the younger brother of Issachar's friend Benjamin Seth Youngs, composed one of many epitaphs:

Issachar Bates Senr was born January 29th 1758. He embraced the gospel in 1801 . . . In the beginning of 1805 he started with his companions, for the Western States, Ohio, Kentucky, &c to open the gospel there. And in them parts he labored upwards of thirty years; through many scenes of hardship, toil and afflictions but he has always borne up with wonderful life and zeal. He was active and powerful; devoted soul and body. He possessed an extraordinary talent for discoursing with persons of all characters on religious subjects whether for inquiry, argument, or opposition: always ready for answer; none at a loss for words; none afraid to meet any man or any subject whatever. It was not an easy matter for any professor of religion to get the better of him or to stand the test against him . . . He was as a battleax to all hypocritical professors — and a thorn to Antichristians. Was very plain and blunt, somewhat humorous; generally setting off his remarks with some very applicable Anecdote, or story, coming just to the case. There seemed rarely an instance but that he should have some entertaining or well adapted remark to make.

His mind seemed to be a great storehouse of information, a museum of intellectual curiosities. With him dies a world of knowledge and information in numerous incidents of his Life and past events, unknown to anyone else; and no small share of common sense, life and animation is buried with him . . . He was, withal, devoted to build up the good and pull down the evil; as his many hymns abundantly indicate. He was remarkably industrious in hand labor, many times going to the extent of his strength to do all the good he could.[1]

Brother Isaac was well positioned to appreciate Issachar's many unique gifts. Having visited the West in 1834, he had witnessed Issachar's influence there. Isaac shared a very close association with Issachar's daughter Sarah, a fellow singer, and he counted other Bates siblings among his friends. He had exchanged correspondence with Issachar over matters relating to hymns and poetry, notes that reflect humor and shared jokes. Because Isaac himself was so notorious for his multiple talents and his tendency for overwork, his depiction of Issachar's "remarkably industrious" character is especially noteworthy. To coin a phrase, it took one "remarkably industrious" Shaker to know one.

Notwithstanding the Shakers' well-established policy of urging members to renounce ties to their non-Shaker biological kindred, one of the earliest notifications of Issachar Bates's death was made to his eldest son, Artemas, who resided over two hundred miles away in northwestern upstate New York and who had recently resumed a cordial relationship with his father. Seth Youngs Wells wrote the letter expressly at the behest of Sarah and Betsy Bates only two days after Issachar's funeral.

> Friend Artemas Bates,
>
> By request of your Sisters Sarah & Betsy, I write to give you notice of your Father's decease. He died the 17th inst., after an illness of ten days in a good old age, being in his 80th year since the 29th of last January. He died as he had lived, beloved and respected by all his faithful brethren and sisters, and is now gone to receive the reward of his faithfulness and zeal, which you may probably remember, was ardent . . .
>
> He had you know, many opposers at his first setting out, and many severe trials to encounter; having to take up his cross and stem a torrent of opposition of his brethren of the Baptist order to which he then belonged, many of whom felt very near and dear to him; yet in the consequence of his faith they became his enemies. But he has triumphed over them all, and maintained his faith to the end. He literally and faithfully forsook all for Christ's sake & the gospel, and . . . he was one of those who preached the gospel to many thousands in the Western states, and thro' his preaching turned many to righteousness, and succeeded in gathering a large body of Believers, who have long honored & respected him as their Father in Christ.
>
> When he was first taken sick he expected to die & chose it. He had done all the good he could do in this world, and he desired . . . that this might be his last sickness, and so it proved. . . .
>
> . . . But your sisters can tell you more about him than I can write at

present, if you come to see them next summer, as I understand your father had invited you to come, & I suppose his death need not hinder your coming.

Your sisters have requested me to convey to you & family their love & respects, and also to your daughter & son in law who made them a visit last fall.

Seth Y. Wells

P.S. I am desired by your sisters, to inform you that if you should think proper to make a visit here, you can receive some small articles that belonged to your father, which, if not of essential value in themselves, may feel valuable to you as a memorial of your Father.

N.B. Your sisters desire to be informed if you receive this letter, as they understand that a former one miscarried.[2]

If Artemas Bates had harbored any resentment against his father for breaking up the family and joining the Shakers, it seems to have evaporated by the time of Issachar's death. It is an indication of the love still shared among the members of the Bates family, Shaker and non-Shaker alike, that Sarah and Betsy were anxious that their brother learn of Issachar's death as quickly as possible. Moreover, their encouragement that Artemas to carry out his planned visit and their intent to share Issachar's remaining possessions with him all serve as earmarks of a father who managed to retain the love of his children, despite turning the family upside down by becoming a Shaker. Considering the outright hostility that existed between many Shakers and their non-Shaker kin, the obvious cordiality seen in the Bates family at the time of Issachar's death is remarkable indeed.

The New Lebanon Shakers were somewhat less efficient in reporting Issachar Bates's demise to the Shaker West. The earliest notification known (there may have been others in missives that have not survived) appears in a letter from Seth Youngs Wells to Elder Mathew Houston at Watervliet, written on April 10, 1837, about three weeks after Issachar's death. Also in that letter Seth enclosed a note for one of the younger brethren at Watervliet, Isaac N. Houston.[3] Letters addressed to Issachar had just been received at New Lebanon, written by Elder Mathew and Brother Isaac, respectively. Elder Seth had to inform both regretfully that their letters had arrived too late.

Beloved Elder Mathew,

About 10 or 12 days ago a letter was received here from Br Isaac N. Houston of Watervliet addressed to Br Issachar; and last Friday another came with the same address, tho without any signature; but . . . that same hand betrayed the author. But they both came too late to reach Brother Issachar before his departure "to that bourn whence no traveler return." The former was mailed at Dayton the day of his funeral (March 18th). This intelligence will doubtless be quite unexpected and prove a disappointment to the writers; but the letters were well received & satisfactory . . . But I must now close for this page is full, and I must reserve the next for a little further communication in behalf of Br Isaac N.H. —

To Isaac N. Houston,

Now Br Isaac, I will write a few lines for you, seeing your good father Issachar for whom you expressed so much love & respect in your letter to him, had gone & left us before the letter arrived; and as I understand you are a good singer, I will send you his last hymn, that you may have it & keep it as a memorial of your faithful father, and learn it, and make it your Nightly Prayer. And I will also inform you that your good father has often been seen since his departure — and once he sung a quick, sharp laboring song to one of the young Brethren which the young Brother had never heard before, and told him there was not half so much indulgence in the world of spirits as there was in this world — that they had to labor very sharp & shuffle half the song for mortification. So I hope Br. Isaac you will improve your time well, and gain all you can in this world, for otherwise you may find it very hard struggling when you come into the world of spirits . . . This, Br. Isaac, you may treasure up in your memory & profit by it.[4]

A novel aspect of Seth's note to Isaac N. Houston is the claim that Issachar Bates remained alive and active in spirit at the New Lebanon community. Even though the spirit manifestations that would characterize the period of "Mother Ann's Work" would not begin in earnest until later that year, Seth nonetheless reported that many people had already seen and communicated with Issachar Bates's spirit, in just the few short weeks since his death. As we will see, recorded spirit visitations would soon become a common feature of nineteenth-century Shakers' engagement with the memory and legacy of Issachar Bates.

There is no question that Issachar Bates left an outsized mark on the Shaker world. In him, a singular set of talents and past experiences, an unusual personality, boundless religious zeal, an adventurous spirit, and energetic tenacity all combined to produce an extraordinary character utterly committed to the furtherance of the Shaker gospel. At the same time, Issachar harbored weaknesses and eccentricities that seemed to contradict the most fundamental features of the Shaker message. In him lies a great irony: that a man who struggled to integrate some of the most vital principles of Shakerism into his own life and who displayed many personality characteristics deeply at odds with the Shaker ideal was nonetheless vital to the expansion of the movement. Another element that distinguishes Issachar from the many influential and laudable figures in Shaker history is the epic scale of his experience. No other Shaker of his time or any other pursued a life journey that passed through such a grand panorama of places, processes, and people. From the battlefields of American independence to the Wilderness Road to the westernmost margin of American settlement, from interaction with celebrated military and political figures and illustrious clergy to imposing Native American leaders, Issachar stood at the fulcrum of many crucial events. His story and the story of Shaker expansion are one and the same. And his story allows us to effectively locate the entire Shaker movement within the context of American expansion during the Early Republic period.

The Shakers have always drawn people from diverse backgrounds. At the turn of the nineteenth century, Shaker ranks held many war veterans, many loving spouses and parents, many excellent singers, many courageous ablebodied men inured to frontier life, many spiritual zealots, many people with tendencies to alcoholism and bawdy speech, and at least a few charismatic preachers and gifted poets. However, it was rare indeed for all of those divergent characteristics to come together in a single individual. Because Issachar Bates embodied all these features and more, his timely conversion in 1801, just as the Shaker movement stood on the cusp of its second great expansion, was serendipitous. He was the right man at the right time.

> He was a powerful minister both in his preaching and singing, of which he had a great gift both natural and spiritual, apt and ready on all occasions either public or private to give a quick answer to any question that might be asked. He had the greatest gift and faculty to combat the world of any among believers, and could not be beat in an argument and always ready to defend the cause of truth and the gospel on all occasions. Altho frequently he had to meet the most learned preachers of the world and particular the New Lights, he would always come off victorious.[5]

The Shakers at New Lebanon seemed to recognize these gifts immediately when he arrived in the summer of 1801 to make inquiries of an elder. The brother who greeted him had barely begun their conversation when he broke away to tell the kitchen sister to prepare a meal "for a man that was going to confess his sins and preach the gospel." From the outset, Issachar's Shaker life was unusual. He was sent out to convert others to a faith to which he himself was relatively new, first in the surrounding region of New York, Vermont, and New Hampshire. Soon the eastern Shaker Ministry expanded its horizons even more, dispatching Issachar and his two spiritually senior companions to the western frontier beyond the Appalachian Mountains. Meanwhile, Issachar was reassured by the conversions of his wife, several children, and branches of his extended family. Nonetheless, the unique combination of gifts that he offered to the Shaker movement doomed him to a life of estrangement from his biological kin.

To meet the challenges of frontier evangelism, the Shakers needed men who could withstand physical hardship, who had been thoroughly grounded in the vices of the world, who understood firsthand the sacrifice of sexuality and family life that the Shakers required, who possessed the backbone to withstand persecution and take on even the most learned disputers, who could inspire complete strangers and persuade them to take life-changing action. Because Shaker worship involved unique applications of music and dance, an effective Shaker frontier evangelist also needed to be a gifted and uninhibited singer and dancer. In an environment of nationalistic fervor when Shakers were commonly denounced as cowardly and unpatriotic because of their avowed pacifism, being a veteran of the American Revolution with direct battlefield experience was also an asset. So was the physical energy and tenacity to be constantly in motion, seeking new audiences, rebounding from failure, returning to nurture new converts, doing the hard work of building that allowed orderly Shaker communities to emerge on the western landscape. To be sure, Shakerism's western expansion was the consequence of the labors of many determined men and women. But few figures from the Shaker West managed to be as instrumental and beloved in so many places at once as Issachar Bates. Ironically, he established himself as a "father" figure in a Shaker world in which he never held the title of "Father."

Issachar Bates's Shaker life was also remarkable because of the extent to which he embodied so many decidedly un-Shaker characteristics. Prior to becoming a Shaker, Issachar had been driven to his first religious conversion out of desperation over his inability to govern his vulgar tongue. Yet he seemed never to have overcome his tendency toward crude speech. For those who knew him best, Issachar's speech and mannerisms could be vexing, as Richard McNemar records in a diary account:

> Elder John in the beginning had often labored to guard him[self] against being tried at Elder Issachar's rowdy sense for he was a real rowdy. But a

singularity, that his spiritual discernment was astonishing that he could rise to almost any degree of spiritual light & again use the most filthy language & show the greatest blackguard . . . [I]t was in vain ever to attempt to check him, that he had not been raised or restricted to a religious life as we had & therefore his gift was not to us but to the lower ranks of mankind whose language was familiar to him & which he could adopt & use without any remorse of conscience.[6]

Clearly, Issachar was a conundrum to even his closest companions. They were baffled that a man capable of such spiritual insight could also sink into what seemed like degraded language and behaviors. But since the frontier folk of the West struck many transplanted New Englanders as representative of "the lower ranks of mankind" anyway, Issachar was well placed in his apparent calling. Many of the westerners among whom Issachar lived were unfazed by his mannerisms but found his personality sufficiently unique among the Shaker leadership to warrant extensive comment:

He was considered more rough than polite in manners and customs, and by his persecutors was called "old rough and ready." Be that as it may, he was without a doubt a very suitable instrument in the hand of God to be a pioneer in the work of God to open the way for the everlasting gospel to be planted in a wild and rough country as this was at that time. He was yet agreeable, lively, and interesting company in almost any class of people and could stir up a lively feeling in almost any company and take their attention in some way or other, sometimes by telling a short story or anecdote to please or cause mirth.[7]

Issachar also deviated from expected Shaker characteristics in his persistent association with the soldiering life. It is true that when the Shakers in Indiana were directly exposed to local military preparations and stood in danger being exploited by the military, Issachar roundly denounced the situation: "There it was drums and fifes — blood and whiskey — alas! alas!"[8] But he also retained certain military mannerisms and figures of speech that he employed liberally in his poetry and hymns as well as in everyday life. When given the opportunity to apply for his military pension, he did so without hesitation. The rich attention Issachar gives his military interlude in his autobiography and pension statement hardly suggests someone who has pushed the experience to the margins of memory, but rather someone who recalls his service with both pleasure and pride. Future Shakers would long recall Issachar's experience as a soldier and as a fifer, and at least one aspect of Issachar's demeanor when elderly — namely, the involuntary "noddle" of his head — was wrongly but inventively attributed to his soldiering life. A Union Village sister asserted in the late nineteenth century that Issachar's "shaking palsy" was "acquired by over exertion during the war, at one engagement he blew on his fife till the blood gushed out from both his ears."[9] And many of Issachar's appearances in visions during the Era of Manifestations in the middle decades of the nineteenth century took on a decidedly military flavor, with Issachar appearing as a soldier or leading soldiers, carrying weapons, or playing the fife. The later Shakers who reported Issachar's associations with fifing and soldiering would have had little reason to do so had he not strongly retained his military mannerisms and spoken openly of his wartime service.

Probably related to his soldiering past, Issachar possessed a profound sense of duty and a related conviction that one should be rewarded fairly, according to one's actions. This conviction is evident in the way he expresses his view of God: "And I had a clear view of God — that he was all fitness and I was just the reverse . . . But it was not comfort and joy that I was seeking after. Nay, it was to come to an honest settlement with God if possible." It is also evident in countless turns of phrase that Issachar used in his hymns and poetry, such as, "If you've been faithful through the day, And done your duty ev'ry way, Now is the time to get your pay, More pow'r against the Devil." This attitude probably also influenced how he approached his military pension: he had performed a duty and deserved the compensation, plain and simple. However, while logical, such an attitude could easily have stood at odds with Shaker principles of obedience to the "lead." The "leading gift," or directives from higher authorities in the Shaker world, did not always seem fair to individuals. And clinging to one's own individual will was considered a great sin. Shaker spiritual discourse is replete with terms such as "old man of sin" or "Great I," which refer to the persistent temptation of one's own will at the expense of obedience to the lead. Being a Shaker meant putting aside one's own ego completely — indeed, putting one's ego or one's "old man of sin" to death.[10] To wit, one Shaker song exclaims "I'll be no companion to Great Big I, For I am determined Old Big shall die." Ironically, while Issachar was among the Shakers' most effective early preachers, he struggled to successfully apply this most basic Shaker principle to all aspects of his own life. He held on to "Great I" in many respects, insisting that his will prevail and lashing out when it did not. Perhaps his greatest heartbreak was his ultimate removal from the West near the end of his life, because he believed at his core that he had *earned* the right to be buried there. After all he had done to launch the Shaker West, he was utterly convinced that he *deserved* to remain there if he chose. Accepting the move — accepting what he regarded as an undeserved consequence to thirty years of unflinching duty — went against every fiber in Issachar's being and was "worse than natural death." In the end, though, he was peacefully reconciled. His final hymn expresses his renunciation of his former habit of demanding just reward for services rendered: "So I'll relinquish all demands, For any good I've ever done."

Another uncomfortable deviation from the Shaker ideal that Issachar was forced to confront in himself during his later years in Ohio was his standing relative to the joint interest, that vital component of Shaker life. In fact, as Issachar assisted Richard McNemar with the work of revising the legal covenants for Union Village and Watervliet, an incongruity presented itself. Until he finally set his name to Richard's revised covenant for Watervliet in 1834, Issachar had only ever signed a single joint-interest document during his entire Shaker life — the relatively short and simple covenant agreement drawn up in 1810 to bind together the first "family" of believers at Turtle Creek, presided over by David Darrow.[11] That document, signed in March 1810 by fifteen men and eighteen women, declared that signatories had the right to take their property with them if they ever withdrew from that family. On that basis, Issachar believed that he was justified in owning property, including "his pension money, the two carriage horses, one cow, and bull" — although he asserted that all of this was simply held by him for the use of the society — as he withdrew from the Turtle Creek family and moved through a succession of churches in the Shaker West. Still, Watervliet Shaker Moses Eastwood clearly saw enough of a discrepancy in Issachar's declared disposition of his property (made in his verbal will in 1834 when he believed he would shortly die) to offer an explanation.

> [Issachar Bates's] last will and testament may seem a contradiction to what he wrote of himself in the sketch of his life, where he says he had owned no property, lands or tenements for more than thirty years and had nothing to bequeath to anybody but his love and blessing. For this property he did not own as personal or private property, for any selfish purpose and only held claim to it for the use of the society. It had been given to him as presents from other societies and different individuals . . . and he only held it for the benefit of this society.[12]

Moreover, Richard McNemar, in writing about the difficulties of the covenant revision, noted that one major sticking point was the fact that Issachar Bates, though respected as one of the founders of the West, continued virtually unbound by a covenant for most of his life in the West,[13] which caused many rank and file Shakers to resent the restrictions of a covenant altogether.[14]

Richard McNemar was one for whom Issachar's eccentricities and personal weaknesses presented a particular dilemma. Both men shared certain key characteristics. Both were preachers, poets, musicians, fathers of large families. Both were figures whom other Shakers looked to for leadership. Because of the extensive poetry and hymns written by each, both played a crucial role in explicating Shaker doctrine for the average believer, brethren and sisters who had not the time, opportunity, nor intellectual tools to wade through such printed tomes as *Testimony of Christ's Second Appearing*. Both were depended upon by the Shaker leadership, east and west, to fulfill certain functions, and in their respective capacities, both enjoyed considerable autonomy at various times. But temperamentally, the two were miles apart. The deeply intellectual Richard could be cold, legalistic, and judgmental. He held his humor privately or shared wry jokes with only a select one or two (sometimes in Latin!). He remained aloof from most Shakers around him; he was smarter than most of the others, and he knew it. Issachar was jovial, empathetic, receptive, and affectionate. He was not standoffish, did not secret away his thoughts in endless notebooks as did Richard (sometimes using Latin!), but expressed himself openly and often with crude bluntness. But Issachar was also aware of his own gifts, which could cause him to discount the contributions of others, as Richard observed: "On the subject of religion he would seem to comprehend all worlds & the state of all the dead, to have all knowledge — to understand all mysteries — that if anything was presented beyond his ken, he could wager it as nonsense, a thing not necessary to know."[15]

Richard McNemar was a historian at heart. In the Ohio covenants, in such printed documents as *A Review of the Most Important Events ... in the West*, and in other accounts that he worked on but never published, he set out to record various aspects of the history of the Shaker West. In an effort to present a correct historical record, he also struggled to clarify the standing and character of key figures. How to present Issachar Bates was particularly puzzling:

[H]ow are we to settle and adjust the leading claims among the several gifts from the Mother church, particularly between David Darrow & Issachar B, the one honored & respected under the title of Father, the other having obtained from his people the superior title of patriarch, a title next to that of Emperor. We have records to show who gave the title of father & Mother to David & Ruth, which might forcibly imply that the individual was first born of many brethren, but at the least hint of such a thing so many adverse claims are waked up that we are admonished to silence lest the house get more dangerously divided against itself. But some how or other, if possible we must fulfill the requirement of the eastern example and get a first somebody for minister, Elder, Trustee, &c prior to the advent of the present incumbents & if we cannot agree among ourselves as to matters of fact let us petition the primary authorities in the east to make the nomination at this late period.[16]

Here we see Richard McNemar grappling with the fact that Issachar Bates was plainly regarded as a father figure by Shakers throughout the West — a western "patriarch" — even though only David Darrow had ever held the title of "Father." This inconsistency annoyed the logical Richard, who implied that Issachar was unfairly accorded too much adulation, and stood in danger of acting like an "emperor." Richard also implies that Issachar became a divisive figure, intentionally or not. For many who had originally confessed their sins to Issachar, he represented their primary connection to the faith, and they simply resisted the spiritual authority of anyone else. Archibald Meacham, who had borne his own share of difficulties while serving alongside Issachar at Busro, empathized with Richard's task of succeeding Issachar at Watervliet and underscored the divisive potential of Issachar's uncommon popularity. Richard related that Archibald, "commented very freely on the subject in this way that as long as Elder Issachar remained on the ground the people would never be gathered to another."[17]

About the time that Issachar Bates and Richard McNemar parted in 1835, Richard tried to sum up his frustrations about his old friend in a poem.

My much esteemed Brother Bates
When you came to the western states
'Twas with a mutual feeling then
We own'd each other mortal men.

We each had got some precious light
Which did our kindred souls unite
But in our mutual free exchange
Were many things both new & strange

In point of order you agreed
That Brother Richard had the lead
And to the hall of social kin
We turn'd the key and let you in.

As fellow servants we went on
Subordinate to Elder John

And every thing I had to spare
I gave you as my Proper heir.

You freely gave me in return
What made my haughty nature burn
'Twas yours to make the bright display
And mine to steer the other way.

You soon possess'd a large estate
And in your order waxed great
Nor did I envy you that crown
While I was lab'ring to get down

When at West Union you were plac'd
Where you were honor'd and caress'd
My humble lot in Father's tribe
I am not willing to describe.

Now on the ancient center plain
Our lot has been to meet again
[E]xchange our gifts But I leave you.
[T]o tell the little story thro.[18]

Richard betrays much about the personalities of both men and the manner in which they had clashed. Looking back to the beginning of their friendship, Richard recalls mutual admiration but also Issachar's deference to Richard's intellectual grasp of Shaker doctrine. He notes they were both subordinate to others. He admits frankly that he was jealous of Issachar: his exuberant public persona ("bright display"), his popularity among the Indiana Shakers. But Richard insinuates that it is he, not Issachar, who is living the more genuine Shaker life (maintaining a "humble lot" and "lab'ring to get down").

Issachar Bates never saw Richard's poem—a good thing, because he likely would have taken umbrage at the portrayal. But it is clear that Issachar was not the only one who spent considerable time after the middle of 1835 coming to terms with the past. Richard was offered a valuable perspective by Elder Rufus Bishop, who wrote reassuringly about the trials that had brought both Issachar and Richard such united vexation: "It is evident that [Issachar's] ready wit and lack of sound wisdom has subjected you to many trials, particularly on account of others who considered him as an old experienced Believer . . . but you know that he was a very young Believer."[19]

This important observation provides a key to understanding a strong theme in Issachar Bates's life as a Shaker. By undertaking the vital task of preaching and drawing converts as soon as his own conversion was concluded, Issachar was placed in the position of representing the insight and wisdom of an "old believer" even though he was himself still a "young believer." And because he was sent out to the frontier before, as Elder Rufus wrote to Richard Mc-Nemar, he was "well milled himself . . . before there was much separation between the wheat and the chaff," he remained in many ways a perpetual young believer. From his young-believer mentality, Issachar derived the necessary zeal and energy to make him an effective preacher–evangelist for thirty years. But because he had only scant initiation into the demands of orderly Shaker life — recall that the eastern communities still lacked the full structure of "gospel order" when Issachar left in 1805 — he continually chafed at order. He not only resisted order over his own actions, he found it difficult to impose order consistently on others when he was placed in positions of authority. Yet Issachar held powerful influence over a multitude of western converts, spiritually and emotionally. One western sister aptly called him "[t]he vessel from whom I first heard the sound of Mother's gospel." For many, he was their path into the Shaker faith, which made him an exemplar in their eyes. But Issachar was well aware of his awkward position of being both "old" and "young" in the faith: "I am called an Old believer here —tho the last and least of all, as pertaining to age and privilege in the gospel — and among all my big feelings, and high sense, I never yet felt myself worthy to be equaled with those who are called Old believers."[20] Though admittedly a man of "big feelings and high sense," Issachar was plagued with the insecurity of not being up to the task, relative to his counterparts among the Shaker leadership in the West. For all his jovial sociability, he stood apart, neither fish nor fowl; and this could be terribly isolating.

Regardless of the many ironies embodied in Issachar Bates, the scope of his influence and his long thirty years as an actor on the western stage made him a linchpin in all accounts of the Shaker West and thus secured him a featured place in the Shakers' own versions of their movement's history. The Shaker movement was early to develop a historicizing impulse, possibly because Shakerism's founding figures in the eighteenth century left behind so little written record. After only a short time, Shakers began to gather and record testimonies and other documentation to establish a durable foundation for the United Society of Believers in Christ's Second Appearing that would sustain it into the future, beyond the lifetime of any single leader. Because even during Ann Lee's lifetime, Shakerism's territorial expansion made it impossible for any individual Shaker to "know" the Shaker experience comprehensively, chronicling the events of Shakerism along its many geographic fronts was all the more important, as it contributed to their collective identity. Recorded experiences of individual Shakers emerged as vital exemplars for believers everywhere, inspiring people to improve their lives and behavior, as well as illuminating and demystifying the more distant settings of the Shaker experience.

Richard McNemar had encouraged Issachar Bates to record his autobiography so that he could publish it from his Union Press at Watervliet, Ohio. Why Richard did not go forward with its printing is unknown. But the substantial manuscript (120-odd pages) was copied at least twice before Issachar left Ohio. In 1833, Issachar carried it with him on his visit to Kentucky, where it was copied at South Union by Benjamin Seth Youngs.[21] Watervliet, Ohio, Shaker Moses Eastwood also made a copy of the manuscript, later adding other material: further reflections on Issachar, copies of letters pertaining to him, and copies of some of Issachar's poems. Meanwhile, Issachar took his original manuscript back to New York. In April 1836 he completed an additional section, and after his death, more ancillary material was written in: more poems and remarks from his funeral. Over the next twenty years or so, many Shakers living at or passing through New Lebanon made manuscript copies of Issachar's original document with its various inclusions. Others may have penned copies from the versions that Benjamin Seth Youngs and Moses Eastwood had completed earlier. Altogether, at least seventeen separate manuscript copies were made,[22] some by Shakers at New Lebanon and Watervliet, New York, others by Shakers in Massachusetts and Maine.

Compared to the reproduction of other Shakers' autobiographies in the period, this number is unprecedented. During the middle decades of the nineteenth century, while scribes and historians within the various Shaker communities made explicit efforts to ensure that the biographical accounts of leading early Shakers were recorded, rank-and-file believers were also urged to write life stories and testimonies. Many of these were copied and compiled into manuscript volumes held by the ministries in various locations. A small number—autobiographies by Ann Lee, Henry Clough, William Leonard, Richard Pelham, and a few others—exist in multiple manuscript copies ranging from two to five. But no other Shaker biography or autobiography was copied and circulated as widely as that of Issachar Bates. The existence of an astounding seventeen manuscript copies, plus the original, scattered across the nineteenth-century Shaker world from Maine to South Union, Kentucky, tell us that Bates's story was sufficiently compelling to warrant the time and effort of many Shakers to reproduce it by hand. Many of these copies number

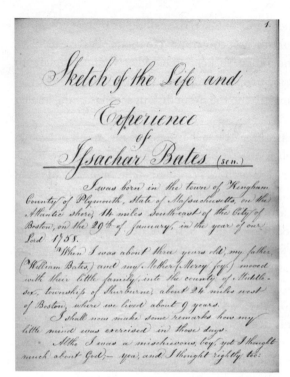

some two hundred pages. Each comprises a slightly different combination of Issachar's core account, together with additional poetry, letters, and assorted writings.[23] In addition, significant portions of the autobiography were extracted and serialized in Shaker publications. Beginning in 1884, New Hampshire elder Henry Blinn produced a series of articles for *The Manifesto*, which presented portions of the autobiography along with Blinn's paraphrased narrative. In the mid-1960s, Issachar's story was serialized again by Brother Ted Johnson in *The Shaker Quarterly*, a journal published by the Sabbathday Lake community in the second half of the twentieth century.

Most of the manuscript copies of Issachar Bates's autobiography reflect meticulous preparation and conscientious handling. One impressive 187-page copy is bound in reverse calfskin, displays careful and consistent calligraphy throughout, and bears subtle evidence of being handled and read by numerous Shakers (figure E.1).[24] The paper on the upper edges of each page bears a slightly darker stain, residue of the fingers that turned the pages. It is inscribed by Betsy Bates, although the character and quality of its calligraphy suggest that Sarah Bates may have helped her sister produce it. The overleaf traces a succession of owners, first from Betsy to Naomi Legier of Union Village, a former Busro, Indiana, Shaker who later rose to the Union Village Ministry. From Eldress Naomi it passed to other members of the Union Village Ministry — Elder William Reynolds and Eldress Adeline Wells. It finally ended up in the possession of Susie Harmston, one of the last Union Village Shakers, who brought it with her back to Canterbury, New Hampshire, where she died in 1926.

The Shakers who read and copied Issachar Bates's autobiography reacted to some of his passages and turns of phrase by making a wide range of editorial changes. For example, in several copies made in the East, passages exposing the rather disorderly state of Watervliet, Ohio, when Issachar arrived there in 1824 are shortened or eliminated. And Issachar's description of how he and Benjamin Seth Youngs attended to a dead body covered in "dung" during the 1805 journey west is eliminated in several copies, perhaps considered too graphic. Betsy Bates's copy rephrases one passage, apparently to eliminate the word "arse." Shaker scribe and antiquarian Alonzo Hollister, who worked tirelessly to collect and organize manuscript material recording various aspects of Shaker history, reacted to the same passage when he read the autobiography as a young man in the Second Order at New Lebanon about 1850. In an undated note addressed to historian John Patterson MacLean sometime after 1903, Hollister reveals how he first made, then stetted, editorial changes.

As you are a man of judgement & our friend & interested in Elder Issacher's writings, I will here tell you something, not to publish, but for your private information. When I first read the story in Elder Issacher's autobio about old Deacon Devon, — I write from memory of what occurred in my 20s — Where it reads that the nabors [sic] reported Issacher Bates had cut Old Devon's arse off, I imagined it was a mistake for ears, & changed the spelling. After I learned what arse stood for, I thot it unbearably vulgar and was loth to change it back. In the meantime, an excellent well written copy was made . . . [How] will Elder Issacher receive it — how will I settle it with him when I come to meet him. Having become satisfied when his intention was, I concluded he could have no cause for dissatisfaction with me for leaving it as I found it — so I endeavored to write the word back there as I found it. You may see that the place has been tampered with. I thot it due to you as historian, to know the facts.[25]

There is no easy explanation for why Issachar Bates's autobiography was so widely copied and read relative to the biographical accounts of other Shakers seemingly far more vital to the movement than he. The life stories of such eminent figures as Ann Lee, Joseph Meacham, and Calvin Green were assuredly recorded and circulated, but to a far lesser degree. What can be said is that Issachar's autobiography—then as now—contains multitudes. It grounds the individual Shaker life in the context of early New England, where the movement began. It incorporates elements that countless Shakers would have directly recalled or at least heard of—the "Dark Day" and other signs and wonders, the Revolutionary War, the early travels of Ann Lee. It includes the wrenching account of one person's spiritual agony and how the Shaker gospel brought relief and transformation. It opens onto the epic of Shaker expansion, integrating to varying degrees reflections on the establishment and growth of each western site, as well as prototypical stories of marvelous spiritual outpourings and public persecution. It candidly addresses the negative and celebrates the positive aspects of Shaker life. And it portrays the struggles of an aging Shaker who faces adversity but manages to retain his faith, the love of his friends, and his union with the authority of the lead. Along the way, because Issachar was an exceptionally fine writer and story teller, it offers drama, entertainment, and colorful poetic asides. Cumulatively, all of these rich elements come together in Issachar's autobiographical account so that it emerged from among other testimonies and biographies as greater than the sum of its parts.

> When we got there . . . they took us up Garret, into a room formerly occupied by Elder Issachar . . . We saw where Elder Issachar used to work in the garden—they gave us two Apples & two Quinces, to take home with us as specimens of Watervliet fruit—the largest we ever saw anywhere without exception . . . In the evening we attended meeting with them . . . Elder Brother James said that Elder Issachar was there—that he had brought a basket of fire to burn up unbelief with.[26]

> We have received love from Mother Lucy, Mother Ruth, how often I know not,—received Songs from very many, say Mother Ann, Father William, Father James, and El. Issachar,—the latter seems to be continually at hand, conducting the visionists, learning them songs, playing the fife &c. &c.[27]

For several decades in the middle of the nineteenth century, worship throughout the Shaker world included various communications and interactions between believers and the spirits of deceased Shakers. During this Era of Manifestations, accounts of communications from Shakers who had been particularly prominent or beloved during their lifetimes—from Ann Lee and other founding figures through recently deceased Shakers—were exceptionally common. The spirit of Issachar Bates was a regular fixture among the visionaries. Shakers throughout the East and West alike reported seeing him,

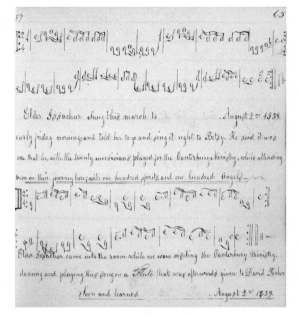

E.2

Songs recorded as having been delivered by Issachar Bates' spirit, August 2, 1839. Mary Hazard hymnal, Item 896, Edward D. Andrews Shaker Collection. (Courtesy, the Winterthur Library: The Edward Deming Andrews Memorial Shaker Collection.)

hearing him singing or preaching, learning songs from him, hearing him play the fife or other instruments, witnessing him dancing or marching or lead armies of angels, and receiving gifts from him. In many of these visionary episodes, Issachar was accompanied by the spirits of other Shakers he had known from his western experience, such as David Darrow, John Meacham, and Andrew Houston.[28] Other visions underscored Issachar's strong association with poetry and humor, such as one vision recorded in verse by Sarah Ann Lewis, who had been a young woman in the New Lebanon Second Order during Issachar's final years there and had participated in the memorable mountaintop outing of September 1836. Written in the voice of an unknown "spirit-friend," the poem concludes,

> Now if you can't remember me
> Just trace it back & you will see
> There are many little funny scrapes
> 'Tis said was done by Issachar Bates.[29]

In fact, many of the "gifts" recorded during the Era of Manifestations were songs or anthems, and many visions of Bates had a distinctly martial flavor. Within the hundreds of individual song books produced by Shakers under inspiration during this period can be found countless short songs marked "Brought by Issachar Bates" or "Learned of Issachar Bates" (figure E.2). Probably because of the common association of Bates with soldiering, some gift drawings depict weapons or military musical instruments labeled as belonging to "Father" Issachar. In many visions, Issachar is portrayed playing his fife: "Elder Issachar came into the room while we were visiting the Canterbury Ministry, singing and playing this song on a Fife that was afterwards given to Daniel Parker. Seen and learned."[30] Some of the visions also integrate details of Issachar's early missionary experiences with his companions: "This march was sung for the Brethren who first went to the West, to open the gospel, the Angels sung this as they were on their Journey. Learn'd of Issachar Bates sen. by some in the Second O."[31] One lively march reportedly delivered by Issachar to an eastern Shaker was accompanied by the observation "In a kind of vision he was seen to march into the West," perhaps a reflection of the visionist's realization of the deep emotional attachment that Issachar had retained for the western communities.[32] And yet other messages evoking experiences consistent with Issachar's missionary adventures were rendered poetically:

> I've crossed o'er the waters I've passd o'er hills and plains
> I've been throughout the desert to sound my Mother's name
> The trump of truth I've sounded & many Souls did hear,
> The everlasting gospel and to the call give ear.[33]

In one interesting text called "Spiglass," alleged to have been brought by Issachar Bates's spirit, Issachar employs a spyglass to discern his own sins. This is an intriguing reference in light of Issachar's documented handling of a spyglass during the September 1836 mountaintop outing with the large group of young sisters, and it suggests the possibility that Issachar owned the spyglass, an unusual item to be found in a Shaker village.

> Poor somebody else has all they can bear
> And now I am determin'd to take my full share
> I know I am lacking in ev'ry respect
> And on my own nature I now can reflect.
> I've look'd at the failings of others so long,
> I hardly can see that I do any wrong
> But since I have turned my spy glass within
> I plainly discover the nature of sin.[34]

An unusual visionary experience of Issachar Bates occurred in 1843, during a visit of Issachar's eldest son, Artemas, to New Lebanon to see his sisters Betsy and Sarah. The often bizarre aspects of Shaker spirituality were seldom revealed to non-Shakers during the Era of Manifestations. Public meetings ceased at New Lebanon between 1842 and 1845. Yet despite the Shakers' efforts to conceal the extraordinary spirit manifestations from outsiders, Artemas Bates was the recipient of one set of messages from his father, through a New Lebanon "visionist."

> Sep. 5th 1843, Tuesday evening . . . In about ten minutes Issachar Bates entered the room and handed me a small letter and said, I have obtained permission to come and visit my natural son Artemas B. who is now in this place and because I cannot have time sufficient to speak to him as I would desire to, I have written this short word as an introduction . . . The next morning I read the letter to him (Artemas) in the presence of Betsy Bates, Semantha Fairbanks, and his companion . . . Soon after the reading was finished, Issachar made himself known addressing himself first to the sisters present saying, I have indeed come in love and peace and not in any wise to terrify any one . . . There was free liberty given and Artemas was asked if he desired to receive a word from his Father, 'I should' was the answer. Issachar then turned to Artemas . . . Yea Artemas . . . I am in reality Issachar your natural Father that once delighted to behold and caress you and speak unto you as unto the fond child of my care and daily concern.[35]

Such visions involving Issachar Bates outlasted the Era of Manifestations itself. By the late 1850s the Shakers' most elaborate visionary experiences of deceased Shaker leaders, historical figures, and assorted heavenly beings had subsided, but occasional striking visions of Issachar persisted. Perhaps one of the most interesting and extensive was recorded in 1862 during the Civil War when Shakers everywhere were concerned about the impact of southern secession on the two Shaker communities in Kentucky, a border state. A sister at Watervliet, New York, recorded a vision in which Issachar Bates played a fife and led a large army of spiritual beings who waged a battle against the "secessionist" army and thereby protected the Kentucky Shakers at South Union, who were concerned about the Confederate occupation of nearby Bowling Green.

> This beautiful and heavenly Army, with Elder Issachar at their head, were dressed in perfect uniform, indescribably curious . . . I saw Elder Issachar step forward, and, raising his hands, he spake aloud in much earnestness. — Our eternal & Heavenly Parents have chosen us from among many, knowing that we have courage that never gives back, and grit that never wears down; they have made us ready, and sent us forth to guard

between their faithful children, and the contending war parties in the south west, where a little branch of lovely Zion is endangered by secession foes and must pass thro' deep tribulation . . . Now Elder Issachar gave a full breath from his fife, as a signal to leave us, when all moved towards the southwest, at which instant Elder Issachar tuned his call for volunteers very loudly & powerfully, thro' his star spangled fife, and all his army now danced out of the room, and with their different music all joined in concert; every sound and step told unwavering courage . . . When Elder Issachar was about leaving our meeting, he sent his bearer to me, with a present of a spy glass. Said he, since then I have seen many interesting things that were going on in the earth . . . While the rebels were at Bowling Green, myself and others felt anxious to know how much they were troubling Believers near . . . I saw the village, but was much astonished to see a great many secession soldiers gathered around. Soon I plainly saw Elder Issachar and his whole army of cavalry, & light infantry throwing bombs among the rebels.[36]

Phebe Ann Smith, the Shaker sister who experienced and reported this vision, had been a young sister recently admitted to the New Lebanon Second Order when Issachar Bates arrived there in 1835. Clearly, Bates's soldiering past continued to inform the Shakers' memories of him, along with his courage, boldness, music-making, and association with his beloved Shaker West. If any Shaker was able to affect the the living Shakers from the spirit world, Issachar Bates would certainly have tried, and reports of visions of him persisted into the 1860s and 1870s.[37] Shortly before his daughter Betsy Bates died in 1869, a group of Shakers reported a vision of his delivery of a song expressly to be sung at her funeral.[38]

The pioneers of our gospel work were gifted in visions but they were at the same time indefatigable workers on the earth. They left their cozy homes and went into the world and preached and prayed and held their meetings from day to day and from week to week and compelled men to believe. John Meacham, Benj. Youngs and Issachar Bates did no less than this on their visit to Ohio. Issachar had visions which comforted him but he also had the confidence that he was a servant of God: and this man could walk from Mt. Lebanon to Ohio and on to Ky. and preach a sermon in every log cabin on the way . . . As Believers grow lukewarm and lose their hold on the various forms of spiritualism which belongs to their own order, they will go out into the world to find them, and so long as the world lasts the magicians will work at their trade.[39]

As the nineteenth century closed, Shakers were enjoined to look back on the example set by Issachar Bates and the other pioneers who carried the Shaker gospel to the West. The writers of the Shaker periodical *The Manifesto* suggested that contemporary believers in their "cozy homes" were "lukewarm," and should work to revive the spiritual zeal of the expansion period. That spiritual zeal was personified in Issachar Bates. As late as January 1898, one hundred and forty years after Issachar's birth, the influence of his memory was still sufficiently strong to generate a poetic exhortation published for the Shakers as an inspirational beginning for the new year ahead.

> In duty enduring, in bearing believe,
> Forgiving if any my spirit should grieve;
> Rememb'ring at all times, as Mother did say,
> To set out anew and begin every day.

How anxiously we have desired that a voice from the unseen might speak a few words, — only a few words, that we might believe. It is in the above quotation that we hear the spirit of our worthy Elder Issachar Bates, and even at this date it gives forth no uncertain sound. Accepting this voice of loving inspiration, let us begin the New Year with a clean record.[40]

Throughout his life journey, Issachar Bates possessed the animation and drive to "set out anew" over and over again. His lifetime of motion helped to expand and shape the Shaker world and ensure that the Shaker movement would remain a vital part of the American landscape.

> The reason why I sing so long And step the notes so quick and strong
> Is just because that God has done What he has promised by his Son.
> He's sent the everlasting Key That opens heaven where I be
> This animates me while I move For this strong Key is truth and love.

Appendixes

	William Bates b. 8-2-1725 Hingham, MA d. 8-9-1803 Plainfield, MA		m. 3-29-1748	Mercy Joy b. 10-1-1732 Hingham, MA d. between 6-11-1776 and 4-26-1777	
Mercy b. 12-18-1751 or 12-17-1752	Noah b. 2-6-1754 d. 5-?-1790	**Hannah** b. 12-31-1755 or 1-8-1756 d. 9-28-1842	**Issachar** b. 1-29-1758 d. 3-17-1837	Sarah b. 6-27-1760	**Theodore** b. 10-11-1762 d. 10-24-1846
	m. 6-22-1778 Ruth Maynard	m. 4-22-1774 **David Train**	m. 4-6-1778 **Lovina** **Maynard** b. 3-23-1760 d. 8-15-1828	m. 2-13-1779 James Wheeler	m. 9-1-1785 Mary Shattuck
	↓	↓	↓	↓	↓
		David b. 1777 d. 1858	*Lovina* b. 1-29-1780		Lucinda b. 1786 d. 1850
		Oliver b. 1779	Artemas b. 3-21-1782		Lydia b. 1787 d. 1864
		Lydia b. 1781 d. 1866	Oliver b. 5-11-1784		
		Hannah b. 1783 d. 1864	*Nahum* b. 3-30-1786		m. 6-29-1792 Abigail Wheeler
		Molly b. 1786	**Polly** b. 6-18-1788 d. 9-14-1823		↓ ↓

Olive	Molly	**Dolly** (Desire)	**Caleb**	William	William
b. 8-27-1764		b. 1-14-1769	b. 9-7-1775	b. 9-7-1775	b. 6-11-1776
		d. 1-1-1841	d. 3-27-1848	d. 2-29-1776	
m. 11-16-1785		m. 5-18-1789	m. **Rebecca**		
Nathaniel Knight		**Jason Harwood**			

↓		↓	↓		
		Justice	**Paulina***		
		b. 1789	b. 12-26-1806		
		Asenath	**Anna***		
			b. 6-6-1809		
			d. 3-16-1825		
		Margaret	*Benjamin*		
			b. 2-22-1814		
			Elizaette		
			b. 10-19-1815		
			John Hall		
			b. 4-23-1820		

A Bates Family Tree (*continued*)

Benjamin b. 1789	**Issachar** b. 11-12- 1790 d. 12-14-1875	*Theodore* b. 4-29-1793 d. 12-24-1869
Abigail	**Sarah** b. 11-29-1792 d. 4-19-1881	Osee b. 1796
Azuba b. 1793 d. 1857	*William* b. 4-23-1796	Abigail b. 1794 d. 1891
Elizabeth b. 1793 d. 1865	**Betsy** b. 6-1-1798 d. 3-3-1869	

William
b. 6-23-1824

Irena*
b. 1824

Names in boldface indicate individuals who converted to the Shakers and remained until death.

Names in italics indicate individuals who converted to the Shakers and later left.

Names that are both italicized and underlined indicate individuals who converted to the Shakers and later disappear from Shaker records.

Names marked with (*) indicate individuals whose paternity is uncertain. Shaker records for Caleb and his wife Rebecca indicate they entered the Shaker community of Watervliet from Jefferson County, New York, in 1825 with four children. However, the number of children and youths named Bates entering Watervliet at that time exceeds four. I speculate that Caleb could have brought kin with him to Watervliet, children of his brother William or of Artemas Bates, Issachar's eldest son, both of whom had also migrated to Jefferson County, New York.

APPENDIX 2 SONGS AND POEMS BY ISSACHAR BATES

Issachar Bates achieved renown across the Shaker world for his songs and poetry. Hymns, namely songs consisting of multi-verse texts of metered poetry with spiritual or doctrinal themes, and ballads, metered multi-verse songs telling a story, were the music genres for which Issachar Bates was best known. But he also contributed liberally to other Shaker genres.[1] Issachar was adept at producing "laboring" songs, short lively tunes sung without words to accompany the different styles of dancing in worship, and many of these bear the earmarks of the fife tunes that he might have played in his youth. He also contributed many "extra" songs, worded songs usually of only one verse, which often accompanied dancing. Probably because of his ability to generate poetry and music nearly spontaneously, Issachar was relied upon for "occasional" songs—songs aimed at specific occasions, such as Christmas, the New Year, funerals, or the greeting and farewell of guests—in most of the communities where he lived. And Issachar's preaching voice echoes through his many "anthems," long meandering songs consisting of narrative prose texts set to irregular non-strophic melodies. He also penned abundant poems that seem to have never been set to music but were recorded throughout Shaker manuscripts nonetheless.

Scarcely any of Issachar Bates' poetry or songs are known outside of the Shaker world. "The Harvest," a selection from his earliest known group of poems (*New Songs, on Different Subjects* [Salem, NY: Dodd, 1800]) was set to music and printed in numerous nineteenth-century hymn books, though never with an attribution to Bates. Of the great multitude of songs and poems he wrote as a Shaker, probably the best known outside of the Shaker world is a short "extra" song—"Come Life, Shaker Life"—that he produced near the end of his life. A version of this song was recorded as the opening track of *Simple Gifts: Shaker Chants and Spirituals* (Joel Cohen and the Boston Camerata, 1995). Many of Bates' hymns have been featured in scholarly studies of Shaker music, but only a scant few have been included in popular recordings of Shaker music,[2] so, as a whole, Issachar Bates's remarkable creative output of songs, hymns, and poetry remains virtually unknown.

A comprehensive compilation of Issachar Bates's work would fill a substantial volume. The samples included here represent songs and poems by Bates that have not been published in other scholarly sources. Most of these songs and poems can be found in multiple Shaker manuscripts, reflecting the popularity of his work within the nineteenth-century Shaker world, although I have cited the specific source from which I have drawn the versions presented here. Because Bates's work is often variously titled by different scribes, I have chosen in many cases to use the first line in lieu of a title.

LIST OF SONGS AND HYMNS INCLUDED

Now by My Motion
The Glory of Zion
The True Spirit of Christ
The Day Star
Ye Stout Ye Hearty and Ye Strong
Salvation by the Cross of Christ in Suffering the Loss of All Things
Issachar's Retreat
Tribulation Worketh Patience
Hail the New Summer
Wake Up My Soul
Nightly Prayer By Issachar Bates Sen.
Flourishing State of Christ's Kingdom
Given By Inspiration
Quick Dance
March (1825)
March (1837)

LIST OF POEMS INCLUDED

On the First Day of the First Month
Ezekiel's Wheel or a Christmas Hymn
A Crown: A Hymn Composed on the Sufferings of Polly Bates;
    Daughter of Issachar Bates, Ohio, 1824
The Morning Pillar
The Letter Kills
A Dialogue on Soldiery and Cross Bearing in Two Parts
The Holy Way

THE SONGS

NOW BY MY MOTION[3]

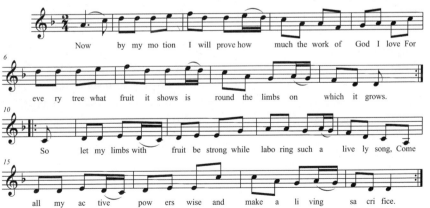

Now by my mo tion I will prove how much the work of God I love For

eve ry tree what fruit it shows is round the limbs on which it grows.

So let my limbs with fruit be strong while labo ring such a live ly song, Come

all my ac tive pow ers wise and make a li ving sa cri fice.

Stand up my soul and clear my way And give me room to dance and play
O cut me loose from every drag As Samuel hew'd the base agag.
For why should sluggish flesh control And bind my ever living soul
Such lawless bondage shall not be As God is true I will be free.

O how I love to feel releas'd From every feeling of the beast
No more to feel one poison dart Of his vile stuff about my heart
But while I'm laboring with my might This nasty beast will heave in sight
And every living step I tread I'll try to place it on his head.

I need not think of gaining much To give the floor an easy touch
Or labor in some handsome form That scarce will keep the ankles warm
For I have not so far increased That I can manage such a beast
Without my blood is neatly het[4] And my whole body flows with sweat.

Tell me no more it is not good To labor sharp and heat the blood
For this is but a vain excuse To let a fleshly nature loose
For I have proved the matter thro' That every work I find to do
Unless I do it with my might It never feels like doing right.

Now here's my faith I'll speak it plain And let my feet the sense explain
With zeal to labor and unite With every gift that comes to light.
If in back order there I'll spring If in step manner or to sing
If shuffling I will do my best To keep my union with the rest.

The reason why I sing so long And step the notes so quick and strong
Is just because that God has done What he has promised by his Son.
He's sent the everlasting Key That opens heaven where I be
This animates me while I move For this strong Key is truth and love.

Now every one that helps me sing May their sweet offerings freely bring
For here's an altar flaming hot To burn the sluggard and the sot.
So let the house be fill'd with smoke That every sluggish beast may choke
Then round the altar we will play And glorify this blessed day.

THE GLORY OF ZION[5]
Issachar Bates constructed this text using 12.11.12.11D meter, not uncommon in folk hymnody, but he adopts an unusual rhyming pattern of ABAB for the first four lines of each
stanza and CCCD for the second four lines. Such texts exhibit his creativity as a poet.

Now my song I'll be gin on the glo ry of Zi on And
tell the in quir er what makes me to sing. 'Tis be cause I have found what at
length has ap pear ed A Church on this earth where Im man uel is King.
Where He reigns in his glo ry the Queen of his plea sure the
king dom of peace he has pur chas'd for e ver, And now is the time he has
come to de li ver And they that are with him are faith ful and true.

Tho his journey was long as he once intimated
His country was far from a blood guilty whore
Yet the time being come which the Father appointed
He's come to his temple to leave it no more
And now we are built on his last revelation
Receiving the kingdom with strength and salvation
And here we have found our eternal relation
So Father and Mother for ever shall reign.

Now the old man awake from his drunken delusion
And cried out alas the deceivers are here
You old drunken Priests this is what you've been reading
I'll come like a thief I'll come like a snare
And now you are taken your house shall be shaken
For strong is the Lord by whom this was spoken
You need not to seek for a sign or a token
I'll cut you asunder and cast you away.

To arms cries the Shepherds of old bloody Zion
We'll warn all the people to flee from the sword
Ye drunkards of Ephraim your lust has deceived you
You cannot escape 'tis the sword of the Lord
And you and your flock shall be broken asunder
'Tis that mighty work which is roaring like thunder

And you and your people shall perish and wonder
And your bloody walls shall come tumbling down.

You are old in your witchcraft your bloodshed and whoredom
You always have hated the light that was new
You have kill'd the just who have strove to retain it
And made humble sinners companions for you
And now your destruction is come to perfection ·
Your old rusty creeds and your fatal election
And your carnal hopes of a flesh resurrection
Shall go with the beast, with the beast whence it came.

O come ye afflicted come out from among them
And leave all your fleshly connections behind
You must hate all the garments of this generation
If ever you mean your redemption to find
Come 'way to the Mount which our parents perfected
And there you'll find peace and be safely protected
Where thousands of souls are already collected
And sing the sweet anthems of new heavn'ly joy.

THE TRUE SPIRIT OF CHRIST[6]

In this text, Issachar Bates explores the Shaker conception of the dual-gendered god-head, along with the notion that the female "Wisdom" element of the godhead is a more recent insight revealed to the Shakers alone. He also touches upon Shaker "Christology," namely, the roles of Jesus and of Mother Ann in the redemption of humankind.

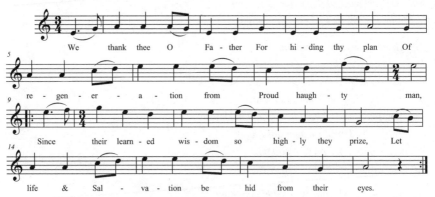

We thank thee O Fa-ther For hi-ding thy plan Of re-gen-er-a-tion from Proud haugh-ty man, Since their learn-ed wis-dom so high-ly they prize, Let life & Sal-va-tion be hid from their eyes.

We thank thee, O Father, that thou hast reveal'd,
The treasures of Wisdom thro' ages conceal'd,
To such simple babes as are open and free,
For so, righteous Father, it seem'd good to thee.

We thank thee, O Father, that judgement is here,
And at thy own house doth the sinner appear,
With open confession of all his base crimes,
We thank thee, O Father, for such blessed times.

We thank thee, O Father, that all must be try'd,
That no human creature from judgement can hide,
We thank thee that judgement with us now begins,
While millions around us are hiding their sins.

We thank thee, O Mother, our eternal Friend,
That thou with the Father didst truly descend,
And in thy sweet wisdom didst purely conceive,
The son of salvation in whom we believe.

We thank thee, O Mother, that Jesus was sent,
And that thou wast with him wherever he went,
Proclaiming salvation to all that are lost,
By full self denial and bearing the Cross.

We thank thee, O Mother, that wisdom is thine,
That thou hast completed thy witty design,
That of male & female in thy prudent plan,
Of twain thou hast formed one perfect new man.

We thank thee, O Father and Mother of man,
We thank thee, Lord Jesus and good Mother Ann,
We thank the whole order consisting of four,
To these we'll sing praises in one evermore.

THE DAY STAR[7]

Issachar Bates probably wrote this "occasional song" in the 1810s or 1820s, possibly at the Busro, Indiana, settlement. The words suggest that it was used to dedicate a newly completed building, a logical assumption considering this was a period of rapid construction throughout the Shaker West. The title echoes a term used in the New Testament (2 Peter 1:19), which refers to Christians' internal realization of Christ's presence.

The day star is ris ing the morn ing is come,So let all cre a tion now wel come the sun.

He's come in his glo ry the na tions to bless, We thank thee, kind hea ven for this day of rest.

Our souls have been waiting for ages that's past,
For thy righteous kingdom and it's come at last:
Altho' our fore Fathers from thee did revolt,
Yet now loving Savior thy horn we'll exalt.

In songs of Thanksgiving thy name we will praise,
For what thou art doing in these latter days;
The kingdom of darkness has now got a shock,
And Zion is built on a permanent rock.

Each part of this building is handsomely laid
The great architecture of Zion hath said;
Her beauty's increasing her glory is come,
Her charms so delightful our spirits are one.

Here stands that great City for which we have prayed,
Her walls they are strong and delightfully made,
Each stone is well hewn by a sharp-edged tool,
And laid in this building according to rule

No City on earth is so clear and so bright
Her lamps are still burning by day and by night
The meek of the earth in her streets may be found,
Her peace like a river shall always abound.

Thy pastures O Zion delightfully green!
Among the gay flowers thy flocks may be seen —
In raptures transporting opposed to all strife,
Thy meadows all smell of the balsam of life.

This hill of salvation's designed for the wise,
Whose eyes are still fix on the heavenly prize;
Come on fellow travelers let's hasten our pace,
And never look back till we've ended our race.

Come into my chamber ye weary and rest,
And at this great banquet I'll make you a guest,
I'll feed you on wisdom I'll lead you in love,
And swiftly conduct you to Zion above.

YE STOUT YE HEARTY AND YE STRONG[8]

Issachar Bates may have directed this short one-verse song at young male converts
who were reluctant to take part in dancing. It probably dates from the late 1810s while
Issachar was at Busro, Indiana.

Ye stout ye hear ty and ye strong Come stir your selves and move a long Why will you hang u pon the song Like weights of hea vy met tle. If you've been faith ful through the day And done your du ty eve ry way Now is your time to get your pay More power a gainst the de vil.

SALVATION BY THE CROSS OF CHRIST IN
SUFFERING THE LOSS OF ALL THINGS[9]

This song is unusual in many respects. It takes the form of a ballad, an uncommon genre in Shaker music, recounting the life experiences of both Jesus and Ann Lee. Prodigiously long even by early Shaker standards, by which twenty-stanza hymns were normal, twenty-six of this ballad's twenty-seven stanzas carry the refrain "And we'll sing the matter thro." The twenty-seventh brings closure to the story with "And we've sung the matter thro." After relating Jesus' life and death, the ballad proceeds to Ann Lee's life in England, including details about her work as a textile laborer and her residence on Toad Lane (stanza 19). Possibly it dates to shortly after 1805, when the missionaries had solicited details of Ann Lee's life to use in their work with converts.[10] Likely this ballad would have been sung alone by Issachar to an audience of listeners. It highlights how important songs and hymns were for inculcating "young believers" in the complexities of Shaker theology and history. Like other didactic hymns by Issachar, this one ends on a note of sarcastic defiance, a reflection of the abrasive preaching demeanor for which he was so well known. Possibly because of its unusual length and poetic complexity, the ballad does not survive in many sources. Significantly, the version here was found and transcribed from a copy of Issachar Bates's autobiography produced by a scribe in the Second Order of the New Lebanon Church Family, where Issachar lived his final years, suggesting that the writer may have found it among his effects or perhaps learned both the words and tune directly from him.

Let those ga-ther near me, Who're friends to the cross, I'll sing if you'll hear me, The suf - fer - ings and loss, That our El - der Bro - ther, In ang - guish went thro', And our Bles-sed Mo - ther, What she suf-fer'd too, And we'll sing the mat-ter thro'.

2nd

'Twas not fear of dying That caused them to sigh
Nor was their strange crying For fear they should die,
But sin on them falling, Constrained them to bleed
For their daily calling, Was dying indeed
And we'll sing the matter thro.

3rd

While Jesus was subject, To his earthly kin
His trade being an object, The world was his friend
By all his employers, His genius was known
And Doctors & Lawyers, Could let him alone
And we'll sing the matter thro.

4th

In Nazareth residing In favour he stands
And no way providing to strengthen his hands
The Priesthood concluded He'd do them no ill
Tho' somewhat deluded, He's harmless and still
And we'll sing the matter thro.

5th

But when he'd completed That order of life
Instead of being seated And choosing a wife
A full separation Forever takes place
He denies all relation, To the fallen race
And we'll sing the matter thro.

6th

In union with heaven He takes up his cross
And soon he was driven To feel his deep loss,
The power of lost nature, Encompass'd him round

He was the first creature Such feelings had found
And we'll sing the matter thro.

7th
O who is sufficient To open his loss
Not one that's deficient In bearing his cross
But faithful crossbearers Can feel every breath
That with him they're sharers In sufferings and death
And we'll sing the matter thro.

8th
He bore the same nature That all others had
But being a flesh-hater They said he was mad,
His whole conversation His life and his way
Was all a vexation To those in that day
And we'll sing the matter thro.

9th
A few honest creatures Came out in that day
Denied their lost natures And walked the same way
And with him were hated In total disgrace
But truly translated From this fallen race
And we'll sing the matter thro.

10th
The basest behavior That ever took place
Was charg'd on the Savior By this fallen race
Tho' he did no evil And they lived in sin
Yet he was the Devil And they honest men
And we'll sing the matter thro.

11th
He was so pestiferious In breaking their peace
His plan so mysterious To stop its increase
Blasphemy & treason Were proved at a breath
And without law or reason They put him to death
And we'll sing the matter thro.

12th
But 'twas not yet ended the work was not thro'
The unction descended In his faithful few
Sedition still spreading All over the land
The Nations still dreading His pestilent band
And we'll sing the matter thro.

13th

With sorrow and trouble They made their complaints
Their forces they double And wore out the saints
The Father's desceased At their bloody hands
And falsehood increased All over the land
And we'll sing the matter thro.

14th

When crossbearing ceased They fix'd a new birth
And converts increased All over the Earth
They fix that base dreamer Whose life they despise
As their great Redeemer Beyond the blue skies
And we'll sing the matter thro.

15th

Now sins are forgiven Tho' they in them lie
And they'll go to heaven As soon as they die
Their fathers kill'd Jesus And they drink his blood
And this fully pleases An angry God
And we'll sing the matter thro.

16th

Thro' twelve gloomy centuries According to John
Religion inventors With fury went on
In Christ's name employing Their swords & their pens
And madly destroying All true godly men
And we'll sing the matter thro.

17th

The time of this slaughter Being come to an end
Then hearken O daughter Was God's last command
The unction descended In Mother to dwell
And Michael contended and overcame hell
And we'll sing the matter thro.

18th

But see the wise Devil Now he is cast out
Tho' he's done in heaven The Earth is his rout
He stirs up the Nations And fills them with rage
Here's a witch for salvation, Against her engage —
And we'll sing the matter thro.

19th

While Mother remained In calling of life
Her name was unstained A decent young wife

She'd one branch of hatting In Manchester then
And wrought at fur cutting And lived in Toad Land
And we'll sing the matter thro.

20th
But when she was wedded To Truth from on high
And went forth to spread it To those who were nigh
Proclaiming salvation Completely from sin
This shook the foundation That Satan dwells in
And we'll sing the matter thro.

21st
The power she received Could not be withstood
Sound reason believed 'Twas surely from God
But their first evasion Was craftily wrought
To blast her reputation And set her at nought
And we'll sing the matter thro.

22nd
Now she whose behavior Was courteous before
Must be like her Savior And call'd her his whore
The basest lewd woman That ever was seen
No act unbecoming But what she was in
And we'll sing the matter thro.

23rd
Their slander diffused All proving a sham
Then how they abused That innocent Lamb
They drove her to prison With clubs & with stones
And bruis'd without reason Her flesh to her bones
And we'll sing the matter thro.

24th
Her life was surrounded As Jesus's was
With threat'nings & woundings All for the same cause
All crimes that's committed By this fallen race
On these two were fitted To bear the disgrace
And we'll sing the matter thro.

25th
If Father and Mother Are equally base
Then Sister & Brother Born of the same race
Must surely be number'd Among the same club
Whose Father & Mother Are call'd Belzabub
And we'll sing the matter thro.

26th

Now who in high station Feels able to come
And own such relation To gain the kingdom
And sacrifice pleasure And honor and life
With all earthly treasure, E'en husband & wife
And we'll sing the matter thro.

27th

Well this is our calling Dear brethren & friends
If this is too galling Then die in your sins
'Twill be made no sweeter It has been tried twice
It can't come no cheaper 'Tis the stated price
And we've sung the matter thro.

ISSACHAR'S RETREAT[11]

This short song uses a tune titled "Pretty Cupid" in a 1777 New England fife manual.
Issachar Bates sang the tune to his companions as he departed the West for the last time
in 1835. He wrote the words later: "I told sister Eunice Bedle . . . I would send her some
words to it, if I should live to get thro. So she learned it, and I sent her the words."[12]
Shaker manuscripts record it using an irregular time signature pattern that seems puz-
zlingly awkward to modern eyes (and likely an alteration from the form that Issachar
would have played on the fife), though such irregularities are fairly common in Shaker
hymnody. In addition to being singular for demonstrating Issachar's clear mental grasp
of music learned some sixty years earlier, it is also highly unusual in another respect.
Shaker songs and poetry texts overwhelmingly take religious themes. This one does not.
Rather, it is a fanciful personal reflection on "time."

So in all my notions tossing up and down,
Puffed with various notions, how I'll win the crown.
Time will still be fleeting, rifles all my plans;
   I am sick of fleeting, let my days be few,
I'll in my last retreating, bid old time adieu.

TRIBULATION WORKETH PATIENCE[13]

Issachar Bates wrote this song soon after returning to New Lebanon in 1835. It is copied in numerous manuscripts, including a hymn book compiled by Hannah Agnew, a young woman from White Water, Ohio, who in 1836 was brought east to live in the New Lebanon Second Order, where Issachar also resided. Several manuscripts indicate they shared a fond relationship. In Hannah Agnew's version, she annotates the hymn with the phrase, "Issachar Bates' worst time, New Lebanon 1835" suggesting her awareness that the song was an expression of his depression upon returning to the East.[14]

And if my suffering hours increase, And sleep forsake my eyes
I'll charge my soul to hold her peace, For murmuring I despise.
Yet Lord in mercy give me strength, To bear this heavy load
That I may dwell with those at length, Who trod this suffering road.

If I with them may find a lot, In mansions where they dwell
I'll gladly leave this dirty spot, And bid the dust farewell
For earth with all her glittering hue, Is but corrupting stuff
To all her sweets I'll bid adieu, I've used them long enough.

HAIL THE NEW SUMMER[15]

Other songs that Issachar Bates wrote after returning to New Lebanon reflect a far more positive frame of mind. This hymn is dated 1835 and probably reflects Issachar's relief at the end of his first summer back at New Lebanon, which was marked by severe thunderstorms.

O God of fore-bear-ance and pit-ty How plea-sant the at-mos-phere feels It makes ev'-ry mus-cle feel pret-ty It warms the cold an-kles and heels. O heels. We've passed the cold drea-ry wet sum-mer Which end-ed just as it be-gan Now hail the right wel-come new-com-er We're glad the old sum-mer is done. We've done.

We thank thee for these pleasant feelings,
While we with weak nature condole;
It shows us thy merciful dealings;
But this is not food to the soul.
We're waiting for something more blessed,
Since thou hast thy kingdom begun,
Altho' our tried souls are oppressed,
We pray that thy will may be done.

Lord Jesus, we long in the spirit
That the final harvest foretold,
May come; that our souls may inherit
A summer that never'll wax cold.
Lord may we now humbly entreat thee,
To hasten thy work to the end,
And we will make ready to meet thee,
In mercy or judgement. Amen.

WAKE UP MY SOUL AND MOVE IN EARNEST[16]
This song likely dates from Issachar Bates's final years at New Lebanon, 1835–1837. It is copied in at least three New Lebanon songbooks, each with attribution to Issachar. The only western hymn book found to contain it is a Watervliet, Ohio, text-only hymn manuscript begun by Moses Eastwood in 1837, suggesting it was learned in the West after Issachar's 1835 departure. Isaac Newton Youngs quoted from it at Issachar's funeral, using it to illustrate Issachar's resilience in overcoming the distress of his forced return to New Lebanon: "He has acted the manly part . . . has not sunk under discouragement nor slackened his pace in running for the prize, but went as a late verse of his says, 'Straight ahead you'll soon be there.'"[17]

Wake up my soul and move in ear-nest You was form'd for end-less day

Soon from flesh you'll be un-har-ness'd Soon you'll burst this clog of clay.

Wide a-wake, Wide a-wake, Wide a-wake and view your kin-dred, Safe in yon-der mansions where

Keep the step, Keep the step, Keep the step and don't be hin-der'd Straight a-head you'll soon be there.

NIGHTLY PRAYER BY ISSACHAR BATES SEN.[18]

Many Shaker music manuscripts, both eastern and western, record this hymn as written by Issachar Bates in 1836 or early 1837, with the request that it be sung at his funeral. Most manuscripts record an entirely different tune in the key of C-major. A version reflecting the major-key tune was published by Roger Hall (2004).[19] However, the earliest known recording of the tune was by Seth Youngs Wells, who incorporated it into the letter he wrote to Mathew Houston and Isaac N. Houston in April 1837 reporting Issachar's death and also that Issachar had sung the hymn several times at union meetings before his death. That is the tune presented here. Because it was set down so soon after Issachar's funeral by his close friend and confidant, it likely is Issachar's own tune and the version actually sung at his funeral.

Al-migh - ty Sa - vior, hear my pray'r, O heal my soul with sor-row torn!

A wound-ed spi - rit who can bear? Yet by thy help it can be borne.

Give me, O Lord, repenting power,
To crush my haughty nature low,
To make me watchful ev'ry hour,
And guard my steps where e'er I go.

Thy mercy Lord from time to time,
Has reached my soul when sore oppress'd.
Thou didst pass by my ev'ry crime,
I with forgiving love was blest.

Once more kind Savior condescend,
To satiate this soul of mine,

And from henceforth till time shall end,
This soul forever shall be thine.

Thou hast declar'd all souls were thine,
And I'll confirm thy righteous claim,
And for a proof I'll give up mine,
In honor of thy sacred name.

So I'll relinquish all demands,
For any good I've ever done:
I'll throw my soul into thy hands,
And trust thy mercy, that alone.

THE FLOURISHING STATE OF CHRIST'S KINGDOM[20]

"Anthems," lengthy non-strophic scripture-based texts set to meandering melodies, were a popular genre among New England choristers of the late eighteenth century. They were produced by both eastern and western Shakers in great abundance (albeit, seldom in harmony), remaining popular among Shakers until the mid-nineteenth century, long after they had fallen out of fashion among mainstream Americans. Issachar Bates produced many anthems, including this one, which probably dates to around 1810.

He will come and save you. Then the eyes of the blind will be o - pen'd and the
ears of the deaf will be un - stopp'd Then shall the lame man leap as a hart
and the tongue of the dumb shall sing. For in the wil-der-ness shall waters break out and
streams in the de - sert. And an high-way shall be there and a way and it shall be
call - ed the way of ho - li - ness The un - clean shall not pass o - ver it.
But the re-deem'd shall walk there And the ran-som'd of the Lord shall re - turn and
come to Zi-on with songs and e - ver las-ting joy u - pon their heads They shall obtain joy and glad - ness and sor - row and sigh - ing shall flee a - way.

GIVEN BY INSPIRATION

This short wordless song is recorded in several manuscripts as having been sung by
Issachar Bates in a spontaneous moment of inspiration during the arduous wintertime
journey to Busro in January 1809. According to a manuscript annotation, this tune was
sung and danced by the trio when they reached the top of a snowy hill in the southern
Indiana wilderness, which allowed them to regain their bearings after having been lost:
"[T]hey . . . travelled till they reached the summit of a hill; at which place they halted,
and Br Issachar received and sung the above tune. And they united in the dance, thank-
ing God in their hearts."[21] Stylistically, it resembles a typical fife or fiddle tune of the
period.

Wordless tunes intended for various dancing styles were produced by the hundreds all over the Shaker world. Despite their abundance, it is common to see individual tunes recopied painstakingly in numerous manuscripts, with the person who originated the tune (or often the location from which it originated) carefully recorded. Issachar Bates produced a multitude of such tunes, such as these three. Of the two identified as "Marches," one dates from 1825 and the other from 1837. Both strongly resemble fife tunes.

QUICK DANCE[22]

MARCH (1825)[23]

MARCH (1837)[24]

THE POEMS

Issachar Bates's poetry is scattered across virtually countless manuscripts, with many recorded in multiple places. He wrote poetry for many specific occasions. The examples presented here include a ballad poem commemorating the 1805 missionary journey, a Christmas poem, and a tribute to his deceased daughter Polly. I have also included several of Issachar's more distinctive spiritual poems that have not been published to date.

ON THE FIRST DAY OF THE FIRST MONTH[25]

On the first day of the first month in eighteen hundred five
The word of God came unto us, that which is alive
Saying arise my chosen messengers go to the western land
Where I've prepared a people by my almighty hand.

The breakers are gone before you my wonders to impart
The spirit of Elisha I have sent to turn the heart
But their rebellious nature will trifle with my love
Therefore be wise as serpents and harmless as a Dove.

You'll find a little number whose heart has been sincere
I've kept a just memorial of their unfeigned prayers.
Their cries came up before me, Lord let thy kingdom come
And now behold I send you to lead my people home.

But there are thousands of them a-feigning the same cry
And shouting singing praying, Lord bring thy kingdom nigh
But by my holy nature, these hypocrites I swear
With all their prayers and shouting shall never enter there.

You and your testimony these scoffers will despise
And view you as deceivers with their adulterous eyes
But fear ye not their terror, but for the truth contend
And soon you shall confound them. I am with you till the end.

We tarried not to reason, but straight took our own way
Let God and the good Angels bear record of that day
In the cold and tedious winter, through water hail and snow
Like pilgrims took our journey from all our friends below.

Led out like faithful Abraham not knowing where we went
But by unerring wisdom a western course we bent
The God of Abram leading us by his unerring hand
On the third month arrived unto the favored land.

Our suffering on our journey a thousand miles and more
Appeared not worth naming to what was still before
A high and lofty people a-riding on the sky
Who on us poor pilgrims looked down with haughty eye.

We viewed the pow'r and wonders there manifest abroad
God working with the people and they with idol gods
Saying climb ye up to heaven, we'll soon be free from sin
By singing shouting praying, while full of lust within.

The Holy ghost forbade us to tarry in that land
But cross the great Ohio before you make a stand
Go to the blest Miami and shortly you shall prove
That I've prepared a people to welcome you in love.

In confidence and patience with weary limbs we went
The spirit of Elijah we found whom God had sent
And there behold we found it when on the spot we came
In one whom God had chosen and Malcolm was his name.

In love he did receive us and told us all his heart
And told how wicked Esau was reigning in that part
Was killing all the preachers and digging altars down
And he alone esteemed as one in darkness bound.

We shortly did inform him that we were sent of God
And came to bring salvation to all the land abroad
That thousands were reserved and he without control
Should shortly see the travel of his afflicted soul.

He and his house believed and brought their deeds to light
Likewise their blessed leader good Richard saw it right
And wisely did maintain it that he who was to come
Had now made his appearance and was received by some.

The gospel of the kingdoms we then did testify
And all the honest hearted the truth could not deny
Some cried with loud Hosannas, the blessed day is come
While others cried, this doctrine has struck the people dumb.

The country was alarmed and in a great surprise
They came upon Mount Carmel to offer sacrifice
And cried what mad delusion, This fire is not good
It does our fire extinguish the altar and the wood.

They are liars! cried the preacher and with a doleful yell
Wolves, liars, and false prophets just from the pit of hell
They've killed all our religion, away with such damn dogs
Go home to your own country, you are the poisonous frogs.

But now we leave the scoffers and speak no more of them
For there unto we're called to suffer pain and shame
But we'll admire the goodness and kindness of our God
Who has sent forth salvation and spread it all abroad.

The everlasting gospel has got a passage through
'Tis planted in Ohio and in Kentucky too
And earth and hell may rage in vain, its course it will pursue
And burn up the old heaven, and earth and hell subdue.

EZEKIEL'S WHEEL OR A CHRISTMAS HYMN[26]
This text exhibits an exceptionally creative and unusual pattern of meter and rhyme.
It also evokes a strong visual picture of the circle dance adopted by the Shakers in the
early 1820s, as reflected in Richard McNemar's written description of 1824,[27] and in
a later published lithograph (figure 12.2). It may well have been intended for singing,
but no tune has been discovered.

   Hosana to the King of Kings
   Whose praise the highest Angel sings
   His birth immortal treasure brings
   And opens up eternal things
His holy birth, Has blest the earth, With joy and mirth,
   And shows us all our duty now.

   In mem'ry of his birth we stand
   United in a loving band
   And only wait the life command
   To see the motion of the hand.
And then we'll play, And spend the day, In any way
   That will display our beauty now.

   Come on we'll move in rank and file
   And worship God in simple style,
   And tread the circle round awhile
   Till all the hosts of heaven smile
To see our zeal, What life we feel, In 'Zekiel's wheel.
   With all the cogs in motion now.

We'll worship God with hands and feet
And every step with joy repeat
That we on Christmas day can meet
And keep our order so complete
That God may see, How glad we be, That we are free
And own our sweet devotion now.

A CROWN: A HYMN COMPOSED ON THE SUFFERINGS OF POLLY BATES; DAUGHTER OF ISSACHAR BATES, OHIO, 1824[28]

Composed a few months after Polly Bates's death and found in only a few manuscripts (each time meticulously dated 1824, and one copied by Issachar Jr.), this poem reflects the grief that Issachar continued to harbor. At first glance, the text appears to address the departed Polly, offering sentiments ennobling her suffering, which Issachar might have longed to share with her directly. But a closer reading suggests another interpretation, namely, that it could have been directed at a living woman who was also grieving for Polly. I believe that Issachar may have been addressing his wife Lovina in this poem, using verse to express his empathy and shared grief, as well as his continued concern for Lovina's emotional well-being (something he had also done several times in letters and postscripts). Shaker culture disapproved of emotional expressions among spouses, so for Issachar to address Lovina openly in a letter to share condolences over Polly's death would have been awkward or impossible. Issachar's skill as a poet would have allowed him to compose an intentionally ambiguous verse, filled with expressions appropriate for either Polly's spirit or for Lovina. Regardless of who the poem addresses, it succeeds in conveying a range of complex emotions with protective ambiguity.

Good sister in thy hour of grief,
The precious Gospel gives relief;
The more we suffer till we die,
The stronger is our gospel tie.

All of the feelings I possess
Now meekly bow and love and bless
Thy faithful soul in mortal clay;
For which I often strive to pray.

Good Angels hover round thee bright
With softest blessings day and night
To guard thy lamb like spirit home
When thou hast truly over come.

Let patience thy distress embrace
It will prepare thee for thy place
Soon will thy worthy soul thro love
Be glorified in bliss above.

Thy faithful cross a crown will gain
Yea, for thy suff'rings then will reign
Sweet pleasures will thy pains destroy
And sorrow cease for endless joy.

So we will patiently endure
All things below, for to secure
A rest in heaven evermore
Beyond the troubles of this shore.

THE MORNING PILLAR[29]

Several elements about this poem deserve mention. It takes its theme from the story
of the Israelites' exodus from Egypt, which set off a forty-year period of wandering in
the desert, with moving "camping places" following a "pillar" of fire and cloud, day and
night. Clearly, Issachar Bates identified with aspects of the story. As a soldier in the
Revolution, he had participated in the rapid set-up of "flying camps." In Issachar's adult
life, "camps" were a familiar fixture, whether the nighttime outdoor encampments that
he improvised alone or with companions during his countless journeys or the revival
"camp" settings where rough preaching stands were fashioned to serve enthusiastic
crowds seeking spiritual renewal. Near the end of the poem, he notes that "Like the
Jews I've been a rover," revealing that he considers his mobility to be one of his defining
features. The poem's use of a repeating chorus suggests it was probably sung, but no tune
has been found.

1st
Sinners hate the true-believer
Moving still from place to place
Who will follow such deceivers
Who this system will embrace
Chorus
O the bright mysterious Pillar
When it moves along the way
When the morning trump is sounded
Then farewell to all who stay.

2nd
Israel started from Rameses
Then to Canaan they go on
But we find their camping places
Were no less than forty one — Chorus

3rd
Passing thro the land of Egypt
All their camps were only three

Then they left the coasts of Pharaoh
Then from bondage they were free — Chorus

4th
Marah gave them bitter waters
Then to Elim they ascend
There they found twelve living fountains
And Palm trees three score and ten — Chorus

5th
Three more camps were formed backward
Many corpses there did stink
Then they journeyed to Rephidim
And found nothing there to drink — Chorus

6th
Next they move to Sina's borders
Where they get the fiery law,
Graves of lust come next in order
Called Kebroth Hattavah — Chorus

7th
As they journeyed to Mount Pisgah
Seven camps were on their way
Then they left their captain Moses
There he dropped his house of clay — Chorus

8th
Their last move was over Jordan
Then they entered into rest
There they found the Promised Garden
There with plenty they were blessed — Chorus

9th
Like the Jews I've been a rover
Never long upon a stand
Until Jordan I passed over
And obtained the Promis'd Land.
Final Chorus
Blessed Pillar keep your station
Faithful Elder give the sign
O the final separation
Egypt now is left behind.

THE LETTER KILLS[30]

In this interesting poem, Issachar Bates seems to be discounting the merits of erudition. Considering that his closest Shaker companions were among the most erudite and learned men in the Shaker world, one wonders if he wrote the poem in a moment of feeling intellectually inferior. One also wonders if his learned friends such as Richard McNemar or Benjamin Seth Youngs would have found this poem insulting.

Still learning learning is the cry!
Now I've got learning, who but I?
I've learned the arts of Earth & hell
And think & think I'm doing well
You'll think & think & think again
But never think the state you're in
Take one degree in Wisdom's school
Then think you are a puffy fool.

The letter kills, this you may read
Still in the letters you'll proceed
And while you plague your restless head
Your stupid soul is worse than dead
Give me thy spirit, God of power
Then while they build the babel tower
I'll hate all books of party names
And gladly see them all in flames

A DIALOGUE ON SOLDIERY AND CROSS BEARING IN TWO PARTS[31]

This poem takes the form of a dialogue, a common technique found in early Shaker hymns and poetry by Issachar Bates as well as other poets. One source notes that this was composed by Issachar in 1817 at Busro, Indiana. Clearly the poem reflects Issachar's intimate familiarity with the soldier's life and his ability to employ martial metaphors for spiritual effect. A close reading effectively illuminates the many dilemmas that western Shaker leaders, at Busro and elsewhere, were confronting as the movement matured in the West, offering a clear window into the perspectives of believers who balked at various aspects of Shaker gospel order. In fact, it stands as one of the most succinct and appealing extant explorations of those problems and therefore warrants examination.

1.   Q.   What times fellow soldiers you seem quite enraged
                Pray tell me old messmate what all this is for
                You had your own choice for the term you engaged
                You entered your name to be during the war.

        A.   I know I enlisted and that to my sorrow
                But I was quite ign'rant of what it was for

And now I have thoughts of deserting tomorrow
For I cannot bear to be during the war.

2.   Q.   Do you not remember in times of recruiting
We both turned out without mention of years
Received our bounty, what drinking and shouting
Hurray for ourselves we are free volunteers.

       A.   All that I remember and I was well suited
My bounty went free at the grog shop and bar
But when a full quota of troops were recruited
Away I must march to be during the war.

3.   Q.   You cannot plead ign'rance, it plainly was told us
When we took our bounty and what it was for
Our Officers stated this money would hold us
As soldiers forever or during the war.

       A.   All that I acknowledge but they have misused me
They've ordered me 'round like a common Jack Tor[32]
And let the proud sargeants and corporals abuse me
Till I have no heart to be during the war.

4.   Q.   No mortals on earth ever treated men better
Than our good commanders have used us thus far
And if they appoint me their corporal or waiter
I mean to stick by them all during the war.

       A.   Well I am too proud to be instantly jogging
When ordered on guard or fatigue or elsewhere
And if I refuse I am sure of a flogging
And this makes me hate to be during the war.

5.   Q.   The life of a soldier consists of subjection
To all his superiors wherever they are
And then he is sure of their aid and protection
For him there's no flogging not during the war.

       A.   But when I am subject my clothing and rations
Are often kept from me while others can draw
And some can get furloughs to see their relations
But I'm kept in bondage enduring the war.

6.   Q.   O quit your complaining 'bout clothing and rations
You've shared with the rest and your sense I abhor
A soldier who cavils 'bout clothing, relations
A free volunteer 'listed during the war.

A.   But I cannot stand it, it's to be kept under
     In hottest of battles I must not withdraw
     When we've took the spoils I've no share of the plunder
     Nor no private property during the war.

7.   CONCLUSION   Our government clothes us and feeds and equips us
     And this is the whole we have any use for
     Tho' they keep the plunder it does not eclipse us
     We've no use for property during the war.

     So stick to your duty and quit your mean story
     And let our commander know who you are for
     And then in bright laurels of vict'ry and glory
     Like heroes we'll shine at the end of the war.

PART SECOND ON CROSS-BEARING

1.   Q.   What grinds you my brother since you have impeached
          Pray tell me what makes you so dry and moross
          You had your free choice when the gospel was preached
          To die in your sins or to take up your cross.

     A.   I know I believed and made my confession
          But I was quite ign'rant in counting the cost
          And now I have thoughts to renounce my profession
          For I have gain'd nothing by bearing my cross.

2.   Q.   You have not forgotten the times of our doubting
          We open'd our minds and dispel'd all our fears
          Receiv'd the good spirit, what dancing and shouting,
          O glory to Jesus, we're free volunteers.

     A.   All that I remember, 'twas joy beyond measure
          I thought I was wholly redeem'd from my loss
          But when some began to give up their whole treasure
          Then I must move forward and bear a full cross.

3.   Q.   This could not be ign'rance, 'twas pointedly told us
          When we heard the gospel the price it would cost
          Our Elders declared the gospel they brought us
          Would fit us for destruction or save by the cross.

     A.   I know what they told us but they have perplext me
          From station to station I'm constantly lost
          They set the trustees and the deacons to vex me
          Till I have no feelings to bear such a cross.

4.   Q.   Could angels or men ever use more forbearance
          Than our loving Elders who feel for our loss
          I mean to submit like a child to its parents
          And love and obey them by bearing my cross.

     A.   Well I'm too important to show such subjection
          Yet when I refuse I am full of remorse
          And this fills the people and me with suspicion
          That I have no notion of bearing my cross.

5.   Q.   What folly to fret about clothes and relations
          Such childish excuses betokens your loss
          For what you call bondage I count my salvation
          I care not how tight I am nailed to the cross.

     A.   I gave up my int'rest and what could come tighter
          I work like a slave tho my labor is lost
          If I could own something 'twould make it some lighter
          But I must claim nothing but faith and the cross.

6.   Q.   Our order supports us with food and with raiment
          And all other plunder I count it as dross
          Since we have no call to make contracts or payments
          We've no other burden but bearing our cross.

     A.   To be reconciled, deny your own pleasures
          And count all behind us as dung and as dross
          Then we shall be bless'd with an immortal treasure
          And a righteous crown at the end of the cross.

THE HOLY WAY[33]

This poem is recorded by Alonzo Hollister in a book of assorted writings he compiled
in 1908. Hollister had copied the poem "from memory" but later discovered that he had
placed many lines out of order, so penned a series of corrections in the margins. The fact
that a poem of Issachar Bates was being copied from memory by a Shaker nearly a full
century after Bates wrote it is powerful testimony to his enduring influence on Shaker
culture.

The way I go full well I know Will take the life of pleasure,
'Twill surely bind the carnal mind And open hidden treasure
This holy way as plain as day By sin cannot be trodden
It will exclude the filthy brood Of Egypt, Rome & Sodom.

If I should run I am undone, I can't escape the battle
I'll bear my cross & burn the dross, Altho the flesh should prattle

In vain should I mount up on high My wicked works to cover
The hand of God that holds the rod Will knock my platform over.

So there will be no way for me, But just to stand & take it —
And drink the cup of sorrow up Just as my works shall make it.
Altho in pain I'll not complain,'Tis just & right & clever,
That God should kill my cursed will And reign in me forever.

NOTES

1. In his monumental work *The Shaker Spiritual,* musicologist Daniel Patterson authoritatively categorized Shaker music into defined genres: solemn songs, laboring songs, ballads, hymns, extra songs, occasional songs, anthems, and gift songs. See Patterson (1979), v–vi.

2. Some of Bates's songs and hymns can be found in Harold E. Cook, *Shaker Music: A Manifestation of American Folk Culture* (Lewisburg, A.: Bucknell University Press, 1973); Patterson (1979); Hall (2004); Goodwillie and Crosthwaite (2009); Medlicott (2011), 'Partake a Little Morsel'; Medlicott and Goodwillie (2013).

3. Item 361, DLCMs, 76.

4. "Het" is used here as a colloquial form of "heated."

5. OClWHi IX B SM 397, 53.

6. OClWHi IX B SM 168, 283.

7. Item 361, DLCMs, 77.

8. Item 361, DLCMs, 380.

9. AIB-NOcaS, 152–160.

10. David Darrow to New Lebanon Ministry, 19 March 1806, OClWHi IV B 66.

11. AIB-KyBgW-K, 111.

12. AIB-KyBgW-K, 99.

13. OClWHi IX B SM 139, 148–49.

14. OClWHi IX B SM 168, 322.

15. OClWHi IX B SM 114, 99–100.

16. OClWHi IX B SM 386, 190.

17. AIB-DLCMs-161, 230.

18. Seth Wells to Mathew Houston, 10 April 1837, Item 247, DLCMs.

19. The major-key version can be found in OClWHi IX B SM 198, 4.

20. OClWHi IX B SM 174, 27–31.

21. DLCM, 2131.S4E5, 50.

22. OClWHi IX B SM 396, 1.

23. OClWHi IX B SM 314, 6.

24. OClWHi IX B SM 51.

25. AIB-ODa, 113–17. This manuscript includes the annotation, "I will hear add another poem written by Issachar Bates on the occasion of his first journey into the West with the first three messengers."

26. OClWHi VI B 54.

27. McNemar to Wells, 23 March 1824, OClWHi IV A 70.

28. OClWHi IX B SM 397, 39.

29. AIB-NOcaS, 178–80.

30. OClWHi IX B SM 344, AIB-NOcaS

31. AIB-ODa, 108. AIB-DCLMs-350d notes that it was composed in 1817 at West Union.

32. "Jack Tor" appears to be a derogatory reference to "Tories" and a reminder that Issachar's Revolutionary War experience informed this composition.

33. OClWHi X B 31, "Poems, reminiscences, and other writings by Alonzo Hollister."

APPENDIX 3 SONGS BY ISSACHAR BATES'S CHILDREN

Shaker music manuscripts reflect numerous songs attributed to Issachar Bates's many family members. Four of the Bates children — Polly, Issachar Jr., Sarah, and Betsy — were all relatively prolific songwriters. Polly and Issachar Jr. were both known for their singing and songwriting at Watervliet, New York, and Sarah was among the leading singers in the New Lebanon Church Family for several decades. Through her role as ministry eldress, Betsy Bates influenced a generation of Shakers with her many pious spiritual songs. None of the Bates children exhibited the same poetic gift as their father, however. Instead of hymns with long poetic texts, the Bates children tended to produce songs in other genres: "extra" songs, wordless laboring songs, anthems, gift songs, and occasional songs.

SLOW MARCH
(Polly Bates, circa 1820)[1]

REMEMBER LORD
(Issachar Bates Jr., 1820)[2]
Written in shape-note notation, this song has been misidentified as the work of Issachar Bates Sr. However, closer study shows Issachar Jr. to be the likely composer. It is addressed to Isaac Newton Youngs, a friend of Issachar Jr., and the handwriting of the accompanying note matches that of Issachar Jr. Finally, the note is signed "Little Issachar," a known nickname used by Issachar Jr. The song is recorded on a five-line staff using shape-note notation in the key of G major, unusual for Shaker practice, which usually transposes major key songs to the key of C for ease of notation.

Re mem ber Lord thy faith ful chil dren Who have kept thy ho ly way, O do pro tect and com fort them, On their jour ney night and day. When they're tried in ev' ry quart er, When they feel thy scour ging rod, O then ap pear for their sal va tion O help them keep the way of God.

SHUFFLE
(Sarah Bates, 1820)[3]

TRUE OBEDIENCE
(Sarah Bates, 1827)[4]

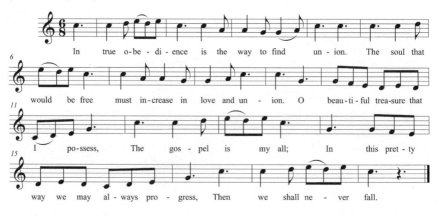

In true o-be-di-ence is the way to find un-ion. The soul that would be free must in-crease in love and un-ion. O beau-ti-ful trea-sure that I po-ssess, The gos-pel is my all; In this pret-ty way we may al-ways pro-gress, Then we shall ne-ver fall.

ANTHEM TUNE
(Sarah Bates)[5]

BEAUTIFUL WORSHIP
(Betsy Bates, 1828)[6]

O the beau - ty, see the beau-ty, beau-ti-ful wor-ship. Glo - ry to God, Glo - ry to Christ, Glo - ry to Mo-ther Ann, For this beau - ti - ful Go - spel.

MY SOUL REJOICES
(Betsy Bates, 1827)[7]

O My soul re - joi - ces, yea my soul re - joi - ces To be set free from the bands of Sa - tan.

TRUE BELIEVER'S HEAVEN
(Betsy Bates)[8]

O my El-ders, O my El-ders, You look like the hea-vens,
you act like the hea-vens, you are the hea-vens! Where
would be my hea-ven, if I was not with you, I
should have no hea-ven, if I could not see you.

QUICK SONG
(Betsy Bates, 1822)[9]

SHUFFLE
(Betsy Bates, October 1822)[10]

HOME WORK

(Eldress Betsy Bates, Holy Mount, September 15, 1858)[11]

"Home Work" is an anthem written by Betsy Bates in 1858, by which time she had achieved the position of Ministry Eldress at New Lebanon, by then called Mount Lebanon, or "Holy Mount." The song reflects the persistent popularity of the Shaker anthem genre, of which Issachar Bates had been a pioneer some fifty years before.

Come home my soul and work with-in This is the way to con-quer sin This pre-cious prize which is in view A love-ly prize to co-vet A prize of pur-i-ty and love This pre-cious gift comes from a-bove So now be free and wor-ship God In ho-li-ness and beau-ty O what a beau-ti-ful gift this home work is! O what a beau-ti-ful gift this home work is! It brings me joy, it brings me peace It brings me hea-ven-ly com-fort O what a beau-ti-ful gift this home work is!

NOTES

1. OClWHi IX B SM 396

2. Letter from Issachar Bates Jr. to Isaac Newton Youngs, undated, WRHS IV A 66.

3. Item 190, DLCMs, Tune No. 118.

4. OClWHi IX B SM 413.

5. OClWHi IX B SM 396.

6. OClWHi IX B SM 413.

7. OClWHi IX B SM 413.

8. OClWHi IX B SM 413.

9. OClWHi IX B SM 51.

10. Item 190. DLCMs, Tune No. 192.

11. OClWHi IX B SM 331 (35).

NOTE ON SOURCES

Scholars of the United Society of Believers in Christ's Second Appearing, or "Shakers," are fortunate that fine collections of Shaker primary sources are held by numerous institutions. Many of these collections include material spanning multiple categories of correspondence, journals, ledgers, hymnals, poetry, spiritual writings, and more. Some focus primarily on a specific community or group of communities within the Shaker world, and some consist of material from a particular time period. I have made use of material from the collections listed below. The reader will find that, throughout the notes to the text, I have used the standard NUC abbreviations for these collections and their holding institutions.

DWint	Andrews Shaker Collection (ASC), Winterthur Museum and Library, Winterthur, Delaware
DLCMs	Library of Congress Manuscript Division Shaker Collection
DLCM	Library of Congress Music Division
OClWHi	Western Reserve Historical Society Shaker Collection, Cleveland, Ohio
ODa	Dayton Metro Library
KyBgW-K	Kentucky Library, Western Kentucky University, Bowling Green, Kentucky
KyLoF	Filson Club, Louisville, Kentucky
NN	New York Public Library Shaker Collection, New York City
N	New York State Library Shaker Collection, Albany, New York
NOcaS	Shaker Museum and Library, New Lebanon and Old Chatham, New York
NCH	Hamilton College Special Collections,Clinton, New York
HSV	Hancock Shaker Village, Pittsfield, Massachusetts
OHi	Ohio Historical Society, Columbus, Ohio

One important primary source for this work has been Issachar Bates's autobiography, a substantial book-length work which he began in 1832 and added to between 1834 and 1836. The location of the original is unknown, and it may not survive. However, as early as 1833, Shakers began making copies. At least seventeen separate manuscript copies of it were completed by various individuals throughout the Shaker world. Each of these contains subtle differences, including minor variations in title, internal organization, spelling, and punctuation. Other less trivial differences exist. Some copyists condense passages, glossing over considerable detail, and some omit entire passages or anecdotes. These changes appear to have been made with the intent of softening or side-stepping certain awkward subjects, or eliminating passages that seem too graphic or vivid for sensitive readers. Finally, most of the different copyists include ancillary material, such as copies of letters, poems, songs, and other miscellaneous writings relevant to Issachar Bates. In consequence, each individual copy is a truly unique work.

I have examined all of the available versions of the Issachar Bates autobiography, but I have relied on just a few for the majority of the quotations and extracts used here. Of these, one was copied from the original by Moses Eastwood of Watervliet, Ohio, where Issachar lived for many years. Eastwood knew Issachar well. Eastwood made this copy prior to Issachar's departure from the West and could therefore have conferred with him directly. I have also extensively used the copy made by Betsy Smith of South Union, Kentucky. I believe that Smith produced this copy from Issachar's original, which was for a time in the possession of South Union Elder Benjamin Seth Youngs. Issachar was a founder of the South Union community and a frequent visitor there. Smith, who was born in 1813, would have had ample opportunity to interact with him during her youth and early adulthood. Third, I have utilized the copy inscribed by Betsy Bates, Issachar's youngest daughter. Its impressive penmanship and meticulous calligraphy suggest that Sarah Bates, who was known for those skills, took a leading role in its production. With its fine materials, careful layout, and creative incorporation of poems, letters, and songs by Issachar, it is a magnificent volume, a powerful testament to the importance that Bates's daughters placed on their father's life story. It also bears evidence of regular handling over the years, including signs that it was read page by page. A fourth copy that has been extremely useful is one produced by Issachar Bates Jr. Finally, I have drawn occasionally from versions made by Benjamin Seth Youngs and by Union Village Shaker Susan Liddell. The version by Liddell is only a partial copy, but it contains annotations found nowhere else.

Within the notes to the text I have used the following abbreviations to reference these different versions of the autobiography of Issachar Bates (AIB).

AIB-ODa	"A concise sketch of the life and experience of Issachar Bates, written by himself. This is copyed from the original manuscript by Moses Eastwood," Item R* 289.8 B32, History Room, Dayton Metro Library.
AIB-KyBgW-K	"Sketch of the Life and Experience of Issachar Bates, sen.," by Betsy Smith. MSS 152 B1, Chambliss Collection, Kentucky Library, Bowling Green, Kentucky.
AIB-DWint	"Sketch of the Life & Experience of Issachar Bates (sen.)," by Betsy (and Sarah?) Bates, ASC 813, Winterthur Museum and Library, Wintherthur, Delaware.
AIB-DLCMs-161	"Sketch of the Life & Experience of Issachar Bates (sen.)," Issachar Bates Jr., Item 161, Shaker Collection, Library of Congress Manuscript Division
AIB-DLCMs-350a	"Sketch of the Life and Experience of Issachar Bates (sen.)," Susan Liddell, Item 350a, Shaker Collection, Library of Congress Manuscript Division.

AIB-NOcaS   "Sketch of the Life and Experience of Issachar Bates," Church,
                   Second Order, Mt. Lebanon New York State, Emma King
                   Library, Shaker Museum & Library, Old Chatham.
AIB-OClWHi VI B 20 "Sketch of the Life & Experience ~~and Travels~~ of Issachar
                   Bates," Benjamin Seth Youngs, Section VI B (Testimonies
                   and Biographies), Item 20, Shaker Manuscripts, Western
                   Reserve Historical Society.

OTHER COLLECTIONS USED

In addition to the Shaker manuscript collections, I have also visited and made use of sources from the following institutions:

American Antiquarian Society, Worcester, Massachusetts.
Athol Public Library History Room, Athol Massachusetts
Cincinnati Historical Society, Cincinnati, Ohio
Dartmouth College
Indiana Historical Society, Indianapolis, Indiana
Indiana State Library, Indianapolis, Indiana
Petersham Historical Society, Petersham, Massachusetts
Records & Library Archives, Warren County Administration Center, Lebanon, Ohio
Warren County History Center, Lebanon, Ohio
Washington County Historical Society, Fort Edward, New York

NOTES

INTRODUCTION

1. Recent critical scholarship by American historians has resulted in reconsideration of the use of such terms as "frontier" and "wilderness." The North American landscape of the eighteenth and early nineteenth centuries was of course a "frontier" and a "wilderness" only for the Euro-American inhabitants and not for native peoples. Throughout this work, therefore, I use such terms to represent the perspectives of Issachar Bates and his Euro-American contemporaries, rather than my own.

2. Glendyne Wergland, *One Shaker Life: Isaac Newton Youngs, 1793–1865* (Amherst: University of Massachusetts Press, 2006), p. x.

3. AIB-ODa, 64.

4. These recollections of an unidentified Union Village sister are recorded in "Miscellaneous writings . . . 1813–1892," Item 353d, Shaker Collection, DLCMs.

5. AIB-ODa, 93. This passage is drawn from a section of reflections by Moses Eastwood, the copyist.

6. "Record of Ancient Songs" by Paulina Bryant, Item 361, p. 76, DLCMs.

7. "Tribe of Issachar," in Geoffrey Wigoder, ed., *New Encyclopedia of Judaism* (New York: New York University Press, 2002).

8. These spellings of Issachar Bates's first name are found throughout "Diary of Nathaniel Taylor," MSS 119, Box 3, Folder 3, OHi.

9. This song was recorded in July 1833 in a South Union, Kentucky, music manuscript, OClWHi, IX.A.3, item 88.

1 EARLY LIFE, SPIRITUAL PREPARATION, AND THE COMING OF THE SHAKERS

AIB-ODa, 1–2.

1. AIB-DWint, 1.

2. George Lincoln, *History of the Town of Hingham Massachusetts, Historical Genealogy, A–Lincoln* vol. 2, (Hingham, MA: Published by the Town of Hingham, 1893), 40.

3. I am grateful to Cohasset town historians for this insight, which is based on the recorded weight of David Bates's fishing boat (seven tons), as well as historical knowledge of the local fishery.

4. Victor E. Bigelow, *A Narrative History of the Town of Cohasset Massachusetts* (Cohasset, MA: Committee on Town History, 1898).

5. George Lyman Davenport and Elizabeth Osgood Davenport, *The Genealogies of the Families of Cohasset Massachusetts* (Cohasset, MA: Committee on Town History, 1909).

6. Thomas W. Baldwin, *Vital Records of Cohasset, Massachusetts to 1850* (Boston: New England Historic Genealogical Society, 1916).

7. By far the most dominant school text of colonial New England for more than a century was the *New England Primer* (Boston: Edward Draper, 1777 edition). It lists about 110 male names "to teach children to spell their own." The text would naturally have been a source that generations of parents would have used in selecting names for their children, helping to account for the popularity of many biblical names that today are very obscure. "Issachar" is not among the names listed in the *Primer*.

8. Baldwin (1916).

9. AIB-KyBgW-K, 7.

10. Bigelow (1898), 378.

11. Davenport and Davenport (1909), 22–23. The second wife of David Bates, and William Bates's stepmother, was a widow with ten children. After David's death in 1760, she married again for a third time. David Bates's sheer number of children and stepchildren suggest that after his death William had little prospect of inheriting any property, which could have had bearing on why he moved his family away from Cohasset.

12. William Biglow, *History of Sherburne, Massachusetts, From Its Incorporation, 1674, to the End of the Year 1830* (Milford, MA: Ballou and Stacy, 1830), 12.

13. Samuel Adams Drake, *History of Middlesex County, Massachusetts*, vol. 1 (Boston: Estes and Lauriat, 1880).

14. *The Boston Evening Post*, February 15, 1768, 3.

15. I am grateful to Sherborn, Massachusetts, town historian Betsy Johnson for the information about the historical absence of brick houses in Sherborn.

16. Issachar Bates identifies eleven children in his family: Mercy, Noah, Hannah, Issachar, Sarah, Theodore, Olive, Molly, Dolly, Caleb, and William. Massachusetts town birth records reflect two Noahs and two Olives born to William and Mercy Bates. But no record has been located for a Molly Bates. Assuming that Issachar's naming of his siblings reflects their correct birth order, Molly would have been born between 1765 and 1768, when the family was living in the Sherborn area or nearby Southborough.

17. Betsy Johnson, town historian, Sherborn, Massachusetts, related this information from tax records kept in Sherborn.

18. James G. Carter and William H. Brooks, *A Geography of Massachusetts for Families and Schools* (Boston: Hilliard, Gray, Little, and Wilkins, 1830). Issachar Bates records that the family moved to Southborough when he was "about eleven." Issachar turned eleven in January 1769.

19. AIB-DWint, 1–2.

20. George H. Martin, *The Evolution of the Massachusetts Public School System: A Historical Sketch* (New York: D. Appleton and Company, 1894), 75.

21. Isaac Watts and John Cotton, *The New England Primer* (Boston: Edward Draper, 1767, M'Alpine edition).

22. Alexander Blaikie, *A History of Presbyterianism in New England* (Boston: Alexander Moore, 1881).

23. Anne Carr Shaughnessy, *The History of Sherborn*, (Sherborn, MA: 300th Anniversary Committee, 1974), 147.

24. Harlan Updegraff, *The Origin of the Moving School in Massachusetts* (New York: Columbia University Contributions to Education Teachers' College Series, 1909).

25. Shaughnessy (1974), 147–48.

26. AIB-KyBgW-K, 4.

27. Although the towns in this area had been laid out in the 1730s, isolation and lingering hostilities with native peoples to the north and west prevented the towns from incorporating until the 1760s. Abijah Perkins Marvin, *History of Worcester County, Massachusetts . . . In Two Volumes* (Boston: C. F. Jewett and Company, 1879), 21–27.

28. Hamilton Hurd, *History of Worcester County, Massachusetts, With Biographical Sketches of its Many Pioneers and Prominent Men*, vols. 1 and 2 (Philadelphia: J. W. Lewis and Co., 1889).

29. See Edmund Morgan, "Masters and Servants," in *The Puritan Family*, 109–32 (New York: Harper and Row, 1966). Although Morgan's work concentrates on the "Puritan" society of seventeenth-century New England, Issachar Bates's family and community in the mid-eighteenth century were clearly the inheritors of that Puritan tradition.

30. The practice of "putting out" children in colonial New England is explored in Helena M. Wall, *Fierce Communion: Family and Community in Early America* (Cambridge, MA: Harvard University Press, 1990), 96–125. The relationship between adolescent boys and their parents, including being sent out as labor, is addressed by Anne S. Lombard, *Making Manhood: Growing Up Male in Colonial New England* (Cambridge, MA: Harvard University Press, 2003), 25–38.

31. "A Short Sketch of a Family Record, by Issachar Bates, Junr," copied in AIB-DL-CMs, 231–32.

32. AIB-ODa, 98.

33. Stephen A. Marini, *Radical Sects of Revolutionary New England* (New York: iUniverse.com, Inc., 1982, 2001), 25–39. Marini argues that the rougher and more isolated geographical conditions of the hill country areas where the northern Appalachians cut through New England — areas opened to settlement in the decades after the French and Indian War — corresponded with areas of more radical religious interpretations.

34. AIB-DWint, 2.

35. Susan E. Schreiner, *The Theater of His Glory: Nature & the Natural Order in the Thought of John Calvin* (Grand Rapids, MI: Baker Academic, 2001).

36. AIB-DWint, 2–3.

37. These accounts are very common, but one unusually detailed example is found in *The Boston Chronicle*, January 8, 1770, 10.

38. Joseph Lovering, "On the Secular Periodicity of the Aurora Borealis," *Memoirs of the American Academy of Arts and Sciences, New Series* 9, no. 1 (1867): 101–20.

39. Sara S. Gronim, "At the Sign of Newton's Head: Astronomy and Cosmology in British Colonial New York," in *Explorations in Early American Culture*, Pennsylvania History, vol. 66, ed. William Pencak and George Boudreau, 55–85(University Park, PA: Pennsylvania Historical Association for the McNeil Center for Early American Studies (1999).

40. Michael Winship, "Prodigies, Puritanism, and the Perils of Natural Philosophy:

The Example of Cotton Mather," *The William and Mary Quarterly* 51, no. 1 (January 1994): 92–105.

41. The pamphlet in Issachar Bates's household was surely Samuel Clarke's *A Short Relation Concerning a Dream Which the Author had ... With some remarks on the late Comet* (Boston: Andrew Barclay, 1769). Issachar's quotations correspond almost exactly with the text of that pamphlet. It was reprinted several times over the next decade, including one edition titled *The American Wonder, Or the Strange and Remarkable Cape-Ann Dream* (Salem, N.E.: Russell Printers, 1776).

42. AIB-DWint, 4.

43. AIB-DWint, 4–5.

44. *The Boston Gazette, and Country Journal* August 19, 1765, 2.

45. AIB-DWint, 7–8.

46. AIB-ODa, 6–7. Note that in AIB-DWint, copied by Issachar's daughter Betsy Bates, a Ministry eldress at New Lebanon, New York, the expression "perfect ass star-gazer" is edited to read "puffed up star gazer," probably because the original expression was considered too crude for the sensitive Shaker eldresses and elders who would circulate and read that version over many years.

47. "The Voice of Wisdom or Mother," by Issachar Bates, OClWHi VII B 242.

48. Edward Deming Andrews, *The People Called Shakers* (New York: Dover Publications, 1963), 16–17.

49. Marini (2001), 40–59.

50. Thomas Brown, *An Account of the People Called Shakers* (Troy, NY: Printed by Parker and Bliss, 1812), 318–25.

51. Ann Lee's two-year period of missionary work in New England, the persecution she suffered, and her death soon after the end of her missionary journey, have been extensively treated in numerous historical works for over 200 years. For an early account, see Brown (1812), 318–25. Major twentieth-century accounts include Andrews (1961), 35–53; Clarke Garrett, *Spirit Possession and Popular Religion: From the Camisards to the Shakers* (Baltimore, MD: Johns Hopkins University Press, 1987), 177–213; and Stephen J. Stein, *The Shaker Experience in America: A History of the United Society of Believers* (New Haven, CT: Yale University Press, 1992), 18–38.

52. Alma White and Leila Taylor, *Shakerism: Its Meaning and Message* (Columbus, OH: Fred J. Heer, 1905), 17.

53. The characteristics of early Shakerism, prior to the establishment of "gospel order" under Joseph Meacham and Lucy Wright are explored in multiple works, including Andrews, Marini, Garrett, Stein, and others such as Priscilla J. Brewer, *Shaker Communities, Shaker Lives* (Hanover, NH: University Press of New England, 1986).

54. AIB-DWint, 5, 26.

2. A FIFER IN THE AMERICAN REVOLUTION

"Rights of Conscience" was printed in the Shakers first hymnal, *Millennial Praises* (Hancock: 1813), 281–85.

1. For background on the fife, I have drawn primarily from Raoul F. Camus, *Military Music of the American Revolution* (Chapel Hill: University of North Carolina Press, 1976); and Warren P. Howe, "Early American Military Music," *American Music* 17, no. 1 (Spring 1999): 87–116.

2. William Windham and George Townshend, *A Plan of Discipline Composed for the Use of the Militia in the County of Norfolk* (London: J. Shuckburgh, 1759), 38.

3. "Diary of Henry Blake," Record ID 271243, American Antiquarian Society, Worcester, Massachusetts.

4. According to records in volume 10 of *Massachusetts Soldiers and Sailors of the Revolutionary War*, Bezaleel Maynard's service overlapped with Issachar Bates's both in 1775 and in 1778, when both served as guards at the barracks in Rutland, Vermont. The rolls of units from Issachar Bates's home area of Athol, Massachusetts reflect several members of the Maynard and Ingalsbe families, all relatives of Lovina Maynard Bates. See Secretary of the Commonwealth, *Massachusetts Soldiers and Sailors of the Revolutionary War* (Boston: Wright and Potter Printing, 1907), 10:391.

5. *Massachusetts Soldiers and Sailors of the Revolutionary War* (1907), 1:797; 16:14.

6. *Massachusetts Soldiers and Sailors of the Revolutionary War* (1907), 1:803.

7. Issachar Bates's account of his wartime service was extracted from his autobiography and reprinted as a pamphlet, *The Revolutionary War and Issachar Bates* (Chatham, NY: Shaker Museum Foundation, 1960), foreword by John S. Williams. His second account, filed with his pension application, was unknown until discovered by the author in the National Archives in 2007. That narrative is written in Issachar's own handwriting, dated September 11, 1832.

8. Among the many manuscript copies of Issachar Bates's autobiography, I have chosen to present the Revolutionary War account as it appears in the version inscribed by Betsy Bates, Issachar's youngest daughter (AIB-DWint). The selection was not entirely arbitrary. The penmanship in this version is pristine and the document is intact and unblemished, allowing clear interpretation of many passages that are nearly indecipherable in other versions. The location of Issachar's original manuscript is unknown, and it may have been lost.

9. It is puzzling that this opening statement is one of the few details of the war that Issachar Bates recalls erroneously. In fact, General Thomas Gage, the highest ranking British military official in the Colonies, had departed Boston in June 1773 to return to England temporarily. Gage returned to Boston with a major contingent of British troops on May 13, 1774.

10. Issachar Bates's original expression was "perfect ass star-gazer," which the copyist, Issachar Bates's pious daughter Betsy, chose to edit, possibly because she found it crude.

11. Captain Ichabod Dexter, of Athol, Worcester County, Massachusetts.

12. John Patterson, who commanded a Massachusetts regiment at Bunker Hill. Brigadier General John Sullivan, present at the siege of Boston in 1775.

13. For reasons unknown, the copyist has edited Issachar Bates's original phrase, "take the bloody track of war."

14. Other versions say "marsh." From maps of the period, it appears that the location would indeed have been marshy.

15. Major General Israel Putnam, of Connecticut, was one of the prominent officers at the Battle of Bunker Hill.

16. Issachar Bates uses many colorful terms (carcasses, stink pots) for the various sizes of ordinance fired by cannon.

17. This officer's identity is a mystery. Other versions of Bates's autobiography read "Baker" or "Boucher."

18. British General Sir William Howe.

19. Issachar Bates's account matches standard accounts of the fortification of Dorchester Heights, regarded as a brilliant and well-executed strategy, down to the detail of the preparation of barrels filled with sand and gravel to roll down onto advancing British troops. Today, a major monument is maintained on the site by the National Park Service.

20. Probably an officer named Phipps, of which there were several in the American Navy.

21. This term *batten* seems to refer to a watercraft, such as a barge or raft, but it is unknown in this context.

22. The island mentioned is the Island of Manhattan.

23. Hessian prisoners were taken at Trenton, but the meaning of "Governor Hessians" is unclear.

24. The location meant here is Walloomsac, New York, adjacent to Bennington, Vermont. The battle at Bennington straddled the two areas. No doubt the passage of time on Bates's part, combined with uncertainty in interpretation by the various copyists, produced the morphing of Walloomsac to "Maloonscoak."

25. "John Bull" is a satirical nickname for the British people collectively, which emerged in early eighteenth-century political cartoons.

3. ISSACHAR BATES AS HUSBAND AND PROVIDER
AIB-ODa, 15.

1. *Vital Records of Athol, Massachusetts, to 1849.*

2. *Vital Records of Phillipston, Massachusetts, to 1849.*

3. The exact date of Mercy Bates's death is unrecorded.

4. In a pioneering study of the domestic lives of men in colonial New England, Lisa Wilson notes that men unlucky enough to be left widowers with young children remarried as quickly as possible, because a wife was so crucial to the household; see Lisa Wilson, *Ye Heart of a Man: The Domestic Life of Men in Colonial New England* (New Haven, CT: Yale University Press, 1999), 144. In *Good Wives: Image and Reality in the Lives of Women in Northern New England, 1650–1750* (New York: Alfred A. Knopf, Inc., 1982), Laurel Thatcher Ulrich makes a similar point, through her analysis of the relative power held by wives within households.

5. AIB-ODa, 15. Garry, or Gerry, was the original name of Phillipston, Massachusetts. Gerry formed in the early 1780s, from land taken from neighboring Athol to the west

and Templeton to the east. See historic map, Herbert Hapgood, *Plan Showing Changes in Boundary Line of Athol*, 1912, Athol Public Library History Room, map cabinet.

6. In *History of Shrewsbury, Massachusetts* (Boston: Samuel G. Drake, 1847), Andrew H. Ward indicates that the Keyes and Maynards were among the towns earliest settlers and that many owned land and held town offices (7–30). In writing about her ancestry in 1775, Sarah Bates, daughter of Issachar, states that her mother's ancestors were "clear English of some rank" and that the family possessed a coat-of-arms from the king; see Sarah Bates to Hulda Bagg, June 28, 1875, ASC 1057, DWint.

7. According to *Massachusetts Soldiers and Sailors in the War of the Revolution*, vol. 10, Gardner Maynard, Artemas Maynard, and Stephen Maynard — all uncles of Lovina Maynard Bates — held officer rank. Sarah Bates notes that several members of her mother's family were officers in the war.

8. Wilson (1999), 46.

9. Daniel Scott Smith, "Parental Power and Marriage Patterns: An Analysis of Historical Trends in Hingham, Massachusetts," *Journal of Marriage and Family* 35, no. 3 (Aug. 1973): 419–28.

10. *Vital Records of Templeton, Massachusetts, to 1849*.

11. Because the birth of the Bates's first living child in January 1780 was Lovina's second pregnancy, following a stillborn child (as opposed to a miscarriage), it is possible that she was already pregnant when they married in May 1778. This raises the prospect that Issachar and Lovina may have shared a passionate youthful romance. For young soldiers in wartime Massachusetts, opportunities for contact with sweethearts would have been fleeting and earnest, contributing to unexpected pregnancies.

12. The birthdates of the nine children of Issachar and Lovina were recorded by Issachar Bates Jr., in "A Short Sketch of a Family Record," contained in AIB-DLCMs-161, 230–31.

13. William G. Lord, *History of Athol, Massachusetts* (Somerville, MA: Somerville Printing Company, 1953), 39–42.

14. Many Bates family events — including the births of the youngest siblings and the mustering into the army of Issachar and his brother Noah — are recorded in Athol. Many Maynard family events — including the mustering into the army of several Maynard men and the 1778 marriages of the Issachar and Noah Bates to Lovina and Ruth Maynard — are recorded in Templeton. It is probable that both families had settled on land in the portions of the two towns that broke away to form the Baptist congregation that was incorporated as the town of Gerry by 1786.

15. AIB-ODa, 17.

16. Thomas J. Campanella, "'Mark well the gloom': Shedding Light on the Great Dark Day of 1780," *Environmental History* 12, no. 1 (January 2007): 35–58. Campanella demonstrates that the darkness likely was the consequence of a huge forest fire in southern Canada that affected the atmosphere for a radius of several hundred miles.

17. Samuel Williams, "An Account of a Very Uncommon Darkness in the States of New-England, May 19, 1780," *Memoirs of the American Academy of Arts and Sciences* (1783), 1:234–246.

18. AIB-ODa, 17–18.

19. Mabel Cook Coolidge, *The History of Petersham, Massachusetts* (Salem, MA: Higginson Book Company, 1948), 234.

20. I am grateful to Nancy Allen and Christine Mandel of the Petersham Historical Society for sharing information on the location of the David Hammond house and the events that occurred there during the period of the Shakers' visit.

21. "Excerpts from the Journal of Sarah Howe (1766–1849), Acc. #PH684, Petersham Historical Society, Petersham, Massachusetts. Howe, a young Petersham woman who was acquainted with the Hammond family, recounts her observations of Shaker worship in her journal.

22. "An Account of Issachar Bates Seeing Mother Ann Lee," undated, Item 353d, DLCMs. This account is contained together with a significant amount of retrospective material probably generated by Ohio Shaker Susan Liddell in the late nineteenth century. Liddell was a child when she arrived at Union Village in the 1830s, when many of the founding generation of Shakers in the West were still alive and active. Her retrospective accounts heavily influenced the first attempts to chronicle Shaker history in the late nineteenth and early twentieth centuries.

23. An account of Ann Lee's ordeal in Petersham, including the attack upon her at the Hammond house, is recorded by Clara Endicott Sears, *Gleanings from Old Shaker Journals* (New York: Houghton Mifflin Company, 1916), 40.

24. AIB-ODa, 18.

25. AIB-KYBGW-K, 24.

26. AIB-KyBgW-K, 24–25.

27. AIB-KyBgW-K, 25.

28. Washington County was incorporated as Charlotte County in 1772. Its configuration changed several times; it briefly included portions of land that became part of Vermont in 1777, and it continued in the early 1780s to claim land that overlapped with the townships of Rutland and Bennington, Vermont. It was renamed Washington County in 1784 in honor of George Washington. See "Chronology of Washington (created as Charlotte)," in "Individual County Chronologies" folders, Washington County Historical Society, 201–5.

29. Isabella Brayton, *"The Story of Hartford: A History," Compiled by Town Historian in collaboration with John B. Norton, Hartford, New York, 1929* (Washington County Historical Society Item 97.31.1), 13.

30. The Ingalsbe and Maynard families both came from Shrewsbury, Massachusetts, and many of their vital records are found in *Vital Records of Shrewsbury, Massachusetts to 1849.* An entry on Issachar Bates's arrival in Hartford in 1786 along with John Ingalsbe and Francis Maynard, and his settlement near Aaron Ingalsbe, is found on page 294 of volume 1 of the *Fitch Gazetteer of Washington County, New York,* a massive nineteenth-century reference work indexed in the late twentieth century. See Kenneth A. Perry, *The Fitch Gazetteer: An Annotated Index to the Manuscript History of Washington County, New York,* vol. 1 (Bowie, MD: Heritage Books, Inc., 1999). The full entry is recorded on page 36 of the Perry index.

31. Joan Patton, "Family Has Been on Farm for Two Centuries," *Hartford Post-Star* 95.72.5 (January 26, 1992), 1–2.

32. This can be inferred from the map of Hartford's original Provincial Patent, reproduced in Fred Patton, "The Provincial Patent: Hartford Might Be Older Than You Think," *Hartford Post-Star* 95.72.5 (January 26, 1992), 2–3. The numbered lots on this map correspond to records of lot numbers occupied by Aaron Ingalsbe and Gardner Maynard, identified in Brayton (1929, 116) and Joan Patton (1992), respectively.

33. Wilson (1999), 24. Wilson's analysis of the challenges faced by New England men in negotiating livelihood choices, parental involvement, kinship networks, fatherhood, widowhood, and aging is useful in assessing the choices and reflections of Issachar Bates, and of his father, William Bates.

34. Wilson (1999), 110.

35. AIB-KyBgW-K, 25.

36. Joan Patton, "For the Sum of a Penny, Foundation Was Laid for Hartford Baptist Church," *Hartford Post-Star* 95.72.5 (January 26, 1992), 1.

37. In his autobiography, Issachar refers to having taught singing for "four winters" by about 1794 or 1795, and to being the "chorister" of the Baptist church in Hartford "for some time." He also refers several times to conversations with the minister "Elder Brown."

38. AIB-KyBgW-K, 25–26.

39. As a choirmaster, Issachar would have possessed deep familiarity with the hymn poets whose work was popular in that period. The verse that he quotes in this reflective passage is the hymn, "The Death of a Sinner" by the popular and prolific early eighteenth-century English hymn writer Isaac Watts.

40. AIB-ODa, 21–22.

41. AIB-ODa, 22–23.

42. AIB-ODa, 24.

43. Norman Penney, *The Journal of George Fox* (Cambridge, MA: Cambridge University Press, 1911).

44. Charles G. Finney, *An Autobiography* (Westwood, NJ: Fleming H. Revell Company, 1908), 12–13.

45. John F. Weishampel Jr., *The Testimony of a Hundred Witnesses* (Baltimore: Blakeman and Co., 1858). This volume consists of scores of short conversion narratives from American and English religious figures of the late eighteenth and early nineteenth centuries.

46. Arnold A. Dallimore, *George Whitefield: God's Anointed Servant in the Great Revival of the Eighteenth Century* (Wheaton, IL: Crossway Books, 2010).

47. AIB-ODa, 24–25.

48. AIB-ODa, 26.

49. A Shaker poem titled "Confession & Remission of Sins," written in Ohio possibly as late as 1832, reflects an experience that matches Issachar Bates's description of his first religious conversion, including a solitary interlude in the forest, going to an elder, and attempting to make a confession. The poem, along with many texts by Bates, is included

in a printed hymn compilation published at Watervliet, Ohio, by Richard McNemar in collaboration with Issachar Bates and others. Though "Confession & Remission of Sins" is unattributed, it's similarity to Issachar's description of his own experience makes it likely that Bates is the author. One striking passage reads: "He did not seek a forest, or go behind a stump / Or like a wholesale merchant, do bus'ness in the lump / But went to the good elder, and bro't his deeds to light / This, holy men have stated, as plain as they could write." See Carol Medlicott and Christian Goodwillie, *Richard McNemar, Music, and the Western Shaker Communities: Branches of One Living Tree* (Kent, OH: Kent State University Press, 2013).

50. AIB-ODa, 27–28. Given the serpent's role in establishing humankind's original sin, Issachar's comparison of his sexual arousal to the bite of a rattlesnake is revealing.

51. AIB-ODa, 27.

52. Sarah Bates to Hulda Bagg, June 28, 1875, New Lebanon New York, ASC 1057, DWint.

53. "A Short Sketch of a Family Record, by Issachar Bates, Junr," copied in AIB-DL-CMs-161, 231–232.

54. For background on William Billings and the nascent American music of his times, see Roger L. Hall, *Majesty: A Discussion of Facts and Fiction about William Billings and the Stoughton Musical Society* (Boston: Pine Tree Press, 2000); George Pullen Jackson, *Spiritual Folk Songs of Early America* (J. J. Augustin, 1937); and George Pullen Jackson, *Down-East Spirituals and Others* (J. J. Augustin, 1939).

55. David Warren Steel and Richard Hulan, *The Makers of the Sacred Harp* (Urbana, IL: University of Illinois Press, 2010). In this important work, Steel and Hulan have compiled short biographies of the most significant among the New England composers whose work is represented in *The Sacred Harp*, a shape-note hymnal in continuous use in America since 1844 that contains a rich selection of late eighteenth-century New England hymnody. Because it was common practice for composers of hymns to also teach singing schools itinerantly, it is quite possible that Issachar Bates had the opportunity to meet some of the notable New England hymn writers who were his contemporaries.

56. It was common practice in the period for hymn books to include song verses only, with no musical scores. Users of the hymn books would simply fit the verses to a familiar tune that shared the right meter.

57. Isaac Orcutt, like so many of Hartford's earliest residents, was a native of Massachusetts, and he may actually have been a distant relative of Issachar Bates. Issachar's maternal grandmother in Hingham, Massachusetts, was Hannah Orcutt, and many Orcutts migrated from Hingham to other parts of the state. It is impossible to know whether or not the two might have been aware of a family relationship and whether that had any bearing on why Issachar immortalized Isaac's death in one of his first poems.

58. Some thirty years later, Issachar would refer to himself as "this old hunter," suggesting that indeed he had counted hunting among his familiar activities. Issachar Bates to New Lebanon Ministry, 11 May 1827, OClWHi IV A 78.

59. Abner Jones, ed., *The Melody of the Heart* (Boston: Manning and Loring, 1804).

60. Jeremiah Ingalls, *The Christian Harmony* (Exeter, NH: Henry Ranlet, 1805). It is unknown whether the tune Ingalls presents for "Harvest Hymn" is the tune that Issachar Bates used.

61. Melvin G. Williams, "Who Was Isaac Orcutt? The History and Origins of an 18th Century New England Ballad," *New York Folklore* 13, nos. 3–4 (1987): 55–71. According to Williams, a version of the ballad was printed in Cincinnati in 1886 as "The Mournful Ballad of Isaac Abbott," with accompanying comical sketches by illustrator E. P. Cranch, indicating that the event had unfolded in Hartford, Connecticut (61–62). Other versions were included in folk music collections in the early twentieth century, some with the location altered from "Hartford" to "Westfield," and others with the names of the principal characters slightly altered. In the article, Williams relates that he ultimately identified Issachar Bates as the ballad's author not through his own research but because Shaker music scholar Daniel Patterson heard of his project and informed him of the existence of Issachar Bates's 1800 booklet of hymn texts, including the Isaac Orcutt ballad (61–62). Williams argues that its textual alteration and the loss of the author's identity is typical of the treatment that songs receive as they are circulated through oral tradition

62. "'Closing Address' from Hannah Agnew to Sister Marietta, White Water, Ohio, 9 May 1868," in "Journal of a memorable journey . . . by Hannah Agnew," Item 50, DLCMs. In this letter, Agnew, a Shaker sister then in her late forties who had known Issachar Bates for several years while she was a teenager prior to his death in 1837, compared her own enthusiasm for poetry with that of "Elder Issachar," whom she quoted as calling such writings "poetry run mad."

63. AIB-ODa, 28–29.

64. One of the Shakers' most vigorous early detractors was Valentin Rathbun, who published *Some brief hints of a religious scheme taught and propagated by a number of Europeans living in a place called Nisqueunia in the state of New-York* (Albany: S. Hall, 1782).

65. "Shakerism: The World's Spiritual Metre," *Shaker Manifesto* 8, no. 3 (March 1878): 67.

66. AIB-ODa, 29–31.

4. SHAKER CONVERSION AND EARLY TRAVELS

AIB-ODa, 32.

1. Mary Dyer, *A Brief Statement of the Sufferings of Mary Dyer, Occasioned by the Society Called Shakers. Written by Herself* (Boston: William S. Spear, 1816), 25. Dyer, a celebrated Shaker apostate, included affadavits from numerous others who claimed to have witnessed scandalous behavior among the Shakers.

2. AIB-KyBgW-K, 39.

3. AIB-KyBgW-K, 40.

4. AIB-DWint, 71.

5. See Wergland (2006), for a thorough discussion of the conversion of the large and important Youngs family, who were related by marriage to the equally important Wells family that came to the Shakers about the same time. Members of both these families

would be counted among Issachar's closest friends and confidants during his entire Shaker life. Benjamin's birth and death dates are found in a manuscript table compiled by Shaker Alonzo Hollister in his "Book of Pioneer Correspondence from the West," OClWHi IV B 34.

6. See a short undated biographical essay on Benjamin Seth Youngs written by Alonzo Hollister, OClWHi IV A 30.

7. Brown (1812) contains a brief physical description of Benjamin Seth Youngs, 349. The small stature and boyish appearance that he retained throughout his life were frequently remarked upon in Shaker writings. His younger brother Isaac Newton Youngs, for example, relates stories of the ridicule that Benjamin often received from crowds, who believed he was just a boy and failed to take his preaching seriously. Isaac Newton Youngs, "Tour thro the States of Ohio and Kentucky, in the Summer of 1834," entries for July 1834, NOcaS.

8. *Massachusetts Soldiers and Sailors of the Revolutionary War* (1907), 1:803.

9. Benjamin Seth Youngs, *Testimony of Christ's Second Appearing* (Lebanon, OH: Office of the Western Star, 1808). Though Benjamin is named as the author, it is widely believed by Shaker scholars that several western Shakers collaborated with him on portions of it, including John Dunlavy, Matthew Houston, and Richard McNemar.

10. From 1787, the primary authority within Shakerism consisted of an appointed "Ministry" of two male and two female leaders who were based at the New Lebanon community. This Ministry orchestrated all the vital aspects of the movement's early expansion, including the dispatching of missionaries. Leadership teams within several individual Shaker communities were also referred to as "ministries." But the New Lebanon Ministry was the presiding authority over the entire Shaker movement. See Stephen J. Paterwic, *Historical Dictionary of the Shakers* (Lanham, MD: The Scarecrow Press, Inc., 2008), 145–146.

11. Brown (1812), 349.

12. AIB-KyBgW-K, 40–41.

13. U.S. Census, 1800, for Pittsford, Vermont.

14. Abiel Moore Caverly, *History of the Town of Pittsford, Vt., With Biographical Sketches and Family Records* (Rutland: Tuttle and Co., 1872).

15. Henry P. Smith and William. S. Rann, *History of Rutland County, Vermont* (Syracuse, NY: D. Mason and Co., 1886). Soon after Issachar and Benjamin's initial missionary journey to Pittsford, other Shaker leaders made visits to work with the new converts there, and they used the Bates home in Hartford, New York, as an overnight stop ("Journal of trips made by Elder Ebenezer and others from Mt. Lebanon to other communities," OClWHi V A 6).

16. Testimony of Eldress Dana Brewster, from "Book of Remembrance" by Alonzo G. Hollister, OClWHi VII B 109, 32–39.

17. OClWHi VII B 109, p. 38.

18. AIB-ODa. Presumably, Artemas and Oliver were the sons with whom Issachar "settled." Born in 1782 and 1784, respectively, Artemas and Oliver would have been nineteen

and seventeen when Issachar became a Shaker. The birthdates of all the Bates children were recorded by Issachar Bates Jr., in "A Short Sketch of a Family Record," AIB-DLCMs, 230–31.

19. The arrival of Issachar Bates and his wife and seven children is noted in New Lebanon's "Domestic Journal of important occurrences," in March 1803, OClWHi V B 60. A brief account is also found in "A Letter Historic & Chronologic, Wisdom's Valley, March 8th 1871," OClWHi VII B 109, a narrative that appears to be written by Shaker Alonzo Hollister and directed to Sarah Bates.

20. Dorothy M. Filley, *Recapturing Wisdom's Valley: The Watervliet Shaker Heritage, 1775–1975* (Albany, NY: Albany Institute of History and Art, 1975).

21. "A Letter Historic & Chronologic," OClWHi VII B 109.

22. In writing of his secret 1801 visit to New Lebanon, Issachar Bates had mentioned encountering one daughter of his sister Hannah Train, who had recently confessed her sins. In the same passage, he mentioned the conversion of his sister Dolly.

23. Brown (1812), 237. This evolution can be inferred from Brown, who, in relating Shaker worship meetings circa 1803, remarks that those reluctant to dance were to "stand in a row with the singers," alongside the wall.

24. At Shaker communities, worship meetings that were open to local spectators were referred to as "public meetings."

25. Brown (1812), 183.

26. Ibid., 278.

27. See entry for "Seth Youngs Wells," Paterwic (2008). The arrival of the Youngs and Wells families is noted in "A Letter Historic & Chronologic, Wisdom's Valley, March 8th 1871," OClWHi VII B 109.

28. Paul Conkin, *Cane Ridge: America's Pentecost* (Madison: University of Wisconsin Press, 1990).

29. John B. Boles, *The Great Revival: Beginnings of the Bible Belt* (Lexington, KY: University Press of Kentucky, 1996).

30. See "General Assembly of the Presbyterian Church," *The Albany Gazette* 19, no. 1627 (June 28, 1802): 2.

31. Sears (1916), 100. Sears' estate was adjacent to the Shaker site at Harvard, Massachusetts, where Ann Lee focused her ministry and established a robust group of converts before her death in 1784. Sears compiled her book using manuscripts and recollections of the events of Ann Lee's final years and the early years of the Harvard community.

32. AIB-KyBgW-K, 43.

33. There is a significant literature on America's early westward expansion into Kentucky and adjacent areas along the "wilderness road" pioneered by Daniel Boone and others. See Thomas Speed, *The Wilderness Road: A Description of the Routes of Travel by which the Pioneers and Early Settlers First Came to Kentucky* (Louisville, KY: John P. Morton and Co., 1886); Otis K. Rice, *Frontier Kentucky* (Lexington: University of Kentucky Press, 1993); Ellen Eslinger, *Running Mad for Kentucky: Frontier Travel Accounts* (Lexington: University Press of Kentucky, 2004).

34. Brewer (1986) presents demographic data on the eastern Shaker communities, including population numbers for each community collected by decade between 1790 and 1880 (209–238).

35. Andrews (1963), 21, 77.

36. Paterwic (2008), 139–140.

37. Brown (1812), 349. In describing the three missionaries, Brown implies that Issachar Bates's "poetical genius" was one of his most winning features and that he was certainly not selected on the basis of his "literary information."

38. AIB-DWint (50).

39. Benjamin S. Youngs to the North Family, New Lebanon, 4 May 1813, copied by Alonzo Hollister in "Book of Pioneer Correspondence from the West," OClWHi IV B 34.

40. "Notes and Writings on Union Village Compiled by Susan C. Liddell," MSS 119, Box 23, Folder 3, 11, OHi.

41. Several hymnals, including Russel Haskell "A Record of Spiritual Songs . . . in Twelve Parts" (WLCM 2131/.S4E5, 302) record this hymn written by South Union Sister Sally Eades for New Years Day 1835: "This day thirty years ago / Was a solemn time we know / When our fathers took the road / Left their friends and best abode."

42. Speed (1886).

43. The term "principal clerk" to describe Benjamin Seth Youngs appears in AIB-DWint, 57.

44. Journal of Benjamin Seth Youngs, 1805, entries for January 12 (9), January 7 (5), January 19 (15), January 29 (22). ASC 859, DWint.

45. ASC 859, DWint, entry for January 18 (14).

46. ASC 859, DWint, entries for February 4 and February 5 (24–25).

47. John Meacham to New Lebanon Ministry, 31 January 1805, OClWHi IV A 66.

48. ASC 859, DWint, entry for February 22 (35).

49. ASC 859, DWint, entry for February 20 (34).

50. ASC 859, DWint, entry for February 23 (36).

51. AIB-KyBgW-K, 43–44.

52. ASC 859, DWint, entry for February 24 (36–37).

53. An 1821 letter discusses a group of some thirty Shaker converts at a settlement on the Clinch River that had been receiving regular visits by leaders at Pleasant Hill. The circumstances of their conversion are not explained. Issachar Bates's autobiography refers to regular preaching trips that he made back into Tennessee, especially during the years 1806–1811, so it is possible that he later returned to the Clinch River settlement, where their act of compassion had made a positive impression in 1805, and made some inroads there. Pleasant Hill Ministry to Comstock Betts, 5 August 1921, ASC 1044, DWint.

54. AIB-KyBgW-K, 45.

55. AIB-ODa, 99. This anecdote is recorded by Moses Eastwood among his own annotations to Issachar Bates's autobiography. In the mid-1830s Eastwood became a chief record-keeper at Watervliet, Ohio, and as such took it upon himself to organize accounts of some of Watervliet's leading figures.

56. AIB-KyBgW-K, 46.

57. Details of Mathew Houston and his family, including their physical descriptions, reputation for fashionable dress, and personality characteristics can be found in "Notes and Writings on Union Village," MSS 119, Box 23, Folder 3, 1–46, OHi.

58. Many Shaker manuscripts record that the ever likable and popular Mathew Houston became uncommonly fat as he aged, and his weight eventually reached three hundred pounds.

59. Ellen Eslinger, *Citizens of Zion: Social Origins of Camp Meeting Revivalism* (Knoxville: University of Tennessee Press, 1999), 209.

60. John Henderson Spencer. "Sects Originating from the Great Revival," in *A History of the Kentucky Baptists* (Cincinnati, OH: J. R. Baumes, 1886), 1:522–34.

61. Barton W. Stone, "History of the Christian Church in the West," *The Christian Messenger* 1, no. 12 (October 25, 1827): 265–69.

62. AIB-KyBgW-K, 46–47.

63. For background on the conversion of Barton Stone, his coming into Kentucky, and his role in the evolution of Presbyterianism in Kentucky, see D. Newell Williams, *Barton Stone: A Spiritual Biography* (Atlanta, GA: Chalice Press, 2000).

64. For a description of the revivals at Cane Ridge, see Conkin (1990).

65. ASC 859, DWint, entries for March 13, March 14, and March 15, pages 49–51. Youngs's journal indicates that John Meacham had been feeling ill for a few days and did not take an active part in the discussions at Cane Ridge.

66. ASC 813, DWint (78–79).

5. SEEKING KINDRED IN THE WEST

AIB-KyBgW-K, 52.

1. Turtlecreek Warren Co., State of Ohio to New Lebanon, 1 June 1805, ASC 1048, DWint.

2. ASC 859, DWint, entry for March 18 (52).

3. The frame structure of Malcolm Worley's house, in contrast to the predominant style of log homes in the area, is mentioned in Lebanon Miami Country, Ohio, to New Lebanon, 17 March 1806, ASC 1048, DWint.

4. AIB-KyBgW-K, 47–48.

5. Richard McNemar, *The Kentucky Revival* (Cincinnati, OH: John W. Browne, 1807), 85.

6. Ellen F. Van Houten and Florence Cole, *Warren County, Ohio Shakers of Union Village 1805–1920* (Lebanon, OH: Cardinal Research, Warren County Genealogical Society 2003).

7. Marriage Records 1803 to 1835, Records and Library Archives, Warren County Administration Center, Lebanon, Ohio, 5.

8. ASC 859, DWint, entries for March 22 and March 27 (54, 57).

9. "Notes and Writings on Union Village," MSS 119, Box 23, Folder 3, p13, OHi.

10. ASC 859, DWint, entry for March 22 (54).

11. ASC 859, DWint, entry for March 22, notes that "we 3 come to one bed."

12. ASC 859, entry for March 23 (54–55).

13. For background on McNemar's early adult life prior to his Shaker conversion, see J. P. MacLean, *A Sketch of the Life and Labors of Richard McNemar* (Franklin, OH: Printed for the *Franklin Chronicle*, 1905), and Hazel Spencer Phillips, *Richard the Shaker* (Lebanon, OH: Typoprint, Inc., 1972).

14. For background on McNemar's varied professional interest and his situation at the time of his conversion, see Christian Goodwillie, "*Custos Sacrorum*: Richard McNemar as Curator and Printer," and Carol Medlicott, "A Window on the West: Unity and Harmony in McNemar's Shaker Zion," in Medlicott and Goodwillie (2013).

15. A description of Richard McNemar's two-story log house is found in Oliver C. Hampton, "Membership list compiled from various sources," OClWHi III B 33, 104.

16. AIB-KyBgW-K, 48–49.

17. ASC 859, DWint, entries for March 25 and March 26 (56).

18. AIB-KyBgW-K, 50–51.

19. A concise expression of the Shaker view of Christ's second appearing was contained in the letter of introduction carried by the three missionaries to Kentucky and Ohio ("The Church of Christ Sendeth unto a People in Kentucky and Adjacent States," 26 December 1804, ASC 1038, DWint), but without any reference to Ann Lee. Youngs (1808) provides an elaborate treatment of the Shaker understanding of Christ's "second coming," including how God in the "latter days" used womankind to reveal the dual-gendered nature of the godhead.

20. AIB-DLCMs-350a, 58.

21. AIB-KyBgW-K, 52.

22. MacLean (1907) includes the full text of Stone's letter to McNemar, sent via Bates in the spring of 1805, 44–45.

23. ASC 859, DWint, entry for March 27 (57).

24. ASC 859, DWint, entries for March 31 and April 1 (59–60).

25. Rufus Bishop and Seth Youngs Wells, comps. *Testimonies of the Life, Character, Revelations and Doctrines of our Ever Blessed Mother Ann Lee* (Hancock, MA: J. Talcott and J. Deming, 1816), 318.

26. The notion of the world turning "upside down" was a strong theme in the popular culture of the Revolutionary period. Tradition has it that the popular ballad, "The World Turned Upside Down," was played during Cornwallis's surrender at Yorktown.

27. ASC 859, DWint, entry for April 6 (67).

28. ASC 859, DWint, entry for April 9 (69).

29. ASC 859, DWint, entry for April 12 (71).

30. Turtlecreek to New Lebanon, 1 June 1805, ASC 1048, DWint.

31. ASC 859, DWint, entry for May 13 (113).

32. "Tour thro the States of Ohio and Kentucky, in the Summer of 1834," entries for July 1834, NOcaS. According to Isaac Newton Youngs, his older brother Benjamin related this story as after-dinner conversation during his visit to South Union in 1834.

33. ASC 859, DWint, entries for March 24 and March 27 (56–57).

34. ASC 859, DWint, entry for April 12 (72).

35. Issachar Dennis's date of birth is recorded along with his date of death by Richard McNemar in "Memorial of Deceases," in *A Review of the Most Important Events Relating to the Rise and Progress of the United Society of Believers in the West* (Union Village, OH, 1831), 32.

36. ASC 859, DWint, entry for April 14 (76–77).

37. Ibid., entry for April 14 (77).

38. Ibid., entry for April 18 (81–82).

39. Ibid., entry for April 8 (66).

40. Ibid., entry for April 20 (86). Benjamin Seth Youngs records that Richard McNemar specifically sought to confess to Issachar Bates and Benjamin together. Richard came to Malcolm Worley's house on April 19 seeking to confess to the two of them, but Bates was absent, having gone to visit another family. Rather than confessing to Youngs alone, McNemar left. The following day, Bates and Youngs went to Richard's home early in the morning, and Richard confessed his sins to the pair.

41. During this period, the term "Miamia" commonly referred to the area that lay in the vicinity of the Great Miami and Little Miami Rivers, tributaries of the Ohio River whose confluences with the Ohio lie in the Cincinnati area.

42. AIB-KyBgW-K, 55.

43. In addition to Benjamin Seth Youngs's 1805 journal and Issachar Bates's autobiography, which record several of the dreams and visions related by converts, the missionaries allude to visions of the Shakers and portents of their work in the letter Turtlecreek to New Lebanon, 1 June 1805, ASC 1048, DWint.

44. ASC 859, DWint, entry for April 21 (90).

45. McNemar (1831), 15.

46. ASC 859, DWint, entry for June 7 (130).

47. Turtlecreek to New Lebanon, 1 June 1805, ASC 1048, DWint.

48. From the Ministry and Elders of the Church in this place, New Lebanon, 19 June 1805, OClWHi IV A 30. Lovina Bates's first name was often spelled "Levina" by various writers, including Issachar himself. The fact that she herself signed documents both "Levina" and "Lovina" makes an authoritative spelling all the more difficult to identify.

49. Turtlecreek to New Lebanon, 1 June 1805, ASC 1048, DWint.

50. AIB-KyBgW-K, 55–56.

51. David Darrow's date of birth, 21 July 1750, is noted by Alonzo Hollister in "Book of Pioneer Correspondence from the West," 1871, OClWHi IV B 34. For Darrow's early conversion and disposition of his land to the Shakers, see Stein (1992), 12; White and Taylor (1905), 71; and Paterwic (2008), 52–53.

52. Rufus Bishop, Records, Book No. 2, "Concise Record of the Succession of Elders in the Church at New Lebanon," Item no. 6, Shaker Collection, NN, 20–21.

53. White and Taylor (1905), 45.

54. Daniel Moseley's date of birth is noted by Hollister in the "Book of Pioneer Cor-

respondence from the West." Mary Moseley's experience with Ann Lee is recounted in Bishop and Wells (1816).

55. "Manuscript history of Union Village, vol. 5," Item 343, 83–84, DLCMs.

56. Hollister, "Book of Remembrance," OClWHi VII B 108, 293–294.

57. "Domestic journal of important occurrences kept for the elder sisters at New Lebanon," OClWHi V B 60. An entry for 1 July 1805, records the departure of Darrow, Moseley, and King, in a loaded covered wagon.

58. ASC 859, DWint, entry for June 26 (156).

59. ASC 859, DWint, entry for August 6 (192).

60. David Darrow, et al, to New Lebanon Ministry, 25 September 1805, OClWHi IV A 66.

61. AIB-DWint, 67–68.

62. White and Taylor (1805), 354–355.

63. Some of Issachar's consultations with elders at New Lebanon are reflected in New Lebanon journals from the period of his visit, though without detail. See OClWHi V B 66, entry for November 5, 1805, "Issachar comes to see Elder Abiathar." This reference is to Abiathar Babbit, who from 1798 to 1807 served alongside Mother Lucy Wright as the principal male lead of the entire Shaker Ministry (see "Statement of the Various Changes of the Ministry from the first organization of the order in New Lebanon to the present date, by Giles Avery, Clerk," found on pages 16–19 of Record Book No. 2, kept by Rufus Bishop, Item no. 6, Shaker Collection, NN). In his consultations, Issachar would have related that in addition to eating with the Worley family, the Shaker missionaries had been relying upon the women converts for washing and mending their clothes, as well as sewing new clothes to replace worn garments, all of which would have emphasized their need to become more autonomous. See ASC 859, DWint, entry for June 26 (156).

64. ASC 859, DWint, entry for September 26 (217).

65. David Meacham to Elder David, 26 October 1805, OClWHi IV A 30. In fact, David Darrow had already negotiated the purchase of the southeastern quadrant of the section on which Worley and Richard's land lay, 160 acres for $440, which he informed the Ministry in a letter written September 25 and carried home by Issachar (Turtle Creek to New Lebanon, 25 September 1805, OClWHi IV A 66). In the same letter, David explains why the quarter section they desired to purchase from Timothy Sewell was priced so high, at $12 per acre.

66. For background on Meacham's function, see Brewer (1986), 22; and Paterwic (2008), 54.

67. David Meacham's letter only mentions the prospect of sending Shaker sisters in June. And in fact, early November entries in a New Lebanon journal for 1805 (OClWHi V B 66) reflect "a gift for the Elder Sister to go to Ohio," mentioning two women by name. But because dispatching a group of sisters alone was unthinkable, the sending of additional brothers also is implied.

68. "Records Kept by the Order of the Church, 1780–1855," Item no. 7, Shaker Collection, NN, 23.

69. See entries in "A domestic journal of domestic occurrences" OClWHi V B 63, and "Records of the Church at Watervliet, New York," OClWHi V B 279, page 7.

70. Benjamin S. Youngs to Ebenezer Bishop, 25 December 1805, copied in "Book of Pioneer Correspondence from the West," OClWHi IV B 34.

71. ASC 859, DWint, entry for December 11 (281).

72. AIB-DWint, 68–69.

73. AIB-DWint, 68.

74. ASC 859, DWint, entry for August 6 (192).

6. THE GROWTH OF THE SHAKER WEST

"New Year's Hymn," by Sally Eades, South Union Kentucky, in Russel Haskell, "A Record of Spiritual Songs . . . Enfield Connecticut, 1845," 2131/.S4E5, DLCM, 302. This hymn, one of many by South Union Kentucky Shaker Sally Eades, commemorates the arrival and early work of the three Shaker missionaries in the West.

1. ASC 859, DWint, entry for December 25 (293).

2. The use of the term "young believers" began at least as early as June 1805 (Turtle Creek to New Lebanon, 1 June 1805, ASC 1048, DWint). The term "old believers" referred collectively to the eastern Shakers sent west and was employed by the late summer of 1807, when it appears on the first map drawn of the Turtle Creek site. See Carol Medlicott, "'We live at a great distance from the Church': Cartographic Strategies of the Shakers, 1805–1835," *American Communal Studies Quarterly* 4, no. 3 (July 2010): 123–60. The terms persisted as an expedient way to differentiate between western-born and eastern-born Shakers in the West. See Carol Medlicott, "'Our Spiritual Ancestors': Alonzo Hollister's Record of Shaker "Pioneers" in the West," *Communal Societies* 31, no. 2 (November 2011): 45–60.

3. Hymn No. 19, OClWHi IX B 391, 47.

4. McNemar (1831), 18. The early land acquisitions at Turtle Creek are discussed in Medlicott (2010).

5. James Flint, "Flint's Letters from America, 1818–1820," from Reuben Goldthwaites, *Early Western Travels, 1748–1846* (Cleveland, OH: Arthur H. Clark Company, 1904), 9:300.

6. Miami Country, Ohio to Deacon Richard Spier, 17 March 1806, ASC 1048, DWint.

7. David Darrow to New Lebanon Ministry, 10 March 1817, in "Book of Pioneer Correspondence from the West," by Alonzo Hollister, OClWHi IV B 34.

8. David Darrow to New Lebanon Ministry, 19 March 1806, OClWHi IV B 66; and New Lebanon Ministry to David Darrow, 15 October 1807, OClWHi IV B 35.

9. See map of lands owned by John Dunlavy and John Knox in Martha Boice, et al., *Maps of the Shaker West: A Journey of Discovery* (Dayton, OH: Knot Garden Press, 1997), 28.

10. ASC 859, DWint, entries for July 30–31 and December 31.

11. South Union Record, vol. 1., Chambliss Collection, Special Collections Library, KyBgW-K, entries for 10–11 February 1805.

12. Benjamin Seth Youngs to Ebenezer Bishop, 2 February 1806, in "Book of Pioneer Correspondence," OClWHi IV B 34, 11–18.

13. South Union Record, vol. 1, KyBgW-K, entry for 13 April 1806.

14. AIB-DWint, 69–70.

15. Ruth Darrow et al., to New Lebanon Ministry, 18 August 1806, KyLoF, Box 18.

16. The furnishings, tools, and supplies taken to the West with this group of nine easterners are detailed in "Book of Records, 1802–1824," kept by Rufus Bishop, OClWHi I B 30.

17. "Concise Record of the Succession of Elders in the Church at New Lebanon, N.Y.," in *Records Book No. 2, Kept by Rufus Bishop, Beginning January 1825*, Item no. 6, Shaker Manuscripts, NN, 20.

18. Vital statistics on all the "old believers" is found in Medlicott (2011), 56–57.

19. Jenny Luckie McNemar to Dear Sisters, 25 September 1805, OClWHi IV A 66.

20. David Darrow and John Meacham to New Lebanon Ministry, 5 June 5 1806, OClWHi IV A 66. This letter is quoted extensively in Jean Humez, *Mother's First-Born Daughters: Early Shaker Writings on Women and Religion* (Bloomington: Indiana University Press, 1993), 133.

21. David Darrow to New Lebanon Ministry, 2 November 1806, ASC 1048, DWint. In this letter, Darrow makes an obvious Biblical reference when he characterizes the old believers' newly constructed dwelling as the "house of David."

22. Benjamin Seth Youngs, "Pamphlet Journal of Union Village, 1806–1807," NOcaS, entries for November 3 and December 15, 1806. The relationship between Edith Dennis and Eunice Bedle is discussed in Medlicott, "A Window on the West: Unity and Harmony in Shaker Zion," in Medlicott and Goodwillie (2013).

23. "Pamphlet Journal of Union Village, 1806–1807," NOcaS, entry for 1 January, 1807.

24. South Union Record, vol. 1, KyBgW-K, entry for 21 November 1806.

25. Ibid.

26. South Union Record, vol. 1, KyBgW-K, entries for 23–24 November 1806.

27. ASC 859, DWint, entry for 20 April 1805 (84).

28. I will use "Indians" to refer to the indigenous people of the region in order to remain consistent with the Shakers' own usage. In a September 1807 letter addressed to the Shawnee Prophet, Issachar Bates wrote that the Shakers "well remember about two years ago when you first came out from among your own people at White River, because they would not put away their wicked deeds," thus indicating that the Shakers had been aware in 1805 of the Indians' spiritual revival. See Benjamin Seth Youngs, Issachar Bates, and Richard McNemar to Lallu'a'tsee'kah, September 9, 1807, OClWHi IV A 67

29. For discussion of Tenskwatawa's conversion and move to Greenville, see R. David Edmunds, *The Shawnee Prophet* (Lincoln: University of Nebraska Press, 1983), 28–48.

30. Alfred A. Cave, "The Failure of the Shawnee Prophet's Witch-Hunt," *Ethnohistory* 42, no. 3 (Summer 1995): 445–75.

31. Benjamin Seth Youngs, "A journey to the Indians, Miami near Lebanon, Ohio, 3d month, 1807," ASC 860, DWint. In fact, David Darrow believed that it was his own

divinely inspired foreknowledge of the Prophet's encampment that led the Shakers to locate him. David Darrow to Lucy Wright, 10 September 1807, KyLoF, Reel 18.

32. The Shakers' March 1807 visit is discussed and Benjamin Seth Youngs' journal account reproduced in full in Edward Deming Andrews, "The Shaker Mission to the Shawnee Indians," *Winterthur Portfolio* 7 (1972): 113–28. The Prophet's name is rendered as "Lallawasheka" in Youngs' journal. R. David Edmunds, biographer of the Prophet, notes his name as "Lalawethika," meaning "noisemaker" before he changed it to Tenskwatawa, meaning "open door." See Edmunds (1983), 28 and 34.

33. ASC 860, DWint, entry for 25 March, 1807, and quoted in Andrews (1972), 125.

34. "Pamphlet Journal of Union Village," NOcaS, entry for 25 May 1807.

35. "Pamphlet Journal of Union Village," entry for 31 May 1807.

36. Historians of philanthropy in America have noticed the Turtle Creek Shakers' deliberate attempts to assist the Shawnee, in the face of local persecution. See Lawrence Jacob Friedman and Mark Douglas McGarvie, *Charity, Philanthropy, and Civility in American History* (London: Cambridge University Press, 2003), 107–10.

37. Lucy Wright to David Darrow, 11 July 1807, OClWHi IV A 31.

38. New Lebanon Ministry to David Darrow, 11 July 1807, OClWHi IV A 31.

39. Union Village Church Record, entry for 10 August 1807, Item 164c, DLCMs.

40. ASC 860, DWint, entry for 18 March 1807.

41. Richard McNemar's account of this visit is summarized by MacLean (1907), 359.

42. Union Village Church Record, entry for 29 August 1807, Item 164c, DLCMs.

43. David Darrow to New Lebanon, 13 September 1807, OClWHi IV A 67.

44. That letter, delivered through Tecumseh and the interpreter George Bluejacket, addresses the Prophet as "Lallu'a'tsee'kah" rather than as "Tenskwatawa," the name used by the Prophet's followers to reflect his spiritual status. To Lalllu'a'tsee'kah from Benjamin Seth Youngs, Issachar Bates, and Richard McNemar, 1 September 1807, OClWHi IV A 67.

45. Turtle Creek Ministry, by Tecumthah and Bluejacket Chiefs, for George Bluejacket, interpreter, 3 September 1807, OClWHi IV A 67.

46. Union Village Church Record, entry for 22 September 1807, Item 164c, DLCMs.

47. David Darrow to New Lebanon Ministry, 12 December 1807, ASC 1048, DWint.

48. South Union Record, vol. 1, KyBgW-K, entries for 27 October and 19 November 1807. A description of the early conversion period for both the Shawnee Run and Gasper River sites can be found in Julia Neal, *The Kentucky Shakers* (Lexington: University Press of Kentucky, 1983), 6–12.

49. AIB-DWint, 70–71.

50. David Darrow to Lucy Wright, 12 January 1807, KyLoF, Reel 18.

51. David Darrow to New Lebanon Ministry, 13 August 1806, ASC 1048, DWint.

52. AIB-DWint, 71–72.

53. AIB-DWint, 72.

54. AIB-DWint, 72–73.

55. I am indebted to Posey's recent biographer, John Thornton Posey, for confirming

after reviewing Issachar Bates's manuscript autobiography that Thomas Posey and Issachar Bates were placed on the same battlefield at Saratoga and in the same encampments at Boundbrook and West Point, while noting that any personal contact between them was highly unlikely.

56. Because of his extensive military service and subsequent political career in Kentucky, Louisiana Territory, and Indiana, the life of Thomas Posey is well-documented, beginning with the publication of his own memoir in 1846: James Hall, ed. "Memoir of Thomas Posey, in *Library of American Biography*, conducted by Jared Sparks (Boston: Charles C. Little and James Brown, 1846), 9:359–403.

57. Detailed discussion and documentation of Thomas Posey's career and travels, as well as the living situation of the Posey family near Henderson, Kentucky in the period of 1800–1810 is found in John Thornton Posey, *General Thomas Posey: Son of the American Revolution* (East Lansing: Michigan State University Press, 1992), 159–85.

58. The religious views of Mary Posey are discussed by Posey (1992), 117–18. Posey quotes Virginia aristocrat Archibald Alexander, remarking on Mary Posey's appearance, 118.

59. I am indebted to John Thornton Posey for his insights on the life and character of Mary Posey. Mr. Posey was not aware of Mary Posey's alleged confession to Issachar Bates, but he confirmed that the story was entirely consistent with her known religious inclinations. He also underscored that General Posey and his wife developed more separate lives after 1809. This was partly brought about by Posey's political career. Mary Posey could have followed him to his residences but chose not to, although there was no indication of strife in their relationship.

60. Issachar Bates's probable intent was to distinguish this man John Thompson from the Ohio New Light preacher of the same name.

61. AIB-DWint, 75–76.

62. This particular sentence is present in AIB-ODa, but is absent from other versions, such as AIB-DWint.

63. AIB-DWint, 75–76.

64. Issachar Bates to Seth Youngs Wells, 24 December 1808, Item 245, DLCMs. Lovina Bates's reply, if any, has not survived.

65. Manuscripts from the period 1805–1810 point to Issachar's increased trouble with his eyesight becoming an impediment to his writing. The immense amount of poetry he generated during this period underscores just how strong his impulse to write poetry must have been, since writing was very difficult for him. (Possibly Issachar dictated his poems to others.) By the early 1830s he had spectacles, but it is unknown when he acquired them. Issachar's eye problems are mentioned in John Meacham to Richard Spier, 19 December 1805, OClWHi IV B 66; and Issachar Bates to Seth Youngs Wells, 24 December 1808, Item 245, DLCMs.

66. Carol Medlicott, "Seeking 'the Cord that Unites' in Shaker Hymnody," in *Partake a Little Morsel: Popular Shaker Hymns of the Nineteenth Century* (Clinton, NY: Richard W. Couper Press, 2011).

67. Begun at Turtle Creek in 1806 and completed there sometime in 1808, in collaboration with John Meacham and others, portions of *The Testimony of Christ's Second Appearing* were sent to New Lebanon for approval before the first edition was printed in Lebanon, Ohio. See discussion of the writing process, David Darrow to New Lebanon Ministry, 12 December 1807, ASC 1048, DWint. After additional consultation with the eastern Ministry, a revised edition was printed in 1810 in Albany, New York.

68. David Darrow to New Lebanon Ministry, 12 January 1807, KyLoF, Reel 18.

69. "Great Shaker" is one among a group of hymns remarkable for their lasting and widespread appeal. See discussion in Medlicott (2011), 42–43.

70. Christian Goodwillie, "Millennial Praises: The Birth of Shaker Hymnody," in Christian Goodwillie and Jane Crosthwaite, eds., *Millennial Praises: A Shaker Hymnal* (Amherst: University of Massachusetts Press, 2009), 1–24.

71. "No Escape from Judgement," in Item 361, DLCMs, 21–23.

72. "Journal of William's Travel to the State of Ohio," entry for 5 July 1810, ASC 818, DWint.

73. "Notes written at Union Village, 7 February 1904," Item 257, DLCMs.

74. See commentary on "Will A Man Rob God? Said the Prophets of Old," in Medlicott and Goodwillie (2013).

75. AIB-ODa, 62.

76. "No Escape from Judgment," in Item 361, DLCMs, 21–23.

7. TRIBULATION ON THE WABASH

"A Winter Journey to Busroe," in AIB-DWint, 166.

1. Turtle Creek Elders to New Lebanon Ministry, 31 July 1808, ASC 1048, DWint.

2. E. Rankin Huston, *History of the Huston Families and Their Descendants, 1450–1912* (Carlisle, PA: Carlisle Printing Co., 1912), 14–15.

3. William Perrin, *History of Crawford and Clark Counties, Illinois* (Chicago, IL: O. L. Baskin and Co., 1883) 140. Robert's sons, John and Alexander Houston, left the Shakers as youths and eventually settled in Crawford County, Illinois, where they became prominent residents. Perrin briefly sketches the background of John and Alexander Houston's father, Robert.

4. For extensive discussion of these routes, see George R. Wilson, *Early Indiana Trails and Surveys* (Indianapolis: Indiana Historical Society Press, 1919), especially "The Buffalo Trace" (16–32), "Yellow Banks Trail" (36–44), "Red Banks Trail" (44–47), and "Salt Route or Trace" (47–49). For official correspondence on securing these routes, see William M. Cockrum, *Pioneer History of Indiana* (Oakland City, IN: Press of Oakland City Journal, 1907), 204–229.

5. *History of Knox and Daviess Counties, Indiana* (Chicago, IL: Goodspeed Pub. Co., 1886), 73.

6. AIB-DWint, 74.

7. Population figures for this early period are notoriously difficult to determine. In 1810, the population of all of Knox County was nearly 8,000 people, according to the U.S.

Census for Indiana Territory. George E. Green, *History of Old Vincennes and Knox County, Indiana* (Chicago, IL: S. J. Clarke Publishing Company, 1911), 1:468.

8. "Journal, Constant Moseley's journeys with the brethren and sisters," entry for 5 June 1808, Item 119, DLCMs.

9. See Green (1911), "The Wabash Creole — An Interesting Character," 88.

10. AIB-DWint, 74–75.

11. Several of Issachar Bates's acquaintances remark on his ability to appeal to any class of people. See AIB-ODa, 98; and "Diaries, memoranda of events, and other writings, by Richard McNemar, ca. 1824–1835," Item 255, DLCMs.

12. Turtle Creek to New Lebanon Ministry, 24 October 1808, ASC 1048, DWint.

13. Robert C. Bray, *Peter Cartwright, Legendary Frontier Preacher* (Champaign: University of Illinois Press, 2005), 56–58; and W. P. Strickland, ed., *Autobiography of Peter Cartwright, the Backwoods Preacher* (New York: Carlton and Porter, 1856), 53–55. According to Bray, Cartwright referred to his 1808 encounter with the Shakers as the "battle of Busro."

14. Issachar Bates, "A Winter Journey to Busro," in "A Record of Spiritual Songs," 2131/.S4E5, DLCM, 281.

15. Joseph Allen to Elder Nathaniel and the Ministry, 10 April 1809, copied in "A Record of Spiritual Songs," 2131/.S4E5, DLCM, 283–84.

16. A line from "A Winter Journey to Busro," by Issachar Bates.

17. Wilson (1919), 4–5, 93.

18. In "A Record of Spiritual Songs," 2131/.S4E5, DLCM, 50.

19. This earliest phase of Busro's organization is recounted in three manuscript sources. One is "South Union Record A, vol. 1, KyBgW-K. Though labeled as a history of South Union, the account's original author, Benjamin Seth Youngs, did not go to South Union as elder until October 1811; thus the earliest years of the account pertain to general events in the gathering of the western communities, with particular emphasis on locations where there was ongoing missionary activity, such as Busro. A second manuscript source is "Union Village Journal or Record, 1805–1889," Warren County Historical Center, Lebanon, Ohio. A third manuscript source is a rough handwritten sketch found in Item 355k, DLCMs, a manuscript that was probably compiled by Ohio Shaker sister Susan Liddell in the 1890s.

20. Benjamin Seth Youngs to Molly Goodrich, 10 February 1811, OClWHi IV B 35.

21. Governor Harrison to the Hon. William Eustis, Secretary of War, Vincennes, 15 May 1810. In *Messages and Letters of William Henry Harrison*, ed. Logan Esarey (Indianapolis: Indiana Historical Society, 1922), 1:421–22.

22. Issachar Bates's exact whereabouts in the first half of 1810 are unrecorded, although he definitely spent time among believers in Kentucky, including Gasper River and Red Banks. Possibly he visited Busro also. One early biography of Harrison alleges that a Shaker who claimed friendship with the Prophet was sent by Harrison as an emissary to Prophetstown in the summer of 1811, but this is not borne out in Harrison's correspondence. It is possible that this biographer conflated Harrison's stated intent to send a Shaker emissary to Prophetstown in 1810 with other dispatches of emissaries and intelli-

gence agents to Prophetstown during 1810–1811. See William O. Stoddard, *The Lives of the Presidents: William Henry Harrison, John Tyler, and James Knox Polk* (New York: Frederick A Stokes and Brother, 1888), 65.

23. James Smith, Esq., "An Attempt to Develop Shakerism," *Vincennes Western Sun* 3, no. 41 (October 10, 1810). I am indebted to Christian Goodwillie, who has shared his insights about James Smith's campaign against the Shakers.

24. South Union Record A, vol. 1, KyBgW-K, entry for 11 November 1810.

25. New Lebanon Ministry to Turtle Creek Elders, OClWHi IV A 32. Although this letter is undated, it can be reasonably dated to the late spring of 1810. It addresses requests made by Turtle Creek in a letter dated March 6, 1810, and it references the imminent arrival of Eliab Harlow, an eastern Shaker who visited the new western communities with William Deming in the summer of 1810. Likely the letter was carried west by Harlow and Deming.

26. Item 164c, DLCMs, entries for 29 August and 24 September 1809.

27. South Union Record A, vol. 1, KyBgW-K, entries for October and November, 1809.

28. "Memorandum of Particular Events Relating to West Union Society, circa 1811," Item 249, DLCMs.

29. That Issachar Bates and Salome Dennis (born Edith Bedle in 1783) developed a close relationship soon after her conversion is suggested by the name of baby Issachar Dennis, who was born in April 1805, probably to her, as she seems to have been the only Dennis woman of childbearing age. Her particular enthusiasm for singing and dancing is also recorded, which would have endeared her to Issachar. And Salome and her sister, Eunice Bedle, had been accorded the privilege of being taken into the household of the old believers in December 1806.

30. Two women named Salome are found in the New Testament, one a wicked temptress and daughter of King Herod and the other a faithful early convert of Paul. Shaker use of the name Salome surely intended to honor the latter.

31. MacLean (1907), 329.

32. A handwritten sketch of early Busro history compiled at Union Village in the 1890s notes, "James Hodge was chosen as (Archibald's) second or aid." Item 355k, DLCMs.

33. AIB-DWint, 78.

34. "Journal of William'sTravel to the State of Ohio," ASC 818, DWint, 20.

35. AIB-ODa, 69. Most of that passage was omitted from the version copied by Betsy Bates, Issachar's daughter and principal Ministry eldress at New Lebanon. Eldress Betsy may have wished to avoid drawing attention to several things: her father's boldness in addressing Darrow, the senior Shaker in the West; Darrow's solicitation of advice; and implied criticism of Archibald Meacham's leadership of Busro.

36. According to an 1812 ledger compiled by Busro's first trustee, John Knox brought well over $500 into the society. See "Indentures, correspondence, and other papers concerning Busro and West Union, Indiana, 1812–1836," Item 249, DLCMs.

37. It is reasonable to assume that David Darrow and Issachar Bates related well on a personal level. Darrow was just a few years older than Issachar, also a Revolutionary War

veteran, and a married man with children. Soon after Darrow's arrival in Ohio, he had been informed of the death of his wife back at New Lebanon, and his loss would have been best understood by Issachar. Later, after Darrow's death, a chair belonging to him came into Issachar's possession, further indication of their friendship.

38. David and Ruth to New Lebanon Ministry, 6 March 1810, OClWHi IV A 68.

39. Issachar Bates to Deacon Richard Spiers, 13 December 1811, OClWHi IV A 68.

40. AIB-DWint, 81.

41. Ironically, melons are the chief crop produced commercially on the farms currently occupying the Busro site in northwestern Knox County, Indiana, as the author learned during a visit to the site in the summer of 2009.

42. William N. Redmon to Eliza Sharp, Watervliet, Ohio, 17 January 1860, Item 245, DLCMs. A transcription of a portion of this same letter also appears in Daniel Patterson, *The Shaker Spiritual* (Princeton, NJ: Princeton University Press, 1979), by way of introducing the early Shaker experience of the frontier, which Patterson argues provided raw material for the writing of ballads (131–32).

43. "Journal, Constant Moseley's journeys with the brethren and sisters," entry for 26 June 1808, Item 119, DLCMs.

44. The life of John Slover was researched by early twentieth-century Ohio historian John Patterson Maclean, who also was among the first non-Shaker scholarly historians of the Shakers. See MacLean, *Some Incidents in the Life of John Slover* (Greenville, Ohio, 1926).

45. Hugh Henry Brackenridge, *Indian Atrocities: Narratives of Perils and Sufferings of Dr. Knight and John Slover Among the Indians During the Revolutionary War* (Cincinnati, OH: U. P. James, 1867), 55.

46. AIB-DWint, 79.

47. Rose Schultheis, "Harrison's Councils with Tecumseh," *Indiana Magazine of History* 27, no. 1 (March 1931): 40–49; Andrew Cayton, *Frontier Indiana* (Bloomington: Indiana University Press, 1996), 216–18; William Henry Harrison to William Eustis, July 10, 1810, in Esarey, ed. (1922).

48. AIB-DWint, 81.

49. Medlicott, " 'Our Spiritual Ancestors,' "(2011), 47.

50. There is a significant literature on the impact of malaria on human history. Some general studies specific to the United States include Erwin Heinz Ackerknecht, *Malaria in the Upper Mississippi Valley, 1760–1900* (New York: Arno Press, 1977) and Margaret Humphreys, *Malaria: Poverty, Race, and Public Health in the United States* (Baltimore, MD: Johns Hopkins University Press, 2001).

51. For a discussion of cultural implications of malaria for early nineteenth-century American settlers, see Conevery Bolton Valencius, *The Health of the Country: How American Settlers Understood Themselves and Their Land* (New York: Basic Books, 2002).

52. Humphreys (2001), 9–15.

53. The ecological reasons for malaria's prevalence in frontier watersheds of the Midwest are well explained by Stephen H. Gehlbach in his chapter "Scourge of the Middle

West: Autumnal Fever and Daniel Drake" in *American Plagues: Lessons from our Battles With Disease* (New York: McGraw Hill, 2005), 69–91.

54. Bates to Spier, 13 December 1811, OClWHi IV A 68.

55. Ibid.

56. Cayton (1996), 217–21.

57. Edmunds (1983), 100–105.

58. Meaning "blamed."

59. Bates to Spier, 13 December 1811, OClWHi IV A 68.

60. Edmunds (1983), 105. In a letter to the Secretary of War dated 25 September 1811, Governor Harrison recounts the theft of four horses "from the Busseron settlement," including details that match those in Issachar Bates's account of the Shakers' attempt to retrieve their stolen horses. This suggests regular contact between the Shakers and the Governor in this period. See Governor Harrison to the Hon. William Eustis, Secretary of War, Vincennes, 25 September 1811, in Esarey (1922), 589–92.

61. Bates to Spier, 13 December 1811, OClWHi IV A 68. Governor Harrison's correspondence reflects a dispatch written from the Army's temporary headquarters at "Bosseron Creek," 27 September 1811. See "General Orders, Headquarters, Bosseron Creek," in Esarey (1922), 592–94.

62. Bates to Spiers, 13 December 1811, OClWHi IV A 68. In fact, unbeknownst to Issachar Bates, the settlement was not then defenseless. On November 26, Governor Harrison wrote to Secretary of War Eustis that he had posted fifty mounted riflemen to patrol the area around the Shaker settlement at "Busseron," it being regarded the outermost perimeter of settlement north of Vincennes. See Harrison to Eustis, 26 November 1811, in Esarey, ed. (1922), 649–52.

63. AIB-DWint, 82.

64. Norma Hayes Bagnall, *On Shaky Ground: The New Madrid Earthquakes* (Columbia: University of Missouri Press, 1996), 100.

65. Issachar Bates to New Lebanon Ministry, 16 December 1811, KyLoF, Reel 18. The effect at Lebanon, Ohio, is noted in Myron Fuller, *The New Madrid Earthquake* (Washington, D.C.: U.S. Geological Survey, 1912), 28.

66. Samuel McCLelland, "Memorandum of Remarkable Events," summary entry for 1812, Item 250, DLCMs.

67. AIB-DWint, 92.

68. See Goodwillie and Crosthwaite, eds. (2009), 199.

69. Richard Spier to Archibald Meacham and Ruth Darrow, 12 May 1812, OClWHi A IV 68.

70. Ibid. Because a fragment of paper is torn away in the last part of this passage, the word "you" is inserted as a guess of how the sentence might read.

71. AIB-DWint, 97.

72. David Darrow to New Lebanon Ministry, 28 November 1812, OClWHi IV A 68.

73. The bloody attack on the large southern Indiana settlement of Pigeon Roost was reported in the *Vincennes Western Sun* on 8 September 1812.

74. David Darrow to New Lebanon Ministry, 28 November 1812, OClWHi IV A 68.

75. "A Funeral Hymn, dated Dec. 27, 1812," in Richard McNemar, *Selection of Hymns and Poems for the Use of Believers* (Watervliet, OH: Philos Harmoniae, 1833). When Richard McNemar composed this funeral hymn, several Shakers had died in a short interval at Union Village, including two of the recently arrived Busro refugees.

8. AN ELDER IN INDIANA

Verse epigraph from "A Lamentation for West Union," in McNemar (1833), 249.

Prose epigraph from AIB-DWint, 90–91.

1. David Darrow to New Lebanon Ministry, November 1812, OClWHi IV A 68.

2. From "Judgment," by Issachar Bates, in Item 361, DLCMs, 215.

3. Union Village Ministry to unknown recipient, September 1813, OClWHi IV A 66.

4. David Darrow to New Lebanon Ministry, December 1812, OClWHi IV A 68.

5. "A Statement of the Provisions &c that the Believers left at Busro, According to their best judgement," in *Records Book No. 2, Kept by Rufus Bishop*, Item no. 6, Shaker Collection, NN, 15. The Shakers' intent to assemble 1,000 spinning wheels in 1812 is put into perspective by one historian's observation that about 1,300 spinning wheels existed in all of Indiana territory in 1810. See Robert Martin Owens, *Mr. Jefferson's Hammer: William Henry Harrison and the Origins of American Indian Policy* (Norman: University of Oklahoma Press, 2007), 166.

6. Entry for December 1812, "Domestic journal of important occurrences . . . New Lebanon," OClWHi V B 60.

7. Eliab Harlow to Archibald Meacham, 26 February 1813, OClWHi IV A 32.

8. Issachar Bates to New Lebanon Ministry, 26 May 1814, Item 351b, DLCMs.

9. See entry for 23 May 1814, *Records Kept by the Order of the Church, New Lebanon*, Item no. 7, Shaker Collection, NN; entry for 27 June 1814, OClWHi V B 60; Union Village Ministry to New Lebanon Ministry, 13 August 1814, ASC 1048, DWint.

10. Issachar Bates to Seth Youngs Wells, 2 September 1817, OClWHi IV A 85.

11. Scholars of the Shakers have long assumed that the Shakers and the Harmonists met in Indiana. However, discovery of the Shaker rendezvous in Pittsburg in June 1814 to transfer relief supplies in 1814, together with careful reconstruction of the timeline of that journey and the timeline of the Harmonist travels, points to their initial meeting taking place in the vicinity of Pittsburg. George Rapp and his companion arrived in Pittsburgh on 4 June 1814 and departed about 14 June. See correspondence reprinted in Karl J. R. Arndt, ed., *A Documentary History of the Indiana Decade of the Harmony Society, 1814–1824* (Indianapolis: Indiana Historical Society, 1975), 1:6–10.

12. The race of one young man at Busro, Abraham (Abram) Jones, was mentioned in both Bates's and Harrison's account of the Shakers' pursuit by the Indians after having horses stolen. In Bates's version, Jones is referred to as a "black man and linguist"; in Harrison's version, he is referred to as a "black and Indian linguist."

13. Carol Medlicott, "Conflict and Tribulation on the Frontier: The West Union Shakers and Their Retreat," *American Communal Societies Quarterly* 3, no. 3 (July 2009): 111–37.

This article argues that the high number of youth who ultimately rejected Shakerism was a factor in the community's demise.

14. Samuel McCLelland, "Memorandum of Remarkable Events," entries for 22 August and 30 August 1814, Item 250, DLCMs.

15. Medlicott, "'Our Spiritual Ancestors'" (2011), observes that the male and female ministry leads in the Shaker West's first few decades were "old believers" from the East, with only occasional exceptions, such as Salome Dennis, who was female lead in West Union's ministry only temporarily.

16. Seth Youngs Wells to Issachar Bates, 18 January 1815, OClWHi IV A 77.

17. Issachar Bates to Seth Youngs Wells, 12 April 1815, Item 245, DLCMs.

18. Humez (1993) reprints a multitude of rich letters written by Shaker women in the West, but only one of these is authored by a western-born woman, as opposed to one transplanted from the East. Glendyne Wergland's *Sisters in the Faith: Shaker Women and Equality of the Sexes* (Amherst: University of Massachusetts Press, 2011) primarily addresses women in the eastern communities.

19. Salome Dennis to Elder Sister Hannah and Elder Sister Patty, 15 April 1815, ASC 1051, DWint.

20. Archibald Meacham to New Lebanon, 23 April 1815, ASC 1051, DWint.

21. Meacham to New Lebanon, 23 April 1814, ASC 1051, DWint.

22. An annotation in "Poems, by Richard McNemar, Issachar Bates, Prudence Morrell, and others," Item 346a, DLCMs, 354.

23. Salome Dennis to Elder Sister Hannah and Elder Sister Patty, 15 April 1815, ASC 1051, DWint.

24. Archibald Meacham and Issachar Bates to George and Frederick Rapp, 30 October 1815, in Arndt, ed. (1975), 146–47. Bates had left Busro on 21 September 1815 to visit the Harmonists, and he apparently fell ill during the visit. See McCLelland, "Memorandum of Remarkable Events," Item 250, DLCMs

25. Archibald Meacham to New Lebanon Ministry, 9 September 1817, OClWHi IV A 85.

26. Issachar Bates to Benjamin Seth Youngs, 10 November 1818, Item 245, DLCMs.

27. Issachar Bates to New Lebanon Ministry, 29 January 1819, OClWHi IV A 69.

28. The Busro Shakers probably suffered from other diseases besides malaria. A hollow tree placed inside a well to stabilize its sides was reportedly the source of water contamination, according to observations from an 1816 traveler. See David Thomas, *Travels Through the Western Country in the Summer of 1816* (Auburn, NY: David Rumsey, 1819), excerpted in Cheryl Bauer, ed., *Shakers of Indiana: A West Union Reader* (Milford, OH: Little Miami Publishing Co.), 83–88. The proximity of cattle and outhouses to the Shakers' water source, together with the high water table, could also have easily caused a variety of water-borne illnesses. See Medlicott (2009) for more discussion of disease at Busro.

29. George Rapp to Frederick Rapp, 22 June 1816, in Arndt, ed. (1975), 228.

30. Bates to Wells, 2 September 1817, OClWHi IV A 85.

31. George Rapp to Frederick Rapp, 22 June 1816, in Arndt, ed. (1975), 228.

32. "Mother's Gospel, Union Village, 1819," OClWHi VII B 242.

33. For a thorough discussion of Richard McNemar's life as a printer, see Goodwillie, "Custos Sacrorum: Richard McNemar as Curator and Printer," in Medlicott and Goodwillie (2013).

34. Issachar Bates to Seth Youngs Wells, 9 September 1817, OClWHi IV A 85.

35. Issachar Bates to Benjamin Seth Youngs, 10 November 1818, Item 245, DLCMs.

36. Though alcoholic cider was not forbidden, Issachar's postscript to this letter implies that it is an indulgence: "David Price made a barrel of cider this fall and we are drinking of it as slow as we can."

37. Archibald Meacham to the Ministry at South Union, 15 November 1818, Item 245, DLCMs.

38. Issachar Bates to Seth Youngs Wells, 2 September 1817, OClWHi IV A 85.

39. Archibald Meacham to New Lebanon Ministry, 20 December 1819, Item 351b, DLCMs. A letter written by Martha Sanford from Busro to two New Lebanon sisters alludes to the possible move to Illinois and suggests that she believed Archibald was seriously considering the move: "But if Illinois is the next place, pray do not forget your little sister. Martha Sanford to Elder Sister Rachel and Sister Olive, 21 December 1819, Item 351b, DLCMs.

40. Issachar Bates to New Lebanon Ministry, 28 April 1820, OClWHi IV A 69.

41. "Reflections by William Redmon," Item 104, DLCMs, 126.

42. Thomas (1819).

43. Absolem H. Blackburn, *A Brief Account of the Rise, Progress, Doctrines and Practices of the People Usually Denominated Shakers* (Flemingsburg, KY: n.p., 1824).

44. Bates to Wells, Sept. 2, 1817, OClWHi IV A 85. There has been some speculation that the reputed lassitude among the Busro Shakers may have been due to the effects of malaria. However, the literature on frontier malaria suggests that malaria survivors could expect lives of normal activity except during periods of relapse, when they could anticipate a specific cycle of chills and fever. See Valencius (2002), 80–84; and Gehlbach (2005), 76–77. For dramatic effect in his novel *Martin Chuzzlewit*, Charles Dickens exaggerated the fictitious "Eden" along the Mississippi as hopelessly squalid, its residents permanently debilitated by malaria.

45. "Industry . . . Elder Issachar Bates, W.U.," in Item 361, DLCMs, 214–15.

46. *Journal of Thomas Dean: A Voyage to Indiana in 1817* (Fort Wayne, IN: Public Library of Fort Wayne and Allen County, 1955), 40–44.

47. Probably this was the same trumpet whose purchase in Vincennes for fifty cents is recorded in the West Union account ledger in August 1815, OClWHi II B 123). Dean's reference to trumpet calls regulating daily activities stands as a rare glimpse of how villages communicated the daily routine prior to the installation of large bells atop village structures (1829 at Union Village and 1835 at New Lebanon). Some scholars assert that eastern Shakers used conch shells for daily signals such as rising, meal calls, etc. I am not aware of any references to trumpets in any other Shaker village. It seems significant that a

trumpet would have been used at Busro while Issachar Bates lived there, considering that he had occasionally served as a "fluglemaster" during the Revolutionary War, along with his duties as a fifer. This raises the possibility that Issachar himself might have blown the trumpet at Busro.

48. *Journal of Thomas Dean*, 42.

49. West Union Ministry to New Lebanon Ministry, 24 March 1821, OClWHi IV A 85. The original letter reflects Issachar Bates's distinctive handwriting. Detailed discussion of the preparation of the stonework—sills, caps, steps, and so on—suggests that Issachar could have been closely involved in the construction project, perhaps using skills he may have learned from his father William Bates, a mason.

50. Union Village Ministry to New Lebanon Ministry, 10 February 1821, ASC 1048, DWint.

51. McClelland, "Memorandum of Remarkable Events," entry for 23 April 1822, Item 250, DLCMs.

52. West Union Ministry to New Lebanon Ministry, 7 June 1822, OClWHi IV A 85.

53. Benjamin's account notes they acquired a Durham bull calf named Comet, which became the progenitor of South Union's highly valued Durham cattle stock.

54. Benjamin Seth Youngs, "Account of a visit to West Union, 3.23.4.1822," ASC 860, DWint.

55. Union Village Ministry to New Lebanon Ministry, 22 October 1822, ASC 1048, DWint.

56. South Union Ministry to New Lebanon Ministry, 3 December 1822, ASC 1047, DWint.

57. West Union Ministry to New Lebanon Ministry, 22 October 1823, OClWHi IV A 85.

58. The letter dated 22 October 1823 from the West Union Ministry to New Lebanon contains a postscript alluding to having just received this news in a letter from the Second Family at Watervliet, NY, where most of Issachar's family resided. At least two letters from the East received earlier in 1823 allude to Polly Bates's deteriorating condition, so Issachar was doubtless aware that his daughter was not expected to live.

59. AIB-DWint, 91.

60. AIB-DWint, 97.

9. THE BATES KINSHIP NETWORK IN THE SHAKER EAST
Seth Youngs Wells to Issachar Bates, 26 July 1817, OClWHi IV A 77.

1. West Union Ministry to New Lebanon Ministry, 7 June 1822, OClWHi IV A 85. This letter is in Issachar Bates's hand, as are many of the letters signed on behalf of the Ministry, suggesting that Issachar was often delegated the task of correspondence.

2. Seth Youngs Wells' phrase is an obvious pun whose humor was based on Issachar's name matching that of one of the Biblical tribes of Israel.

3. AIB-DWint, 22–23.

4. "A Letter Historic & Chronologic, Wisdom's Valley, March 8th, 1871," OClWHi VII B 109.

5. AIB-DWint, 47.

6. The only known reference to Issachar's eldest daughter being a Shaker is an anthem attributed to Lovina Bates, Jr., recorded in the Elizabeth Garvey hymnal, NCH.

7. OClWHi V A 6.

8. Malcom Worley to New Lebanon Ministry, 9 September 1807, ASC 1048, DWint.

9. Daniel Moseley to David Darrow, 26 February 1813, OClWHi IV A 32. "Elder Brother" probably refers to Seth Youngs Wells, who regularly corresponded with Issachar Bates.

10. Hannah and David Train married in Athol, Massachusetts, in 1774, and four of their nine children were born before Issachar and Lovina Bates moved to Hartford, New York, in 1786.

11. "The Covenant of the Second Family of the Society of Believers at Watervliet," 5 March 1815, Reel 3, Shaker Collection, N.

12. For a study of the Eunice Chapmen case, see Ilyon Woo, *The Great Divorce: A Nineteenth-Century Mother's Extraordinary Fight Against Her Husband, the Shakers, and Her Times* (New York: Atlantic Monthly Press, 2010).

13. Eunice Chapman's own account of her short stay at Watervliet in 1814, including seeing James Chapman conversing with his "spiritual wife" and her physical removal by Hannah Train and other sisters is included in her published statement of grievances against the Shakers, *Account of the Conduct of the Shakers, In the Case of Eunice Chapman & Her Children* (Lebanon, OH: Van Vleet and Camron, 1818).

14. Eunice Chapman's case against the Shakers is discussed in the Watervliet Church Family records, entries for February and March 1817, OClWHi V B 279.

15. Goodwillie, in *"Millennial Praises*: The Birth of Shaker Hymnody," in Goodwillie and Crosthwaite (2009) presents evidence from Shaker manuscripts showing that *Millennial Praises* was brought home from the bindery on April 6–7, 1813. He notes that the manner of distributing the hymnal is not clear. I am grateful to Goodwillie for sharing his further insights on the distribution, including his observation that copies were commonly distributed to rank-and-file Shakers and that while signature inscriptions are common, copies inscribed with dates corresponding to the volume's publication period are less so.

16. New Lebanon Ministry to Pleasant Hill Ministry, 25 December 1828, OClWHi IV B 7. Lovina Bates's death is listed along with several others who had recently died "from consumption and other complaints."

17. The copy of *Millennial Praises* inscribed with Lovina Bates's signature is in the Shaker collection of Western Reserve Historical Society, call number BX 9786 P7M6a Pts. 3–4 Copy 2. Beneath Bates's inscription is the name "Olive Wicks," who was an adolescent girl in the Watervliet Second Family at the time of Lovina's death ("List of Believers at Watervliet, New York, 1829," in Item 255, DLCMs).

18. "The Covenant of the Second Family of the Society of Believers at Watervliet," 5 March 1815.

19. "A Letter Historic and Chronologic," OClWHi VII B 109. The fact that the Lane family was "colored" is mentioned in many passing references to individual members of the Lane family in Watervliet, New York, manuscripts.

20. Salome Dennis to Elder Sister Hannah and Elder Sister Patty, 15 April 1815, ASC 1051, DWint.

21. Shaker Biographical Card File Collection, Wallace Cathcart, OClWHi, Reel 123.

22. New Lebanon Ministry to West Union Ministry, 22 May 1823, OClWHi IV A 34.

23. "Daily journal of the Second or West Family," OClWHi V B 300.

24. "A Memorandum Book Beginning in the Year 1818," entry for 16 July 1823, Reel 3, Shaker Collection, N. Other visits, including that of Theodore Bates, are recorded in OClWHi V B 300.

25. New Lebanon Ministry to Union Village Ministry, 11 August 1823, OClWHi IV A 34.

26. Entries for 13–15 September 1823, OClWHi V B 300.

27. Salome Dennis to Elder Sister Hannah and Elder Sister Patty, 15 April 1815, ASC 1051, DWint.

28. Issachar Bates to Benjamin Seth Youngs, 10 November 1818, Item 246, DLCMs.

29. Financial records for the Watervliet, New York, community, OClWHi II B 97, entries for 1832–1833, indicate that Issachar Bates Jr. produced great quantities of both lumber planks and braided whips.

30. Issachar Bates to Isaac Youngs, undated, OClWHi IV A 66. Though the date is not known, "1820?" is written on the outside of the letter, an estimate. "Little" Issachar writes the text and tune of a song on the second page of the letter, rendering the song with four-shape notation (see appendix 3, "Remember Lord"). Use of four-shape noteheads was a common form of musical notation that the senior Issachar Bates, a choirmaster, would have known and used. How Issachar Jr. learned it is unknown. Isaac Newton Youngs occasionally employed it in some of his many music manuscripts. This letter, originally collected by the Western Reserve Historical Society in the early twentieth century, is catalogued with manuscripts pertaining to Union Village, Ohio, evidence that earlier ar-chivists assumed its author was the senior Issachar Bates. I also assumed that until closer analysis revealed the almost certain attribution to Issachar Jr.

31. Wergland (2006) analyzes the various struggles with obedience and sexuality that Isaac Young experienced in his early twenties, especially in chapter 3, "Youth and Lust," and chapter 4, "Rebellion in Shaker Society."

32. "A Daily Journal of Passing Events," entry for 1 September 1834, Rufus Bishop, Item no. 1, Shaker Collection, NN.

33. See "Roll of members of the South Family or Gathering Order," OClWHi III B 36; and entry for 24 January 1833, "Records of the Church at Watervliet, N.Y.," OClWHi V B 279.

34. During 1834 and 1835, for example, Issachar Bates Jr. made several trips to New Lebanon to talk about Garret Van Houten, a Shaker in Watervliet's gathering order, who had left but was despondent and wished to return.

35. Most recipients of the Sacred Role were prominent U.S. politicians and foreign dignitaries. Recipients are listed in OClWHi II B 97.

36. OClWHi II B 97 records the expenses of Issachar Bates Jr. for his trip to Jefferson County to deliver the Sacred Role to Artemas Bates. He also delivered a copy to a Meth-

odist minister in Schenectady, New York, named Harwood, who was likely a cousin as the Harwoods and Bateses were related by marriage.

37. Sarah Bates to Hulda Bagg, June 28, 1875, ASC 1057, DWint. In this letter, Sarah notes that she and her brother Issachar are the only surviving siblings, that none of the siblings died earlier than in their thirties, and that she and Issachar have both outlived their oldest brother, who lived to be seventy-seven.

38. Sarah Bates and Betsy Bates both lived long enough to have been photographed. I have been unable determine if they are included in any group photos of Shakers.

39. Issachar Bates to Sarah Bates, 9 September 1807, OClWHi IV A 67.

40. Issachar Bates's letter to his daughter is dated just a few days after his letter written to the Shawnee Prophet, and at the end of a tense period during which he and Richard McNemar had visited the Shawnee, followed by the arrival of 50 Shawnee at Turtle Creek, whom they hosted amid threats from local militia to disassociate from the Indians. Shortly Issachar and Richard would start for Kentucky and Tennessee on a major preaching circuit. The letter mentions nothing of these activities.

41. Entry for 16 November 1808, OClWHi V B 279.

42. "Records Kept by the Order of the Church," entry for 20 February 1811, New Lebanon, New York, Item no. 7, Shaker Collection, NN. The entry notes that Sarah Bates was brought to New Lebanon by Jesse Wells.

43. See entry for "Seth Youngs Wells," Paterwic (2008).

44. As early as 1810, Seth Youngs Wells served as superintendent of the town schools in New Lebanon, New York, of which the Shaker school was a part, as indicated in "School Record for District No. 12, Town of New Lebanon, Kept Agreeably to the 23rd Article of the Act for the Support of Common Schools, passed April 12th, 1819," OClWHi I B 32. For evidence of Wells's work in organizing Shaker schools, as well as traveling throughout the northeast to make recommendations on school administration, see "A few remarks upon learning and the use of books, for the consideration of the youth among Believers," Seth Youngs Wells, 1825. OClWHi VII B 255.

45. Account of Rhoda Blake, ASC 846, DWint. Note that ASC 846 is designated "Autobiography of Richard Pelham," but the same volume contains the autobiographical account of Rhoda Blake, written in at a different time.

46. Wergland (2006) briefly discusses the teaching career of Isaac Newton Youngs, 150–51.

47. Wergland (2011), 65–66.

48. Sarah Bates to Hulda Bagg, June 28, 1875, ASC 1057, DWint.

49. Many examples have been preserved. See "Rewards of Merit," OClWHi XIV 15.

50. Daniel Patterson, *Gift Drawing and Gift Song* (Sabbathday Lake, ME: United Society of the Shakers, 1983), 61–65.

51. This phase of Shaker history has received considerable attention, both from later Shakers who produced historical accounts and from non-Shaker scholars from the mid-twentieth century forward. See for example, Henry C. Blinn, *The Manifestation of Spiritualism Among the Shakers* (East Canterbury, NH: The Shakers, 1899); White and Taylor

(1905), 219–52; Andrews (1953), "Mother Ann's Work," 152–76; Stein (1992), 165–200; and Wergland (2006), "Shaker Worship, Isaac Newton Youngs, and the Era of Manifestations," 109–25.

52. The inspired art of the Shakers has attracted significant scholarly attention. See David Sellin, "Shaker Inspirational Drawings," *Philadelphia Museum of Art Bulletin* 57, no. 273 (Spring 1962), 93–99; Edward Deming Andrews and Faith Andrews, *Visions of the Heavenly Sphere: A Study in Shaker Religious Art* (Charlottesville: University Press of Virginia, 1969); Sally Promey, *Spiritual Spectacles: Vision and Image in Mid-Nineteenth Century Shakerism* (Bloomington: Indiana University Press), 1993; France Morin, ed., *Heavenly Visions: Shaker Gift Drawings and Gift Songs* (New York: The Drawing Center, 2001).

53. For analysis of Hannah Cohoon's artwork, see Ruth Wolfe, "Hannah Cohoon," in Jean Lipman and Tom Armstrong, eds., *American Folk Painters of Three Centuries* (New York: Hudson Hills Press, 1980), 58–65.

54. Sally L. Kitch, "'As a Sign That All May Understand': Shaker Gift Drawings and Female Spiritual Power," *Winterthur Portfolio* 24, no. 1 (Spring 1989): 1–28.

55. "Shaker Biographies and Spirit Messages," 1867, ASC 1073, DWint.

56. "Narrative of Various Events," Isaac Newton Youngs, entry for 8 April 1819, Item 42, DLCMs.

57. Since the eighteenth century, the term "class" is commonly applied to any group of singers engaging in sight-singing using the shape-note system. This term is a residue of that system having been taught by choirmasters in "singing schools." That the New Lebanon Shakers used the term "class" is a reminder of the orientation of their singing to this existing regional choral tradition.

58. The singers in each "class" are identified in "Journal kept by Betsy Bates," entry for September 13, 1835, OClWHi V B 128. Sarah Bates's status as a singer is also mentioned in several places in "Journal kept by Henry DeWitt," OClWHi V B 97.

59. "Journal kept by Annie Williams," entries for 1836, OClWHi V B 127.

60. Shakers were encouraged to compile songbooks for their own use and to share with friends. Typically an individual songbook contains material authored and composed by many different Shakers in several communities. Surviving Shaker manuscript songbooks number in the thousands and are, as a whole, an incredibly diverse manifestation of Shaker creativity. See Carol Medlicott, "Innovation in Music and Song," in R. Stephen Miller, *Inspired Innovations: A Celebration of Shaker Ingenuity* (Hanover, NH: University Press of New England, 2010), 199–206.

61. The account of the child Betsy Bates bidding tearful farewell to Issachar in 1805 attests to her strong affection for her father, at least in childhood.

62. Sarah Bates to Issachar Bates, 20 May 1823, OClWHi IV A 34. A postscript in the same letter, which conveys greetings to the rest of the ministry at Busro, Indiana, is signed by both Sarah Bates and her sister Betsy, evidence that Betsy was aware of Sarah writing to their father.

63. Several examples of letters copied by Sarah Bates on behalf of the Ministry can be found in "Copies of letters sent by the Ministry to various communities," OClWHi IV B 8.

64. "A Concise view of the Various Changes In the Order of Office Deacons & Deaconesses of the Church," 32–37, in *Records Book No. 2, Kept by Rufus Bishop*, Item no. 6, Shaker Collection, NN.

65. "Journal of daily events kept by Betsy Bates," entry for 10 April 1835, OClWHi V B 128.

66. "Records Kept by the Order of the Church," entry for 24 April 1811, New Lebanon, New York, Item no. 7, Shaker Collection, NN. The entry notes that the New Lebanon Ministry returned from Watervliet, bringing Betsy Bates with them.

67. Entry for 1 December 1808, OClWHi V B 279.

68. "Sheets containing poems, verses, lyrics, and prayers," OClWHi X A 1.

69. "My Soul Rejoices," Betsy Bates, 1827, in "Book of Songs, by Isaac Newton Youngs to Alonzo Hollister, 1864," OClWHi IV B SM 413. This volume contains many short songs attributed to Betsy Bates.

70. While Daniel Patterson (1979, 217) describes Betsy Bates by way of an 1828 visitor's account of a middle-aged Shaker eldress (Anne Royall's encounter with the hospitable, tall, and handsome "Miss Betsy"), the woman described was probably not Issachar's daughter. Betsy Bates was neither middle-aged nor yet an eldress during Royall's 1828 visit, and with a recorded height of 5'3" she was average height. Several other women named Betsy at New Lebanon fit Royall's description more closely.

71. Wergland (2011) analyzes the importance and meaning of women's caps in Shaker culture (73–84). The experience of Shaker women in designing caps and bonnets for their own stimulated a bonnet industry that made various kinds of bonnets for sale to the world (148–60).

72. "Journal of daily events kept by Betsy Bates," entries for April 1835, OClWHi V B 128.

73. The several offices held by Betsy Bates in the New Lebanon Church Family and Ministry are detailed in Rufus Bishop, Records, Book No. 2, "Concise Record of the Succession of Elders in the Church at New Lebanon," Item no. 6, Shaker Collection, NN.

74. "True Believer's Heaven," by Betsy Bates, OClWHi IV B SM 413.

75. "Records of the Church at Watervliet, N.Y.," entries for March 1860, OClWHi V B 281.

76. "Book of Sacred Hymns, Hancock," ASC 888, DWint, 129.

77. "Eldress Betsey Bates, in the Spirit Land," *Shaker and Shakeress* 4, no. 2 (February 1874): 15.

78. Shaker scholars have noticed members of the Train family, who exhibited disruptive and deranged behavior from time to time, causing speculation that some of the Trains were mentally ill. See for example, Stephen J. Stein, "The 'Not-So-Faithful' Believers: Conversion, Deconversion, and Reconversion Among the Shakers," *American Studies* 38, no. 3 (Fall 1997): 5–20.

79. U.S. Census, 1820.

80. "Records of the Church at Watervliet, N.Y." entry for 4 February 1825, OClWHi V B 279, and entries for Bates, Microfilm Reel 123, OClWHi.

81. New Lebanon Ministry to West Union Ministry, 30 July 1825, OClWHi IV A 35.

82. "Register of Members of Various Communities," members lists for Watervliet, New York, 1827, OClWHi III B 42.

83. Paulina Bates, *The Divine Book of Holy and Eternal Wisdom... In Two Volumes* (New Lebanon, NY, 1849). Paulina Bates's work is addressed at length in Humez (1993), who analyzes it (220–21) and presents an extensive transcription (258–67).

84. Seth Youngs Wells to Issachar Bates, 25 February 1815, OClWHi IV A 77.

85. Note from Issachar Bates to Seth Youngs Wells, appended to letter from Salome Dennis to Hannah Wells and Patty Carter, 15 April 1815, ASC 1051, DWint.

86. Seth Youngs Wells to Issachar Bates, 26 July 1817, OClWHi IV A 77.

87. Issachar Bates to Seth Youngs Wells, 2 September 1817, OClWHi IV A 85.

88. This claim is widely repeated by the earliest historians among the Shakers, including White and Taylor (1905), 314.

89. See discussion of brooms in M. Stephen Miller, "Health and Sanitation," in Miller (2010), 149–67.

90. "Watervliet: signed by members, 1801," Reel 3, Shaker Collection, N.

91. "Journal of trips made by Elder Ebenezer and others," OClWHi V A 6.

92. *Vital Records of Templeton, Massachusetts.*

93. Sears (1916), 41.

94. *Vital Records of Phillipston, Massachusetts.*

95. *Vital Records of Templeton, Massachusetts.*

96. "The Covenant of the Second Family of the Society of Believers at Watervliet," 5 March 1815, and "Roll of Members of the South Family or Gathering Order," OClWHi III B 36.

97. Immediately upon the death of her husband in 1846, Theodore Bates's widow Abigail Wheeler filed an application in Albany to receive the widow's survivor benefits of Theodore's Revolutionary War pension. Theodore had never claimed his pension. See Pension Application for Theodore Bates (Massachusetts), Records Relating to Revolutionary War Pension Applicants, National Archives.

98. "Records Kept by the Order of the Church," entry for 1 April 1827, Item no. 7, Shaker Collection, NN.

99. "Record of clothing & articles given to apostates from Watervliet," OClWHi II B 98.

100. Watervliet Church Record, entry for 10 August 1827, OClWHi V B 279.

101. "Records Kept by the Order of the Church," entry for 23 September, Item no. 7, Shaker Collection, NN

102. New Lebanon Ministry to Issachar Bates, 12 January 1824, OClWHi IV B 7.

10. TRANSFORMATIONS IN THE SHAKER WEST

"The Cockatrice Routed" appears as Hymn 25, Part 3, in McNemar (1833), 183. The text is unattributed, but believed to be the work of Issachar Bates. See Medlicott and Goodwillie (2013).

1. From "The Daystar" by Issachar Bates, from Item 361, DLCMs. Attributed to Issachar Bates but undated, "The Daystar" probably comes from the late 1810s or early 1820s, periods of rapid building both at Union Village and throughout the Shaker West. For tune and full text, see appendix 2.

2. Although Union Village did not exert hierarchical authority over all the western Shaker communities, it was nonetheless repeatedly referred to as the "Center of Union" in the West because it was the first seat of the gospel and because its initial leaders, David Darrow and Ruth Farrington, were accorded by New Lebanon the rare parental titles of "Father" and "Mother."

3. Issachar Bates to the New Lebanon Ministry, 29 January 1819, OClWHi IV A 69.

4. For discussion of Union Village's layout and structures in the early 1820s, see Cheryl Bauer and Rob Portman, *Wisdom's Paradise: The Forgotten Shakers of Union Village* (Wilmington, OH: Orange Frazer Press, 2004),

5. See "Sketches of the Various Situations of Union Village," part of a series of maps produced in 1835 by eastern Shaker George Kendall, after sketches completed in 1834 by Isaac Newton Youngs during his visit to the western Communities. The collection can be found as *Sketches of the Various Societies of Believers*, Library of Congress.

6. In "Membership list compiled from various sources," OClWHi III B 33, 2.

7. "Map of Ohio," in H. C. Carey and I. Lea, *A Complete Historical, Chronological, and Geographical American Atlas* (Philadelphia: T. H. Palmer, 1822). The Union Village location is identified by only a single word, misspelled on the map as "Uinon." Ironically, the state maps in the Carey and Lea atlas mark more western than eastern Shaker sites, correctly locating the four villages that had ministries: Union Village, Ohio, Pleasant Hill, Kentucky, South Union, Kentucky, and West Union, Indiana. The three latter are marked as "Shaker T," "Shakertown," and "Shaker Town," respectively. Of all the eastern Shaker villages in 1822, only the village at Enfield, Connecticut, is marked in the Carey and Lea maps, denoted with the word "Shakers."

8. Robert B. Gordon, *Natural Vegetation of Ohio, At the Time of the Earliest Surveys* (Ohio Biological Survey, 1966).

9. AIB-ODa, 75.

10. McNemar's exact reasons for adopting the pseudonym are murky, notwithstanding a late nineteenth-century explanatory anecdote repeated in Phillips (1972). Careful attention to the body of early western Shaker documentation points to this story being a fabrication. However and whenever Richard arrived at the pseudonym, friends and the community in general were nearly universal in using "Eleazar" (or the initials E. W.) to refer to him from the 1820s on.

11. Indiana had become a state in 1816, while Issachar Bates was living at Busro. The work with the Darby Plains community, the beginning of the White Water Shaker community, and the beginning of the North Union Shaker community all occurred simultaneously, as explained in letters by Mathew Houston and Richard McNemar. See Houston to Seth Youngs Wells, 23 September 1823, KyLoF, Reel 18; and McNemar to Procter Sampson, 4 July 1824, Item 245, DLCMs.

12. "Diary of Nathaniel Taylor," entries for January 1823, MSS 119, Box 3, Folder 3, OHi.

13. Richard McNemar to Seth Youngs Wells, 23 March 1824, OClWHi IV A 70.

14. From 1821 to 1825, Malcom Worley was elder at the "Brick House," one of three dwellings that comprised the Center Family at Union Village. From 1814 until sometime in 1824, Mathew Houston was elder at the "East House," the site of McNemar's original property.

15. "Daily journal of events and activities by John Wallace and Nathan Sharp," entries for February and March 1824, OClWHi V B 236.

16. *Testimony of Christ's Second Appearing* (Union Village, OH: B. Fisher and A. Burnett, Printers, 1823). These editions and their differences are identified in Mary Richmond, *Shaker Literature: A Bibliography*, vol. 1 (Hanover, NH: Shaker Community, Inc. and University Press of New England, 1977), R1469, R1470, R1471.

17. A letter states that the Elder's Shop was Issachar Bates's lodging in early 1824. Richard McNemar to Seth Youngs Wells, 23 March 1824, OClWHi IV A 70.

18. Entry for 22 March 1824, OClWHi V B 236.

19. Richard McNemar to Seth Youngs Wells, 23 March 1824, OClWHi IV A 70.

20. Ibid.

21. It was common in most Shaker communities for singers to secretly prepare celebration hymns for special occasions, unveiling them at a specified times, often in special processions.

22. McNemar to Wells, 23 March 1824, OClWHi IV A 70.

23. Richard, who knew Hebrew, was referring to a manner of circular dancing from ancient Jewish tradition. The Hebrew word that he renders as "Hag" is one of several Hebrew words meaning "dance." See Julian Morgenstern, "The Etymological History of the Three Hebrew Synonyms for 'To Dance,' HGG, HLL and KRR, and Their Cultural Significance," *Journal of the American Oriental Society*, 36. (1916): 321–32. The circle dance became a favorite form throughout the Shaker world (see figure 12.2). Manuscripts reflect that Shakers came to see the circle dance as a physical expression of the Old Testament story of "Ezekiel's Wheel" (see appendix 2, "Ezekiel's Wheel, or A Christmas Hymn."

24. McNemar to Wells, 23 March 1824, OClWHi IV A 70.

25. After its early appearance at Union Village, this manner of circular dancing, with alternating wheels of men and women marching in opposite directions around a center point, became widespread throughout the Shaker world. It was famously rendered as a lithograph by a visitor to New Lebanon and published in *Frank Leslie's Illustrated Newspaper*, 1 December 1873 (see figure 12.2). See discussion of the "round dance" and "circular march" in Patterson (1979), 178 and 265–67.

26. McNemar to Wells, 23 March 1824, OClWHi IV A 70.

27. Entry for 28 March 1824, OClWHi V B 236.

28. AIB-DWint, 98–99.

29. Philip E. Webber, "Jakob Sylvan's Preface to the Zoarite Anthology *Die Wahre Separation, oder die Widergeburt* as an Introduction to Un(der)studied Separatist Principles," *Communal Societies*, 19 (1999): 101–28, 102.

30. Webber (1999), 101. The Zoar Separatists were initially assisted by Quakers, who sympathized with their antipathy towards the liturgical formality of German Lutheranism.

31. AIB-DWint, 100. Issachar mentions his "bursted" foot and his complete loss of hair and nails, which later grew back.

32. "Journal of Passing and Important Events at Union Village, Ohio," entry for 11 May 1824, by Daniel Miller, OClWHi V B 237.

33. MacLean (1907), 352. reports that both Morrell and Hampton had worked as physicians.

34. AIB-DWint, 99.

35. E. O. Randall, *History of the Zoar Society* (Columbus, OH: Press of Fred J. Heer, 1900), 96.

36. Entry for 27 May 1824, OClWHi V B 236.

37. "Hymnbook, Richard McNemar, nephew of the preacher Richard McNemar, 1823," Item 193, DLCMs.

38. AIB-DWint, 100.

39. Entry for 4 July 1824, OClWHi V B 237. The number of people at Union Village on that day was estimated at an even higher 2,000 by David Darrow in a letter to the New Lebanon Ministry, 31 July 1824, 112–18, OClWHi IV B 34.

40. AIB-ODa, 69–70. This particular passage, and the one that follows, reveal evidence of how Bates's biography was later edited. At least two versions copied later by other scribes, including two by Bates's own children (AIB-DWint and AIB-DLCMs-161), omit remarks that disparage conditions at Watervliet and reveal Bates's misgivings.

41. Issachar Bates to the New Lebanon Ministry, 28 April 1820, OClWHi IV A 69.

42. "Documents copied from church records at Watervliet, Ohio," entry for 24 October, 1824, Item 263, DLCMs. This remark suggests that instituting a separate ministry for Watervliet was considered. It was never accomplished, however.

43. AIB-ODa, 70.

44. Richard McNemar recorded extensive notes on the history of the Watervliet society in his manuscript diaries, Item 255, DLCMs. See also Item 263, DLCMs, and MacLean (1907), 194–97.

45. "Dates of buildings and time they were erected," by Charles Sturr, OClWHi I A 21, and "Journal of Peter Pease," entries for 1813, Item 232, DLCMs.

46. "Diary of Nathaniel Taylor," Mss. 119, Box 3, Folder 3, OHi.

47. David Darrow to the New Lebanon Ministry, 7 June 1824, ASC 1048, DWint.

48. Bates's visits to Watervliet in January 1819 and January 1823 are recorded in OClWHi V B 237 and in "Diary of Nathaniel Taylor," MSS, Box 3, Folder 3, OHi.

49. Entry for 25 November 1827, OClWHi V B 236.

50. AIB-ODa, 70.

51. Pleasant Hill Ministry to New Lebanon Ministry, April 12, 1825, ASC 1044, DWint.

52. "Extract on the Death of David Darrow," Item 348b, DLCMs, 398.

53. Union Village Ministry to New Lebanon Ministry, 4 July 1825, ASC 1048.

54. Ibid.

55. Entry for 1 September 1816, OClWHi V B 236.

56. In a letter to Seth Youngs Wells written from Busro on April 12, 1815, Issachar Bates states that he is writing from his room on the second floor of the community's log meeting house. One passage that confirms that David Darrow lodged above the meeting house can be found in Item 346a, DLCMs, 374. In this passage discussing the first performance of a Christmas song at Union Village in the early 1820s, Susan Liddell recalls that it was sung as the singers processed around the meeting house, stopping beneath Father David's window.

57. Issachar Bates to the South Union Ministry, 29 January 1834, quoted in AIB-DWint, 131–35.

58. Writings of Richard McNemar concerning Union Village, Item 347a, DLCMs.

59. AIB-ODa, 72.

60. A letter written about a year after David Darrow's death and signed jointly by some of the senior members at Union Village officially names Solomon King as his successor but declares that the "titles of Father and Mother have become obsolete." Union Village to New Lebanon Ministry, 3 July 1826, ASC 1048, DWint.

61. AIB-KyBgW-K, 78.

62. "Diary of Nathaniel Taylor," entries between July 1825 and August 1826, MSS 119, Box 3, Folder 3, OHi.

63. Biographical background on Andrew Houston is included in "Notes and Writings on Union Village," MSS 119, Box 23, Folder 3, OHi, 30–46.

64. There is no simple explanation for the closure of Busro. The reasons for its demise are analyzed at length in Medlicott (2009). David Darrow's death was likely a factor, as he had been an enthusiastic advocate of Busro in correspondence with the New Lebanon Ministry.

65. AIB-ODa, 73.

66. Salome Dennis (born Edith Bedle) and Eunice Bedle were kin, probably sisters. Their relationship with Issachar Bates is discussed at length in Medlicott, "A Window on the West," in Medlicott and Goodwillie (2013).

67. AIB-ODa, 78.

68. In addition to Issachar's own discussion of his illness, the Nathaniel Taylor diary notes that the Watervliet Shakers learned by letter that Issachar was suffering a severe bout of seasonal fever, an indication of malaria. "Diary of Nathaniel Taylor," entries for September 1826, MSS 119, Box 3, Folder 3, OHi.

69. AIB-KyBgW-K, 79.

70. "Diary of Richard McNemar, retrospective remarks about 1826–1827," Item 256, DLCMs, 18–20.

71. Entry for 13 April, 1823, Item 263, DLCMs.

72. New Lebanon Ministry to Union Village Ministry, 2 March 1827, OClWHi IV B 7.

73. "Account of West Union, by William Redmon," Item 104, DLCMs, 121–122.

74. Watervliet Ministry to New Lebanon Ministry, 22 January 1828, and 15 April 1828, OClWHi IV A 78.

75. "Diaries . . . and other writings," Item 256, DLCMs, 18–20.

76. AIB-ODa, 75.

77. Samuel Turner to Eleazar Wright, 26 April 1827, copied in "Book of Pioneer Correspondences," OClWHi IV B 34, 144–150.

78. AIB-DWint, 115–116, 119.

79. Issachar Bates to eastern friends, 11 May 1827, OClWHi IV A 78.

80. AIB-KyBgW-K, 81.

81. Medlicott, " 'We live at a great distance from the Church' " (2010), 19–20.

82. "List of changes in the ministry and eldership in the Church, between 1788 and 1845," OClWHi III B 16.

83. "Elders Solomon King & Issachar Bates" and "Issachar Bates Preaching," in "Book of Remembrances," OClWHi VII B 108, 274.

84. Issachar's own account of his 1830 eastern interlude is one of the only ones to survive. Though several eastern journals contain passing references to his arrival, departure, and presence, few recorded much detail.

85. The trip, including the visit to the Watervliet cemetery on August 10, is chronicled in Rufus Bishop, "A Daily Journal of Passing Events," Item no. 1, Shaker Collection, NN, entries for June–August, 1830. Anna Bates was a niece of Issachar, and probably the daughter of one of his youngest two brothers, Caleb or William. Her death in 1825 was reported in a letter to Busro, which identified her as "the neice of Elder Issachar," New Lebanon Ministry to West Union Ministry, 26 September 1825, OClWHi IV B 35. Possibly the writer did not realize that Issachar was no longer residing at Busro to receive the news. The exact locations of the Bates family graves are recorded on "Map of the Believers Burying Ground in Watervliet," ASC 1075, DWint.

86. Issachar Bates to New Lebanon Ministry, October 30, 1830, ASC 1050, DWint.

87. Entry for 31 August, OClWHi V B 236.

88. AIB-ODa, 71.

89. Entries for January 1831 and May–June 1832, OClWHi V B 237.

90. "Diaries . . . and other writings," Item 256, entry for 22 February 1829, DLCMs.

91. AIB-ODa, 79.

92. Richard McNemar to Seth Youngs Wells, 7 January 1832, Item 245, DLCMs.

93. "Diaries . . . and other writings," entries for December 1831, Item 255, DLCMs.

94. Ibid.

95. AIB-ODa, 81.

11. A BITTER CLOSE IN THE WEST

AIB-DLCMs-161,139. (Emphasis in the original.)

1. "Miscellaneous writings . . . Union Village," Item 353d, DLCMs.

2. "Diaries . . . and other writings," Item 255, DLCMs, [68]. Large portions of manuscript Items 253–56, DLCMs, are not paginated. Page numbers in brackets [ ] were added to the research copy made by Christian Goodwillie and shared with me.

3. Richard McNemar to Rufus Bishop, 28 November 1833, OClWHi IV A 84.

4. Ibid.

5. "Diaries . . . and other writings," Item 255, DLCMs, [70–71].

6. Ibid., [102–3]. Richard McNemar's propensity for using Latin phrases in his personal writings is seen here.

7. See Goodwillie, "Custos Sacrorum: Richard McNemar as Curator and Printer," in Medlicott and Goodwillie (2013).

8. "Diaries . . . and other writings," Item 253, DLCMs, [28].

9. Richard McNemar to Seth Youngs Wells, 17 July 1833, Item 245, DLCMs.

10. From remarks made by Issachar Bates and others close to him, it is evident that he carried on private correspondence with both Shakers and non-Shakers. However, its extent is a matter of speculation.

11. From "Remarks Extracted from a Journal of Issachar Bates's Funeral, Written by Isaac Newton Youngs," in AIB-DLCMs-161, 228–31.

12. AIB-DWint, 108–9.

13. AIB-ODa, 87–88.

14. Richard McNemar to Rufus Bishop, 28 November 1833, OClWHi IV A 84.

15. This volume, its production, and its impact on the Shaker world are thoroughly explored in Medlicott and Goodwillie (2013).

16. McNemar (1833), 3.

17. Goodwillie, "Custos Sacrorum" (2013).

18. "Diaries . . . and other writings," entries for 14–15 July 1832, Item 255, DLCMs, [107].

19. Ibid., entry for 12 November 1832, Item 255, DLCMs, [89].

20. Ibid., entry for 10 December 1832, Item 255, DLCMs, [90].

21. Ibid., entry for 18 December 1832, Item 255, DLCMs, [91].

22. Richard McNemar to Seth Youngs Wells, 13 February 1833, Item 245, DLCMs.

23. Revolutionary War Service-Pension Act of June 7, 1832 (4 Stat. 529), see *War Department Report From the Secretary of War, . . . in Relation to the Pension Establishment of the United States*, 1835 (23d Cong., 1st sess., S. Doc, 514; serials 249–51).

24. "Diaries . . . and other writings," entry for 13 September 1832, Item 255, DLCMs.

25. "Diaries . . . and other writings," entry for 13 September 1832, Item 255, DLCMs, [93].

26. Pension Application for Issachar Bates (Massachusetts) Record Number S2360, Records Relating to Revolutionary War Pension Applicants, National Archives.

27. Augustus Waldo Drury, *History of the City of Dayton and Montgomery County, Ohio* (Chicago, IL: S. J. Clarke Publishing Co., 1909), 1:791.

28. "Diaries . . . and other writings," entry for 13 September 1832, Item 255, DLCMs, [93].

29. Watervliet Church Record, entry for 23 January 1833, Item 263, DLCMs.

30. AIB-KyBgW-K, 91–92.

31. AIB-ODa, 87.

32. New Lebanon Ministry to Union Village Ministry, 2 May 1827, OClWHi IV B 7.

33. AIB-KyBgW-K, 92.

34. Entries for July and August 1833, OCLWHI V B 237.

35. OClWHi IX B 198, 37–38.

36. Songs dating from the 1830s in two- and three-part harmony, many by Sally Eades and her son Harvey Eades, can be found in "A Collection of Hymns, Anthems & Tunes; Adapted to Worship . . . 1835," compiled by Betsy Smith, Coke Collection, Special Collections Library, KyBgW-K.

37. Many manuscript versions of "Ode to Contentment" give dual attribution to Issachar Bates and Richard Pelham, who converted at Union Village in 1817 and served as an elder at North Union in the 1830s. However, neither the circumstances of the song's origin nor the likelihood of a connection between Bates and Pelham have been deeply scrutinized by scholars, and it is not uncommon to discover attributions in Shaker hymnals contradicted by other facts. Significantly, the earliest version of "Ode to Contentment"— the one annotated at South Union on June 20, 1833, during Issachar Bates's visit—does not include an attribution to Pelham, and although Issachar Bates and Richard Pelham both lived in Ohio, they rarely crossed paths. Both wrote autobiographies, but neither mentions the other even once. There is in fact no evidence, apart from attributions in some manuscript versions of the song that the two men ever collaborated.

38. OClWHi IX A 3, 88.

39. Union Village Ministry to New Lebanon Ministry, 3 July 1826, ASC 1040, DWint.

40. AIB-KyBgW-K, 92–93.

41. AIB-KyBgW-K, 93–94.

42. This reference to a letter prepared by Issachar is one of many indicating his active correspondence to individual Shakers, relatively little of which has apparently survived.

43. Richard McNemar to Seth Youngs Wells, 2 October 1833, OClWHi IV A 84.

44. Ibid.

45. In September 1824 a "great conflagration of books" had been held at Union Village, the first in a series of efforts to curb the believers' consumption of outside literature that was considered unwholesome (OClWHi V B 237). Later in 1829, Solomon King delivered a sermon in which he urged believers to burn their inappropriate books, a category that covered topics other than horticulture, farming, or other purely practical topics; see Item 255, DLCMs.

46. As Benjamin Seth Youngs was one of the recipients of this letter, Issachar is probably alluding to a trunk that had been in his possession for a great many years, and possibly one that had been carried on one of his journeys with Benjamin.

47. Extract, Issachar Bates to the Ministry of South Union, 29 January 1834, copied into AIB-KyBgW-K, 133–35.

48. New Lebanon Ministry to Union Village Ministry, 6 November 1833, OClWHi IV B 8.

49. Richard McNemar to Rufus Bishop, 28 November 1833, OClWHi IV A 84.

50. New Lebanon Ministry to Union Village Ministry, 3 January 1834, OClWHi IV B 8.

51. "Extracts from a journal kept by Moses Eastwood," OClWHi VI B 54; and AIB-ODa, 87–88. This passage is recorded in both manuscripts with slight variations.

52. Issachar Bates, "Wooden Thunder," 29 January 1834, Item 350d, DLCMs. This essay is also copied into AIB-DWint, 126–30.

53. Item 353d, DLCMs.

54. Josiah Morrow, *The History of Warren County* (Chicago, IL: W. H. Beers Co, 1882; reprint, Mt. Vernon, IN: Windmill Publications, 1992), states that the "Thompsonian" system promoted by the New England physician Samuel Thompson, was introduced into Warren County, Ohio, around 1826.

55. This line and the previous quotation from AIB-KyBgW-K, 95–96.

56. Isaac Newton Youngs, "Tour thro the States of Ohio and Kentucky in the Summer of 1834," July 9–10, NOcaS.

57. "Diaries . . . and other writings," entry for 17 September 1834, Item 253, DLCMs, [54].

58. Notes from Richard McNemar, 13 September 1834, Item 347b, DLCMs.

59. Notes of Richard McNemar, 27 August 1834, Item 347b, DLCMs.

60. Richard McNemar's detailed analysis of the transfer of the eldership "gift" at Watervliet is found in his "Diaries . . . and other writings," Item 253, DLCMs, [100–101], [105–6]. It is obvious in Richard's account that Issachar was conflicted about the role of Salome Dennis and Eunice Bedle, whom he seemed to blame in some respects, even though they were clearly brought to Watervliet through his express request, and according to Richard, their "study & labor day & night is to make Elder Issachar comfortable." Nonetheless, Richard and others (such as Solomon King) believed that their overprotection of Issachar was "cruel as the grave."

61. AIB-KyBgW-K, 96.

62. Ebenezer Bishop to Issachar Bates, 9 March 1835, OClWHi IV A 79.

63. Richard McNemar to Solomon King, 24 March 1835, copied into Richard Mc-Nemar's "Diaries . . . and other writings," Item 255, DLCMs, [210–12].

64. Ibid.

65. AIB-KyBgW-K, 99.

66. Jane Patterson to Issachar Bates, 12 May 1835, copied into AIB-DLCMs-161.

67. McNemar to King, 24 March 1835.

68. Ibid.

69. "Documents copied from Church records at Watervliet, Ohio," Item 263, entry for 16 April 1835, DLCMs.

70. This song, later recorded in several music manuscripts as "Issachar's Retreat," takes its tune from a fife retreat well known among New England fifers during the American Revolution. The tune appears in the 1777 manuscript music book of Giles Gibbs, a Connecticut fifer, under the title "Pretty Cupid." See Kate Van Winkle Keller, *Fife Tunes from the American Revolution* (Sandy Hook, CT: Hendrickson Group, 1997), 14, 34. See appendix 2.

71. AIB-KyBgW-K, 99.

12. JOURNEY'S END AT NEW LEBANON

The words and tune for "Nightly Prayer" are copied into Seth Youngs Wells to Isaac N. Houston, 10 April 1837, Item 246, DLCMs.

1. AIB-KyBgW-K, 102.

2. "Account of the rise and progress of the Church at North Union," entry for 21 May 1835, OClWHi V B 177. The presumption that Issachar Bates visited North Union in May 1835 where Richard Pelham was an elder has been the chief evidence, other than some manuscript annotations, that Bates and Pelham collaborated on the unusual hymn "Ode to Contentment." See Roger Hall, *"Come Life Shaker Life": The Life and Music of Elder Issachar Bates* (Stoughton, MA: Pinetree Press, 2004), 27. But because Bates never, in fact, went to North Union in 1835 and his encounter with the North Union elders was rushed and awkward, a creative collaboration with Pelham was unlikely, if not impossible.

3. Benjamin Seth Youngs to Molly Goodrich, 29 May 1835, OClWHi IV B 19. This letter has been copied by a later scribe and wrongly dated as 29 May 1833.

4. "Records of the Church at Watervliet, N.Y.," entry for 30 May 1835, OClWHi V B 279. The scribe was apparently unaware that Issachar had not come all the way from South Union as his companions had.

5. "Records of the Church at Watervliet, N.Y.," entry for 9 June 1835, OClWHi V B 279.

6. "Diary of Giles Avery," entry for 9 June 1835, OClWHi V B 105.

7. AIB-KyBgW-K, 102.

8. Richard McNemar to Solomon King, 24 March 1835, copied into "Diaries . . . and other writings," Item 255, DLCMs, [210–12].

9. After March 1835, no further mention of Issachar Bates's pension money appears to have been made. It is doubtful whether he continued to collect it after his move to New Lebanon.

10. New Lebanon Ministry to Eleazar Wright, 5 August 1835, OClWHi IV B 8.

11. AIB-KyBgW-K, 103. Issachar compares himself to Rachel of the Bible, an archetypal figure of parental mourning, who, according to the prophet Jeremiah, "refused to be comforted for her children, because they were not" (Jeremiah 31:15). A "harrow" refers to an archaic piece of farm equipment consisting of a broad and flat tool for raking or shallow plowing, on which multiple close-set spikes protruded towards the ground. It offers a potent metaphor for Issachar's psychological state at that time.

12. I am indebted to Stephen Paterwic for helping me to better understand the complexities of the New Lebanon Church Family. In the minds of individual rising leaders, the First Order may have carried an aura of spiritual superiority where none was intended. For summary background on the Church Family see entry "First Order of the Church," in Paterwic (2008), 79–80.

13. "Records Kept by Order of the Church," entry for 31 December 1835, Item no. 7, Shaker Collection, NN.

14. "Map of New Lebanon, Columbia Co., N.Y.," attributed to Isaac Newton Youngs representing the period between 1827 and 1838 is pictured in Robert P. Emlen, *Shaker Village Views* (Hanover, NH: University Press of New England, 1987), 60–61. The original is in a private collection.

15. Issachar Bates to Beloved Friends at Watervliet & Union Village, 27 June 1835, copied in AIB-DWint, 155–60.

16. Details on Daniel Moseley and Constant Moseley were compiled, along with vital statistics of all the "Old Believers" in the West, by Shaker brother Alonzo Hollister. Vital statistics on all the old believers, including Daniel and Constant Moseley, is found in Medlicott, "'Our Spiritual Ancestors'" (2011), 56–57.

17. Hiram Rude's Shaker life got off to a rocky start. His mother, Patty Rude, had entered Union Village briefly, but left. Union Village journals record that she returned several times in the 1810s to try and take her children away. On one occasion, Hiram hid in the tall grass of a meadow to evade his mother. Patty Rude came periodically to disrupt Union Village Sabbath meetings and on one Sunday in August 1817 "carried on like a bitch which created considerable debate." Hiram was just short of his eighteenth birthday when he traveled to New Lebanon in May 1820, along with Elder Peter Pease. See "Journal of a trip to the western societies by Hiram Rude" (in which he reminisces about his early life at Union Village), OClWHi V B 161; entry for 31 August, 1817, OClWHi V B 236; and entry for 28 May, 1820, OClWHi V B 237. As an adult, Hiram was of unusual height, standing 6'2".

18. When recounting his first 1801 visit to New Lebanon seeking information, Issachar notes that he had encountered "a sister's daughter of mine, also Hannah Train," by whom he met his niece who was his sister's namesake. She had encouraged Issachar, telling him where to go and who to ask for.

19. "Records Kept by the Order of the Church," entry for 11 June 1835, Item no. 7, Shaker Collection, NN.

20. "Diary of Giles Avery," entry for 15 June 1835, OClWHi V B 105.

21. "Issachar Bates to Beloved Friends at Watervliet & Union Village, 27 June 1835," copied in AIB-DWint, 155–160.

22. "Diary of Giles Avery," entries for 12–13, June 1835, OClWHi V B 105. Other New Lebanon journals also make reference to the same severe storm, which awakened people in the early morning; see the journal of Annie Williams, who wrote of a massive storm that "routed us from our beds" (OClWHi V B 127).

23. AIB-KyBgW-K, 104.

24. "Map of New Lebanon, Columbia Co., N.Y.," in Emlen (1987), 60–61.

25. "Records Kept by the Order of the Church," entry for 25 July 1835, Item no. 7, Shaker Collection, NN.

26. "Issachar Bates to Beloved Friends, Watervliet and Union Village, Ohio, 27 June 1835," copied in AIB-DWint, 155–158.

27. "Journal of daily events kept by Betsy Bates," entries for June 1835, OClWHi V B 128.

28. Tailoring record for New Lebanon, OClWHi III B 9. Entries for 1835 and 1836 reveal that Issachar Bates had many new garments made in addition to striped linen trousers.

29. "Diary of Giles Avery," entries for June 1835, OClWHi V B 105.

30. Ibid.

31. "Diary of Giles Avery," 16 August 1835, OClWHi V B 105.

32. Ibid., entry for 6 September 1835, OClWHi V B 105.

33. Patterson (2000, 209) notes that "The Stubborn Oak was sung in the East as early as 1823 and was attributed to Susanna Barret of the Shirley [Massachusetts] community." One wonders whether Issachar Bates, with his known fondness for applying tree metaphors to his own spiritual life as a Shaker, identified personally with the words "I will not be like the stubborn oak, But I will be like the willow tree." After all, Issachar had specifically asked to be buried in the very spot where he himself had removed a large — possibly stubborn — oak, while clearing land for the graveyard at Watervliet, Ohio.

34. AIB-KyBgW-K, 102–5.

35. The arrival of this group of New Lebanon representatives was awkward for many Ohio Shakers, because it was clear their visit had been necessitated by mismanagement of affairs over many years since the death of David Darrow. Although this episode requires further study to be fully understood, one source that sheds light on it is the journal of Joanna Kitchel, OClWHi V B 238. Significantly, the New Lebanon Ministry chose to include Joanna Kitchel, an Ohio native in her thirties who had converted as a child at Turtle Creek in 1808 and had been taken to New Lebanon at the age of twelve in 1810, in the visiting group.

36. Ruth Johnson's use of "Eldress Rachel" during her years in office at Union Village is noted by Alonzo Hollister in his tables of vital information on all the "Old Believers." See Medlicott, "'Our Spiritual Ancestors,'" (2011), 56–57.

37. Because Richard McNemar's printing press at Watervliet had served as the platform for his accumulation of a huge repository of Shaker records and historical material, Richard was not able to quickly relocate back to Union Village. Rather, he lingered at Watervliet until early in 1836. See Medlicott and Goodwillie (2013).

38. Issachar Bates to Salome Dennis, 30 July 1835, enclosed in "Writings on the Scriptures by Issachar Bates," OClWHi VII B 254.

39. Issachar's use of "grandfather" is puzzling. He may be referring to Father David Darrow, who, by virtue of his spiritual leadership to Issachar might be someone whom Salome would think of as a metaphorical "grandfather."

40. AIB-KyBgW-K, 104–5.

41. Martha Wetherbee and Nathaniel Taylor, *Shaker Baskets* (Sanbornton, NH: Martha Wetherbee Basket Shop, 1988).

42. Background on the natural history of "basket willow" in America can be found in William F. Hubbard, *The Basket Willow* (Washington, D.C.: U.S. Department of Agriculture, 1909), 7–11.

43. "Journal of Barnabas Hinckley," entry for 20 May 1836, ASC 831, DWint.

44. Writing in 1877, Elder Frederick Evans notes that white willow grew around ponds at Mt. Lebanon. Presumably it would have been native to the area in the 1830s as well. See F. W. Evans, "Mt. Lebanon," *The Shaker* 7, no. 1 (January 1877): 6.

45. Issachar Bates to Watervliet, Ohio, 25 February 1837, copied in AIB-ODa, 103–107.

46. Hannah Agnew had been chosen as female travel companion for Eldress Joanna Kitchell for her return trip to New Lebanon in the spring of 1836. Hannah lived the rest of her life in New Lebanon, except for a visit back to Ohio in 1856.

47. "Closing Address to Sister Marietta, May 9, 1868," in "Journal of memorable journey... by Hannah Agnew when 16 years of age 1836, and other writings," Item 50, DLCMs. In this short note, Agnew apologizes for her poetry, remarking that Elder Issachar used to joke with her about "poetry run mad."

48. "Diary of Giles Avery," entry for 4 July 1836, OClWHi V B 106.

49. "Journal of Asenath Clark," entry for 13 August 1836, Item no. 9758 C592, ID no. 1480, HSV.

50. The U.S. Census of 1820 places Artemas Bates in Lorraine, New York, a tiny community some ten miles from the eastern end of Lake Ontario.

51. "Domestic Journal of Important Occurrences," entry for 13 August 1836, OClWHi V B 60.

52. Seth Youngs Wells to Friend Artemas Bates, 20 March 1837, copied in AIB-DWint, 163–165.

53. "Journal of Barnabas Hinckley," entries for August and September 1836, ASC 831, DWint.

54. This song is found in several manuscript song books, including one begun by Watervliet, Ohio, Shaker Moses Eastwood in 1837 (Item 173, DLCMs), and at least three New Lebanon songbooks begun in the mid-1830s (OClWHi IX B SM 33, OClWHi IX B SM 386, and ASC 936, DWint), where it is copied together with the tune that Issachar likely sang with it.

55. "Various Lists of Births and Deaths," OClWHi III B 14. New Lebanon's Second Family was an entirely separate family of New Lebanon Shakers, distinct from the Church Family.

56. "Journal Kept by Annie Williams," entry for 22 September 1836, OClWHi V B 127.

57. The ages of the outing's participants can be calculated from information tabulated by Rachel Cottrell, in "Shaker Death Records," *New England Historical and Genealogical Record* 115 (January 1951).

58. Issachar Bates to Watervliet, Ohio, 25 February 1837, copied in AIB-ODa, 103–107. By "old eyes," Issachar is referring to his spectacles, previously forgotten in Ohio, which by now he had gotten back, probably via one of the other travelers journeying from Ohio to New Lebanon. His reference to opium is a reminder that opium was grown and used by the Shakers in a range of medicinal preparations in both East and West for a good part of the nineteenth century.

59. Eleazar Wright to Rufus Bishop, 19 October 1836, OClWHi IV A 71.

60. After accompanying Issachar back to the East in May 1835, Benjamin Seth Youngs returned to the West, but only briefly. He too was summoned back, at the comparatively young age of sixty-two. He arrived at Watervliet, New York, in early November 1836, and died there in 1855. See Medlicott, " 'Our Spiritual Ancestors,' " (2011), 55–56.

61. Richard's "Alpha and Omega" remark is extracted from Eleazar Wright to Rufus Bishop, 19 October 1836, OClWHi IV A 71. That Richard printed "Eli's vision" is surmised from Issachar's reference to "that little printed sheet." No existing copy has been found. Possibly only a few copies were printed and none have survived. The exact nature of Eli's

"vision" can only be extrapolated from the context of the correspondence and events during this period.

62. Issachar Bates to Eleazar Wright, 27 December 1836, Item 246, DLCMs.

63. Seth Youngs Wells to Eleazar Wright, Item 246, DLCMs. The letter is undated, but the posting date is named in a postscript as 17 February 1837.

64. Seth Youngs Wells to Mathew Houston, 10 April 1837, Item 246, DLCMs.

65. "Diary of Giles Avery," entry for 16 March 1837, OClWHi V B 106.

66. "Remarks from the Funeral of Issachar Bates by Isaac Newton Youngs," copied in AIB-DLCMs-161, 228–31.

67. Rufus Bishop to the Harvard Ministry, 17 March 1837, OClWHi IV B 8.

68. "The following is extracted from the speaking at Brother Issachar's Funeral," copied in AIB-DWint, 160–62.

69. Seth Youngs Wells to Mathew Houston, 10 April 1837, Item 246, DLCMs.

70. The "Burying Ground" is clearly visible on "Map of New Lebanon, Columbia Co., N.Y.," (reprinted in Emlen [1997, 60–61]), along the village road running straight west from the Second Order buildings alongside the large medicinal garden. Later in the nineteenth century, the New Lebanon Shakers ceased using this small cemetery. Today it is overgrown, and its location is not marked.

71. Alan Lomax, probably America's most prominent twentieth-century folk musicologist, chose this song to represent the Shakers in his landmark anthology *Folksongs of North America in the English Language* (Garden City, NY: Doubleday and Company, Inc., 1960), 68, 73.

EPILOGUE

AIB-ODa, 98.

1. "Remarks extracted from a Journal of Issachar Bates's funeral, Written by Isaac N. Youngs," AIB-DLCMs-161, 228–31.

2. "Copy of a Letter Sent to Artemas Bates, respecting the Death of Issachar Bates," in AIB-DWint, 163–65.

3. Manuscript evidence suggests that Isaac N. Houston was a mixed-race Shaker. At the time of Mathew Houston's Shaker conversion in 1805, his household included a "mulatto" servant, Isaac Newton, probably the same individual named in Union Village records as Isaac N. Houston, born in 1795, and known at Turtle Creek as early as 1805. Union Village Shaker Susan Liddell identifies Isaac Newton as harboring lifelong devotion to Mathew and insisting upon living with Mathew. Isaac was present when he died in 1853. Considering the closeness of Issachar Bates and Mathew Houston and the fact that they shared residential quarters in Ohio from time to time, anyone close to Mathew would have had ample opportunity to also develop an intimate friendship with Issachar. Therefore it is probable that the mixed-race Isaac Newton and Isaac N. Houston are one and the same person.

4. Seth Youngs Wells to Matthew Houston, 10 April 1837, Item 246, DLCMs.

5. AIB-ODa, 98.

6. Diaries . . . and other writings," Item 255, DLCMs.

7. AIB-ODa, 98.

8. Issachar Bates to Richard Spiers, 13 December 1811, OCIWHi IV A 84.

9. "Miscellaneous Union Village Writings," Item 353d, DLCMs.

10. In Shaker thought, the idea of annihilating one's ego or putting to death "Great Big I" or one's "old man of sin" is comparable metaphorically to Jesus' death on the cross.

11. Turtle Creek's first covenant is dated 14 March 1810, and its signatories included mostly the "old believers" together with a few of the western converts or "young believers" living together in joint interest in the household of David Darrow. This covenant is printed in John Patterson MacLean, *A Bibliography of Shaker Literature* (Columbus, OH: Fred J. Heer, 1905), 14–16.

12. AIB-ODa, 90.

13. Issachar Bates's office of Second Elder was written into the West Union Covenant of 1815. However, named office-holders were not signatories to Shaker covenants.

14. "Diaries . . . and miscellaneous writings," Item 256, DLCMs.

15. Ibid., Item 253, DLCMs.

16. Richard McNemar to Joshua Worley, 13 June 1837, Item 347b, DLCMs.

17. "Diaries . . . and miscellaneous writings," Item 253, DLCMs, [100–101].

18. Ibid., Item 255, DLCMs, [112].

19. Rufus Bishop to Richard McNemar, November 1835, Item 245, DLCMs. This letter is extracted in Lee Johnson, *The Struggle for Watervliet, Ohio* (Washington, D.C.: Spirit Tree Press, 1999), 28–29.

20. Issachar Bates to the New Lebanon Ministry, 28 April 1820, OCIWHi IV A 69.

21. AIB-OCIWHi VI B 20. On the overleaf of this copy is written "S.Union Copied July 1833 B.S.Y." A letter from Benjamin indicates that Issachar had left his "Sketch" at South Union at the close of his extended visit there in the summer of 1833, suggesting that others may have wished to examine and copy it, too. Benjamin Seth Youngs to Eleazar Wright, 14 December 1833, OCIWHi IV B 19.

22. Of the seventeen known copies made by Shakers, eight are held in the Western Reserve Historical Society, two are in the Library of Congress, two are held by the Shaker Museum and Library at Old Chatham, and the following collections each hold one: Public Library of Dayton and Montgomery County History Room, Kentucky History Library, New York State Library, Andrews Shaker Collection at Winterthur, and Sabbathday Lake Library. A copy at Ohio Historical Society is the work of the non-Shaker historian J. P. MacLean at the turn of the twentieth century. The location of the original is unknown, and it is possible that it has not survived.

23. Depending upon which version was the basis for subsequent copies, individual copies bear a range of interesting variations. For example, a copy made in the West from the version created by Moses Eastwood prior to Issachar's 1835 departure from Ohio does not contain the additional material Issachar added at New Lebanon in April 1836.

24. AIB-DWint.

25. Undated note from Alonzo Hollister to J. P. MacLean, OCIWHi IV A 30. A separate

source (MSS 119, Box 3, Folder 1, OHi), shows that MacLean was unaware of the existence of Issachar Bates's autobiography until 1903.

26. "Journal of James Prescott, North Union, Ohio, 1842," MSS 119, Box 4, Folder 1, 24–28, OHi.

27. Andrew C. Houston to D. A. Buckingham, 21 March 1839, ASC 1048, DWint.

28. Andrew Houston, the son of Matthew Houston and a popular rising leader at Union Village, died relatively young from an accidental fall in 1844. Spirit visitations from Brother Andrew were commonly reported, especially in the West.

29. "A Poem on Life's Journey," given to S.A.L., in manuscript hymnal inscribed to Jessie Campbell, Violetta Platt, and Sister Emily Wilkinson, H-3, NCH, 81–85.

30. Annotation in "Hymn book of Mary Hazard," ASC 896, DWint.

31. Annotation in "Hymns by inspiration to various instruments," OClWHi IX B SM 192.

32. "Tune book of Giles Avery," Tune 402, Item 190, DLCMs.

33. "Febry. 4th 1851 . . . Sent from Issachar Bates to Mary Ann," OClWHi IX B SM 83.

34. "Spiglass . . . Given by Issachar B. Senr., Feb. 17th 1851," OClWHi IX B SM 29.

35. "A Message from Issachar Bates to Artemas Bates, his son," copied in AIB-Ky-BgW-K, 118–20.

36. "An Open Vision of an army of spirits Under command of Elder Issachar Bates, all of whom were volunteers, enlisted to fight for the safety of Zion, to the end of the Present War . . . by Phebe Ann Smith, January 1, 1862," OClWHi VIII A 59. Curiously, this vision of Smith, who lived in the New Lebanon Second Order with Issachar, also includes another explicit reference to Issachar handling a spyglass, further indication that he might have actually possessed one.

37. Issachar Bates was named as the source of the song "Three polish'd birds in brilliant hue," delivered in 1871 at New Lebanon and copied into several other manuscripts. See Folder 38–7, NOcaS; the "Vision of John Gildersleeve, OClWHi III B 46; and "Words Spoken by John Gildersleeve when under the power of God," Special Collections, NCH.

38. "Book of Sacred Hymns, Hancock," ASC 888, DWint, 129.

39. *The Manifesto* 14, no. 7 (July 1884): 159–60.

40. *The Manifesto* 28, no. 1 (January 1898): 14.

BIBLIOGRAPHY

Ackerknecht, Erwin H. *Malaria in the Upper Mississippi Valley, 1760–1900*. New York: Arno Press, 1977.

Andrews, Edward D. *The People Called Shakers: A Search for the Perfect Society*. New York: Dover Publications, 1963.

———. "The Shaker Mission to the Shawnee Indians." *Winterthur Portfolio* 7 (1972): 113–28.

Andrews, Edward D., and Faith Andrews. *Visions of the Heavenly Sphere: A Study in Shaker Religious Art*. Charlottesville: University Press of Virginia, 1969.

Arndt, Karl J.R., ed. *A Documentary History of the Indiana Decade of the Harmony Society, 1814–1824, Volume I*. Indianapolis: Indiana Historical Society, 1975.

Bagnall, Norma Hayes. *On Shaky Ground: The New Madrid Earthquakes*. Columbia: University of Missouri Press, 1996.

Baldwin, Thomas W. *Vital Records of Cohasset, Massachusetts to 1850*. Boston: New England Historic Genealogical Society, 1916.

Bates, Issachar. *New Songs, on Different Subjects*. Salem, NY: Dodd, 1800.

Bates, Paulina. *The Divine Book of Holy and Eternal Wisdom . . . In Two Volumes*. Arranged and Prepared for the Press at New Lebanon, NY, 1849.

Bauer, Cheryl, and Rob Portman. *Wisdom's Paradise: The Forgotten Shakers of Union Village*. Wilmington, OH: Orange Frazer Press, 2004.

Bauer, Cheryl, ed. *Shakers of Indiana: A West Union Reader*. Milford, OH: Little Miami Publishing Co., 2009.

Bigelow, Victor E. *A Narrative History of the Town of Cohasset Massachusetts*. Cohasset, MA: Committee on Town History, 1898.

Biglow, William. *History of Sherburne, Massachusetts, From Its Incorporation, 1674, to the End of the Year 1830*. Milford, MA: Ballou and Stacy, 1830.

Bishop, Rufus, and Seth Youngs Wells. *Testimonies of the Life, Character, Revelations and Doctrines of our Ever Blessed Mother Ann Lee*. Hancock, MA: J. Talcott and J. Deming, 1816.

Blackburn, Absolem H. *A Brief Account of the Rise, Progress, Doctrines and Practices of the People Usually Denominated Shakers*. Flemingsburg, KY, 1824.

Blaikie, Alexander. *A History of Presbyterianism in New England*. Boston: Alexander Moore, 1881.

Blinn, Henry C. *The Manifestation of Spiritualism Among the Shakers*. East Canterbury, NH: The Shakers, 1899.

Boice, Martha, et al. *Maps of the Shaker West: A Journey of Discovery*. Dayton, OH: Knot Garden Press, 1997.

Boles, John B. *The Great Revival: Beginnings of the Bible Belt*. Lexington: University Press of Kentucky, 1996.

Bray, Robert C., and Peter Cartwright. *Legendary Frontier Preacher*. Champaign, IL: University of Illinois Press, 2005.

Brayton, Isabella and John B. Norton. *The Story of Hartford: A History*. Hartford, N.Y. [Glen Falls, N.Y., Bullard Press]1929. Washington County Historical Society Item 97.31.1.

Brackenridge, Hugh H. *Indian Atrocities: Narratives of Perils and Sufferings of Dr. Knight and John Slover Among the Indians During the Revolutionary War*. Cincinnati, OH: U.P. James, 1867.

Brewer, Priscilla J. *Shaker Communities, Shaker Lives*. Hanover, NH: University Press of New England, 1986.

Brown, Thomas. *An Account of the People Called Shakers*. Troy, NY: Parker and Bliss, 1812.

Campanella, Thomas J. '"Mark well the gloom': Shedding Light on the Great Dark Day of 1780." *Environmental History* 12, no. 1 (Jan. 2007): 35–58.

Camus, Raoul F. *Military Music of the American Revolution*. Chapel Hill: University of North Carolina Press, 1976.

Carey, Henry Charles, and Isaac Lea. *A Complete Historical, Chronological, and Geographical American Atlas*. Philadelphia: T.H. Palmer, 1822.

Carter, James G., and William H. Brooks. *A Geography of Massachusetts for Families and Schools*. Boston: Hilliard, Gray, Little, and Wilkins, 1830.

Cave, Alfred A. "The Failure of the Shawnee Prophet's Witch-Hunt." *Ethnohistory* 42, no. 3 (Summer 1995): 445–75.

Caverly, Abiel Moore. *History of the Town of Pittsford, Vt., With Biographical Sketches and Family Records*. Rutland, VT: Tuttle and Co., 1872.

Cayton, Andrew. *Frontier Indiana*. Bloomington, IN: Indiana University Press, 1996.

Chapman, Eunice. *Account of the Conduct of the Shakers, In the Case of Eunice Chapman & Her Children*. Lebanon, OH: Van Vleet and Camron, 1818.

Clarke, Samuel. *A Short Relation Concerning a Dream Which the Author had . . . With some remarks on the late Comet*. Boston: Andrew Barclay, 1769.

Cockrum, William M. *Pioneer History of Indiana*. Oakland City, IN: Press of Oakland City Journal, 1907.

Conkin, Paul. *Cane Ridge: America's Pentecost*. Madison: University of Wisconsin Press, 1990.

Cook, Harold E. *Shaker Music: A Manifestation of American Folk Culture*. Lewisburg, PA: Bucknell University Press, 1973.

Coolidge, Mabel C. *The History of Petersham, Massachusetts*. Salem, MA: Higginson Book Company, 1948.

Cottrell, Rachel. "Shaker Death Records." *New England Historical and Genealogical Record* 115 (Jan. 1951): 35–45, 118–35.

Dallimore, Arnold A. *George Whitefield: God's Anointed Servant in the Great Revival of the Eighteenth Century*. Wheaton, IL: Crossway Books, 2010.

Davenport, George L., and Elizabeth Osgood Davenport. *The Genealogies of the Families of Cohasset Massachusetts*. Cohasset, MA: The Committee on Town History, 1909.

Drake, Samuel A. *History of Middlesex County, Massachusetts*, Vol. 1. Boston: Estes and Lauriat, 1880.

Drury, Augustus W. *History of the City of Dayton and Montgomery County, Ohio*. Vol. 1. Chicago, IL: S. J. Clarke Publishing Co., 1909.

Dyer, Mary. *A Brief Statement of the Sufferings of Mary Dyer, Occasioned by the Society Called Shakers*. Boston: William S. Spear, 1816.

Edmunds, R. David. *The Shawnee Prophet*. Lincoln: University of Nebraska Press, 1983.

Esarey, Logan, ed. *Messages and Letters of William Henry Harrison*. Vol. 1. Indianapolis: Indiana Historical Society, 1922.

Eslinger, Ellen. *Citizens of Zion: Social Origins of Camp Meeting Revivalism*. Knoxville: University of Tennessee Press, 1999.

———. *Running Mad for Kentucky: Frontier Travel Accounts*. Lexington: University Press of Kentucky, 2004.

Filley, Dorothy M. *Recapturing Wisdom's Valley: The Watervliet Shaker Heritage, 1775– 1975*. Albany, NY: Albany Institute of History and Art, 1975.

Finney, Charles G. *An Autobiography*. Westwood, NJ: Fleming H. Revell Company, 1908.

Friedman, Lawrence J., and Mark Douglas McGarvie. *Charity, Philanthrophy, and Civility in American History*. London: Cambridge University Press, 2003.

Fuller, Myron. *The New Madrid Earthquake* (Bulletin 4). Washington, D.C.: U.S. Geological Survey, 1912.

Garrett, Clarke. *Spirit Possession and Popular Religion: From the Camisards to the Shakers*. Baltimore, MD: Johns Hopkins University Press, 1987.

Gehlbach, Stephen H. *American Plagues: Lessons from Our Battles with Disease*. New York: McGraw Hill, 2005.

Goldthwaites, Reuben. *Early Western Travels, 1748–1846*. Vol. 9. Cleveland, OH: Arthur H. Clark Company, 1904.

Goodwillie, Christian, and Jane Crosthwaite, eds. *Millennial Praises: A Shaker Hymnal*. Amherst, MA: University of Massachusetts Press, 2009.

Gordon, Robert B. *Natural Vegetation of Ohio, At the Time of the Earliest Surveys*. Ohio Biological Survey, 1966.

Green, George E. *History of Old Vincennes and Knox County, Indiana*. Vol. 1. Chicago, IL: S. J. Clarke, 1911.

Gronim, Sara S. "At the Sign of Newton's Head: Astronomy and Cosmology in British Colonial New York." *Pennsylvania History* 66 (1999): 55–85.

Hall, James, ed. "Memoir of Thomas Posey." In *Library of American Biography*. Conducted by Jared Sparks. Vol. 9. Boston: Charles C. Little & James Brown, 1846.

Hall, Roger L. *Majesty: A Discussion of Facts and Fiction about William Billings and the Stoughton Musical Society*. Stoughton, MA: Pine Tree Press, 2000.

———. *"Come Life Shaker Life": The Life and Music of Elder Issachar Bates*. Stoughton, MA: Pinetree Press, 2004.

History of Knox and Daviess Counties, Indiana. Chicago, IL: Goodspeed Pub. Co., 1886.

Howe, Warren P. "Early American Military Music," *American Music* 17, no. 1 (Spring 1999): 87–116

Hubbard, William F. *The Basket Willow* (Farmer's Bulletin 341). Washington, D.C.: U.S. Department of Agriculture, 1909.

Humez, Jean. *Mother's First-Born Daughters: Early Shaker Writings on Women and Religion.* Bloomington: Indiana University Press, 1993.

Humphreys, Margaret. *Malaria: Poverty, Race, and Public Health in the United States.* Baltimore, MD: Johns Hopkins University Press, 2001.

Hurd, Hamilton. *History of Worcester County, Massachusetts, With Biographical Sketches of Its Many Pioneers and Prominent Men.* Vols. 1–2. Philadelphia: J. W. Lewis and Co., 1889.

Huston, E. Rankin. *History of the Huston Families and Their Descendants, 1450–1912.* Carlisle, PA: Carlisle Printing Co., 1912.

Ingalls, Jeremiah. *The Christian Harmony.* Exeter, NH: Henry Ranlet, 1805.

Jackson, George P. *Spiritual Folk Songs of Early America.* N.p.: J. J. Augustin, 1937.

———. *Down-East Spirituals and Others.* N.p.: J. J. Augustin, 1939.

Johnson, Lee. *The Struggle for Watervliet, Ohio.* Washington, D.C.: Spirit Tree Press, 1999.

Jones, Abner, ed. *The Melody of the Heart.* Boston: Manning and Loring, 1804.

Journal of Thomas Dean: A Voyage to Indiana in 1817. Fort Wayne, IN: Public Library of Fort Wayne and Allen County, 1955.

Keller, Kate Van Winkle. *Fife Tunes from the American Revolution.* Sandy Hook, CT: The Hendrickson Group, 1997.

Kitch, Sally L. "'As a Sign That All May Understand:' Shaker Gift Drawings and Female Spiritual Power." *Winterthur Portfolio* 24, no. 1 (Spring 1989): 1–28.

Lincoln, George. *History of the Town of Hingham Massachusetts.* Vol. 1, *Historical,* and vol. 2, *Genealogy, A–Lincoln.* Hingham: Published by the Town of Hingham, 1893.

Lipman, Jean, and Tom Armstrong, eds. *American Folk Painters of Three Centuries.* New York: Hudson Hills Press, 1980.

Lombard, Anne S. *Making Manhood: Growing Up Male in Colonial New England.* Cambridge, MA: Harvard University Press, 2003.

Lord, William G. *History of Athol, Massachusetts.* Somerville, MA: Somerville Printing Company, 1953.

Lovering, Joseph. "On the Secular Periodicity of the Aurora Borealis." *Memoirs of the American Academy of Arts and Sciences,* n.s., 9, no. 1 (1867): 101–20.

MacLean, John P. *A Bibliography of Shaker Literature.* Columbus, OH: Fred J. Heer, 1905.

———. *A Sketch of the Life and Labors of Richard McNemar.* Franklin, OH: Printed for the *Franklin Chronicle,* 1905.

———. *Some Incidents in the Life of John Slover.* Greenville, OH, 1926.

Marini, Stephen A. *Radical Sects of Revolutionary New England.* New York: iUniverse .com, Inc., 1982, 2001.

Martin, George H. *The Evolution of the Massachusetts Public School System: A Historical Sketch*. New York: D. Appleton and Company, 1894.

Marvin, Abijah P. *History of Worcester County, Massachusetts . . . In Two Volumes*. Boston: C. F. Jewett and Company, 1879.

McNemar, Richard. *The Kentucky Revival*. Cincinnati, OH: John W. Browne, 1807.

———. *A Review of the Most Important Events Relating to the Rise and Progress of the United Society of Believers in the West*. Union Village, OH, 1831.

———. *Selection of Hymns and Poems for the Use of Believers*. Watervliet, OH: Philos Harmoniae, 1833.

Medlicott, Carol. "Conflict and Tribulation on the Frontier: The West Union Shakers and Their Retreat." *American Communal Societies Quarterly* 3, no. 3 (July 2009): 111–37.

———. "Innovation in Music and Song." In *Inspired Innovations: A Celebration of Shaker Ingenuity*. Ed. R. Stephen Miller, 199–206. Hanover, NH: University Press of New England, 2010.

———. "'Our Spiritual Ancestors': Alonzo Hollister's Record of Shaker 'Pioneers' in the West." *Communal Societies* 31 no. 2 (Nov. 2011): 45–60.

———. *Partake a Little Morsel: Popular Shaker Hymns of the Nineteenth Century* Clinton, NY: Richard W. Couper Press, 2011.

———. "'We live at a great distance from the Church': Cartographic Strategies of the Shakers, 1805–1835." *American Communal Studies Quarterly* 4, no. 3 (July 2010): 123–60.

Medlicott, Carol, and Christian Goodwillie. *Richard McNemar, Music, and the Western Shaker Communities: Branches of One Living Tree*. Kent, OH: Kent State University Press, 2013.

Morgan, Edmund. *The Puritan Family*. New York: Harper and Row, 1966.

Morgenstern, Julian. "The Etymological History of the Three Hebrew Synonyms for 'To Dance,' HGG, HLL and KRR, and Their Cultural Significance." *Journal of the American Oriental Society*, 36 (1916): 321–32.

Morin, France, ed. *Heavenly Visions: Shaker Gift Drawings and Gift Songs*. New York: The Drawing Center, 2001.

Morrow, Josiah. *The History of Warren County*. Chicago, IL: W. H. Beers Co, 1882. Reprint, Mt. Vernon, IN: Windmill Publications, 1992.

Neal, Julia. *The Kentucky Shakers*. Lexington: University Press of Kentucky, 1983.

Owens, Robert M. *Mr. Jefferson's Hammer: William Henry Harrison and the Origins of American Indian Policy*. Norman: University of Oklahoma Press, 2007.

Paterwic, Stephen J. *Historical Dictionary of the Shakers*. Lanham, MD: Scarecrow Press, Inc., 2008.

Patterson, Daniel. *The Shaker Spiritual*. Princeton, NJ: Princeton University Press, 1979.

———. *Gift Drawing and Gift Song* Sabbathday Lake, ME: United Society of the Shakers, 1983.

Patton, Fred. "The Provincial Patent: Hartford might be older than you think," *Hartford Post-Star* 95.72.5 (January 26, 1992), 2–3.

Patton, Joan. "Family has been on farm for two centuries," *Hartford Post-Star* 95.72.5 (January 26, 1992), 1–2.

———. "For the sum of a penny, foundation was laid for Hartford Baptist Church," *Hartford Post-Star* 95.72.5 (January 26, 1992), 1.

Penney, Norman. *The Journal of George Fox*. Cambridge, MA: Cambridge University Press, 1911.

Perrin, William. *History of Crawford and Clark Counties, Illinois*. Chicago, IL: O. L. Baskin and Co., 1883.

Perry, Kenneth A. *The Fitch Gazetteer: An Annotated Index to the Manuscript History of Washington County, New York*. Vol. 1. Bowie, MD: Heritage Books, Inc., 1999.

Phillips, Hazel S. *Richard the Shaker*. Lebanon, OH: Typoprint, Inc., 1972.

Posey, John T. *General Thomas Posey: Son of the American Revolution*. East Lansing: Michigan State University Press, 1992.

Promey, Sally. *Spiritual Spectacles: Vision and Image in Mid-Nineteenth Century Shakerism*. Bloomington: Indiana University Press, 1993.

Randall, E. O. *History of the Zoar Society*. Columbus, OH: Press of Fred J. Heer, 1900.

Rathbun, Valentin. *Some brief hints of a religious scheme taught and propagated by a number of Europeans living in a place called Nisqueunia in the state of New-York*. Albany, NY: S. Hall, 1782.

Richmond, Mary. *Shaker Literature: A Bibliography*. Vol. 1. Hanover, NH: Shaker Community, Inc., and University Press of New England, 1977.

Rice, Otis K. *Frontier Kentucky*. Lexington: University of Kentucky Press, 1993.

Schreiner, Susan E. *The Theater of His Glory: Nature & the Natural Order in the Thought of John Calvin*. Grand Rapid, MI: Baker Academic, 2001.

Schultheis, Rose. "Harrison's Councils with Tecumseh." *Indiana Magazine of History* 27, no. 1 (March 1931): 40–49.

Sears, Clara E. *Gleanings from Old Shaker Journals*. New York: Houghton Mifflin Company, 1916.

Secretary of the Commonwealth. *Massachusetts Soldiers and Sailors in the War of the Revolution*. Vol. 10. Boston: Wright and Potter Printing Company, 1902.

Sellin, David. "Shaker Inspirational Drawings." *Philadelphia Museum of Art Bulletin* 57, no. 273 (Spring 1962): 93–99.

Shaughnessy, Anne C. *The History of Sherborn*. Sherborn, MA: 300th Anniversary Committee, 1974.

Smith, Daniel S. "Parental Power and Marriage Patterns: An Analysis of Historical Trends in Hingham, Massachusetts." *Journal of Marriage and Family* 35, no. 3 (Aug. 1973): 419–28.

Smith, Henry P., and William S. Rann. *History of Rutland County, Vermont*. Syracuse, NY: D. Mason and Co., 1886.

Smith, James Esq., "An Attempt to Develop Shakerism," *Vincennes Western Sun* 3, no. 41, October 10, 1810.

Speed, Thomas. *The Wilderness Road: A Description of the Routes of Travel by which the Pioneers and Early Settlers First Came to Kentucky*. Louisville, KY: John P. Morton and Co., 1886.

Spencer, John H. "Sects Originating from the Great Revival." In *A History of the Kentucky Baptists*. Vol. 1. Cincinnati, OH: J. R. Baumes, 1886.

Steel, David W., and Richard Hulan. *The Makers of the Sacred Harp*. Urbana, IL: University of Illinois Press, 2010.

Stein, Stephen J. *The Shaker Experience in America: A History of the United Society of Believers*. New Haven and London: Yale University Press, 1992.

———. "The 'Not-So-Faithful' Believers: Conversion, Deconversion, and Reconversion Among the Shakers." *American Studies* 38, no. 3 (Fall 1997): 5–20.

Stoddard, William O. *The Lives of the Presidents: William Henry Harrison, John Tyler, and James Knox Polk*. New York: Frederick A Stokes and Brother, 1888.

Stone, Barton W. "History of the Christian Church in the West." *The Christian Messenger* 1, no. 12, Oct. 25, 1827.

Strickland, W. P., ed. *Autobiography of Peter Cartwright, the Backwoods Preacher*. New York: Carlton and Porter, 1856.

Systematic History Fund. *Vital Records of Athol, Massachusetts, to the Year 1849*. Worcester, MA: Franklin P. Rice, 1910.

Systematic History Fund. *Vital Records of Phillipston, Massachusetts, to the Year 1849*. Worcester, MA: Franklin P. Rice, 1906.

Systematic History Fund. *Vital Records of Shrewsbury, Massachusetts, to the Year 1849*. Worcester, MA: Franklin P. Rice, 1904.

Systematic History Fund. *Vital Records of Templeton, Massachusetts, to the Year 1849*. Worcester, MA: Franklin P. Rice, 1907.

Thomas, David. *Travels Through the Western Country in the Summer of 1816*. Auburn, NY: David Rumsey, 1819.

Ulrich, Laurel T. *Good Wives: Image and Reality in the Lives of Women in Northern New England, 1650–1750*. New York: Alfred A. Knopf, 1982.

Updegraff, Harlan. *The Origin of the Moving School in Massachusetts*. New York: Columbia University Contributions to Education Teachers' College Series, 1909.

Valencius, Conevery B. *The Health of the Country: How American Settlers Understood Themselves and Their Land*. New York: Basic Books, 2002.

Van Houten, Ellen F., and Florence Cole. *Warren County, Ohio Shakers of Union Village 1805–1920*. Lebanon, OH: Cardinal Research, Warren County Genealogical Society, 2003.

Wall, Helena M. *Fierce Communion: Family and Community in Early America*. Cambridge, MA: Harvard University Press, 1990.

Ward, Andrew H. *History of Shrewsbury, Massachusetts*. Boston: Samuel G. Drake, 1847.

Watts, Isaac, and John Cotton. *New England Primer*. Boston: Edward Draper, 1777 edition.

Webber, Philip E. "Jakob Sylvan's Preface to the Zoarite Anthology *Die Wahre Separation, oder die Widergeburt* as an Introduction to Un(der)studied Separatist Principles." *Communal Societies* 19 (1999): 101–28.

Wetherbee, Martha, and Nathaniel Taylor. *Shaker Baskets.* Sanbornton, NH: Martha Wetherbee Basket Shop, 1988.

Weishampel, John F., Jr. *The Testimony of a Hundred Witnesses.* Baltimore, MD: Blakeman and Co., 1858.

Wergland, Glendyne. *One Shaker Life: Isaac Newton Youngs, 1793–1865.* Amherst: University of Massachusetts Press, 2006.

———. *Sisters in the Faith: Shaker Women and Equality of the Sexes.* Amherst: University of Massachusetts Press, 2011.

White, Alma, and Leila Taylor. *Shakerism: Its Meaning and Message.* Columbus, OH: Fred J. Heer, 1905.

Wigoder, Geoffrey ed. *New Encyclopedia of Judaism.* New York: New York University Press, 2002.

Williams, D. Newell. *Barton Stone: A Spiritual Biography.* Atlanta, GA: Chalice Press, 2000.

Williams, John S., ed. *The Revolutionary War and Issachar Bates.* Chatham, NY: The Shaker Museum Foundation, 1960.

Williams, Melvin G. "Who Was Isaac Orcutt? The History and Origins of an 18th Century New England Ballad." *New York Folklore* 13, nos. 3–4 (1987): 55–71.

Williams, Samuel. "An Account of a Very Uncommon Darkness in the States of New-England, May 19, 1780." *Memoirs of the American Academy of Arts and Sciences* 1 (1783): 234–46.

Wilson, George R. *Early Indiana Trails and Surveys.* Indianapolis: Indiana Historical Society Press, 1919.

Wilson, Lisa. *Ye Heart of a Man: The Domestic Life of Men in Colonial New England.* New Haven, CT: Yale University Press, 1999.

Windham, William, and George Townshend. *A Plan of Discipline Composed for the Use of the Militia in the County of Norfolk.* London: J. Shuckburgh, 1759.

Winship, Michael. "Prodigies, Puritanism, and the Perils of Natural Philosophy: The Example of Cotton Mather." *The William and Mary Quarterly* 51, no.1 (Jan. 1994): 92–105.

Woo, Ilyon. *The Great Divorce: A Nineteenth-Century Mother's Extraordinary Fight Against Her Husband, the Shakers, and Her Times.* New York: Atlantic Monthly Press, 2010.

Youngs, Benjamin Seth. *Testimony of Christ's Second Appearing.* Lebanon, OH: Office of the Western Star, 1808.

NEWSPAPERS REFERENCED

The Albany Gazette
The Boston Evening Post
The Boston Chronicle

The Boston Gazette, and Country Journal
Frank Leslie's Illustrated Newspaper
Hartford Post-Star
Shaker and Shakeress
Shaker Manifesto
Vincennes Western Sun

INDEX

Bates, Issachar, Jr., 182, 185–187, 225, 258, 385n34; as "Little Issachar," 160, 161, 186–187; musical ability of, 191–192, 385n30; occupations, 185–186, 385n29

Bates, Lovina Maynard, 21, 37–38, 54, 64, 66, 106, 178–179, 180–182, 225, 369n48; death of, 182, 256, 384n16; kin of, 37, 46, 56, 357n4, 359n6–7, 359n14; relationship with Issachar Bates, xiv, 37, 59, 95, 100–101, 122, 179–180, 359n11

Bates, Mercy Joy, 2–5, 9, 36–37, 42, 354n16, 358n3

Bates, Molly, 5, 356n16

Bates, Noah, 3, 5, 16, 38, 42, 354n16, 359n14

Bates, Olive, 5, 258, 354n16

Bates, Paulina, 199, 389n83

Bates, Polly, 66, 160–161, 165, 179, 182–184, 185, 187, 206, 225, 256; death of, 176, 184, 186, 383n58

Bates, Sarah, 66, 187–194, 194, 197, 281; art and calligraphy, 189–191, 192, 193, 298; correspondence, 55, 67, 359n6, 365n19, 386n37, 387n62; as family member, 179, 198, 272, 285–286, 302; as singer, 191–192, 225, 285, 387n58;

Bates, Sarah Potter, 200

Bates, Sarah Stockwell, 37

Bates, Theodore, 5, 16, 21, 42, 63, 184, 198, 199–200, 225, 258; physical appearance of, 21, 63

Bates, Theodore, Jr., 199, 200

Bates, William (brother of Issachar), 36, 198, 271, 394n85

Bates, William (father of Issachar), 2–6, 16, 36–37, 58, 180, 354n16, 361n33, 383n49

Bates, William (son of Issachar), 66, 179, 200

Baxter, Robert, 220, 249, 255

Beaver Creek, 93, 107, 112, 117, 213. *See also* Watervliet, OH

Bedle, Edith. *See* Dennis, Salome

Bedle, Francis, 239, 252, 253

Bedle's Station, 89

Bennington, VT, 21, 32

Billings, William, 55, 362n54

Bimeler, James, 210, 211

Bishop, Rufus, 225, 249, 251, 281, 295–296

Blake, Rhoda, 189, 386n45

Blinn, Henry, 298

Bluejacket, Chief, 112

Bluejacket, George, 112, 115, 373n44

Boler, Daniel, 282

Bound Brook, 32

Brewster, Cassandana, 65–66

broom making, 199, 200, 204, 247, 389n89

Brotherton Indians, 272

Brown, Amasa, 47, 54

Brown, Thomas, 67–68, 365n23, 366n37

Bunker Hill, Battle of, xiv, 20, 26, 27

Busro, IN: covenant of, 158, 159, 162, 220; description, 142–144, 159–160; 171; dissolution of, 202, 218–220, 221, 230, 241, 242, 267–268, 393n64; earthquake at, 130, 150–151; expansion of, 172–174, 219, 383n49; founding of, 131–133; hymns at, 159, 160–161, 175; Indians at, 142–145, 149, 150, 152, 153, 172; Issachar's journeys to, 134–136, 139–140, 218–219; leadership of, 137–140, 168–169, 212, 376n19; malaria at, 146–147, 158, 164, 167–169, 175, 219, 378n53, 381n28, 382n44; melons at, 143, 378n41; mixed-race Shakers at, 139, 158, 380n12; spiritual warfare at, 161–164, 169; trumpet at, 171, 382–383n47; war preparations at, 152–153, 155–156; worship at, 161–163, 169, 171.

Busseron Creek, 130, 131, 141, 147

Campbell, Cornelius, 89

canal travel, xiv, 223–225, 255, 257–258

Cane Ridge, 69, 79–80, 85–89, 105, 137, 367n64–65

Canterbury, New Hampshire, 299, 304

oak as metaphor, 256, 266, 400n33.
  See also "Stubborn Oak"
obedience, 141, 154, 168–169, 216, 259, 282,
  291–292
O'Brien, Lydia, 189, 261, 264
"Ode to Contentment," 243–244, 396n37,
  398n2
Ohio River, 83, 84–85, 95, 110, 116, 119, 131,
  134–135, 243
old believer(s), 104–105, 108–110, 117–118,
  126–127, 165–166; Joseph Allen as, 134,
  146; Issachar Bates as, 177, 212–213, 215,
  256, 267, 295–296; at Busro, 138–141,
  146, 160; first women among, 99,
  108; as group in West, 174–175, 242,
  261, 371n2, 372n18, 381n15, 403n11;
  as transmitters of Shaker doctrine,
  208–209, 212
opium, 274–275, 276, 401n58
Orcutt, Isaac, 56–57, 362n57, 363n61

Paint Lick, 78–79, 106, 109, 117
Pease, Peter, 107, 399n17
Pelham, Richard, 297, 396n37, 398n2
Pension Act, 23, 238
pension controversy, 228, 238–240,
  248–249, 254, 259, 290, 291, 292
persecution: of Ann Lee and Shakers, 13,
  14, 41–42, 356n51; in Shaker West, 102,
  104, 117, 121–122, 124, 128, 139, 282, 289,
  373n36
Phillips, William, 235
Phillipston, MA, 38, 358n5
Picket, Job, 50
Pickett, Mercy, 166, 255
Pleasant Hill, 128, 196, 209, 245–246,
  390n7; elders at, 209, 223, 261; and
  evacuation of Busro, 152, 155; unrest
  at, 219–220, 222, 226. See also Shawnee
  Run
poetry, 55–57, 58, 122–125, 165, 211, 235–237,
  243, 257; of Bates children, 182–183, 186,

189–192, 194; for Polly Bates, 184, 206;
  military metaphors in, 22–23, 290–291;
  of spirits, 301, 302, 305
Posey, Mary, 119–121, 374n58–59
Posey, Thomas, 119–121, 373–374n55–57;
  374n59
Potawatomies, 148–149, 152, 171
prayer, 211; for Busro, 156, 159; for healing,
  163, 164
preaching: of Issachar Bates, xiv, 51–52,
  54–55, 59, 62, 64–65, 67–69, 86–88,
  109–110, 118–119, 235; at Busro, 132,
  167; of Mathew Houston, 78–79, 87,
  110, 212; by Indians, 111, 112; to Indians,
  112, 113; of Ann Lee, 13–15, 40–41, 65;
  limitations of, 117, 221, 264; of Richard
  McNemar, 85–86, 89, 92, 205, 227; of
  New Lights, 80, 86–87, 92–93, 107, 118;
  of Benjamin Seth Youngs 63, 71, 106,
  107, 118, 199, 213, 364n7
preaching stand, 69, 78, 87, 91, 97, 99, 109
Price, David, 382n36
Prophet, the, 172, 375n, 376n. See also
  Lalawethika (Lallawasheka);
  Tenskwatawa

Quakers, 12, 74, 83, 91, 105, 171, 392n30

Rankin, Daniel, 222
Rankin, John, 116
Rapp, George, 154, 157–158, 164, 209,
  380n11
Red Banks, 116–119, 120–121, 130–133, 136,
  137, 144, 376n22
Redmon, William, 142–144, 169, 378n42
religious revival, among Indians, 111–112
"Rights of Conscience," 17, 124, 211
Rollins, Samuel, 86
Rollins family, 106
Rude, Hiram, 261, 273, 399n17
Rutland, Vermont, 21, 32, 33, 357n4,
  360n28

sacramental meeting, 92–93, 107

Sacred Role, 187, 385n35–36

Sanborn, Martha, 160, 167, 175, 184, 205

Saratoga, NY, xiv, 21, 33, 44, 373–374n55

Selection of Hymns and Poems for the Use of Believers, 228, 235–237, 238, 243

sexuality, 15, 49, 53–54, 57, 61, 80, 90–91, 179–180, 187, 289, 362n50, 385n31

Shaker communities mapped, 204, 390n7

Shaker population, eastern, 70–71

Shaker theology, 14, 59, 63, 87–88, 123, 162, 165, 206, 208–209, 242; dual-gendered godhead, 123, 368n19

Sharp, Nathan, 267

Shattuck, Elizabeth, 199

Shattuck, Mary, 199

Shawnee, 111–115, 128, 130–131, 137, 142–145, 154, 171–172, 372n28–29, 373n32, 373n36, 386n40

Shawnee Run, 107, 109, 117, 127, 373n48. *See also* Pleasant Hill

Sherborn, 3–5, 354n15–16

Shrewsbury, MA, 37, 359n6, 360n30

sickness: at Busro, 155, 157, 162–164, 165, 167–168, 169, 218, 219; at New Lebanon, 280, 281; tuberculosis, 176, 182, 183–184, 384n16

Slover, John, 143–145, 378n44

Smith, James, 137, 377n23

Smith, Lucy, 107, 223

Sodus Bay, 223

Somerset (HMS), 25–26

Southborough, MA, 4, 6, 9, 354n16

South Union, 128, 143, 152, 155, 196, 303, 383n53, 390n7; Issachar Bates's visits to, 165–167, 174–175, 243–245, 403n21; elders of, 174, 223, 242, 247, 297, 368n32, 376n19; music at, 243–245. *See also* Gasper River

Spencer, Salome, 138

Spier, Richard, 150, 151

Square House, 14, 40

steamboat travel, xiv, 243

Stewart, Amos, 261

Stone, Barton, 79–81, 84, 85, 86–88, 131, 367n63,

Stout, Joseph, 239, 252, 253

"Stubborn Oak," 266, 400n33

Taylor, Nathaniel, xxii, 231

Tecumseh, xiv, 111–114, 145, 147–148, 171–172, 373n44

Templeton, MA, 6, 14, 17, 38, 40, 199, 359n14

Templeton Pond, 24

Tenskwatawa, 111–112, 114–115, 137, 145, 148, 149, 171–172, 372n29, 373n32. *See also* Lalawethika (Lallawasheka); Prophet, the

Testimony of Christ's Second Appearing, 123, 206, 233, 293, 364, 375n67, 391, 412

Thompson, John, 81, 83, 91–93, 107, 121

Thompson, John (of Indiana territory), 121, 374n60

Thompsonian order, 250, 397n54

Thruston, Robert, 240

Train, David, 21, 37, 67, 179, 180, 384n10

Train, Hannah, 180, 181, 261, 365n22, 384n13 *See also* Bates, Hannah

Train, Hannah, Jr., 58, 181, 261, 365n22, 399n18

tree husbandry, 126, 159, 160, 170, 238, 262

trumpet, 20, 171, 382–383n47

tuberculosis, 176, 182, 183

Turner, Jethro, 264

Turner, Samuel, 107, 241

Turtle Creek: arrival of Shaker missionaries at, 83–84, 206–208; growth of Shaker community at, 104–106, 108–109, 126–128, 203–204, 371n4, 403n11; Indians visiting, 112, 114; and launching of Busro, 136, 138; persecution at, 112, 114, 127, 139, 373n36

Tyringham, MA, 146, 225